Women Leaders of Africa, Asia, Middle East, and Pacific

Women Leaders of Africa, Asia, Middle East, and Pacific

A Biographical Reference

Guida M. Jackson

Library of Congress Control Number:		2009907480
ISBN:	Hardcover	978-1-4415-5844-2
	Softcover	978-1-4415-5843-5

This book was printed in the United States of America.

To order additional copies of this book, contact:
Xlibris Corporation
1-888-795-4274
www.Xlibris.com
Orders@Xlibris.com
52111

For John Hume

Preface

The first part of this book has at its core the African women rulers of the original *Women Who Ruled*, although half again as many completely new biographical entries were added for the second book, entitled *Women Rulers Throughout the Ages*. These included not only women rulers who had come upon the scene in the decade since the publishing of the original work, but many more culled from historical records by dedicated researchers and from oral tradition by translators and field anthropologists. In addition many entries in the original work were revised, expanded, and updated. The result was a biographical listing of every known ruling queen, empress, woman prime minister, president, regent ruler, defacto ruler, constitutional monarch, and verifiable ruler from the oral tradition of the world's kingdoms, islands, empires, nations, and tribes since the beginning of both recorded and recaptured oral history down to the time of the publication of *Women Rulers Throughout the Ages*.

In the decade since the appearance of the second volume, women's participation world-wide in all levels of government has mushroomed, such that it seemed logical to include not only rulers, but other leaders in government. The entries in this two-volume collection are arranged regionally: African, Asian—which includes India, the Middle East and the Pacific in the first volume, and European and the Western Hemisphere in the second. Within these geographical sections, the entries are arranged alphabetically according to leaders' names, dictionary style. Each entry is supported by suggestions for further reading.

In the case of rulers, the name of each woman ruler is followed by a title or titles and, in parentheses, the year(s) during which she ruled. In the case of entries that give more than one title, the additional title will help to distinguish that ruler from other women in history with similar names; to designate either a title different from that which the ruler held while ruling or a title that was not the usual one held by a ruler of that particular place; or to clarify for the reader the type of title used in a certain time and place.

Such a compilation could not possibly be a history based on original research of primary sources in their hundreds of languages. It must rather be a gathering together from secondary sources, from the works of others from many cultures. As such, if it cannot be an original scientific work, it carries an added obligation that a history does not, and that is to provide information in some cases even beyond historical fact, so called.

Since grey areas are inherent in a categorization as broad as "women rulers," there will be questions about certain inclusions or exclusions. In broad terms, I have sought to include the name (or when the name has not survived, the identifying clan, dynasty, or even locale) of any woman who held the reins of power, regardless of the extent to which she exercised it, and regardless of her official sanction to do so. To include only those who presided from a recognized seat of government, however, would omit certain tribal leaders.

In addition, with some ambivalence, I have included the names of a very few legendary rulers about whom no firm historical or archeological evidence survives, whose embroidered histories may or may not have been based on the lives of actual (albeit far less colorful) persons. These inclusions are clearly labeled as legendary and are included because of the unique information that they provide, which in some cases may link the historical to the legendary or may contain some elements that coincide with known historical data. There are others, such as Herodotus' two "queens" named Nitrocris, that I feel a responsibility to include, if only to clear up confusion and to present the possibilities as to the historical counterpart of one of these women. Historians sometimes disagree as to the authenticity of a person, i.e., Dido; my stance is that exclusion of such a controversial legendary figure would be to have settled a matter without corroborating evidence to do so.

Diacritics, particularly in accounts of rulers of recent times, have been kept to a minimum for the sake of a particular fluid robustness which a clean page allows; however, in the case of certain of the more exotic and distantly removed entries, where names have not been Anglicized by current usage, the use of diacritics seems preferable and even unavoidable. It is hoped that what fluidity is lost due to their inclusion is compensated for by the edaphic flavor they lend.

In this ongoing endeavor, I am indebted to those who brought newly elected rulers to my attention, who lent or located research materials, and who offered editing assistance, inspiration, and encouragement: John Hume, William H. Laufer, James Tucker Jackson, Patty Wentz, William A. Jackson, Mary Gillis Jackson, Jeffrey A. Jackson, Linda J. Jackson, Annabeth Dugger,

Steve Dugger, Glenda Miller Lowery, Davis Lowery, Daniel Ramos, Julia Mercedes Castilla de Gomez-Rivas, Ida H. Luttrell, Gregory A. Jackson, Jeana Kendrick, Ashley D. Ramos, Chichi Layor Okoye, Elizabeth A. Jackson, Patsy Ward Burk, Karen Stuyck, Jackie Pelham, Vanessa Leggett, Louise Gaylord, Sue Volk, Lynne S. Gonzales, Mattie R. Jackson, Troy B. Lowery, Ann Anderson, Christopher Michael Ramos, Irene Bond, Bobbi Sissel, Eleanor Frances Jackson, Stephanie L. Noggler, David Bumgardner, Jim Elledge, Ron Pearson, Linda Helman, Jan Matlock, Kenny Noggler, Rance J. Lowery, Trinity Alexis Noggler, Jace Lowery, Olivia Orfield, Gloria Wahlen, Carol Rowe DeBender, Joyce Pounds Hardy McDonald, Donn Taylor, Joy Ziegler, Beverly Herkommer, Judith Sherbenou, Bob Davis, Addison McElroy, George Thomen, Joan Winkler.

Houston, Texas 2008

PART I

African Women Leaders

Women rulers, what pitifully few there have been in our long recorded history, have only rarely come to power through the front door, and that, fairly recently. True, some have been born inside the walls, inherited the scepter by divine right, but still more arrived via the alley door or over the basement transom, as queen mothers, regents, widowers, even concubines. A handful of the most daring have been gate crashers, usurpers who took their lives in their hands in their lust for power. Some of those have been assassinated for their trouble. Many have been allowed to share authority with another, usually a spouse. Others were summoned to fill a void by machinators who expected them to behave like puppets, but sometimes the puppets cut their own strings. In recent years a growing number have knocked politely on the portals of power and have been invited in via the front entrance by an ever more tolerant electorate.

Much as we would like to fantasize that at some time in the peaceful idyllic past, vast numbers of matriarchs presided over happy, bucolic subjects, there is no anthropological evidence to prove a universal prehistoric matriarchy, although there was a time when women were held in awe for their magical ability to bleed and not die, to reproduce seemingly at will, and to manufacture food from their bodies. Mother-goddesses abounded, and doubtless women had much more bargaining power, but evidence that they used it to rule is scant.

There were isolated exceptions, however; some West African nations at one time had only women rulers. The Baule tribe came into being under the rule of a woman (Awura Pokou), as did Zaria (Turunku Bakwa). At least three women in a row ruled the Hausa state of Zaria in its prime, and one of them in fact gave the tribe her name. The late Jomo Kenyatta, founder of Kenya, related the origin of the Gikuyu clans, originally named for daughters of the founder and all ruled by women. While holding a superior position in the community, the women practiced polyandry and became domineering and ruthless. Men were put to death for committing adultery or for minor infractions of the civil law. Finally, the men plotted, overthrew the women, and took command, becoming for the first time the heads of their families. This event doubtless coincided with realization of their role in procreation. Immediately the men took steps to abolish polyandry and establish polygamy. They planned to change the clan names as well, but the women, infuriated by this ultimate insult, threatened that they would bear no children if the clan names, which stood as proof that women were their founders, were changed. The men backed down and the female clan names stand today.

On the East African islands of Zanzibar, Pate, and its neighbors, as late as the 18th century there was a tradition of women rulers, many called Fatima, but few of whose birth names remain on record. Since only the names of outstanding leaders have survived, it is not known how many African tribes may have been matriarchal for at least some period.

Appearance of a number of queens in a row doesn't necessarily indicate existence of a matriarchy, but it might. The Lovedu of South Africa were ruled by at least four women who carried the dynastic title of Mujaji. On the South Pacific island of Tonga, there were at least four ruling queens who took the name of Pomare, and at least one by that name on Tahiti.

Many matrilineal societies have existed, particularly near forested areas where domesticated animals were not present. However, matrilinearity, polyandry, or matrilocality also do not necessarily indicate the existence of a matriarchy. In Buganda, for example, among the Babito people, the kings perpetuated the long-held custom of adopting the clan of their mothers. Mothers were honored, but men ruled.

In ancient Egypt, full-blooded consanguineous marriage among royalty became common during the late 17th c. B. C. or early 16th c. B. C. This practice reflected the belief in divine rule, but in addition, Egyptian kings married their royal sisters because they wished to partake of the family inheritance that often passed from mother to daughter. The Greek historian Diodorus Siculus, writing in the 1st. c. B. C., described the matriarchal character of the Egyptian royal family. His *Bibliotheca Historica* was compiled from earlier works which have not survived. While every royal Egyptian princess bore the titles and dignities of the office from birth, a man only acquired them at his coronation, and could do so only by becoming the consort of a royal princess.

The queen bore the title of God's Wife of Amon. Even after the practice of full-blooded consanguineous marriage was abandoned in the mid 16th c. B. C., the title of God's Wife remained. It was bestowed in childhood upon the pharaoh's legitimate heiress. The incoming pharaoh, to secure his right to the throne, generally—but not always—married the God's Wife. Some variations of this tradition have been practiced in many other parts of the world. Often these unions resulted in co-rule by both king and queen; other times certain duties were assigned to each. In the case of Cleopatra II, when she was divorced by Eurgetes in favor of her daughter, Cleopatra III, the cast-aside queen revolted and in 130 B.C. became queen of parts of Upper Egypt on her own, ruling it alone until 118 B.C. There is at least one instance where the queen (Arsinoe II) ruled the land while the king (Ptolemy II) engaged in cultural pursuits.

In addition to establishing a precedent on the African continent for the occasional sole woman ruler, Egypt is credited with the concept of an "official woman" within the government, a model followed down to recent times in some African kingdoms. This office carries in some instance the weight of vice-ruler, in others that of prime minister or secretary of state.

Africa has always boasted a large number of women leaders, from tribal times onward. This volume attempts to include, in addition to African rulers, significant woman leaders as well. Since history is a shifting affair, leaders often come and go without our noting their contributions. We have attempted to right this injustice with the inclusion of at least a few of the leaders who have made an impact on African society.

Africa: Where It All Began

Charity Kaluki was born in 1955, the ninth of 13 children of a minister of the Ebenezer Gospel church in Kenya. Because school was free before Kenya's independence in 1983, she received a good education. She became a secretary and later got a job at the Central Bank. In the 1970's she married an electrical engineer, Michael Nguli, who financed her way to college, where she earned a degree in business administration. She established a successful bakery and a plumbing supply company and managed to rear three children and become involved in projects to improve things in her home district, Kitui, headquarters of the Akamba tribe, where primitive conditions had not changed since her childhood. She worked with the women to build better health clinics and raised money to build a water system for Kitui so the women wouldn't have to carry water on their backs for miles to their homes.

In 1992, when Kenya held its first multi-party elections, Charity Kaluki Nguli was in her kitchen washing dishes when a group of women approached her back door. They had come to ask her to run for Parliament. Buoyed by her own outrage at the large sums politicians were wasting while the poor got poorer, she agreed to represent the women. In an unusual grass-roots uprising, she won the election and soon became a thorn in the side of President Daniel arap Moi, who had been in office since 1978, for his complete inattention to the problems of the poor, especially women.

"Instead of putting priorities right, (Moi) spends a colossal sum of $60 million to buy himself a presidential jet," she said. " . . . Then he has the audacity to go in front of women to say, 'Please vote for me.' The women he is telling that to are walking naked and carrying sick children on their back and their homes have holes in them that you can see through . . . ."

After serving five years in the Parliament, still dissatisfied with Moi's performance, she announced her candidacy for president, promising to serve only one term and to demystify power: "Presidents are to serve and not to be served. I am demystifying that office." Three days after her announcement, she was attacked and wounded by thugs with machetes, and she was harassed by threatening phone calls. Although she did not win that election, which was marred by fraud and violence, she continued her outspoken championship of the rights of the poor. She had already gained more clout than most women in a country where politics have traditionally been run by and for men. Kenya had only one woman minister and very few women in the Parliament—roughly the same make up as the United States government during the same period. (1) She may very well run again.

When Ellen Johnson-Sirleaf was inaugurated as president of Liberia in 2006, newspapers hailed her as the first woman president on the continent of Africa. In fact, she was not the first woman president on the continent, nor even the first woman president of Liberia. That designation goes to Ruth Perry, who was elected, not in a general election, but by a committee, something like presidents are elected in the United States today. The entrance of women into the affairs of Black African governments is not new. Egypt's long and well-documented history of ruling dynasties dipping deep into antiquity has so overshadowed the histories of other African cultures that we sometimes overlook the fact that there have been many other empires on the continent—and many other women rulers. Certainly, Egypt's long tradition has influenced other cultures within her sphere of influence. Other than establishing a precedent for the occasional sole woman ruler, Egypt is responsible for the concept of an "official woman" within the government of a ruling man, an office bearing in some instances the weight of co-ruler, in others that of "vice-ruler," in others that of "prime minister" or "secretary of state."

First, addressing governments other than those presided over by a woman exclusively: In ancient Egypt, full-blooded consanguineous marriage among royalty, instituted during the late 1600s or early 1500s B.C., reflected the belief in divine rule. The queen bore the title of God's Wife of Amon. Even after the practice of full-blooded consanguineous marriage was discontinued in the mid-1500s B.C., the title of God's Wife remained. It was bestowed in childhood upon the pharaoh's legitimate heiress. The incoming pharaoh, to secure his right to the throne, generally married the God's Wife. Some variation of this procedure has been practiced in many other parts of the world. Often these unions resulted in co-rule by both king and queen; other times they did not. There is at least one instance where the queen ruled the land while the king engaged himself in cultural pursuits. There are other instances where the queen was given one state, city, principality to govern while the king took command of another.

Greek historian Diodorus Siculus, who traveled in Egypt during 60-57 B.C. and commented in his *Bibliotheca Historica* on the matriarchal character of the Egyptian royal family, also noted of the commoners: "Among private citizens, the husband by the terms of the marriage agreement, appertains to the wife, and it is stipulated between them that the man shall obey the woman in all things." (2) Diodorus noted that, while every Egyptian princess of the royal house was born a queen and bore the titles and dignities of the office from the day of her birth, a man only acquired them at his coronation, and could do so only by becoming the consort of a royal princess. Those features of the constitution of Egyptian royalty are substantially the same as those in most other African kingdoms, even the Muslim ones. (3)

Medieval traveler Ibn Batuta described the custom of joint rule in Islamic Mali where, to show obeisance to and acceptance of the queen, the noble ladies would throw earth on their own heads. In Mali it was the custom for the Empress to be crowned with the *Mansa* and to share the imperial power. However, her ability to rule depended upon this vote of confidence from the other noble women. Empress Bendjou, for example, not receiving that homage, went after blood. Mali is not the only Islamic country which practiced liberal treatment of women. In Sudan the ruler Shehu Usman cited the Koran as the source of his liberalism. He pointed out that the Koran had not assigned to women the tasks of cooking or washing clothes, and that it was necessary for them to receive an education in order to know the teachings of God and the laws of the Prophet. (4) By contrast, in the Songhay, where a full-fledged Moslem kingdom also existed, and in the Fulani Empire, women played essentially no part at all.

West Africa is the site of several ancient kingdoms of certain sophistication and boasts the most African women rulers of record, although many others doubtless existed whose identities are not known, since detailed written history began so relatively recently. In Bornu and Haussa the queen mother and the queen held important posts in the court. The Bornu queen mother, *Maguira*, acquired great prestige and power, even having veto power over the acts of the emperor. She also played an important role in the ceremonials of the court. The empress, *Gousma*, also had a role of authority. Among the Mossi, the queen was also crowned, and shared in a joint rule. Among the Akan, which includes the Ashanti and Baule, the title of Queen Mother likewise refers to an office, not a familial role, although in fact she was invariably related to the chief. Often among Ashanti she would be the sister of the chief. The Queen Mother, elected by the council, acted as head of state in the absence of the ruler; at his death, she nominated the next ruler. She was usually the instigator of all diplomatic exchange with other governments.

Some West African nations had only women rulers. The Baule tribe came into being under the rule of a woman (Awura Pokou), as did Zaria (Turunku Bakwa). At least three women in a row ruled the Hausa state of Zaria during its prime. Kanem-Bornu records at least one sole woman ruler. Since only the names of outstanding leaders have survived in this region, it is not known how many other women ruled African kingdoms.

However, in 20th century Sierre Leone, there have been at least two tribal chiefs (Honoria Bailor-Caulker of the Shenge and Madame Gulama of the Mende) (5), and in Swaziland a queen mother (Mdluli Gwamile) ruled as regent until her grandson came of age (6). Madame Gulama gained much of her power from arranging marriages between men in important positions and graduates of her famed Sande Bush, a female society whose students are instructed in strategies of leadership. This school is so reknown that mothers vie for acceptance of their daughters in its program.

A comparable program for training young women for positions of leadership does not exist on any other continent.

Traditionally, much of Central and Eastern Africa was matrilineal: the original inhabitants of Angola and the Kongo kingdom, as well as later Bantu people, such as the Lunda, were matrilineal. Nzinga Mbandi, who inherited leadership of the Mbundu at a time when the Portuguese and Dutch were vying for slave trade in Angola, spoke to the foreigners in a language they could understand: she put on a gory display of dance for a Dutch captain designed to encourage him keep his distance, and, by one account, for her first humiliating audience with the arrogant Portuguese overlord who refused her the courtesy of a chair, she sat on her own slave, whom she then had hacked to death when she had finished with him. All nine clans of the Gikuyu tribe were named for daughters of the original founder of the tribe. In Buganda, among the Babito people, the Babito kings perpetuated the long-held custom of adopting the clan of their mothers. The Basaigi clans of the Ababito tribe employed a system of governing similar to that prevalent in West Africa. In addition, among the families of the Babito kings of Kitara there would be many princesses—as many as 60. One would be elected *Rubuga*, Official Queen-Sister of the King. She would have an official position and/or seat on the king's council. In Sudan also, the pre-eminent offices were nearly always those of the queen mother, the queen sister and a limited number of titled "great wives" of the ruler. In Kitara because the queen mother was an indispensable figure in the government, in some ways more pivotal than the king, she was greeted in a special way. She might be greeted in the same way as the king. "You who are better than all men in this village" or "The savior of the people in the country." (7)

Madagascar has a minor tradition of women rulers—at least four in a row at one point. However, the real power in each case rested with the Queen's consort, the same man in three cases.

Zanzibar (where Queen Fatima reigned) and other small kingdoms along the South Central African coast had several women rulers during the 17th and 18th century. As on Madagascar, these kingdoms were of mixed African and Indonesian extraction. (8)

African women have a tradition of bravery and aggression. In eighteenth century Dahomey (Benin), a corps of women warriors was formed. Originally, women caught in adultery or found guilty of other crimes had the option of being executed or joining the army. The ruler Agaja was so impressed by the bravery of the women soldiers that he made them a regular unit of the army, called the Amazons. The group soon became a *corps d'elite* and the criminal elements were then eliminated from the corps. A law was passed requiring every notable to present one daughter to the king for service in the Amazons, which was divided into five corps: the Infantry, the Elephant Huntresses, the Razor Women, the Archers, the Blunderbuss Women. (9) Their strenuous training would make a U.S. Marine blanch. They became the most dreaded, terrible force in West Africa. The last Ashanti war against the British is called the Yaa Asantewaa War, named for the feisty Ohemaa of Edweso, Yaa Asantewaa, who, even though she was 50 years old at the time, led the fight. In this century, a young Senegalese queen, Aline Sitoe, mounted such a revolt against the French that she had to be deported when she was finally captured, to keep her from continuing her fight even from prison. In North Africa, the Berber tribes of the Aures mountains combined under the leadership of a woman named Al-Kahina to sweep down repeatedly on the Arabs who had taken Carthage (traditionally said to have been established, by the way, by Queen Dido) from the Byzantine forces in 695. The actions of these warriors against the Arabs were not unlike the guerilla attacks of the Vietnamese Trung sisters in ca. A.D. 39 or those of Queen Mawia, who first nattered away at the Romans and later even chilled the blood of the barbarous Goths.

The late Kenyan founder Jomo Kenyatta told the story of the Gikuyu clans, which, being named originally for the nine daughters of the founder, were all ruled by women: while holding a superior position in the community, the women became domineering and ruthless fighters and practicers of polyandry. Many men were put to death for committing adultery or other minor offenses. Finally the men plotted, overthrew the women and took command, becoming for the first time the heads of their families. Immediately they took steps to abolish the system of polyandry and establish polygamy. They planned to change the clan names as well, but the women, infuriated by this final and ultimate insult, threatened that if the clan names, which stood as proof that women were the original founders of the clan system, were changed, they would bear no more children. The men, frightened by the women's strong stand, elected never to change the clan names. Those names stand today. (10)

Acts of courage and defiance by women in South Africa did not begin with the twentieth century. When the British defeated the Zulu army in 1879, a tribal elder, Mkabi, called her people together and told them that, having seen the glory of the Zulus, she could not bear to see their king Cetewayo become a hunted fugitive. In protest of the British degradation of their illustrious and gallant leader, in front of the assembled tribe, she cut her own throat. (11) Nor was her act of bravery the first of its kind in this region. The Zulu Chronicles relate at least one story of a young maiden who killed an enemy soldier and won for herself a warrior's insignia and an official praise name. The official organ of the African National Congress of South Africa perhaps most succinctly describes African women, both rulers and commoners in what may only be termed masterful understatement: "African women are not fragile flowers." (9)

A case in point: during the turbulent six years of the bloody Liberian civil war, when many lawmakers and private citizens fled for safety to neighboring countries, Ruth Perry (b. 1939), legislator and later senator, remained in the country. In 1996 she was elected president of Liberia, head of a six-member collective governing body that was charged with bringing order to the war-torn country. She assured the assemblage that although she had the "touch of velvet", she could be "as hard as steel." In the elections of the following year another woman, Harvard-educated Ellen Johnson-Sirleaf, presented herself as the obvious choice to continue Perry's non-violent approach to problem-solving. Although Johnson-Sirleaf did not win in 1997, Perry's principle of non-violent means of conflict-resolution was adopted by a United Nations-sponsored conference of some 60 women involved in government in various African countries. When Johnson-Sirleaf tried again in 2005, running against a popular football player, George Weah, she won the election and became Liberia's first president to be elected by the people in a general election. (13)

Notes:

(1) McKinley Jr., James C. "A Woman to Run Kenya? One Says, 'Why Not?'" *The New York Times International.* 3 August 1997: 3.

(2) Robert Briffault. *The Mothers.* (New York: The Macmillan Co., 1931), 279

(3) W. T. Balmer. *A History of the Akan Peoples of the Gold Coast.* (New York: Negro Universities Press, 1969), 176-177; John G. Jackson. *Introduction to African Civilizations.* (Secaucus: The Citadel Press, 1970), 95.

(4) K. Madhu Panikkar. *The Serpent and the Crescent, A History of the Negro Empires of West Africa.* (Bombay: Asia Publishing House, 1963), 327.

(5) John Reader. *Africa.* (New York: Alfred A. Knopf, 1998), 377-379; Sylvia Ardyn Boone. *Radiance From the Waters.* (New Haven: Yale University Press, 1986), 86, 146.

(6) Mark R. Lipschutz and R. Kent Rasmussen. *Dictionary of African Historical Biography.* (Berkeley: The University of California Press, 1986), 220.

(7) J. W. Nyakatura. *Anatomy of an African Kingdom, A History of Bunyoro-Kitara.* (Garden City, NY: Anchor/Doubleday, 1973), 191; Roland Oliver and J. D. Fage. *A Short History of Africa.* (Harmondsworth, Middlesex: Penguin Books, 1970), 45, 129.

(8) Alvin M. Josephy, Jr., ed. *The Horizon History of Africa.* (New York: American Heritage Publishing Co., McGraw Hill, Inc., 1971), 369-370.

(9) Panikkar, *The Serpent and the Crescent,* 162.

(10) Jomo Kenyatta. *Facing Mount Kenya.* (New York: Vintage Books, 1965), 8.

(11) Wilfred Cartey and Martin Kilson, eds. *The African Reader: Independent Africa.* (New York: Vintage Books, 1970), 315.

(12) "The Defiance of Women." *Sechaba* 1 9 August 1967.

(13) "Half the World" *Guardian Weekly.* 16-22 June 2006.

African Leaders Section A

Adame, Mama

Mansa (ruler) of Niumi Bato at Bakindiki, West Africa

The history Niumi Bato, occupied by a Mandika-speaking people in the northern coastal regions of Niumi in the Lower Gambia, is still passed down by *griots*, oral historians, who take great pride in memorizing vast quantities of information and passing it down to the next generation.

Although great kingdoms had arisen in West Africa as early as the 12th and 13th centuries there were many villages ruled by local kings or queens, just as was the case in feudal Europe.

South of the Gambia the country had been under the control of the Mandika since early times, but no accurate dates can be assigned to their leaders. Oral tradition as recounted by current *griots* mentions that when the Sonko people first came from Fulbe to the Gambia, the Jammeh people were already there. The Sonka found a woman ruling in the village of Bakindiki.

This same tradition names Mama Adame as the first woman *mansa* there, although at the time women had been *mansa* in other villages. At that time, when a woman ruled, "the men slept behind the women."

At the time of the arrival of the Sonko, the Jammeh were fighting against the people of Saloum, who were "tricksters and good fighters." The queen lodged the Sonko newcomers, who said to her, "Since these people are fighting against you, we wish to help you."

She answered, "Thank you, but before you help us, wait until they have almost finished us off."

The Sonko disagreed: "No, that is not safe. Unity is not a bad thing. But if we should overcome them we could intermarry, but that is not enough. We must share your position—that is, we must rotate *mansaya*."

Thereafter the Janneh, the Sonko, and another tribe which arrived from Kabu, the Manneh, all rotated the rule peacefully. However, Mama

Andame decided that no more women should rule. She said, "Underwear is not strong, but trousers are."

Suggested Reading:

(1) Wright, Donald R. *Oral Traditions from the Gambia*. Athens: Ohio University Center for International Studies, 1980, vol. 2. pp. 76-79.

Afua Koba

Asantehemaa [Queen Mother] of the Asante Empire (c. 1834-1884)

The Asante Empire comprised at that time most of the present-day West African nations of Ghana and Togo and portions of Ivory Coast and Dahomey. The office of Asantehemaa, or Queen Mother, was an elected position of great importance and influence. The holder of this office nominated the Asantehene, or leader of the chiefs, and she might serve during several administrations, in some cases.

Accession to the Golden Stool, or throne, was matrilineal. Afua Koba, whose second husband, Boakye Tenten occupied the Boakye Yam Panin okeyeame stool, was the mother of Kofi Kakari, occupant of the Golden Stool from 1867 to 1874, and Mensa Bonsu, occupant of the Golden Stool from 1874 to 1883. She was a powerful and influential figure in a troubled period in the history of Asante. During the reign of her first son, the British general asked Kofi Kakari that, as a condition of his not advancing to his city, the Queen Mother and Prince Mensa, next heir to the throne, be sent to him as hostages. The general did not understand that in the eyes of the Asante, these were the most important persons in the kingdom, and it was not within Kofi Kakari's power to surrender them, even if he had been so inclined.

In 1881, her intervention in the interest of peace with the British invaders was instrumental in preventing bloodshed for a time. She held the office of Queen Mother during the reign of several of her royal family members. In 1884, after Kwaku Dua was poisoned and the governmental system was in disarray with several outlying areas threatening to secede, she put forth, as candidate for the office of Golden Stool, an unpopular candidate, Kwasi Kisi, who she knew had no chance of winning. This nomination was a gesture to win British assistance and to bring the outlying rulers into the capital for council deliberations. The ploy was unpopular; she was deposed in late 1884 and was succeeded by Yaa Akyaa.

Suggested Reading:

(1) Lewin, Thomas J., *Asante Before the British*. Lawrence, KS: Regents Press of Kansas, 1979. pp. 49, 74, 82.
(2) Balmer, W. T., *A Brief History of the Akan Peoples*. New York: Atlantis Press, 1925. p. 167.

Ahhotpe I

Queen of Thebes (c.1570-c.1548 B.C.)

She was the wife of Seqenenre Ta'a II ("the Brave") and the mother of Egyptian King Kamose (d. c. 1570), King Ahmose I (r. c. 1570-1546 B.C.), who succeeded him and who is generally given credit for founding the Eighteenth Dynasty in Egypt, and Ahmose-Nofretari, their younger sister, whom Ahmose I married. On the doorway at Buhen an inscription alludes to Ahhopte I and Ahmose I in such a manner as to suggest that a co-regency existed during the early years of Ahmose's reign when he was too young to rule alone.

Later, while Ahmose I was driving the Hyksos kings out of Egypt, Queen Ahhotpe ran the government in Thebes, which is near modern day Luxor. On King Ahmose's stele in the temple of Amon-Re at Karnak, her achievements are commemorated. She is given credit for having "taken care of Egypt," of having "watched over her twoops and protected them," of having "pacified Upper Egypt and hunted down rebels." The latter refers to the fact that she helped to quell an uprising until her son could arrive with reinforcements. Her efforts, added to his, reunited Egypt under one rule.

She died c. 1548.

Suggested Reading:

(1) *The Cambridge Ancient History*, 3rd. ed., 2 vols. Cambridge: Cambridge University Press, 1970-1971. vol. 1, pp. 40, 62.
(2) Grimal, Nicolas, *A History of Ancient Egypt*. tr. Basil Blackwell Ltd. New York: Barnes & Noble, 1997. pp. 190, 200, 201.
(3) Carpenter, Clive. *The Guinness Book of Kings, Rulers & Statesmen*. Enfield, Middlesex; Guinness Superlatives Ltd., 1978. p. 68.

Ahmose-Nofretari

Queen, co-ruler of Egypt (c. 1552-1546 B.C.)

During the Second Intermediate Period of Egyptian history (c.1674-1553 B.C.), which was characterized by turbulence and regional rulers, the Hyksos, from Asia, invaded. Ahmose I, Nofretari's brother and husband, continued the fight against the invaders which his brother King Kamose had begun, eventually defeating the Hyksos and founding the Eighteenth Dynasty. He married his sister, Ahmose-Nofretari, who, in Ahmose's 16th or 22nd. year of reign, renounced the title of Second Prophet and received instead the title of God's Wife of Amon, through which the matrilineal dynasty would succeed. She was the first queen to hold this title.

The couple had a son, Amenhotep I (Amenophis), who succeeded to the throne upon his father's death, and a daughter, Ahmose, who received the title God's Wife as well. She outlived her husband and became regent for her son, who was too young to rule.

Ahmose-Nofretari was an influential and highly honored queen, as evidenced by depictions at Thebes of later pharaohs making offerings to her as a goddess. After her death she became the object of a religious cult, the center of which was at Deir el-Medina. Her name appears in at least fifty private tombs and on more than eighty monuments.

Suggested Reading:

(1) Grimal, Nicolas, *A History of Ancient Egypt*. tr. Basil Blackwell Ltd. New York: Barnes & Noble, 1997. pp. 190, 195, 200-202, 283.
(2) White, J. E. Manchip, *Ancient Egypt*. New York: Dover Publications, 1970. pp. 164-165.

Aissa Koli (Aisa Kili Ngirmaramma)

Ruler of the Kanuri Empire of Bornu, West Africa (c. 1562/3-1570, or 1497-1504)

Kanem-Bornu was located in West Africa. While some descrepancy exists about the dates and parentage of Aissa, substantial evidence of her reign exists among local tradition.

Arabic historians, who routinely ignored women sovereigns, failed to record her rule. Too, history records that her successor, Idris Aloma, imposed a Muslim bureacracy upon previously pagan subjects, all the more reason for Islamic sources to ignore her rule.

By some accounts she was the daughter of Ali Gaji Zanani, who died in c. 1545/47 (or 1497, according to Panikkar) after ruling only one year. By this account, when Ali Gaji Zanani died, he was succeeded by Dunama, a relative, who also died in 1497. Aissa Koli then ruled alone for seven years, because it was believed that there was no male heir.

However, she was unaware of the existence of a brother, whom his mother, a Bulala, had sent to the Bulala court because the interim ruler had threatened to kill all the former king's sons. The boy, Idris, was five years old at the time that Aissa Koli's rule began. When he reached the age of twelve, he wrote his mother and his sister the Queen, informing them of his existence. Aissa Koli's term being up—the rulers of many of the African nations had a fixed term of seven years—she asked him to come home. By this account, he was crowned king in 1504. Aissa Koli continued in a position of influence and authority, advising her long-exiled brother.

Other sources say that she was the daughter of a relative of Ali, King Dunama, who succeeded Ali and reigned until c. 1562/63. This version says that Ali had left a young son of five, Idris, who had been spirited away to live with his mother's Bulala relatives in Kanem for fear that Dunama would have him killed. After Dunama's death, Aissa assumed the throne and ruled for seven years, as it was generally believed that there was no male heir. When Idris was twelve, he wrote to his mother and his sister (by some accounts) Aissa, informing them of his existence. When the queen's seven-year term was up, she invited him to come home. He was crowned king (*mai*) in c. 1570 and went on to become the most famous king in the 1000-year Sefawa dynasty of Kanem-Bornu.

This version also maintains that Aissa continued in a position of influence and authority, as advisor to her brother on government procedures and the ways of his subjects, strengthening his position against inter-dynastic strife, until he grew to manhood.

Suggested Reading:

(1) Ajayi, J. F. A. and Michael Crowder, eds. *History of West Africa*. New York: Columbia University Press, 1972. vol. 1. "Songhay, Bornu and Hausaland in the 16th Century" by John Hunwick. pp. 101-139.

(2) Panikkar, K. Madhu, *The Serpent and the Crescent: A History of the Negro Empires of West Africa*. Bombay: Asia Publishing House, 1963. p.104.

Akawkis Candace

Queen of Ethiopia (343-333)

All queens of the period were called Candace. Akawkis ascended the throne after the death of King Basyo.

Aline Sitoe (Queen Sitoe)

Queen of the Diola Tribe, Casamance (c. 1936-1943)

Casamance was located in modernday Senegal, West Africa.

Aline-Sitoe was born ca. 1920 in Kabrousse. Beginning in 1942, she turned her people against the French who ruled her country. She gained renown as far away as Mauritania, Mali, and Guinea-Bissau for her battle-cry, "The white man is not invincible." She instigated a boycott of French products, encouraging instead local artisans to produce more. She discouraged use of the French language and exhorted her people to develop their intellectual capacities and resurrect their own culture. She sought to strengthen community life by giving women a more vital role. She announced a return to the use of the Diola six-day-week calendar, which was based on the annual rainy season, harvest season, dry season and pre-rainy season.

When Diola warriors ambushed a truck and killed four men, three of them soldiers, the French advanced upon Kabrousse and held it under seige from Jan. 13 to Jan. 29, 1943, when the Queen surrendered to prevent the French from burning the town to the ground. She was arrested and condemned to ten years in exile in Timbuktu; however, she died on May 22, 1944 after a long bout with scurvy.

She was buried in Timbuktu's Sidi el Wafi Cemetery, but plans were made in 1983 to return her remains to Senegal, which became independent from France 19 years after her death.

Legend claimed that Queen Sitoe could change herself into a bird whenever she liked.

Suggested Reading:

(1) "Mystery Finally Solved: Rebellious Queen Sitoe Succumbs to Scurvy," *The Houston Post* Associated Press. 27 October 1983: W3.

Amanipilade

Queen Regnant of Meroë (308-320)

Meroë was located in present-day Sudan. The kingdom declined under attacks by petty invaders, desert nomads called the Blemyes and Nobatae. By 200 Meroë was finally taken over and absorbed by Axum (Aksum).

Amanishakhete (Candace)

Queen, ruler of Kush in Meroë (c. 24-23 B.C.E.)

Queens were called "Candace" in Kush, which gave rise to the assumption by conquering Romans that "Candace" was her name. The Merotic people adopted an African-style matriarchal regime and set up a dynasty of queens, known collectively as the Candaces.

When the Romans under Petronius attacked the northern Kushian city of Napata, they were met by a "one-eyed lady of masculine status" who retreated to a neighboring fort, probably Meroë, and sent envoys to negotiate, hoping to dissuade them from destroying the religious capital. Petronius brushed aside her pleas and destroyed the town and the great temple of Amun at Jebel Barlal.

Two years later she returned to attack Petronius, but the Romans held their ground. The Romans then withdrew to Nubia, finding nothing more to interest them.

After 27 B.C. the Ethiopian "Candace" maintained diplomatic relations with Augustus.

Amanishakhete was succeeded by Queen Amantari and King Natakamani (Nelekamani), probably not only husband and wife, but brother and sister as well: Queen Amanishakhete's offspring. These two were able to carry on some measure of restoration of Napata.

Suggested Reading:

(1) Grimal, Nicolas, *A History of Ancient Egypt*. tr. Basil Blackwell Ltd. New York: Barnes & Noble, 1997. p. 387.
(2) Fairservis, Walter A., Jr., *The Ancient Kingdoms of the Nile*. New York: Mentor/NAL, 1962. p. 193.
(3) Cooke, S.A., F. E. Adcock, and M. P. Charlesworth, *The Cambridge Ancient History*. London; Cambridge University Press, 1971. vol. 10, pp. 42, 243, 778.
(4) Josephy, Alvin M., *The Horizon History of Africa*. New York: American Heritage Publishing Co., 1971. pp. 61-63.

Amina

Queen of Zaria (Zauzau) in Hausaland, Nigeria (15th or 16th c.)

One source postulates that Amina was the daughter of Turonku Batwa, who founded the city of Zaria, West Africa, in 1536, and therefore gives her rule as the end of the sixteenth century.

Amina succeeded her mother as ruler, but she had no husband. She is credited in oral tradition with expanding the empire of Zaria to include Nupe and Kororofa (Kwararata), a Jukun kingdom. Her influence also extended over Kano and Katsina.

She encouraged trade and built many of the famous Hausa earthworks. Under her remarkable leadership, Zaria became the most powerful state in Haussaland. Eventually her holdings stretched down to the sea.

The Chronicles of Kano speak of her with great respect: "At this time Zaria under Queen Amina conquered all the towns as far as Kwarafara and Nupe. Every town paid tribute to her. The Sarikin Nupe sent forty eunuchs and ten thousand kolas to her. She was the first to have eunuchs and kolas in Haussaland. Her conquests extended over 34 years."

The kola nut which she introduced is one of the great luxuries of Western Sudan; it is prized for its bitter taste, slightly aphrodisiac properties and its ability to quench thirst.

It was said that, although Amina never married, she took a new lover every night.

After Amina's death, her sister Zaria succeeded to the throne, but Zaria, the kingdom, soon faded from history as a great West African power.

Suggested Reading:

(1) Ajayi, J. F. A. and Michael Crowder, eds. *History of West Africa* vol. 1. "Hausaland and Bornu, 1600-1800" by R. A. Adeleye. New York: Columbia University Press, 1972. pp. 485-530.

(2) Panikkar, K. Madhu, *The Serpent and the Crescent: A History of the Negro Empires of West Africa*. Bombay: Asia Publishing House, 1963. pp. 113-114, 273.

Amanitore

Queen of Meroë or Nubia (B.C. 12-C.E.12)

She was the daughter of Queen Amanishaketo (ruled B.C.E. 41-12) and the wife of King Natakamani. She and her husband succeeded her mother. She is mentioned in the Bible in Acts 8: 26-40. She was succeeded by Queen Nawidemak.

Anches-en-Amen

See Ankhesenamun

Ankhesenamun (Also Ankhesenaton or Anches-en-Amen)

Egyptian Queen, widow of Tutankhaten (c. 1336-1327 B.C.)

Formerly named Ankhesenpaaten, she married Tutankhaten ("Living image of the Aten") who changed his name to Tutankhamun ("Living image of Amun"), while her name became Ankhesenamun. The couple had no living male heirs, although two foetuses found in the king's tomb might have been their two stillborn babies.

After the king's death in 1336 B.C., Queen Ankhesenamun, learning of the conquest of Amka, or Amki (adjacent to Lebanon) by the Hittites, wrote to Hittite King Suppiluliumas I (r. c. 1375-1335 B.C.): "My husband has died, and not one son do I have. But of you it is said that you have many sons. If you will give me a son of yours, he could be my husband. For how may I take one of my slaves and make him a husband and honor him?" Under Egypt's laws of matrilinear succession, the new husband would be the pharaoh.

The Hittite king was skeptical, commenting to the envoy he sent to investigate, "Perhaps they only wish to deride me." The queen sent an ambassador in return with the letter, "Why have you spoken these words: 'They wish only to deride me'? I have not written to any other country. To you alone have I written. It is said that you have many sons. Give me a son of yours; he shall be my husband and king over Egypt!"

Suppiluliumas agreed to send a son, Prince Zennanza, but he was murdered before he reached Egypt. Queen Ankhesenamun then married Ay, the vizier of her dead husband (1327 B.C.), leading to speculation ages hence that Zennanza's murderers might have been followers of the vizier. Ay was pharaoh of Egypt for four years.

After the so-called "marriage", Ankehesenamun disappeared from the scene, further fueling speculation among historians as to Ay's mode of ascension to power. In his tomb Ay is depicted accompanied by his wife, Tiy II.

Suggested Reading:

(1) Grimal. Nicolas. *A History of Ancient Egypt*. New York: Barnes & Noble, 1997. pp. 204, 241-242.
(2) Ceram, C. W. *The Secret of the Hittites*. New York: Dorset Press, 1990. pp. 161-162.

Ankhnesneferibre

Queen of Egypt (584-525 B.C.)

Ankhnesneferibre was the granddaughter of Wahibre Necho II who ruled from 610-595 B.C. and who was succeeded by his son Neferibre Psammetichus II, who ruled from 595-589 B.C.

Ankhnesneferibre ("Neferibre lives for her") was the daughter of King Neferibre Psammetichus and Queen Takhut. Before he died in 589, the king made sure that his daughter was adopted by the Divine Adoratarice Nitocris, whom she succeeded in 584.

Ankhnesneferibre held the office until the conquest of Egypt by Persia in 525 B.C.

Suggested Reading:

(1) Grimal, Nicolas. *A History of Ancient Egypt.* tr. Basil Blackwell Ltd. New York: Barnes & Noble, 1997. pp. 360-361.

Ankyeaa Nyame

Legendary Queen of Kumasi in West Africa (c. 17th c.)

The so-called Kumasi Stool family are members of the Oyoko family of Asante.

Ankyeaa Nyame is credited by oral tradition with being the founder of the tribe at Asumennya-Santemanso. Tradition says she simply appeared there, accompanied by an executioner, a court crier, and a stool carrier (throne carrier) named Taasiri. She came with her own stool as Queen, in other words.

According to the account of her origins authorized by the *Asantehene* (ruler) Osei Agyeman Prempe II (r. 1931-1970), she is said first to have appeared at a place located in Akyem Abuakwa called Toaa-ase, ruled by Chief Ntoni, "descended from the skies in a large Brass-pan suspended by a strong gold chain."

After eating, she disappeared, later to arrive at Asumennya-Santemanso.

Suggested Reading:

(1) Barber, Karin and P. F. de Moraes Farias, ***Discourse and Its Disguises***. Birmingham, England: University of Birmingham Centre of West African Studies, 1989, p. 76.

Arsine I (Arsinoë)

Queen of Egypt (284/281-ca. 274)

She was born ca. 305/295, the daughter of Lysimachus, king of Thrace and Macedonia. She married Ptolemy II Philadelphia and the mother of Ptolemy III Lysimachus and Berenice Phernophorus. In the 270s she was charged with and found guilty of plotting against her husband and exiled to Copts ca. 274/3.

Arsinoë II

Queen first of Thrace, then of Macedonia, then of Egypt, co-ruler of Egypt (277-270 B.C.).

Arsinoë was born c. 316 B.C., the daughter of Berenice and Ptolemy I Soter of Egypt.

In 300 B.C. she married Lysimachus, King of Thrace. Thrace was located in Asia Minor bounded by the Aegean and Black seas on the east and south, and by the Danube River on the north.

Arsinoë left her Egyptian homeland far behind when she married the King of Thrace. But as she was not his first wife, she had little prospect of furthering the futures of her offspring. Lysimachus already had an heir to the throne, his son Agathocles.

In the same year that her father Ptolemy I died in Egypt (283 B.C.), Arsinoë orchestrated the demise of Agathocles, Lysimachus' son by his first wife. In an attempt to advance the rights of succession of her own three sons, Arsinoë accused Agathocles of treason, hoping to discredit him. An angry Lysimachus, believing her accusations, ordered his own son Agathocles executed. In the outbreak of violence that followed, which escalated into a war involving Agathocles' avenging allies in Selucia, Lysimachus was killed in battle (281 B.C.).

Arsinoë, a consummate survivor, escaped from Ephesus, taking her sons to safety in Cassandrea where her exiled half-brother and new King of Macedonia, Ptolemy Ceraunus, cajoled her into marrying him—or vice versa. Thereafter, her new husband murdered two of her sons, his nephews.

When Ptolemy Ceraunus died fighting the Gauls in 279, Arsinoë attempted to have her remaining son Ptolemaeus installed on the Macedonian throne, but she failed and was forced to flee to Egypt.

There, in c. 276, now forty years old, she married her brother, Ptolemy II, and became in every sense co-ruler. It was due largely to her diplomatic skill that Egypt won the First Syrian War (c. 274-271). Following it, she was deified as Philadelphus (meaning "brother-loving") and displayed on the coinage of the realm.

The new Queen ruled the empire and managed its wars, meanwhile gathering around her such notable men of letters as the poet Callimachus. Ptolemy, also called Philadelphus, reigned among the chiefs and scholars of the court, while Queen Arsinoë, a woman of great intelligence and mature experience, is thought to have played the dominant role in the formulation of royal policy so long as she lived.

Several cities were named for her. Her interest in cultural pursuits led to the founding of a museum at Alexandra. She died in 270 B.C., but even before her death, she was being worshipped as a goddess, an incentive which she herself may have initiated. The king erected a monument in her honor in Alexandra known as the Arsinoeum.

This elevation to divinity of both king and his sister-queen might have ameliorated the deep Hellenistic taboos against incest. The precedent of marriage between siblings had already been set by Egyptian pharaohs. Thereafter, the practice of Hellenistic rulers of proclaiming their own divinity became commonplace.

Suggested Reading:

(1) Rawlinson, George. *Ancient History.*New York: Barnes & Noble, 1993. pp. 198, 200.
(2) Bowder, Diana, *Who Was Who in the Greek World*. New York: Washington Square Press, 1984. pp. 101-102.
(3) Peters, E. E. *The Harvest of Hellenism*. New York: Barnes & Noble Books, 1970)
(4) Langer, William L, ed. *World History*. Boston: Houghton Mifflin Company, 1940, 1980. p. 96.

Awura (or Aura) Pokou (or Queen Pokou)

Queen of the Baule tribe in West Africa (c. 1730-1750)

Awura Pokou ruled over one branch of the Akans' great Ashanti kingdom, which moved into the southeast part of the Ivory Coast region early in the eighteenth century.

Following a dispute over leadership, in which she refused to join the Ashanti confederacy in what is now Ghana, Awura Pokou took her followers and struck out south to the banks of the Komoe River. When she questioned her priest about the hazardous crossing of the river, he informed her that if she offered a sacrifice, all would go well for her tribe's crossing.

She offered her own son as a sacrifice, calling out, "Baouli—the child is dead." To this day, her descendants are called Baoules.

Queen Pokou and her tribe crossed the river and cultivated the savanna which lay on the other side. This was the beginning of the Baule (Baoule) tribe, which populate the area between the Komoe and Bandama Rivers. Eventually her clan assimilated many of the pre-existing tribes of the area to become the largest, most powerful tribe on the Ivory Coast. Although it lost much of its political power during the nineteenth century, it remains the largest tribe in the Ivory Coast today.

Suggested Reading:

(1) Kirtley, Michael and Aubine, "The Ivory Coast, African Success Story." *National Geographic.* July 1982: 95-125.

Section B

Bailor-Caulker, Honoria

Paramount Chief of the Shenge, Sierra Leone (fl. 20th c.)

Madame Honoraria Bailor-Caulker has been influential in Sierra Leone politics for several decades. Her family, the Caulkers, were slavers who ruled the coast of Yawri Bay in the vicinity of Freetown. Through slave trading, the Caulkers grew rich and powerful. While she was Paramount Chief, Madame Bailor-Caulker frequently mentioned this fact in public speeches, not only to assure some of her audiences that she had much for which to atone, but also because she said that powerful chiefs prefer that their ancestry be rooted among the strong who ruled rather than the weak who were enslaved.

She was a flambouyant leader who dressed in voluminous silk gowns and wore a turban adorned with ornate jewelry. She would be carried through the village in a palanquin, borne by relays of her subjects, and accompanied by a large entourage of singers, drummers, and dancers. At public meetings she would promise her subjects who had elected her that she would soon bring water and electricity to the area. She presided over Shenge District Court, where she heard cases involving local grievances and dispensed judgments.

In 1977 she traveled to the United States to speak at an American Anthropological Association meeting on women in government and politics. In 1997, although no longer holding office, she was still an outspoken champion for the Shenge.

Suggested Reading:

(1) Reader, John, *Africa*. New York: Alfred A. Knopf, 1998, originally London: Hamish Hamilton, Ltd., 1997. pp. 377-379.

Bakwa (Bazao)

See Turunku, Bakwa.

Balkis (Balqis, Bilqis, also Makeda)

Queen, ruler of Axum, Legendary name of the Queen of Sheba (10th c. B.C.)

Conflicting legends abound concerning the Queen of Sheba. Arab historian Sir John Glubb believes the Queen of Sheba was from Yemen.

Although she is not mentioned by name in the Koran, sura 27, "The Ant," describes her meeting with King Solomon. The king, noticing that one of the birds, the hoopoe, was missing from review, vowed to punish it if it could not justify its absence. When the bird arrived (verse 22), he said, "I have found out a thing that thou apprehendest not, and I come to thee with sure tidings. (verse 23) Lo! I found a woman ruling over them [the people of Sheba, or Saba], and she hath been given [abundance] of all things, and hers is a mighty throne."

The Yemenis honor all their queens by calling them *balqis al-sughra*, meaning "little queen of Sheba."

According to the Muslim legend, the king's demons, fearing he might marry the Queen of Sheba, told him that she had the hoof of an ass and hairy legs. The king had glass installed in the floor in front of his throne so that the Queen, mistaking it for water, raised her skirts, revealing that she did not have hairy legs.

Fage mentions the existence in southwestern Arabia (in present-day Yemen) of a number of major kingdoms, among which Saba, or Sheba, was the most powerful for some period in pre-Islamic times. Between the 6th c. B.C. and the 1st. c. A. D., Sabaean influences reached Ethiopia, which included among its traditions the story of the Queen of Sheba.

African legend says that in the tenth century B.C. an Ethiopian king on his deathbed named his daughter Makeda as his successor, and that Makeda ruled as Queen of Sheba.

According to an Ethiopian manuscript now in the British Museum, when an Ethiopian merchant named Tamrin took building materials to Jerusalem for the construction of King Solomon's temple, as a show of gratitude, Solomon sent with him valuable gifts for the queen. She was so impressed by the merchant's account of Solomon's wealthy court that she organized a large caravan laden with precious gifts and went to see for herself. A romance developed, resulting in the birth of a son whom Makeda named David, who ruled as Menelik I.

John Reader recounts a legend that Menelik went to the court of his father for a year, and on his departure, took the Ark of the Covenant from the temple and brought it to Axum. [However, while Solomon was alive, Axum, of Aksum, did not exist.]

Later, during the time of Queen Judith, Axum was destroyed, but monks carried the Ark to an island in Lake Zewai.

By another account, Solomon recognized Menelik as his first-born son and decreed that only Menelik's male heirs would rule Ethiopia. Emperor Haile Selassie claimed direct lineage from Menelik.

Hirtle points out that if Makeda were a contemporary of Solomon's, she would have lived in the 9th century B.C., but the ruins of the ruins of her purported palace at Axum have been dated from a few centuries A.D. to 500 B.C., "maybe further."

By yet another account mentioned by Vansina, the Kingdom of Rozwi, a Shona clan in Zimbabwe, was the true land ruled by the Queen of Sheba.

Suggested Reading:

(1) Mernissi, Fatima, *The Forgotten Queens of Islam*. tr. mary Jo Lakeland. Minneapolis: University of Minnesota Press, 1993. pp. 9, 43-44, 89, 118-119, 141-144.

(2) Jackson, John G., *Introduction to African Civilizations*. (Secaucus, NJ: Citadel Press, 1970. pp. 268-269.

(3) Glubb, Sir John, *A Short History of the Arab Peoples*. New York: Dorset Press, 1969. p. 24.

(4) de Villiers, Marq and Sheila Hirtle, *Into Africa*. Toronto: Key Porter Books, Ltd., 1997. pp. 23, 336-337, 346.

(5) Josephy, Jr., Alvin M., ed., *The Horizon History of Africa*. "Inner Africa" by Dr. Jan Vansina. New York: American Heritage Publishing Co., McGraw-Hill, Inc., 1971. p. 270.

(6) Reader, John, *Africa*. New York: Alfred A. Knopf, 1998; originally published in London: Hamish Hamilton, Ltd., 1997. pp. 220-222.

(7) Fage, J. D., *A History of Africa*. New York: Alfred A. Knopf, 1978. pp. 54-55.

Ballinger, Margaret

ANC Parliamentary Leader (1953-1960)

Born Margaret Hodgson in Scotland in 1894, she emigrated to South Africa as a child. She took her higher education in England, then returned to Johannesburg, where she taught history. She married W. P. Ballinger, a British labor organizer who had come to South Africa to assist Clements Kadalie's labor movement.

In 1953, Ballinger and Alan Paton and others founded the Liberal Party. She became its first president. The 1936 "Representation of Natives Act" had taken Black Africans off the common voting roles in the Cape Province, so Margaret Ballinger was asked by leaders of the African National Congress to stand for one of the four parliamentary seats set aside for non-white voters. She was the only member of the Liberal Party to serve in the parliament. She held this seat until it was abolished in 1960, then retired from public office.

During her political career, Ballinger was one of the few outspoken advocates of Black Africans' rights in the South African parliament.

She died in 1980.

Suggested Reading:

(1) Ballinger, Margaret. *From Junta to Apartheid: A Trek to Isolation.* Cape Town: Juta, 1969.
(2) Saunders, Christopher. *Historical Dictionary of South Africa.* Metuchen: Scarecrow Press, 1983.

Bazao (Also Bazao-Turunku)

See Turunku, Bakwa

Bendjou, Empress

Joint ruler of Mali (ca. 1345)

Bendjou was a commoner and the second wife of Emperor Sulayman (Suleymon), who ruled Mali from ca. 1341 to 1360. Sulayman had divorced his first wife, Kossi, in order to marry Bendjou.

However, either because of her commoner origins or because of Queen Kossi's popularity, when Bendjou met the noble ladies in the audience chamber, none would pay homage to her by throwing earth on their heads. They only threw it on their hands, a sign of disrespect.

Ibn Battuta, observing the customs of Mali in 1352, described this practice of groveling before the ruler: "If one of [the sultan's attendants] addresses the sultan and the latter replies, he uncovers the clothes from his back and sprinkles dust on his head and back, like one washing himself with water . . . ."

When the ladies of the court refused to throw dirt on their heads to honor Bendjou, she complained to the sultan [emperor], whose anger was incited against his ex-wife.

The incident, a reflection of a greater struggle for political power in Mali, escalated into a minor civil war which pitted Sulayman against the relatives of his ex-wife. Queen Kossi and a prince launched an unsuccessful coup attempt, but Sulayman and his chiefs defeated the opposition which she spearheaded, and Bendjou assumed joint rule of Mali without further incident.

Suggested Reading:

(1) Dunn Ross E., *The Adventures of Ibn Battuta*. Berkeley: The University of California Press, 1986. p.302.

(2) Panikker, K. Madhu, *The Serpent and the Crescent: A History of the Negro Empires of West Africa*. Bombay: Asia Publishing House, 1963. p. 60.

Berenice III (Cleopatra Berenice)

Queen of Egypt, co-ruler (101-88), then sole ruler (81-80 B.C.)

Berenice was the daughter of Ptolemy Lathyrus (Ptolemy IX), who ruled from 117 to 81 B.C. Her mother was either Cleopatra IV or Cleopatra Selene, who first (prior to 101 B.C.) married her to her uncle, Ptolemy Alexander (Ptolemy X).

Although the reign of her father Lathyrus totalled 36 years, for the first seven years (117-107 B.C.), his mother Cleopatra ruled for him, and for the next eighteen years (107-89 B.C.) he was a fugitive, ruling only over Cyprus, while his brother Alexander ruled Egypt, with the dowager queen, Cleopatra III.

When Cleopatra III died in 101, Berenice became full queen and co-ruler of Egypt.

However, Alexander was suspected of having assassinated Cleopatra III and was driven from Egypt. He raised an army and attempted to return, but when it was learned that he had robbed the tomb of Alexander the Great to finance his army, he was once again driven out.

Berenice accompanied him, but when he died, she returned to Egypt.

Meanwhile, Lathyrus had returned and had been restored as king. When Lathyrus died, he left only one legitimate heir, Berenice. She succeeded him on the throne and ruled for six months as sole monarch.

The Roman dictator Lucius Cornelius Sulla arranged for Ptolemy Alexander X's son, her first cousin, to return to Egypt to marry her. It was his intent that they would rule jointly.

However, Berenice had no intention of dividing her power and refused his proposition, so he simply had her assassinated (80 B.C.). The enraged populace, with whom Berenice had been very popular, killed Alexander, thus eliminating the last Ptolemaic ruler of Egypt.

Suggested Reading:

(1) Rawlinson, George. *Ancient History*. (New York: Barnes & Noble, 1993. pp. 206-207.
(2) Egan, Edward. W., et. al. *Kings, Rulers and Statesmen*. New York: Sterling Publishing Company, 1976. p. 125.
(3) Bowden, Diana. *Who Was Who in the Greek World*. Ithaca, NY: Cornell University Press, 1982. p. 405-406.

Berenice IV

Ruler Egypt (58-55 BC)

Berenice was the eldest daughter of Ptolemy XII Auletes (called "the flute player" because of his frivolous pursuits), Macedonian king of Egypt, and Cleopatra V Tryphaeana. Berenice was the older sister of the famous Cleopatra VII.

When Berenice's father went to Rome in 58 B.C. to seek military aid against an Alexandrian insurrection, he left the government in the hands of Berenice and her mother.

The mother died shortly thereafter, and Berenice was proclaimed queen of Egypt. She ruled alone for three years.

In 56 B.C. the Alexandrians, anxious to replace the absent Ptolemy XII Auletes, found a suitable marriage candidate for Berenice in Archelaus, a Pontic prince.

However, in 55 B.C. her father returned with Syrian reinforcements, regained control of the throne and executed Berenice and her supporters.

Suggested Reading:

(1)   Rawlinson, George. *Ancient History*. New York: Barnes & Noble, 1993. pp. 208-209.

(2)   Bowden, Diana. *Who Was Who in the Greek World*. Ithaca, NY: Cornell University Press, 1982. p. 406.

(3)   West, John Anthony. *The Traveler's Key to Ancient Egypt*. New York: Alfred A. Knopf, 1985. pp. 428-429, 446.

Bilqis

See Balkis

Section C

Cahina

Sse Khahina, al-

Candace

Traditional name for a dynasty of queens who ruled Meroë, Ethiopia and Kush. Also see *Amanishakhete*, whom Romans called Candace.

Candace

Queen of Ethiopia and Meroë (A.D. 42-52)

This particular Queen Candace is said to have learned of the new religion called Christianity from her treasurer, who had made a pilgrimage to Jerusalem and there had been baptized by Philip the Apostle. The episode is depicted in the book of Acts in the New Testament, where the treasurer is described as "a eunuch of great authority under Candace, queen of the Ethiopians, who had the charge of all her treasures, and had come to Jerusalem to worship."

Suggested Reading:

(1) Peters, F. E., *The Harvest of Hellenism*. New York: Barnes & Noble Books, 1996. p. 389.
(2) de Villiers, Marq and Sheila Hirtle. *Into Africa*. Toronto: Key Porter Books, Ltd., 1997. p. 340.

Cleopatra of Cyrene (Cleopatra Selene)

Ruler of Cyrene (ca. 33-31 B.C.)

Cyrene, originally a Greek colony, was located off the coast of Libya. In 74 B. it was incorporated as a province of Rome.

Cleopatra Selene was born in 40 B.C., the daughter of Mark Antony and Cleopatra VII and the twin sister of Alexander Helios, who ruled Armenia, Media, and Parthia. Another brother, Ptolemy Phoenicia, ruled Syria and Cilicia.

Her parents gave her Cyrene to rule ca. 33, but Octavian restored the lands to Roman rule after the battles of 31 B.C.

In compensation, Octavia, Octavian's sister and a wife of Mark Antony's, arranged a marriage for the deposed Cleopatra Selene with Juba of Mauretania, the king of Numidia, one of the most gifted rulers of his time.

Suggested Reading:

(1) Peters, F. E., *The Harvest of Hellenism*. New York: Barnes & Noble Books, 1996. pp. 385, 510fn.
(2) Langer, William L., ed. *World History*. Boston; Houghton Mifflin, 1980. p. 97.
(3) West, John Anthony, *Traveler's Key to Ancient Egypt*. New York: Alfred A. knopf, 1985. p. 26, 420.

Cleopatra I

Co-ruler (193-181 B.C.), Regent of Egypt (181-173 or 176 B.C.)

Cleopatra was the daughter of Antiochus III, Seleucid king of the Hellenistic Syrian Empire, which had long been at war with Egypt. Her mother was Laodice, a princess of Pontus.

Cleopatra was given in marriage to Ptolemy V Epiphanes in 199 or 196 B.C. but the marriage was not celebrated until 193 B.C. Ptolemy V. Epiphanes ruled from 203-181. The marriage, a political move as a result of a peace treaty with Antiochus, also made Egypt a protectorate of Seleucia. Cleopatra ruled at Epiphanes' side.

In ca. 189 B.C. the couple had a son who was to become Ptolemy VI Philomater (also Philometor, "loving mother") and later, a daughter, Celopatra II. Philomater was still a child when his father was poisoned and died in 181 at the age of 28.

Cleopatra I then became regent and kept an iron grip on the government until her death in 173 B.C. She also taught her son well; Ptolemy VI is mentioned in the Egyptian ruin Kom Ombo as a kind, wise, and tolerant ruler. However, because of what was seen as his cowardice during the war with Antiochus (171-168), the people of Alexandria demanded that he include his brother, Ptolemy VII, in his rule. His brother eventually expelled him.

Suggested Reading:

(1) Peters, F. E., *The Harvest of Hellenism*. New York: Barnes & Noble Books, 1996. pp. 178-179, 256, 272fn, 381fn.
(2) Rawlinson, George, *Ancient History*. New York: Barnes & Noble Books, 1993. p. 204, 205.
(3) Langer, William L., ed. *Encyclopedia of World History*. Boston: Houghton Mifflin, 1980. p. 97.

Cleopatra II

Co-ruler of Egypt (176-130 and again in 118-116 B.C.), sole ruler of Upper Egypt (130-118 B.C.)

Cleopatra II was the daughter of Ptolemy V Epiphanes. She married her brother, Ptolemy VI Philomater (or Philometor), who ruled Egypt from 180 to 145 B.C. She became co-ruler and bore him a daughter, Cleopatra III, and a son, Neos Philopater.

During the war with Antiochus IV, (171-168 B.C), Philomater displayed such cowardice that thereafter the people of Alexandria insisted that the couple share the rule with their younger brother, Ptolemy VII Euergetes (Physcon). This arrangement lasted until 164, when Euergetes expelled Philomater. To settle the quarrel between the two brothers, the Roman Senate restored Philomater, giving him and his wife Egypt to rule, and giving Cyrene and Cyprus to Euergetes.

In 145 B.C., while on a campaign in Syria, Philomater died. Their son was to share the throne with Cleopatra, but Euergetes came back to Egypt, killed Neos Philopater, and married Cleopatra II. Thus the empire was united, but only briefly.

Euergetes divorced his sister and married her daughter, Cleopatra III. In 130 B.C. Cleopatra revolted against him and became queen of parts of Upper Egypt, which she ruled alone until 118 B.C., when she and her brother signed a peace and amnesty agreement. They both died in 116 B.C.

Suggested Reading:

(1) Peters, F. E., *The Harvest of Hellenism*. New York: Barnes & Noble Books, 1996. pp. 181, 182, 269fn.
(2) Rawlinson, George, *Ancient History*. New York: Barnes & Noble Books, 1993. pp. 206-207.
(3) West, John Anthony, *Traveler's Key to Ancient Egypt*. New York: Alfred A. Knopf, 1985. p. 446.

Cleopatra III

Co-ruler of Egypt (116-101 B.C.)

Cleopatra III was the daughter of Cleopatra II and Ptolemy VI Philomater, who was also her mother's brother. She married her uncle, Ptolemy VII Euergetes II, and had two sons, Soter II Lathyrus and Alexander.

When her father died in 116, he bequeathed the throne to her and her sons jointly. Soter II, being the elder, ruled with his mother from 116 to 110, as Ptolemy VIII. However, Cleopatra favored her younger son and doubtless encouraged him to expel his brother.

Alexander, as Ptolemy IX, ruled briefly with his mother in 110, but Soter II gathered his forces and returned the next year to oust his brother.

Two years later Alexander was again able to expel his brother and join Cleopatra in ruling Egypt until her death in 101 B.C.

Suggested Reading:

(1) Peters, F. E., *The Harvest of Hellenism*. New York: Barnes & Noble Books, 1996. pp. 181, 182.
(2) Rawlinson, George, *Ancient History*. New York: Barnes & Noble Books, 1993. p. 207.

Cleopatra VII

Queen of Egypt (74-31 B.C.)

Cleopatra VII was born in 69 B.C., the daughter of Ptolemy Auletes. Although probably born in Egypt, she was not Egyptian, but Macedonian, Persian, and Greek.

When she was 14, Mark Antony visited Alexandria and the couple may have met then for the first time. Her father had previously been forced to flee an incensed populace in Egypt because of high taxes he had imposed, and he had only just been restored to the throne at the time of Mark Antony's visit.

When her father died in 51 B.C., as the oldest surviving daughter, Cleopatra became, at 18, joint ruler and bride of her younger brother Ptolemy XII, the oldest surviving son. Their father's will made Rome the guardian of Egypt, for by this time, the dynasty of the Ptolemys had become weak.

Plutarch described the young queen as the epitome of beauty, and she obviously had great powers of persuasion.

The chief ministers, Pothinus and Achillas, plotted to get rid of Cleopatra so that they could rule in her younger brother's name, and for two years they thwarted her attempts to rule and at last succeeded in expelling her to Syria. There she raised an army and set out for Egypt.

Her forces met the opposition at Perlusium in 48 B.C., but before a battle could be waged, Julius Caesar arrived in Alexandria, and Cleopatra decided on a new tack. She concealed herself in a rolled-up rug and had herself delivered to Caesar's headquarters so that she could petition him to intervene in her behalf. The old general—he was 56—was charmed by the young queen, and he quickly ordered that Cleopatra be restored to the throne.

Pothinus, believing that he was too far away from Caesar to be challenged, instigated a rebellion against Caesar's forces which lasted three months and resulted in Pothinus' death. During the final battles, Ptolemy drowned while trying to escape down the Nile on a barge.

Caesar, who had originally traveled to Egypt to do battle with his former son-in-law Pompey, whom Pothinus had already killed, had no further reason to remain in Egypt except for his infatuation with the young queen, who even bore him a son. Caesar chose another of her younger brothers, Ptolemy XIII, then ten, to be her co-ruler.

Although there is not complete agreement on the activities of Cleopatra, at least one legend claims that she followed Caesar back to Rome, arriving in 46 B.C. with a large retinue which included her brother and her baby. She moved into Caesar's villa and entertained him frequently, by this account.

He was assassinated in 44 B.C., and one of the versions of the reason for that murder was that he asked the Senate to pass a special law enabling him to divorce his wife so that he could marry Cleopatra, declare himself king, and make their son heir to the Roman Empire. He also placed a gold statue of her in the temple of Venus, an unpardonable sacrilege, since Cleopatra was a barbarian.

In the civil war that raged after his death, Cleopatra fled to Egypt, but she did not remain neutral in that struggle. She sent a fleet and four legions against Brutus and Cassius, Caesar's murders, but her forces were intercepted and conscripted for Cassius. Again she raised a fleet, but it was turned back by a storm.

The three victors of that war divided their spheres of influence such that Octavian stayed in Rome, Lepidus took Spain and France, while Mark Antony took the east.

One of Mark Antony's first acts, on arriving in Tarsus, was to summon Cleopatra to answer charges of conspiracy, since her troops had been used by Cassius. Cleopatra was prepared; she had not been idle in the meantime. Before her younger brother could reach the legal ruling age of 14, she had had him poisoned and had named her son Caesarion as her co-ruler.

At 28, she had gained great confidence and theatrical timing. She took her time answering Mark Antony's summons and eventually arrived, just as he was holding audience, dressed as Venus aboard a gaudily festooned boat. The crowds turned from him and rushed to the bank of the Nile, where she waited, like a hostess, for him to come to her.

Mark Antony did indeed come to her, and she gave him a queenly reception and proposed a great feast. By the time the revelry ended, Cleopatra had even managed to convince him to order the death of her one remaining sister, Arsinöe, so that no other threats remained to her sovereignty.

The relationship between Antony and Cleopatra lasted for 12 years, although in its midst he returned to Rome and in 40 B.C., as a political move, married Octavius' sister, Octavia. He probably also married Cleopatra in 36 B.C. so as to legitimize the couple's three children.

Together the couple ruled Egypt and most of Asia Minor. Mark Antony designated her "Queen of Queens" and appointed her and Caesarion as joint rulers of Lybia, Cyprus, and Coelesyria. They parceled out other lands to their children: Alexander, the older son, was made ruler of Armenia, Media, and Parthia; while his twin sister Cleopatra was made ruler of Cyrene, and their brother Ptolemy Phoenicia was made ruler of Cilicia and Syria.

Octavian then denounced Mark Antony in the Senate and in 32 B.C. declared war on Cleopatra. The couple ignored the threat and spent the winter in feasting and revelry on the island of Samos. Octavian advanced across their lands, claiming them for Rome, until he met Antony's troops near Actium in Greece in 31 B.C. Although Antony had superior troops, Cleopatra persuaded him to fight a naval battle against Agrippa, Octavian's naval commander.

During the battle, Cleopatra's boat sailed away, and Antony, thinking that she had fled, was so distraught that he left his command and sailed after her. His forces were defeated, so Cleopatra left for Alexandria to raise another fleet.

There she met Octavian. She offered to abdicate in favor of Caesarion, but Octavian was not interested. He offered her favorable treatment if she would kill Antony. After yet another losing battle, Cleopatra retreated to a mausoleum she had built for her own death and sent a messenger to tell Antony that she was dead. Distraught, he stabbed himself, but he didn't die immediately. When he learned that Cleopatra was still alive, he had servants carry him to her mausoleum, where they raised him by ropes so that he could see her looking out the window.

Plutarch said, "Those who were present say that there was never a more pitiable sight than the spectacle of Antony, covered with blood, struggling in his death agonies and stretching out his hands towards Cleopatra as he swung helplessly in the air."

She pulled him up through the window and Antony died in her arms. The year was 30 B.C.

When Antony died, Cleopatra, then 39, again tried to beguile Octavian, but she could see that he was not easily entranced by a middle-aged woman. Fearing poor treatment as a hostage in Rome, she attempted suicide, but Octavian removed all knives and weapons and threatened to harm her children when she went on a hunger strike. Legend maintains that loyal servants smuggled an asp into her mausoleum in a basket of figs. She held it to her breast until it killed her. To the Egyptians, the asp was the divine minister of the sun god. The symbolic meaning of an asp bite was that the sun god had rescued his daughter from humiliation and taken her to himself.

Suggested Reading:

(1) Peters, F. E., *The Harvest of Hellenism*. New York: Barnes & Noble Books, 1996. pp. 183, 314fn, 381, 384-387, 402fn, 436.
(2) Ludwig, Emil, *Cleopatra*. New York: Viking Press, 1937.

Cleopatra VI Tryphaena

Co-ruler of Egypt (58 B.C.)

Cleopatra Tryphaena was married to Ptolemy XI Auletes (the flute player), who ruled from 80 to 58 B.C. and from 55 to 51 B.C. Ptolemy had an illegitimate claim to the throne, so he faced much opposition to his rule. When he was driven into exile in 58 B.C., Cleopatra Tryphaena and his daughter Berenice took turns ruling. Cleopatra died shortly after he left, and Berenice was elected queen.

Suggested Reading:

(1) Langer, William L., ed., *Encyclopedia of World History*. Boston: Houghton Mifflin, 1980. p. 97.
(2) Peters, F. E., *The Harvest of Hellenism*. New York: Barnes & Noble Books, 1996. pp. 380-381.

Section D

Daurama, Queen (Magajiva)

Ruler of Daura state (c. 9th c.), Founding Queen-grandmother of the Hausa States of Northern Nigeria and Niger. (10th c.)

Daura is a town and emirate in present-day Kaduna State, Northern Nigeria, West Africa. "Magajiva" means "the senior princess."

A queen was founder of Daura, and she began a lineage of ruling queens that, according to de Villiers and Hirtle, lasted for several hundred years. According to Davidson, the last queen of Daura was the last of a line of only nine queens in the area; however, it is possible that each of these queens ruled for many decades. Another source sets the number of successive Habe Queens who ruled Daura in the tenth and eleventh centuries at seventeen. Oral tradition lists these women as: Kurfuru, Shata, Gino, Walzama, Shawata, Daura, Batatume, Yanbamu, Innagari, Gamata, Sandamata, Jamata, Zama, Yakumo, Yukuna, Gizirgizir, and Hamata. The queenly tradition survives to some extent even today in Islamic Daura, for the senior princess in the Daura emir's household holds the title "Magajiva"

According to Hausa lore, the last queen of Daura, Magajiya Daurama, had offered half her realm to the person who killed Sarki, the huge fetish snake living in Daura's well. A son of the king of Baghdad, Bayajida (or Anuyazidu), was traveling through the area with his wife, a princess of Bornu to the east, and stopped for water at the well. He killed the snake, cutting off its head, which he kept, and throwing the body onto the ground. When the feat was reported to the queen, she called for Bayajida to appear before him with proof of his deed. When he produced Sarki's head, she offered to give him half of her town. He answered, "Do not divide the town because I . . . will be amply rewarded if you will . . . take me as your consort." She married him and he was given the title "Makas-Sarki", "slayer of the snake."

The most popular version of the legend says that she and Bayajida had seven children, one of whom was named Daura. A son was named Bawogarior

("Give back the town"). Another version says that their six grandsons, plus a son of Bayajida's other wife, Magasram, became the Seven Rulers of the Hausa Bakwai, the Seven True Hausa Kingdoms (10th c.).

Sarki's well is still in use in Daura. Women still draw water daily from the well.

Suggested Reading:

(1) de Villiers, Marq, and Sheila Hirtle. *Introduction to Africa*. Toronto: Key Porter Books, Ltd., 1997. p. 287.

(2) Josephy, Jr., Alvin M., ed. *The Horizon History of Africa*. "The Niger to the Nile" by Basil Davidson. New York: American Heritage Publishing Co., McGraw-Hill, Inc., 1971. pp. 241-242.

(3) Layor, ChiChi. *The Land of the Long Horn*. Hausa epics. Ebo State, Nigeria. In manuscript form, 1996. Also published in *Leopards, Oracles and Long Horns: Three West African Epic Cycles*. Spring, TX: Panther Creek Press, 2001: "Abuyazidu and the Queen of Daura" pp. 138-141.

Dido (Also Elissa)

Queen of Phoenicians, founder of Carthage (ca. 814 B.C.)

The oldest version of the event of the founding of Carthage by Dido is from a history of Sicily by Timaeus in the early part of the 3rd century B.C. The founding date is cited variously as 825 or 814 B.C.

Dido is also called Elissa in Greek tradition and is associated with Tanit, tutelary goddess of Carthage. Dido, or Elissa, was said to be the daughter to Mutton, King of Tyre, and the sister of Pu'myaton (Pygmalion), who ruled the Sidonian state (r. 820-774 B.C.). She married Acerbas, who was killed by her brother. To escape her brother, during the seventh year of his reign, she fled to northern Africa, near modern day Tunis, where a local chief, Iarbus, sold her a piece of land upon which she founded a settlement which became Carthage.

Carthage became the most important outpost of Phoenician civilization in the Western Hemisphere, with almost a million people within its walls. In the sixth century it was the wealthiest city in antiquity.

To keep from having to marry Iarbus, Dido stabbed herself in the presence of a host of witnesses atop her own funeral pyre which she herself had caused to be constructed.

Virgil's version is that Dido met Aeneas when he landed in Africa and killed herself with his sword when he left her. She cursed him and his descendants, saying they would always be enemies of Carthage.

Ovid tells the story of Dido's sister Anna who came to Italy after Dido's death and many other misfortunes. There she was welcomed by Aeneas, but Lavinia was jealous. Anna warned of Lavinia's jealousy by Dido's ghost, left and disappeared in the Numicus River.

Morford and Lenardon suggest the story may be genuine to a point.

Suggested Reading:

(1) Ben Khader, Aïcha Ben Abed, and David Soren. *Carthage: A Mosaic of Ancient Tunis*. New York: The American Museum of Natural History and W. W. Norton, 1987. pp. 25-26, 100.

(2) Watts, A. E., tr. *The Metamorphoses of Ovid*. San Francisco: North Point Press, 1980. p. 319.

(3) Morford, Mark P. O., and Robert J. Lenardon. *Classical Mythology*. New York: Longman, 1977. pp. 2f, 257, 261, 453, 455, 488.

Luísa Dias Diogo

Prime Minister of Mozambique (2004-)

Luísa Dias Diogo, the first woman prime minister of Mozambique, was born April 11, 1958 in the remote Mague district of the central province of Tete. She went to school in Tete before moving to Maputo, where she studied accountancy at the Maputo Commercial Institute. She studied economics at Maputo's Eduardo Mondlane University, graduating with a bachelor's degree in 1983.

Meanwhile, in 1980, she began working in Mozambique's Ministry of Planning and Finance, while the country was in economic chaos, struggling to overcome the effects of colonial rule, and mired in civil war that would continue for another ten years. She became head of the department in 1986.

At the war's end, Mozambique was a devastated nation, strewn with land mines and facing disasters from floods to soaring rates of HIV/AIDS infection.

In 1989 Diogo was named National Budget Director.

She went on to obtain a master's degree in financial economics at the University of London in 1992. Then she worked for the World Bank as program officer in Mozambique.

In 1994 she joined the Frelimo Party's government as Deputy Minister of Planning and Finance, then in 2000 became Minister of Planning and Finance, a position she continues to hold.

After three years as Mozambique's finance minister, in February of 2004, Diogo, 46, was tapped by President Joaquim Chissano to become Mozambique's first woman Prime Minister, replacing Pascoal Mocumbi, a medical doctor by profession, who left the post he had held for nine years for a top position in an international health body.

Diogo's appointment represented a changing of the guard in Mozambican politics. Longtime President Joaquim Chissano later announced that he would not run for reelection, giving Diogo an opportunity to influence national affairs far greater than her predecessors. She immediately focused on improving an economy weakened by a series of major floods and double-digit inflation. Diogo consistently used her contagious passion for Mozambique to drive real economic change. She became an outspoken advocate of transparency, accountability and good governance in a region long victimized by corruption.

On a continent where women rarely reach the highest rungs of politics, Prime Minister Diogo now heads a government that was once written off as a failed state but that now posts healthy economic growth rates. Income per capita in Mozambique has doubled over the past decade.

Her achievements attracted global attention. She was singled out by the World Bank for her efforts in poverty reduction and later served on the United Nations Commission on the Private Sector and Development, helping to map out a vision of how even the poorest countries could unleash entrepreneurship and mobilize the private sector to meet their development challenges. In 2004, Elizabeth MacDonald and Chana R. Schoenberger, in a special report to *Forbes* Magazine, named her one of the top 100 most powerful women in the world. In September 2005, she was the international guest speaker at the British Labour Party Conference.

Diogo is married to an attorney and is the mother of three children.

Suggested Reading:

(1) "Luisa Diogo Advocate for Africa" by Mark Malloch Brown. *Time Magazine*, April 26, 2004.

Dola (Iye Idolorusan)

Queen of the Itsekiri kingdom in Nigeria (c. 1850)

Dola was the half-sister of *Olu* (king) Akengbuwa, who died in 1848. Following his death, a dispute broke out among several contenders for the throne. Dola finally set up an interregnum council of state, which she headed, in an attempt to hold the kingdom together.

However, the Itsekiri divided into vying trade groups which Queen Dola was powerless to control. Her "Governor of the River", or minister of trade, became the most influential person in the kingdom.

Queen Dola's influence quickly diminished, but no new *olu* was elected until 1936.

Suggested Reading:

(1)   Crowder, Michael and Obaro Ikime, eds. *West African Chiefs*. New York: Africana Publishing Company, 1970. pp. 289-311, Ikime, Obaro. "The Changing Status of Chiefs among the Itsekiri".

Domitien, Élisabeth

Prime Minister of the Central African Republic (1975-1976)

The Central African Republic is a landlocked nation, bordered on the north by Chad, on the east by Sudan, on the south by Congo, and on the west by Cameroon. It is ruled by a Head of State (president and briefly, emperor) and a Head of Government (prime minister).

The country gained independence from France in 1960 with David Dacko as president. Five years later, Dacko's cousin Jean-Bedel Bokassa seized power in a military coup. In 1972 the sole political party declared Bokassa president for life.

Thus he was still in power when, on January 1, 1975, Élisabeth Domitien began her term as prime minister, the first woman so designated on the continent. The choice of a woman Head of Government was particularly unusual in a dictatorship that was growing more repressive each year, but Bokassa had displayed one degree of sensitivity toward the plight of women. For example, in 1971, in commemoration of Mother's Day, he had released all women prisoners at the same time ordering the execution of men accused of serious crimes against women.

Élisabeth Domitien served until April 7, 1976. Then, in September, Bokassa dissolved the government. In December he renamed the country "Central African Empire" and gave himself the title of Emperor Bokassa I. His coronation the following year cost some $30 million. His eccentric behavior finally led Dacko to head another (French-supported) coup, toppling Bokassa in 1979 and returning Dacko to power.

Suggested Reading:

(1) Lipschutz, Mark R. and R. Kent Rasmussen. *Dictionary of African Biography*. Berkeley: University of California Press, 1989. pp. 51, 261.

(2) Delury, George E. *The World Almanac and Book of Facts*. New York: Newspaper Enterprise Association, Inc., 1980. p. 523.

Dzeliwe Shongwe

Queen Regent of Swaziland (1982-1983)

Dzeliwe was the senior wife of King Sobhuza II (Mona) (1899-1982), who ruled for sixty years and died at the age of 82. It had been arranged that Dzeliwe was to act as Regent until Sobhuza's handpicked successor, Prince Mokhesetive (Mswati III, b. 1968), came of age. A fifteen-man National Council (Liquqo) and an "Authorized Person", Prince Sozisa Dlamini, were appointed to assist her.

In 1983, Swaziland's first Prime Minister, Prince Mbandla (Makhosini) N. F. Dlamini, a great-grandson of Sobhuza I and the nephew of Sobhuza II, was ousted from his post by Dzeliwe and the Liquqo for his resistance to recognizing the authority of the Liquqo. Additionally, his reformist and modernist views clashed with the conservative and traditional Liquqo. He was forced to flee into Bophuthatswana while a more conservative candidate, Prince Bhakimpi Dlamini, was appointed Prime Minister.

However, the Liquqo kept asserting its authority and in August, 1983, prepared a document for the Queen Regent to sign which would acknowledge the Supreme Authority of the Liquqo. When Dzeliwe refused to sign, she was physically removed as head of state and ordered out of the

Royal Compound. She was suceeded by Queen Ntombi Thwala, mother of the king-designate.

Suggested Reading:

(1) Blaustein, Albert P., and Gisbert H. Flanz, eds. *Constitutions of the Countries of the World: A Series of Updated Texts, Constitutional Chronologies, and Annotated Bibliographies.* Dobbs Ferry, New York: Oceana Publications, 1991.

Section E

Eji (Also called Mutnedjmet or Metnedjenet)

Co-ruler of Egypt (c. 1351-1350 B.C.)

She was the eldest sister of Queen Nefertiti, wife of King Akhenaton, whose rule Egyptologists place variously from c. 1378-1352 B.C. to 1379-1362 B.C. Nefertiti had either died or fallen out of favor with her husband about the twelfth year of his reign. Toward the end of his reign, their oldest daughter Meritaton's husband Sakere (or Smenkhkare) was asked to co-rule, probably because of an infirmity of Akhenaton's. When Sakere died, c. 57 or 61, his child-brother Tutankhamen ruled (c. 1362-1352 B.C.). He was also married to a daughter of Akhenaton, Ankhesenpoaten. During Tutankhamen's rule, the actual power rested with his elderly regent Ay and with General Horemheb, the royal deputy. When King Tut died ca. 1352 or 1351, the elderly Ay continued to hold power while the widow queen looked for a husband-successor. It is likely that Horemheb had a hand in the void which led to his own ascension, since the widow's husband-to-be was murdered, Ay died, and so, apparently, did Tut's widow. During this void, Queen Eji, as the sister of the late queen, was left as ruler for only a year or two. Horemheb married her to secure a claim to the throne, and Eji seemed to play little part in the government following the marriage. Although he was an elderly man, Horemheb ruled for over a quarter of a century, but he and Eji had no children. This rule marked the end of the Eighteenth Dynasty.

Suggested Reading:

(1) Grimal, Nicolas. *Ancient Egypt*. New York: Barnes & Noble Books, 1997. pp. 214, 226, 312, 317, 318.
(2) Egan, Edward W. et. al., eds. *Kings, Rulers, and Statesmen*. New York: Sterling Publishing, 1976. p. 123.

Ras Ela Giudit

Ruler of Axum or Aksum, Ethiopia (846-885)

Axum, located in northern Ethiopia, was one of the most powerful kingdoms in sub-Saharan Africa. The kingdom of Axum thrived from about A.D. 100 to 800. Ela Giudit was the granddaughter of Ras Demawedem Wechem Asfare, who ruled Aksum from 790 to 820. She was also known as Terdáe Gomaz Yodit.

Elissa

Legendary founder of Carthage. See *Dido*

Esato (or Esat)

See Judith

Section F

Fatima

Queen of Zanzibar (c. 1652-1696)

For over a century the small kingdoms on the South Central coast of Africa were harassed by the Arabs and the Portuguese, each fighting for control. Several women ruled during this period, making their kingdoms easy targets, in the eyes of the Arabs. In 1652 the Sultan ibn Seif of Oman drove the queen of Zanzibar off the island. For the next forty years, however, the Portuguese continued to maintain the upper hand and the queen returned to Zanzibar. In 1696 the Arabs lay seige to Fort Jesus at Kilindini in Mombasa, where many of the local citizens had taken refuge. The Portuguese dispatched ships from Goa and Mozambique to intercept the Arabs, but the Omani slipped through. Queen Fatima had been attempting to send supplies to Fort Jesus, which was so undermanned that the women had to take turns as sentries. The Arabs captured Zanzibar and took the queen prisoner, deporting her to Muscat. After ten years, however, she was allowed to return.

Suggested Reading:

(1) Josephy, Jr., Alvin M., ed., *The Horizon History of Africa*. Clarke, Prof. John Henrik, "Time of Troubles". New York: American Heritage Publishing Co., McGraw-Hill, Inc., 1971. pp. 369-370.

Section G

Garsemot Kandake

Queen Regnant of Ethiopia (ca. 50-60)

No information has been found on her relation to other rulers of the era.

Gokare

Queen Regnant of the Kuba, Congo (ca. A.D. 950)

She led the Kuba during a period of expansion into its territory by new settlers, who arrived in the Congo region between 1000 and 1500 to form small communities.

Gudit

Warrior-Queen Regnant of Bahi al-Hamusa (ca. 980-1000)

Bahi al-Hamusa of Demot was located south of the Nile River and southwest of Shava. Gudit was probably Jewish. She led her people in an attack against the Axumite (Aksumite) Dynasty that ruled Ethiopia. There are a number of queens with similar names in this region at approximately the same time. There is not enough archeological evidence to ascertain whether or not some of them may in fact be the same ruler by a different appellation. However, this queen appears not to have been a ruler of Axum, but an invader.

Gulama, Madame

Mende Chieftain in Sierra Leone, West Africa (1960's-1986)

For more than thirty years, Madame Gulama was a prominent and controversial leader in Sierra Leone affairs. Much of her power stemmed from arranging marriage between graduates of the Sande Bush (female initiation society, of which she herself was a graduate and then director) and men in strategic positions who could help her in her own ambitious plans. Graduates of the Sande Bush are always influential in their own right and thus a great asset to men in positions of leadership.

Suggested Reading:

(1) Boone, Sylvia Ardyn, *Radiance From the Waters*. New Haven: Yale University Press, 1986, pp. 86, 146.

Gwamile Mdluli

Queen, Chief Regent of Swaziland (1899-1921)

She was the wife of King Mbandzeni (c. 1857-1889), who reigned from 1874 until his death. Gold was discovered in 1882, bringing more and more Europeans into the area, so that, during the last five years of his reign, he signed almost 400 concessions granting the newly arrived Europeans sundry privileges. Shortly before his death in 1889, he signed one final concession granting Europeans control of Swaziland in return for twelve thousand pounds a year. Upon his death, his son Bhunu (b. 1873) succeeded as king at the age of sixteen. During his short life, Bhunu and his regents worked futilely to regain control of Swazi rights that his father had signed away. Bhunu died in 1899, leaving a newborn son Sobhuza II (Mona) to inherit the throne.

Sobhuza's grandmother Gwamile served as Chief Regent, working to reverse the "sellout" of Swazi rights perpetrated by her husband. One of her first acts was to dissolve the concessionaires' committee.

In 1899 the Boer War began between Britain and the Transvaal and the Orange Free State. On October 1, 1899 the Transvaal government surrendered its powers over Swaziland to Queen Regent Gwamile. But by that time, the white man's encroachment into Swazi life could not be reversed.

In 1903, after the war was over, Swaziland became a British protectorate. Gwamile continued as regent until her grandson was formally installed (1921). Swaziland would not gain full independence again until 1968.

Suggested Reading:

(1) Blaustein, Albert R. and Gisbert H. Flanz, eds. *Constitutions of the Countries of the World: A Series of Updated Texts, Constitutional Chronologies, and Annotated Bibliographies.* Dobbs Ferry, New York: Oceana Publications, 1991.
(2) Lipschutz, Mark R. and R. Kent Rasmussen. *Dictionary of African Historical Biography.* Berkeley: The University of California Press, 1986, p. 220.

Section H

Hadina Za Hadena

Queen of Ethiopia (390-380)

Bayo, her successor, reigned for seven years and was succeeded by Queen Akawa Candace, who ruled for ten years.

Hatshepsut (Or Hatasu)

Queen of Egypt (1479-1458 B.C.)

Other sources list 1505-1484, 1503-1482, 1501-1480, or 1473-1458, Eighteenth Dynasty. Hatshepsut was the daughter of King Thutmose I and Queen Ahmose I. She married her half-brother, King Thutmose II. When their father died in ca. 1493 B.C., the couple ascended to the throne. Thutmose II died ca. 1479, before Hatshepsut could bear him a son, and a boy of six by a minor wife of his became Thutmose III. Hatshepsut assumed the regency, but very shortly usurped the throne and ordered herself crowned pharaoh, as selected by the god Amon-Re. She adopted the false beard signifying wisdom worn only by pharohs. Occasionally she was depicted wearing masculine garb as well.

An extraordinary and able monarch, she forswore the military conquests of her forebears and concentrated instead on commercial enterprises. Her greatest economic triumph was the reestablishment, in the ninth year of her reign (c. 1471 B.C.), of trade with the land of Punt, which was probably on the Somali coast along the Gulf of Aden, although scholars differ as to its exact location. Because the Nubians controlled the Nile route between Aswan and Khartoum and demanded toll to use it, another route had to be found. Hatshepsut's Chancellor Nehsy led the trade expedition of five provision-laden ships that had to be carried across the desert from Thebes to the Red Sea to reach Punt. The chief of Punt, Parahu, and his wife, Atiya, met the expedition with gestures of great obeisance. In exchange for bread, beer, wine, meat and fruit, the ships brought back "green" gold, ivory, ebony, herbs, myrrh, baboons, monkeys, hounds, servants and their children. Many of the treasures collected in Punt were used to adorn the impressive edifices and monuments built during the queen's approximately 20-year reign.

The military leaders chafed under her indifference and lack of military ambitions and rallied around Thutmose III, waiting for him to grow to manhood. Encouraged by them, Thutmose III became bent on acquiring a reputation as an empire-builder, and he rose to become head of the army, occupying himself with foreign wars, while Hatshepsut occupied herself constructing monuments. Some of those monuments which survive are small chapels dedicated to the great architect of the day, Senmut, who rose to a position of eminence in her court. Their location within her temple suggests that Senmut must have been her lover. However, if he had the memorials placed there without her knowledge, as some suggest, she must have discovered them and hacked them from the walls of niches. Five years prior to the end of her reign, all record of Senmut's activities ceases.

In the last five years of her reign, Hatshepsut's power waned. Prince Thutmose III, doubtless irked by the usurpation of his aunt, either came to the throne in a *coup d'etat* or acceded at the time of her death. Evidence of his vendetta against her memorials is irrefutable. Hatshepsut died in about 1458 B.C.

Suggested Reading:

(1)   Josephy, Jr., Alvin M., ed. *The Horizon History of Africa*. New York: American Heritage Publishing Co., McGraw-Hill, Inc., 1971. pp. 73-74. Shinnie, Margaret, "Civilizations of the Nile".

(2)   Rawlinson, Nicolas. *Ancient History*. New York: Barnes & Noble Books, 1997. pp. 77, 163, 174, 176, 200-217, 246, 262-264, 274, 295, 297, 300-202, 313.

(3)   Grimal, Nicolas. *A History of Ancient Egypt*. New York: Barnes & Noble Books, 1988. pp. 163, 174, 176, 200 fl.-217, 246, 262, 264, 274, 295, 297, 300-302, 313.

(4)   Reader, John, *Africa*. New York: Alfred A. Knopf, 1998; published in London: Hamish Hamilton, Ltd., 1997. pp. 196-197.

(5)   White, J. E. Manchip. *Ancient Egypt: Its Culture amd History*. New York: Dover Publications, 1970. pp. 165-167.

(6) Fairservis, Walter A. Jr. *The Ancient Kingdoms of the Nile*. New York: Mentor/NAL, 1962. pp. 133-134, 141, 165.

(7) West, John Anthony. *The Traveler's Key to Ancient Egypt*. New York: Alfred A. Knopf, 1985. pp. 342-343.

Hetepheres I

Queen mother of the fourth dynasty, Egypt (c. 2613-2494 B.C.)

Because of Egypt's law of matrilineal succession, Hetepheres I bore the title of Daughter of God. She was the daughter of Huni and half-sister of Meresankh, who was not of royal blood. Meresankh was the mother of Sneferu (Snofru), whom Hetepheres married and who ruled after Huni's death. Among the couple's children was Khufu (Cheops), who succeeded upon the death of his father. Hetepheres outlived her husband and was buried with great honors by her son.

Suggested Reading:

(1) Grimal, Nicolas. *The History of Ancient Egypt*. New York: Barnes & Noble, 1997. pp. 67-68, 128)

Hoho

South African Khoi chiteftainess (fl. 1750)

Although no written history existed at the time of Hoho's reign, evidence of the existence of this ruler of a Khoi, or Hottentot, clan are found in at least two old texts, one by Juju (1880), another by J. H. Soga (1930). Both describe the advance of the Xhosa people into Khoi territory. Sometime after 1750 the Xhosa warriors led by Rharhabe (d. 1782) a son of Xhosa chief Phalo, crossed the Kei river and encountered three of Hoho's men, whom, tradition states, he incorporated into his chiefdom as the isi'Thathu clan, *isithathu* meaning three. It is not known what her clan was called prior to that time. According to Soga, Hoho peacefully surrendered the Amatola Mountains to Rharhabe in exchange for tobacco, dagga and dogs; however, Juju describes a battle against her which Rharhabe waged in order to bring about that surrender.

Suggested Reading:

(1) Peires, J. B. *The House of Phalo*. Berkeley: The University of California Press,1982, p. 23, 200.
(2) Juju. "Reminiscences of an Old Kaffir". *Cape Monthly Magazine*, 3rd series, 3. 1880: 289-294.
(3) Soga, John Henderson. *The South-Eastern Bantu*. Johannesburg: Witwatersrand University Press, 1930. p.130.

Section I

Isato ("Fire")

Queen of the Falasha Agaw of Abyssinia. See Judith.

Section J

Jinga (also Jingha)

See Nzinga

Jodit

See Judith, Abyssinian queen

Johnson-Sirleaf, Ellen

President of Liberia (2006-)

Ellen Johnson-Sirleaf was born in Monrovia on October 29, 1938. Three of her grandparents were indigenous Liberians and the fourth was a German who married a marketwoman from a rural village. In 1917, when the United States declared war on Germany, Liberia, out of loyalty to the U.S., also declared war on Germany, and that grandfather was forced to leave the country. Liberia had maintained close ties to the States since it was established by former U.S. slaves whom the country relocated to the West African shores. Her election victory was formally announced by the Liberian elections commission on November 23, 2005, and she was sworn in in January, 2006. She is the world's first elected black female president and likewise Africa's first elected female head of state. Her vice president is Joseph Boakai.

Johnson-Sirleaf graduated from the College of West Africa in Monrovia, then studied in the United States, receiving a BBA in Accounting in 1964 at Madison Business College in Madison, Wisconsin, an economics diploma fron the University of Colorado in 1970, and a Master of Public Administration in 1971 from Harvard University.

When she returned to Liberia, she entered Liberian politics, becoming the Assistant Minister of Finance in President William Tolbert's administration.

She held that position until 1979, when she was named Minister of Finance of the Government of Liberia. In 1980, Tolbert was overthrown and killed by army sergeant Samuel Doe, who represented the Krahn ethnic group. Doe was the first Liberian president who was not descended from the elite ex-American slave community which had established Liberia. This ushered in a ten-year period during which Doe allowed the Krahns to dominate public life. During the multiple civil wars in the 80s and 90s, Johnson-Sirleaf spent time in jail, was exiled to Kenya, and ended up in 1982 working for the World Bank.

After the overthrow of Tolbert, Johnson-Sirleaf went into exile in Nairobi, Kenya, where from 1982 to 1985, she was Vice President of the Africa Regional Office of Citibank. She returned to Liberia in 1985 to run for the Senate, but she was jailed for speaking out against Doe's military regime and sentenced to ten years in prison. Released after a short period, she moved to Washington, D.C., where, from 1986 to 1992, she was Vice President and Member of the Executive Board of Equator Bank. Liberia was torn with multiple civil wars in the 80s and 90s. She initially supported Charles Taylor's bloody rebellion against Samuel Doe in 1990, but later she opposed him. She returned to Liberia again in 1997 in the capacity of an economist, working for the World Bank and Citibank in Africa and immediately ran against the warlord Taylor in the 1997 presidential elections. She received only 10% of the votes to Taylor's 17%, and Taylor charged her with treason. She campaigned for the removal of President Taylor from office, playing an active and supportive role in the transitional government, as the country prepared itself for the 2005 elections. With Taylor's departure, she returned to take over the leadership of the Unity Party.

In the first round of 2005 voting, she came second with 175,520 votes, putting her through to the runoff vote on November 8 against former football star George Weah. On November 11, the National Elections Commission of Liberia declared Johnson-Sirleaf to be president-elect of Liberia. On November 23, they confirmed that Johnson-Sirleaf had won with a margin of almost 20% of the vote. Independent, international, regional, and domestic observers declared the vote to be free, fair, and transparent. Her inauguration took place on January 16, 2006. Both Condoleezza Rice and Laura Bush were on hand for the ceremony. Now, Johnson-Sirleaf faced one of the largest tasks of any leader in the world: rebuilding her homeland after decades of civil war.

Two months later, President Johnson-Sirleaf addressed a joint meeting of the U.S. Congress, asking for American support to help her country "become a brilliant beacon, an example to Africa and the world of what love of liberty can achieve."

Former President Charles Taylor's followers remain in large numbers in Liberia's government. Edwin Snowe, current Speaker of the House (third in the government), is Taylor's son-in-law and was prominent in his government. Taylor's estranged wife, Jewel Howard Taylor, is in the Legislature. So is Prince Johnson, whose gruesome torture and murder of President Samuel Doe in 1990 was captured on a widely-distributed videotape. Nevertheless, on March 17, 2006, President Johnson-Sirleaf submitted an official request to Nigeria for Taylor's extradition.

Only a few months into her presidency, on July 26, 2006, the Executive Mansion caught fire while she hosted the hosted the leaders of Ivory Coast, Ghana, and Sierra Leone. Police did not rule out sabotage and Johnson-Sirleaf subsequently said that some of her closest aides would be screened before they could return to work.

Johnson-Sirleaf is the mother of four sons, two of which live in the United States, and two live in Liberia) and has six grandchildren, some of whom live in Atlanta, Georgia. She is often referred to as the "Iron Lady." In 2006 Forbes Magazine named her 51st on the list of the most powerful women in the world.

Johnson-Sirleaf has also been: Founding Member of the International Institute for Women in Political Leadership, Member of the Advisory Board of the Modern Africa Growth and Investment Company, Member of the Finance Committee of the Modern Africa Fund Managers, President of the Liberian Bank for Development and Investment, President of the Kormah Development and Investment Corporation, Senior Loan Officer of World Bank and Vice President of Citibank. She is the author of: *From Disaster to Development* (1991) and *The Outlook for Commercial Bank Lending to Sub-Saharan Africa* (1992), and co-author of: *Women, War and Peace: The Independent Experts' Assessment on the Impact of Armed Conflict on Women and Women's Role in Peace-building* (2002), a project of UNIFEM (the United Nations Development Fund for Women) She is the recipient of the 1988 Franklin Delano Roosevelt Freedom of Speech Award, the Ralph Bunche International Leadership Award, the Grand Commander Star of Africa Redemption of Liberia, the Commandeur de l'Ordre du Togo (Commander of the Order of Togo), the 2006 Common Ground Award, the 2006 laureate of the Africa Prize for Leadership for the Sustainable End of Hunger, and the 2006 Distinguished Fellow, Claus M. Halle Institute for Global Learning, Emory University.

Suggested Reading:

(1) *The New Yorker.* March 27, 2006.

Judith (also Jodit, Esato, Esat, Isato, or Yehudit)

Queen of the Falasha Agaw of Abyssinia (10th c.).

Historical records do not make it clear when the Agaw became the monarchs of old Abyssinia (now Ethiopia). However, it is fairly certain that the Zagwe Dynasty of the Agaw of Lasta held power in Abyssinia from A.D. 1137 to 1270. In the south of Ethiopia, between the fault of the lakes and the loop of the Blue Nile, lay the great Damot kingdom. The Damot are possibly identical to the Demdem people, who are known to have been near Lake Abaya, the homeland of the Galla people. A part of these turbulent populations, who to some degree converted to Judaism, launched frequent attacks against the Amhara-Tegre power, the Christian provinces of Ethiopia. The most serious of these attacks, led by a Felasha queen named Esato (Judith) in ca. A.D. 976, devastated the Christian empire as far as the mountains of Tigre.

Judith, or Esato ("the Monster") or Isato ("Fire") was the daughter of Gedeon, a member of the Falasha (Falasha Agaw) tribe, the black Jews of Ethiopia, who claim descent from Solomon. Judith launched her attack against the Christians of Axum when their king, Anbessa Wudim, was only ten years old. The Ethiopians saw Esato's invasion as a heavenly punishment for their having failed to be obedient to their Coptic patriarch, and they fled as her armies neared. Queen Judith did not stop until Axum was reduced to ruin, its churches destroyed and its holy relics looted. The one exception, according to legend, was the Ark of the Covenant, which monks had carried south to an island in Lakeewai.

Queen Judith ruled for the next forty years, wreaking havoc and killing many thousands of Christians. Only the rock churches of Tigrai survived her onslaught. Legend says she died while returning to her palace following a church-burning expedition, when God misdirected her to a place called Adi Nefas. There a whirlwind picked her up and dropped her from a great height to her death. Her burial place, marked only by a pile of stones, is at Ade Kaweh near Wukro.

Once the local Ethiopian Christians were delivered of Esato's terrible wrath, they tightened their bonds with the Egyptian Church. While the

Agaw held political control, the Amhara and Tegre culture entered what has been described as a "dark age" about which little is known. A large part of the Ethiopic civilization was lost or destroyed during this time.

Suggested Reading:

(1) Gamst, Frederick C., *The Quemant: A Pagan-Hebraic Peasantry of Ethiopia*. New York: Holt, Rinehart and Winston, 1969. pp. 13, 14, 124.

(2) de Villiers, Marq and Sheila Hirtle, *Into Africa*. Toronto: Key Porter Books, Ltd., 1997. p. 341.

Judith

See Zauditu

Section K

Kahina, Al—(or Cahina, Dhabba, or Dahiya al-Kahina)

Priestess-queen of North African Berbers (c. 695-703)

Prior to the capture of Byzantine-held Carthage by the Arabs and the establishment of the new Arab city of Tunis, the pastoral Berbers, the original inhabitants of northern Africa, had remained aloof from the struggle between Muslims and Christians, probably in the hope of benefiting from the aftermath. But around A.D. 695, the independent Berber tribes of the Aures mountains, part of the Atlas range in northern Africa, joined under the leadership of a queen of the Jerna tribe whom Gibbon called "Cahina," meaning "priestess." Shortly after the capture of Carthage, Al-Kahina and her tribes swept down upon the Arabs with savage ferocity. In 703 the Berbers defeated the Arabs under Hassan ibn No'man near Mons Aurasius and drove the Saracens back to Egypt. After the victory, Al-Kahina assembled the Moorish chiefs and, according to Gibbon, suggested that, because the gold and silver in their cities attracted the Arabs, they should burn the cities and bury the "vile metals" in their ruins. The fortifications from Tangier to Tripoli were burned. Even the fruit trees were cut down, leaving a desert. The populace was so devastated that the general of the Saracens was welcomed back. Al-Kahina was killed in the first battle against him. By one account, she took her own life after her defeat, instructing her sons to go to the Arab camp, make peace, and learn the ways of Islam. She died near a well that is still known as "Bir al-Kahina." Thereafter the Berbers became allies of the Arabs, and they participated in the invasion of the Iberian Peninsula. For her valiant effort, the priestess-queen earned the title of Queen-Mother of the Berbers. She is celebrated in Maghreb (Maghrib) epic literature.

Suggested Reading:

(1) Oliver, Roland and J. D. Fage. *A Short History of Africa*. Harmondsworth: Penguin Books, 1970. p. 71.

(2) Gibbon, Edward. *The Decline & Fall of the Roman Empire*. New York: The Modern Library, Random House, n.d. Vol. 3, p. 190.

(3) Langer, William L., ed. *Encyclopedia of World History*. Boston: Houghton Mifflin, 1980. p. 202.

(4) Marrouchi, Mustapha. "Breaking Up/Down/Out of the Boundaries: Tahar Ben Jelloun." *Research in African Literature*. vol. 21 no. 4, 1990: 79.

Kanza

Regent of Idris of Saghir (793-ca. 810)

Saghir was located in present-day Morocco. Kanza was the wife of King Idris of Saghir and the mother of Idris II ibn Idris of Saghir (793-823) who at his birth was heir apparent.

Kassi

Empress of Mali (1341-?)

Kassi was the principal wife and paternal cousin of Emperor Suleyman, who ruled Mali from 1341 to 1360. According to Mali custom, the emperor and his principal wife ruled jointly. Kassi was extremely popular with the royal court, many members of which were her relatives. She was not, however, as popular with her husband as was a commoner named Bendjou. Eventually the emperor divorced Kassi in order to marry Bendjou. Kassi rallied support of the noble ladies of the court, who refused to pay homage to the new empress. Instead, Kassi was still regarded as empress by the noble ladies, who would do obeisance by throwing earth on their heads and who showed their disdain for Bendjou by throwing earth on their hands. This insubordination angered both Bendjou and the emperor, and Kassi was forced to seek sanctuary in the mosque. From this vantage, she incited the nobles, particularly her cousins, to revolt. The struggle which followed was actually a reflection of the larger division into two ideological factions vying for ascendancy. One party in the empire supported Suleyman, while the other supported the sons of the former ruler, Mansa Maghan I,

Suleyman's nephew. The latter faction also supported Kassi. Suleyman and his military chiefs eventually defeated Kassi and her cousins. This he did by discrediting her with her party by proving that she was intriguing with her cousin, Djathal, who had previously been expelled for treason. Suleyman was succeeded by Kassi's son, Kassa, who ruled only nine months before his cousin Mari Diata seized power.

Suggested Reading:

(1)   Panikker, K. Madhu. *The Serpent and the Crescent: A History of the Negro Empires of West Africa*. Bombay: Asia Publishing House, 1963. p. 60.

Khentkaues (also Khentkawes or Khamerernebti II)

Co-ruler of Egypt (c. 2494 B.C.)

She was the daughter of Khafre, also called Cephren (r. c. 2520-2494 B.C). Her mother was most likely the king's sister, Khamerernebti I, his first wife. She was the sister and wife of Mycernius (also called Menhaure or Menkure), fifth ruler of the Fourth Dynasty (r. c. 2494-2472 B.C.). Mycernius began construction on the third and smallest pyramid of Giza. Although the king was supreme, sculpture which survives indicates that Khentaues shared the rule. In the Fourth Dynasty kingship reached the peak of centralized authority. According to Herodotus, Mycernius only had one child, a daughter, who died. The king had a hollow wooden cow made, plated with gold, to hold her. The cow was still standing during Herodotus' time (c. 490-425 B.C.). In an adjoining chamber from the one housing the cow were some statues representing, by one account, concubines of Mycernius. By a second account, the daughter hanged herself because her father had violated her, so her mother cut off the hands of the servants who allowed the king access to her. The statues in the adjoining chamber, with missing hands, represent the servants.

Suggested Reading:

(1)   Grimal, Nicolas. *A History of Ancient Egypt*. New York: Barnes & Noble Books, 1997. pp. 68, 72, 74-75, 115-116, 128.
(2)   West, John Anthony. *The Traveler's Key to Ancient Egypt*. New York: Alfred A. Knopf, 1985. p. 110, 134.

Kimpa Vita (Dona Beatrice)

Prophetess and religious leader in the Kongo kingdom (c. 1704-1706)

After a long period of political decline among the Kongo, Kimpa Vita, using her Christian name, Dona Beatrice, rose to prominence, claiming to be the incarnation of the Portuguese Saint Anthony. Preaching an anti-Catholic but Christian message, she relied heavily on traditional Kongo symbolism and cultural roots. Under pressure from Catholic missionaries, Kongo's King Pedro IV had her burned at the stake as a heretic.

Her martyrdom gave strength to her Antonian church, which for a time encouraged the revitalization of the kingdom in the 18th century.

Suggested Reading:

(1)   Balandier, Georges. *Daily Life in the Kingdom of the Kongo.* tr. H. Weaver. New York: Pantheon Books, 1968.

Kinigi, Sylvie

Prime minister of Burundi (1993-1994)

Burundi, located in central East Africa, is bounded on the east and south by Tanzania, on the north by Rwanda, and on the west by Zaire and Lake Tanganyika. During the entire time that it has been a political entity since the fifteenth century, first as a kingdom, now as a republic, a power struggle between the Hutu and the Tutsi tribes has characterized its government.

Kinigi was born in 1952 of a prominent Bujumbura family, a member of the Tutsi ethnic group. Her husband, with whom she had five children, was a member of the Hutu ethnic group, which tradidionally had poor relations with the Tutis. Kinigi graduated from Burundi University, having studied economic management, and worked in the Burundi civil service. She was a chairperson in women's organizations concerned with health and education before entering the national political arena. She eventually became a senior advisor in the Prime Minister's office, focusing on economic policy.

In 1981 a new constitution confirmed its status as a one-party state. At that time, the Tutsi faction held power over the majority Hutu peasants. In 1987 the president was ousted in a military coup headed by Major Pierre Buyoya, and this was followed within the year by ethnic violence that left 5000 dead.

In 1993 when Melchior Ndadaye, a Hutu, was elected President of Burundi, he appointed Silvie Kinigi as his Prime Minister, hoping to build unity between the country's two ethnic groups. She was nominated from a field of clashing factions within her party as a compromise candidate. Kinigi, the first woman to serve her country's government, stated that reconciliation between the two ethnic groups would be her highest priority.

But on October 21, 1993, President Ndadaye and six of his ministers were captured and killed by Tutsi insurgents, marking the beginning of the Burundi Civil War, with widespread ethnic violence breaking out. Kinigi and other senior government figures took refuge in the French embassy. On November 1, she attempted to gather together a new administration, effectively becoming acting President. Her position was bolstered when former presidents Pierre Buyoya and Jean Baptiste Bagaza gave their support to her government.

In January of 1994, Parliament declared that Cyprien Ntaryamira, the former agriculture minister, would serve as President for the remainder of Ndadaye's term. As Ntaryamira was a Hutu, the appointment generated hostility from many Tutsis. Kinigi, however, recognised Ntaryamira as President, and retained her position as Prime Minister.

At approximately the same time that Kinigi had become Prime Minister, neighboring Rwanda had also elected a woman Prime Minister, and the two women looked forward to amicable relations. But Kinigi's election had been greeted with surprise and hostility even from within her own party. In placing herself in public service, she was aware of the danger accompanying victory. She served only a matter of months before the political upheaval that removed Ndadaye from the presidency also forced her out. In February, 1994, she was replaced by another Tutsi, Anatole Kanyenkiko, but she was more fortunate than her Rwandan counterpart, Agathe Uwilingiuamana, who was assassinated. Kinigi then then took a position in Burundi's banking sector.

Suggested Reading:

(1) "Women on the Run". *World Press Review*. February 1996: 38-39.

Section L

Lenshina, Alica

Religious and Political Leader in Zambia (1953-1975)

She was born in 1924 and raised a Presbyterian under the Church of Scotland mission. In 1953 she had a vision which inspired her to organize a witchcraft eradication movement which swept through what was then called Northern Rhodesia and the central Copperbelt region. By 1957 she claimed to have 50,000 followers; by 1961 she had twice that number. In 1963, the Presbyterians ex-communicated her, so she organized the Lumpa church.

The following year Zambia became independent and Kenneth Kaunda's United National Independence Party came into power. Lenshina's new Lumpa church opposed Kaunda and refused to pay taxes, fortifying their villages in resistance. Kaunda's government reacted with violence, killing over 700 church adherents and banning the church altogether. Many members fled to Zaire, while Lenshina was arrested. She was placed in restriction, but was in and out of captivity from 1964 to 1975, when, in December of that year, she was finally released. Even after her death in 1978, her Lumba church continued as a viable underground movement.

Suggested Reading:

(1) Grotpeter, John J. *Historical Dictionary of Zambia*. Metuchen: Scarecrow Press, 1979.

Lobama

Queen Regnant of Kuba (ca. 490)

The Kuba settled in the area known as Congo-Brazzaville. Before they migrated to their present location, the Kuba state developed east of the confluence of the Kasai and Sankuru rivers. Lobama was the daughter of Loko Yima who ruled prior to ca. 490. After he died, Lobama was Queen Regent until Woto succeeded her.

Section M

Maathai, Wangari

Kenyan MP (2002-), Deputy Minister for the Environment and Natural Resources (2003-2005), Nobel Peace Prize Winner (2004)

Wangari Muta Maathai was born to Kikuyu parents on April 1, 1940 in Ihithe village in the Nyeri District of Kenya. The family lived in a mud hut with thatched roof and slept on mattresses stuffed with leaves and grass. In a country where women are seldom afforded an education, Maathai was the first in East and Central Africa to earn a PhD. She traveled to Atchison, Kansas to study at Mout Saint Scholastica College where in 1964 she earned a BS in biological sciences. From there she went to the University of Pittsburgh where she received a Master's degree in 1966. She then studied in Germany but returned to Nairobi to complete her doctoral studies in 1971. She remained at the University of Nairobi teaching in the Department of Veterinary Anatomy, to which she was named head in 1976. She was made an Associate Professor the following year.

Maathai was active in the National Council of Women of Kenya from 1976 to 1987, serving as its chair from 1981 to 1987. In 1977 she founded the Green Belt Movement in Kenya, mobilizing the women to plant more than thirty million trees since then, in an effort to restore the country's indigenous forests.

Although she was jailed and beaten on several occasions, Maathai continued her efforts to save Kenya's forests and to restore democracy to Kenya. In 2002, receiving 98 percent of the vote, she was elected to Kenya's Parliament in the first free elections in a generation. In 2003 she became Deputy Minister for the Environment and Natural Resources in the government of President Mwai Kibaki between January 2003 and November 2005. In 2004 she became the first African woman to receive the Nobel Peace Prize, awarded for "her contribution to sustainable development, democracy and peace."

Suggested Reading:

(1) Maathai, Wangari, *Unbowed, A Memoir*. New York: Alfred A. Knopf, 2006. Also published in London by William Heinemann, 2007.

(2) *Les Prix Nobel: The Nobel Prizes 2004*, Ed. Tore Frangsmyr [Nobel Foundation], Stockholm, Sweden, 2005.

Magajiya Kofana

Queen of the Kofana (Kufuru) in Nigeria (ca. 700)

She was the first of fifteen successive queens of her people. According to oral tradition, she was succeeded by: Gufano (Gino), Yakunya (Yfakaniva), Waizam (Walzamu), Yanbam Gizirigzit (Gadar-Gadar), Imagari (Anagiri), Dura, Gamata, Shata, Batatume, Sandamata, Hamata, Zama, and Shawata (ca. 1000).

Makeda (Also called Balkis, or Balqis)

Queen, ruler of Axum; believed by some to be the Queen of Sheba (9th. B.C.). See Balkis.

Malegorobar

Queen Regnant of Meroë (266-283)

Meroë was located in present-day Sudan. Malegorobar was also known as Malegereabar.

Mansarico

Mani warrior queen in West Africa (mid-16th c.)

The Mani (Mane) were a Mandinko (Mande-speaking) people arising from the Mali Empire. Queen Mansarico, who had perhaps been exiled by the *Mansa* (king) of Mali, left that country and led her followers south, then west, eventually establishing, by the mid-1540's, a base of operations in the vicinity of Cape Mount in Liberia. From there, she dispatched her armies into the borderland of present day Sierra Leone, subjugating the local populace and establishing sub-kingdoms which were forced to pay tribute to her. This pattern of waves of invasions eventually had the result of developing the Mende as the largest ethnic group in Sierra Leone.

Mansarico and other Mani women were equipped for leadership because they apparently possessed not only such essential skills as knowledge of herbal medicine and agriculture and such serendipitous skills as knowledge of the fine arts, but also expertise in statecraft. The basis for this knowledge and expertise appears to have been education obtained through a hierarchical initiation society. Thus Mani women were always powerful, often regents or rulers in their own right.

Suggested Reading:

(1) Boone, Sylvia Ardyn. *Radiance From the Waters*. New Haven: Yale University Press, 1986, pp. 4, 25, 246.

Mamochisane (Ma-Muchisane)

Queen of the Kololo in Zambia (1851)

The Kololo are a Sotho people who, under Chief Sebitwane, fled in ca. 1839 from the advancing Mfecane, crossing the Zambizi and occupying western Zambia. There they conquered the Lozi (Barotse) kingdom, but during the fighting, the Lozi captured Sebitwane's daughter, Mamochisane (c. 1840). However, they released her to her father unharmed, and the Lozi's kind treatment of her apparently influenced King Sebitwane to deal leniently with the Lozi. He divided the conquered territory, known as Bulozi or Barotseland, into four provinces and appointed Mamochisane as governor of a central province. Apparently she was an able leader, for before the king died in 1851, he nominated her to succeed him. Mamochisane ruled briefly, but soon abducated in favor of her brother, Sekeletu, ostensively so as to marry and have a family.

Suggested Reading:

(1) Lipschutz, Mark R. and R. Kent Rasmussen. *Dictionary of African Historical Biography*. Berkeley: University of California Press, 1978, 1986.

Mantantisi (Mmanthatisi, Mma Ntatisi, Matatisi)

Queen-regent of the baTlokwa in South Africa (c.1817-c.1824)

She was born c. 1780, a member of the Sia, a branch of the Sotho-speaking people of present-day Orange Free State. She married Mokotjo, chief of the Tlokwa branch, and in c. 1804 had a son, Sekonyela. When her husband died (c. 1817), she sent her son to live with her people while she remained to rule the Tlokwa.

In c. 1820 a Nguni army under Mpangazitha invaded from the east coast, driving the Tlokwa westward. Mantantisi then led her people in a series of raids against neighboring armies that lasted several years and became known as the Difaqane. Soon her reputation as a predator was widespread. A corruption of her name, "Mantatee," became the term for the various predatory bands that ravaged the region of the Orange and Vaal Rivers.

She is described, in epic literature about the exploits of the Zulu Emperor Shaka the Great (r. 1816-1828), as a fierce woman who personally led her army, raiding and terrorizing the Maluti nations of the Sothos. She fought not only Shaka's chief enemy, Matiwane, but also conquered the army of Shaka's ally, the great king of the Bathos and founder of the Sotho nation, Moshoeshoe (Mshweshwe). She subdued the fierce nation of the Fukengs as well, and defeated the army of the Kwena nation. Only the Hlubis of Mpangazitha were able to withstand her army's onslaught. After her defeat, Shaka, pleased to hear people "rain curses against Queen Mantantisi", is reported to have said, "I always marvel at how men could be terrorized by a woman . . . ." Shaka's commander-in chief, Mdlaka, reporting her various brave exploits to his emperor, said that the entire southern region of Khahlamba mountains "curses her very name and ancestry." Shaka commented, "How strange is all this courage in a woman!" He termed her a "homeless vagabond."

Eventually she settled in northern Lesotho, where, in c. 1824, her son joined her and assumed the kingship. She continued to play a central role in Tlokwa affairs until the mid-1830s; after c. 1836 no more is known.

Suggested Reading:

(1) Lipschutz, Mark R. and R. Kent Rasmussen, *Dictionary of African Historical Biography*. Berkeley: University of California Press, 1986. pp. 148-149.

(2) Kunene, Mazisi, *Emperor Shaka the Great*. tr. Mazisi Kunene. London: Heinemann Educational Books, 1979. pp. 112, 253-254.

Mantsebo

Queen Regent of Lesotho, or British Basutoland (1940-1960)

She was born in 1902 and became a wife of Paramount Chief Seeiso Griffith (1905-1940), who ruled the South African British Protectorate from 1939 to 1940. When Griffith died after only one year as king, his son and heir, Constantine Bereng Seeiso (1938-), was only two years old. Mantsebo, his step-mother, was named regent, a post she held until 1960, when Constantine reached the age of 20 and assumed the throne as Moshoeshoe II. She died in 1964, too soon to see Basutoland gain independence (1966) and her step-son become the Constitutional Monarch.

Suggested Reading:

(1)   Haliburton, Gordon M. *Historical Dictionary of Lesotho.* Metuchen: Scarecrow Press, 1977.

Mavia (or Mawai)

Queen Regnant of the Saracens (ca. 370-380)

Mavia may be the same person called Mawi or Mawia, Queen of Syria, possibly a Ghassanid. Ghassar was an Arabian kingdom bounded on the northeast by the Euphrates River and extending into the Sinai Peninsula (Egypt). She was the wife of a Bedoin chieftain there and succeeded him when he died. She led raids against Rome's eastern outposts in Palestine and Phoenicia and demanded, as her price for peace after defeating a Roman army, that a certain hermit named Moses be forcibly consecrated as Bishop of her tribe. She married her daughter to a Roman commander-in-chief, Victor, a Samartian from across the Danube. In 378 she sent her Arab cavalry to aid the Romans in defending Constantinople. Its shockingly bloodthirsty mode of fighting intimidated even the Goths.

Suggested Reading:

(1)   Bowder, Diana, ed. *Who Was Who in the Roman World.* Ithaca, NY: Cornell University Press, 1980. pp. 335, 575.

Mawia

Queen of Syria. See Mavia.

Mawa

Leader of Zulu political refugees (c. 1842-1848)

Mawa was born c. 1770, the youngest sister of regent Mnkabayi and of Senzangakhona, who became the father of three Zulu kings. During the reigns of two of her nephews, Shaka (r. c. 1815-1828) and Dingane (r. 1828-1840). she served as royal liason in a British military town. In 1840 another nephew ousted Dingane and, in c. 1842, had his brother Gqugqa assassinated. Mawa, who apparently had supported Gqugqa's bid for the throne, fled with several thousand followers to Natal. There she gathered additional supporters and eventually negotiated a treaty with the new British administration to settle permanently in Natal.

She died in 1848.

Suggested Reading:

(1)   Bryant, A. T. *Olden Times in Zululand and Natal.* London: Longman Green, 1929.

Menetewab (or Mantuab)

Empress of Ethiopia (1730-1769)

She was born Walata Giorgis or Berhan Mogasa, and claimed descent in part from Portuguese settlers who had come to Ethiopia during the reign of Galawdewos (c. 1522-1559). In the 1720's she became the wife of Emperor Baqaffa (Bakaffa), who ruled Ethiopia from 1721 to 1730. During his reign she watched over the reestablishment of Christianity in the southern provinces, a duty she was to continue for the rest of her life. When Baqaffa died in 1730, she served as regent during the minority of her son Iyasu II. When Iyasu came of age, he showed little interest in government, so she continued to wield power, promoting various relatives into positions of influence, and angering much of the nobility. With Menetewab, Iyasu had the splendid Abbey of Kusquan built. To free himself of his mother's rule, he married the daughter of one of the Gullas chiefs and introduced Gallas warriors into the capital. When Iyasu died in 1755, Menetewab helped to bring her infant grandson, Ioyas, to the throne and again served as regent. During the reign of Ioyas, who ruled from 1755 to 1769, a rival faction arose headed by Mikael Sehul. Sehul had Ioyas assassinated in 1769, removed Menetewab and put Tekle-Haimanot II on the throne. She retired to Gojjam and later met a Scottish explorer, who wrote about her life.

Suggested Reading:

(1) Lipschutz, Mark R., and R. Kent Rasmussen, *Dictionary of African Historical Biography*. Berkeley: University of California Press, 1989. p. 145.
(2) Budge, E. A. *A History of Ethiopia*. London: Methuen, 1928. pp. 221-222.
(3) Egan, Edward. W. et. al., eds. *Kings, Rulers, and Statesmen*. New York: Sterling Publishing, 1976, p. 130.

Meryit-Net (or Merneith)

Queen, ruler of Egypt (c. 300 B.C.)

According to Manetho, it was during the reign of Neteren that is was decided that women might occupy the throne; however, there is evidence that has convinced some historians to suppose that Meryit-Net ("beloved of Neith") was the successor of Zir (Djer) and possibly the third sovereign of the First Dynasty. She was likely Djer's daughter, the wife and apparent co-ruler of his successor Wadjit, and the mother of Den, the fourth king of the dynasty.

Since among the royal ladies of the dynasty, Meryet-Nit is the only one to have great monuments both at Abydos and Sakkara adjascent to those of kings, it could be surmised that she herself was a reigning monarch. Her Abydos monument is one of the largest and best built of all.

Suggested Reading:

(1) Grimal, Nicolas. *A History of Ancient Egypt*. New York: Barnes & Noble Books, 1997. pp. 50, 52.
(2) Emery, W. B., *Archaic Egypt*. Harmondsworth: Penguin Books, 1987. pp. 32, 65, 66, 68, 69, 94, 126.

Suggested Reading:

(1) Biersteker, Ann and Mark Plane. "Swahili Manuscripts and the Study of Swahili Literature" *Research in African Literature*. vol. 20 no. 3. Fall 1989: 449-472; specifically, 468.
(2) Mtoro bin Mwinyi Babari. *The Customs of the Swahili People. The Desturi za Waswahili*. ed, and tr. J. W. T. Allen. Berkeley: University of California Press, 1981. pp. 305, 307.
(3) Davidson, Basil. *African History*. New York: Collier/Macmillan Publishing Co., 1991. p. 196.

Mnkabayi (Mkabayi, Mkhabayi)

Regent ruler of the Zulus (c. 1780s)

Described as the most important political figure in Zululand, she was born a Zulu princes c. 1760. She was the older sister of the future Zulu Chief Senzangakhona, for whom she served as regent after their father died. She remained single in order to retain her political independence and her influence over her brother. Shortly before he ascended to the throne, Senzangakhona disgraced himself by impregnating his lover Nandi before their wedding, but he married her anyway, and she bore a son, Shaka (c. 1787). The Zulu chief married others and had other sons, who would eventually succeed him. His harsh treatment of Nandi and Shaka, however, caused them to leave. Mnkabayi remained friendly with Nandi, and following Senzangakhona's death in c. 1815, she encouraged Shaka to return and seize power from his half-brother Sigujana, which he did. In 1827 Nandi died, and Mnkabbayi is believed to have blamed Shaka for her death. She encouraged two other nephews, Dingane and Mhlangana, to assassinate him. Later she persuaded Dingane to eliminate Mhlangana as well.

She was last reported alive in 1835. At the time she was said to be extremely old.

Suggested Reading:

(1) Lipschutz, Mark R. and R. Kent Rasmussen, *Dictionary of African Historical Biography*. Berkeley: University of California Press, 1986.
(2) Kunene, Mazisi, *Emperor Shaka the Great*. tr. Mazisi Kunene. London: Heinemann Educational Books, 1979.

Mfalma Fatima

Ruler of Pate in East Africa (early 18th century)

Pate is an island off the coast of Kenya, part of the Lamu archipeligo. it is located northeast of the mouth of the Tana River as it empties into the Indian Ocean. pate is also the name of the town on the island.

According to *The Pate Chronicles*, the existence of *jumbes* (Swahili for chiefs) in the southern Swahili world is evidence that the area was once ruled by Pate, since these *jumbes* were all originally part of the Pate *yumbe* (council of elders). If thie were indeed the case, the ruler would have had a wide sphere of influence. There is certainly evidence that the rulers of Pate played a significant role in East Africa's resistance to Portuguese rule.

From the 15th century onward, the Nabahani Dynasty, of Omani origin, ruled Pate; therefore there were close ties between the East Africans and the Iman of Oman. When the Portuguese exercised authority over East Africa in 1652, the Omani, in response to a Mombasan request, sailed into Pate and Zanzibar and slaughtered the Europeans. From that time forward, Pate became the center of resistance to Portuguese rule and would maintain its pre-eminence in the Lamu islands for more than a century and a half. In 1669, the Iman of Oman returned, in answer to an appeal from the ruler of Pate, and attacked the Portuguese in Mombasa and Faza. In 1669 he attacked Mozambique.

As Pate continued to court the Omanis, in 1678 Portuguese forces attacked Pate and executed its ruler. However, the return of the Omani in 1679 caused the Europeans to withdraw. By 1686, however, the Portuguese had stepped up their encroachment and Pate again rebelled. But its ruler was eventually captured, sent to Goa, in Portuguese India, and executed in 1688. Once more Pate called upon the Iman of Oman, who, in 1696, attacked Mombasa with a fleet of over three thousand men. In 1698 Sayf ibn Sultan brought about a Portuguese surrender, ousting the Europeans from Fort Jesus, the great Mombasan castle.

However, soon the Omani developed imperial ambitions and attempted to dominate the Swahili seacoast and monopolize oceanborne commerce. In 1727 Pate, anxious to preserve its independence, switched allegiance and joined with the Portuguese to oust the Omani.

It was during this latter period that Mfalma Fatima ruled Pate. Two of her letters, written in Swahili, are among a collection of fourteen, dating between 1711 and 1729, preserved in the Historical Archives of Goa. Portuguese translation describes her only as "a female ruler of Pate."

Moremi

Semi-legendary savior of the Yoruba Ife people (fl. 15th century)

When the Ife were being terrorized by the ferocious-looking neighboring Igbo people, Moremi, who was a renoun beauty, infiltrated enemy lines by allowing herself to be captured by the Igbo. She found favor with the Igbo king, who confided to her that his warriors were ordinary men disguised in raffia to make them look fierce. Moremi escaped and returned to her people, whom she told about the deception. The Ife set fire to the Igbo costumes and defeated the offending army. But in order to pay the Ife deity for her success, Moremi was forced to sacrifice her own son.

Suggested Reading:

(1) Smith, R. S., *Kingdoms of the Yoruba*. London: Methuen, 1976.

Mother of the King of Kongo

Queen, ruler of Mpemba Kazi (c. 12th c.?)

Long before the Kongo coalesced into a kingdom in the 14th century, there is a tradition as to its beginnings. Although this queen carried the title Mother of the King of Kongo, she may or may not have been the Queen-mother of Mbene, founder of the Kongo kings, but she was doubtless the strongest person and the one whom Mbene (Motinobene or Mutinu Mbene) most trusted.

With ambitions to expand his area of influence, Mbene married the daughter of ManiKabungo and set about founding a dynasty. He conquered all the indigenous chiefs in the area except Mbata, with whom he made an alliance. In the future all Kongo kings were to marry daughters of the ManiMbata.

Mbene established his first capital at Mpemba Kazi. As he sought to enlarge his territory, it became his custom to conquer one area, then leave a local ruler in charge and move on. When he moved farther south to M'banza Congo, he left the queen to rule at the old capital, giving her the title Mother of the King of Kongo.

Suggested Reading:

(1) de Villiers, Marq and Sheila Hirtle, *Into Africa*. Toronto: Key Porter Books, Ltd., 1997. p. 159.

Mout

Queen of the Sudan (fl. 730 B.C.)

Mout is mentioned in accounts of the life of Egyptian commander Taharqa (Khunefertemre Taharqa, the Biblical Tirhakah, r. 689-664 B.C.), who led the Egyptian forces into Asia against the Assyrian Sennachirib. Queen Mout was married to King Piankhi of Sudan (c. 751-716 B.C.), who laid the foundation for his brother Shabaka to found the Twenty-fifth Egyptian Dynasty by invading and subduing the various rebel forces in Lower Egypt. Taharqa was the youngest son of Mout and Piankhi. After Piankhi's death, Shabaka became Pharaoh of Egypt. After Shabaka died in 701, his nephew Shabataka became Pharaoh. In 689, Taharqa had Shabataka assassinated and ascended the throne, proclaiming himself the son of Mout, Queen of the Sudan, and erecting a temple in her honor.

Suggested Reading:

(1) Diop, Cheikh Anta. *The African Origin of Civilization*. tr. Mercer Cook. Chicago: Lawrence Hill Books, Chicago Review Press, 1974.

Mujaji I, II, III, IV

"Rain Queen" of the Lovedu in South Africa (19th-20th centuries)

The Lovedu (Lobedu) are a Bantu-speaking people of the northern Transvaal. Mujaji is the dynastic title of the female rulers. According to legend, King Mugodo's father, to deceive people, had treated his son with disrespect in public but privately had taught him the secrets of the tribe's rain charms. When Mugodo came to the throne, his people refused to respect him, because of his own father's apparent disrespect, and his reign ended in confusion, ushering in the reign of queens. Mugodo went to one daughter with a plan to save the kingdom by fathering a child by her, but she refused his proposal, which she considered a sin. He then went to his next daughter,

Mujaji, who agreed to give birth to an heir to the throne, with Mugodo as the father. She gained ascendancy while Mugodo was still on the throne, but she remained in seclusion and the people began to believe in her great wisdom and immortality. They called her "white-faced", "radiant as the sun", and "one who gives water to wash the face." Word of her powers spread south to the Zulus and north to the Sothos, both of which sent emissaries bearing gifts to the great queen.

Mujaji II's reign was less successful. When Zulus invaded her land, she attempted to conjure a drought to destroy them. White men, Europeans came next, encroaching on her territory, desecrating the tribe's holy places. She went into seclusion and induced a half-sister to present herself as "She Who Must Be Obeyed." Her ploy did not keep the Europeans at bay, and despondent, in 1894 she took poison and died.

The Europeans had discovered Mujaji II's deception and, to punish the Lovedu, refused to recognize the next queen, Mujaji III, until the bogus "She Who Must Be Obeyed" had died. Still, it was only Mujaji who inherited the secret medicines and objects for making rain and for denying it to their enemies, and so her people recognized her as their divinely ordained ruler, although they did not rebel against their overlords. The Lovedu, a peaceful people, practice the ideals of co-operativeness and reciprocity.

Mujaji IV, the current queen, is called "Transformer of Clouds" and functions more as a rainmaker than a monarch. With the assistance of her rain-doctor, who uses medicine to help remove the forces that occasionally block the queen's powers, she guarantees the cycle of the seasons, bringing rain throughout the year. Her health is of utmost importance to the tribe. In times of great drought, people bring gifts and long dances are performed. Her ability to control the rain depends on cooperation from her ancestors, whose skins she uses in her rain-pots.

Suggested Reading:

(1) Krige, E. J. and J. D. Krige, *The Realm of a Rain-Queen*. London: Oxford University Press, 1943.

(2) Parrinder, Geoffrey, *African Mythology*. New York: Peter Bedrick Books, 1982. pp. 120-121.

Section N

Nandi

Queen Mother of the Zulus (c. 1815-1827)

Nandi was born c. 1760, a member of the Langeni tribe in South Africa. In c. 1787 she had an illicit affair with Zulu Chief Senzangakhona and became pregnant. Although pregnancy out of wedlock was considered a tribal disgrace, the king nevertheless married her, and she bore a son, Shaka. The Zulu people treated Nandi and Shaka badly and forced her out of the capital, so she took her son and returned to her people, who treated her no better. She then took Shaka to the Mthethwa people, where he grew to manhood and served in the army of Chief Dingiswayo, rising to a high position. When Zulu Chief Senzangakhona died in ca. 1815, Shaka returned to claim his throne. Nandi, as Queen Mother, wreaked retribution on those who had previously mistreated her. Shaka, the empire builder, was frequently absent during military maneuvers. He never married, so Nandi exercised full authority during his absence. She remained the king's most important influence until her death in 1927. When she died, Shaka and the entire nation went into protracted mourning: "a fearful mourning exploded throughout the land." The king called in his couselors and told them: "There have been two rulers in Zululand:/ One gentle, who excelled in her kindness and generosity . . . . Such duality has never been known in all history."

Suggested Reading:

(1) Kunene, Mazisi, *Emperor Shaka the Great*. London; Heinemann, 1979. pp. 2fl-422.
(2) Lipshutz, Mark. R., and R. Kent Rasmussen. *Dictionary of African Biography*. Berkeley: University of California Press, 1986. p. 169.

(3) Josephy, Jr., Alvin M., ed., *The Horizon History of Africa*. Clarke, Prof. John Henrik, "Time of Troubles." New York: American Heritage Publishing Co., McGraw-Hill, Inc., 1971. pp. 374-375.

Na Wanjile

Assassin who changed Dahomey history (1797)

Na Wanjile was a resident of King Agonglo's court who opposed the ruler when, at invading Portugal's demand, he converted to Christianity in exchange for a promise of increased trade with the Portuguese. After she assassinated Agonglo, a brief civil war ensued. Agonglo's son Adandozan prevailed and was crowned the new king. In punishment Na Wanjile and the other conspirators were buried alive.

Suggested Reading:

(1) Akinjogbin, I. A., *Dahomey and its Neighbors*. Cambridge: Cambridge University Press, 1967.

Nawidemak (Also called Naldamak)

Queen Regnant of Meroë (ca. C.E. 12)

Meroë (Nubia) was located in present-day Sudan. She was the daughter of Queen Amanitore who ruled from B.C.E. 12 to C.E. 12). She was married to Prince Apedemakhe. Her son, Arikharer (or Arikhankharer), began his reign in C.E. 10 with his mother as regent.

Nefrusobek (Also called Sebekkare, Sebeknefru, Skemiophris or Sobekneferu)

Last queen of the Theban Twelfth Dynasty, Egypt (ca. 1790/87-1785/83 B.C.).

Nefrusobek, or Sobkneferu ("the beauty of Sobek") was the daughter of Amenemhet (Ammenemes) III who ruled from ca. 1844/42 to 1797 B.C., and the half-sister of Amenemhet (Ammenemes or Aman-m-he) IV, who succeeded his father at an elderly age after his father's 45-year reign. When her brother died approximately a decade later, the absence of a male heir made Nefrusobek the next in line of succession. She ruled as king and full pharoh but did not attempt to depict herself as a man as did Queen Hatshepsut (Eighteenth Dynasty). In her titulature, she was described, for the first time in Egyptian history, as a woman-pharoh. Her father had enabled a long period of peace and prosperity for Egypt. Although White termed her "insignificant," she did maintain the peaceful and prosperous rule set by her predecessors, until she was ready to choose a successor. The kingship was inherited through the daughter of the monarch. In order to preserve the royal succession within the same family, the custom was adopted of having the oldest son of the king marry his oldest sister, which Amenemhet had done. Since he died childless, Nefrusobek was privileged to select the next king by marrying him. She was expected to marry a member of the Theban nobility and elevate him to the throne, but she had other ideas. Instead, she married a commoner from Lower Egypt. Her choice so enraged the citizenry that civil war broke out, since the northerners believed that they were far superior to the southerners. However, the sides were too evenly matched, and no one could gain a decisive victory. While this senseless war raged on, a tribe of nomads from Asia, the Hyskos ("shepherd kings") invaded and took over. Nefrusobek died ca. 1783 B.C. and the Twelfth dynasty ended.

Suggested Reading:

(1) Grimal, Nicolas, *A History of Ancient Egypt*. New York: Barnes & Noble Books, 1997. pp. 118, 171, 179, 182, 391.
(2) Rawlinson, George, *Ancient History*. New York: Barnes & Noble Books, 1993. p. 60.
(3) White, J.E., *Ancient Egypt: Its Culture and History*. New York: Dover Publishing, 1970. p. 158.
(4) Jackson, John G., *Introduction to African Civilization*. Secaucus, NJ: Citadel Press, 1970. pp. 107-108.

Ngirmaramma, Aisa Kili

Ruler of the Kanuri Empire of Bornu. See Aisa Kili Ngirmaramma.

Ngokay (also Gokadi)

Queen Regnant of the Kuba (ca. 575)

The Kuba are located in modern-day Congo-Brazzaville. Ngokay's reign belongs to that legendary period when the Kuba migrated to its present West African location. She was succeeded by King Bonga Mashu Mashi, possibly her son.

Nitrocris

Queen of Egypt (c. 2475 B.C.)

Although no archaeological evidence has survived of her reign, the Turin Canon lists her as the last ruler of the Sixth Dynasty and the wife of Merenre II, whom she succeeded. She was the first known queen to exercise political power over Egypt. She is associated with the legendary courtesan Phodopis, mythical builder of the third pyramid of Giza. Herodotus (b. c. 484 B.C.), who traveled in Egypt after 454 B.C. and received much of his information from word of mouth, tells of an Egyptian queen, Nitrocris. To avenge the murder of her brother-king, whom she succeeded, she built a huge underground chamber. As an inaugural ceremony she held a banquet and invited all those responsible for her brother's death. When the banquet was in full swing, she opened a large concealed conduit and allowed her guests to drown in river water. To escape her punishment, she threw herself into a roomful of ashes. No other source supports Herodotus' account.

Suggested Reading:

(1) Herodotus, *The Histories*. tr. Aubrey de Sélinourt. New York: Penguin Books, 1954. p. 166.
(2) Grimal, Nicolas. *A History of Ancient Egypt*. New York: Barnes & Noble Books, 1997. p. 89.

Nongqause

Prophetess, advisor to Gcaleka Xhosa King Sarili (1856-1857)

The teen-aged niece of the prophet Mhlakaza, in 1856 Nongquase told her uncle of a millenarian vision she had. Xhosa's ancestors had described to her a way the Xhosa could escape their many difficulties. The ancestors promised a millennium free of Europeans in exchange for purifying themselves and sacrificing all their material wealth, which consisted of cattle and grain crops. For ten months in 1856 and 1857 the Gcaleka Xhosa and some of their neighbors slaughtered 150,000 cattle and destroyed most of their grain. As a result, thousands of people had to escape to Cape Colony to avoid starvation. After her prophetic advice failed to protect the tribe from the approaching British, Nongquase was forced to flee and King Mhlakaza soon died. The British captured Nongquase and another young prophetess, Nonkosi, placing them in protective custody. Eventually Nongquase was released and allowed to return to the eastern Cape Colony where she lived quietly in obscurity until her death, either in 1898 or after 1905.

Suggested Reading:

(1)   Meintjes, Johannes. *Sandile: the Fall of the Xhosa Nation*. Cape Town: T. V. Bulpin, 1971.

Ntombe Twala (or Thwala)

Queen Regent of Swaziland (1983-1986); iNlovukazi, or Ndlovukazi (Queen Mother) (1986-)

Swaziland is a landlocked independent kingdom bounded on three sides by South Africa and on the east by Mozambique. Ntombe was the mother of King designate, Prince Mokhesetive (b. 1968) and a junior wife of King Sobhuza II. When the king died in 1982, his senior wife, Queen Dzeliwe, was so act as regent for the king's hand-picked successor, Mokesetive. However, in August of 1983, Dzeliwe was removed by the Liqoqo, or National Council, for refusing to sign a paper acknowledging the council as the Supreme Authority. She was replaced by Crown Prince Mokhesetive's mother, Ntombe, who signed a decree in September of 1983, which apparently gave the Liqoqo (or Libandla) the Supreme Authority to act. Constitutional matters continued to be vested in the king.

That same month, the Crown Prince returned from England, where he had been in school, to preside over his first official function. In a traditional ceremony at Lobamba, he was formally introduced to the chiefs and the

Swazi people. In April of 1986 he was crowned King Mswati III, at age eighteen, the youngest monarch (Ngwenyama) to rule Swaziland. His first order of government was to restore support for the crown that had eroded by power-hungry members of the Council. He dissolved the Liqoqo and dismissed the Prime Minister.

In Swaziland power is shared between the King and the Queen Mother. "Ngwenyama" signifies "hardness" as typified by thunder. "iNdlovukazi" signifies "She Elephant" as typified by the softness of water. The National Council (Liqoqo, or Libandla), the traditional side of government, is appointed by the king and headed by the King and Queen Mother. Her main duty is to uphold the traditional and cultural elements of Swazi society; however, she may make diplomatic foreign policy decisions and national executive decisions. She is present at all policy-making meetings and is the first addressed by the King in all his public speeches. The governing power is vested in the King, who appoints a Prime Minister. A People's Parliament was re-established in 1988. It is an open forum which offers the public an opportunity to express their views on policies of the Swazi nation.

Each year, in August of September, the young maidens of Swazi congregate from every part of the kingdom to honor the Queen Mother with the Umhlanga, or Reed Dance, a celebration which takes more than a week to prepare.

Suggested Reading:

(1) Hussey, Hazel. "Ceremonies", "Choosing the King of Swaziland" and "Umhlanga Reed Dance." *Swaziland Jumbo Tourist Guide*, 1997.

(2) Blaustein, Albert P. and Gisbert H. Flanz, eds. *Constitutions of the Countries of the World: A Series of Updated Texts, Constitutional Chronologies and Annotated Bibliographies*. Dobbs Ferry, New York: Oceana Publications, 1991.

Ntsusa

Chief of the South African amaRharhabe/Ngqika (1782)

Ntsusa was the daughter of Xhosa chief Rharhabe who, along with his Great Son (eldest and heir) Mlawu, died in battle against the Thembu tribe in 1782. Mlawu's son Ngqika was only four years old at the time. The age of Ntimbo, Mlawu's other son, is not known. One tradition reported by Stephen Kay says Nysusa was appointed chief by King Khawuta, while two factions squabbled over which of Mlawu's sons should be chief. Most of the former chief's councillors supported Ntimbo, while Rharhabe's son Ndlambe and his party backed Ngqika. Ndlambe secured the king's support and thereafter ruled as regent for his nephew, even continuing to exercise real power after he installed Ngqika as chief. It is Ndlambe who is credited as the architect of Rharhabe greatness. Eventually, however, Ngqika rebelled and tried to wrest control from his uncle, enlisting support from the Boer colonists. War broke out between the two factions that continued for years. Meanwhile, a clan with many chiefs had developed under Ngqika's aunt Ntsusa, whom Ngqika's son Tyhali accused in the theft of some Boer military horses, calling Ntsusa's clan "the terror of the country." As a result, a Boer commando group was sent out against the Ntsusa. Ntsusa died in 1826.

Suggested Reading:

(1) Peires, J. B. *The House of Phalo*. Berkeley: The University of California Press, 1982, pp. 49, 81, 212.

(2) Kay, Stephen, *Travels and Researches in Caffraria*. London: John Mason, 1833, p. 152.

Nyakaima

Queen, founder of the Bunyoro, or Babito dynasty (c. 16th c.)

The Babito dynasty was located in the Great Rift area of East Central Africa between the Great Lakes. Nyakaima was a member of the Luo group of Nilotic-speaking tribes of southern Sudan. A member of the MuChwezi tribe from East Central Africa migrated to her area and married her. The couple established a clan which became the ruling Bunyoro dynasty known as Babito. Eventually the kingdom absorbed the BaChwezi people and inherited their kingdom. The Babito dynasty endured for some ten generations.

Even today, priestesses who claim descendance from Nyakaima, still attend a shrine honoring her located at the base of a 400-year-old, 130-feet tall "witch tree". The tree is located on the top of Mubende at the center of the Great Lakes region. There, the priestesses make offerings and sacrifice white chickens.

Suggested Reading:

(1)   de Villiers, Marc and Sheila Hirtle, *Into Africa*. Toronto: Key Porter Books, Ltd., 1997. p. 351.

Nyamazana

Queen of the Ngoni in East Africa (1835-1890's)

The Ngoni people, more than a million strong, consist of a dozen subgroups of Bantu-speaking people scattered throughout eastern Africa, each forming an independent state with its own ruler. Nyamazana was reputedly the niece of Zwangendaba, who led a migration from Zululand c. 1819, and in Zimbabwe became leader of a branch of the Ngoni. In 1835 he led his Ngoni across the Zambezi River, but his niece remained behind with her followers. One story alleges that Zwangendaba barred her from coming farther with him, possibly for reasons having to do with logistics.

For approximately the next two years, Nyamazana led her Ngoni tribesmen through Shona territory, pillaging native settlements until, in c. 1839, the warriors of King Mzilikazi (c. 1795-1868), founding king of the Ndebele state, arrived in Zimbabwe. Nyamazana surrendered to them, married the king, and allowed her followers to be integrated into the Ndebele state. She is said to have outlived the king by more than three decades, dying in the early 1900's.

Suggested Reading:

(1)   Lipschutz, Mark. R. and R. Kent Rasmussen. *Dictionary of African Historical Biography*. Berkeley: University of California Press, 1986.
(2)   Rasmussen, R. Kent. *Mzilikazi of the Ndelebe*. London: Heinemann Educational Books, 1977.

Nzinga Mbandi (Also called Singa, Jinga, Zhinga, Nzinga Pande, Ann Zingha, Njinga Oande, and Dona Ana de Sousa)

Queen, or *ngola*, of the Mbundu in the kindoms of Ndongo (1624-1626) and Matamba (c. 1630-1663) in northwest Angola)

Nzinga was born c. 1580, the daughter and sister of kings. One of her predecessors was Nzinga Mhemba, baptised in 1491 by the Portuguese as Alfonso, who came to the throne in 1507 and ruled as an "ardent and enlightened Christian" until he died in 1543. In 1618 the Portuguese finally conquered the Ndongo kingdom in Angola. ("Angola" comes from "ngola", meaning ruler.) Nzinga's early attempts to become the ruler of her tribe failed, and her brother was made ngola in the early 1620s. In c. 1622 he sent her to Luanda to negotiate with the imperious Governor de Sousa. The governor sat upon a throne while Nzinga was expected to stand before him. She ordered a slave to kneel so that she could sit. According to one account, when the interview was at an end, she ordered the slave slaughtered before the horrified governor's eyes to show him that she never had to sit in the same chair twice. Nzinga first attempted to use the Portuguese to secure her leadership, even allowing herself to be baptised and to take the name "Dona Ana de Sousa," being named after the Portuguese governor. Her sister Mukumbu had become "Lady Barbara" and her sister Kifunji had become "Lady Grace." Her brother died in 1624 as did his son, both possibly at Nzinga's instigation, and Nzinga became the undisputed queen. Two years later the Portuguese drove her out and installed a more cooperative ruler. Nzinga went east into the interior and recruited a powerful army. In the early 1630's she conquered the kingdom of Matamba and made herself queen. From there she continued to harass the Ndongo kingdom and to control the interior slave trade, so that the Portuguese were still required to negotiate with her. She dressed as a male chief and was accompanied by an entourage of concubines, who were young men dressed as women. She was the first monarch to initiate a policy of aggressive military expansion, hence the term "jingoism."

She could be diplomatic if it suited her purposes, or she could put on a great show of barbarism, which seemed to work more effectively to gain respect from the European intruders. Once, across the river from the horrified Dutch she had put on such a show of savagery, in the form of a gory ceremonial dance, that she could be certain of not being hindered by them. In 1626 the Portuguese decided to drive Nzinga out and set up a puppet ruler.

"Lady Grace" was taken prisoner, but from captivity she supplied Nzinga with intelligence for years concerning Portuguese affairs. Nzinga's people remained loyal to her and refused to obey the puppet chief. In retaliation for the Portuguese attempt at a coup, Nzinga made an alliance with the neighboring kingdom of Kasanji, closing the slave routes to the Portuguese. She then moved eastward and conquered the kingdom of Matamba. From there, she developed her own powerful slave trading center.

In the 1640's she formed an alliance with the Dutch, who had forced the Portuguese out of Luanda in 1641. In 1648 the Portuguese recaptured Luanda and began waging war on the inland kingdoms, including Matamba. In 1643, 1647, and 1648 she attacked the Portuguese and drove them back each time. On one of these raids the Portuguese drowned their prisoner "Lady Grace" as they retreated, and on one "Lady Barbara" was captured. In 1648 the Portuguese reconquered Luanda and were thus free to reconsolidate their hold on their African possessions. In 1656/9 they finally negotiated a treaty with Queen Nzinga in which she would engage in slave trade with the Portuguese and assist them in their military campaigns. She signed this treaty in 1659 at over the age of 75, having dealt with incursions by the white man all of her life. She also agreed to accept missionaries in Matamba, once again embracing Christianity herself. One term of the official peace with the Portuguese was the release of "Lady Barbara" in exchange for 130 slaves. Nzinga, a Roman Catholic, continued to rule well into her eighties until her death, collaborating with the Portguese in slave trade. She never married, but was said to keep as many as 30 slaves as sexual partners, supposedly killing them off when she had finished with them.

Upon her death in 1663, she was given a Christian burial.

Suggested Reading:

(1) Lipschutz, Mark R. and R. Kent Rasmussen. *Dictionary of African Historical Biography*. Berkeley: University of California Press, 1986. pp. 181-182.

(2) Gray, Richard, ed. *The Cambridge History of Africa*. London: Cambridge University Press, 1975. vol. 4, p. 8.

(3) Birmingham, David, *Trade and Conflict in Angola: The Mbundu and Their Neighbors Under the Influence of the Portuguese*. Oxford: Oxford University Press, 1966. pp. 6, 226, 236-246, 268, 270.

(4) de Villiers, Marq and Sheila Hirtle, *Into Africa*. Toronto: Key Porter Books, Ltd., 1997. pp. 13, 15, 154, 168-169.

(5) Fage, J. D., *A History of Africa*. New York: Alfred A. Knopf, 1978. pp. 303-304, 316.

(6) Josephy, Jr., Alvin M., ed., *The Horizon History of Africa*. New York: American Heritage Publishing Co., McGraw-Hill, Inc., 1971. Clarke, Prof. John Henrik, "Time of Troubles". pp. 320, 365-357, 405.

Section P

Patrapeameni

Queen Regnant of Meroë (300-308)

Meroë was located in present-day Sudan. Patrapeameni was alwo known as Nahidemani. During her era the Meroeans developed a unique art form uniting styles of Black Africa and Mediterranean Egypt.

Pemba, Queen of

Ruler of Pemba (?-c.1679)

Pemba is an island off the coast of East Africa near the part of Tanga, Tanzania. During the 17th century queens ruled on several of the islands in the area. In c. 1679 a queen was ruling, but an antagonistic faction from a distant branch drove her into exile. In 1687 she went to the Portuguese colony of Goa, seeking refuge. There she ended all chance of regaining her throne by becoming a Christian. Nevertheless, the queen continued to speak for her people on Pemba. In an act of gratitude for the refuge she had received, she willed her kingdom to the Portuguese upon her death, but they were never able to claim this inheritance. In 1694, with conditions on Pemba still in a state of upheaval, the Portuguese discontinued its attempts to subject its populace. The queen died about 1694.

Suggested Reading:

(1) Josephy, Jr., Alvin M., ed., *The Horizon History of Africa*. Clarke, Prof. John Henrik, "Time of Troubles". New York: American Heritage Publishing Co., McGraw-Hill, Ltd., 1971. pp. 369-370.

Perry, Ruth

President of Liberia (1996-1997)

Liberia, located on the west coast of Africa, was founded in 1822 by United States black freedmen. Modeling its government after that of the United States, it became a republic in 1847.

Ruth Perry was born in 1939, received a good education, and married. She was first elected to the legislature. During the military rule of Samuel Doe, Ruth Perry served as a senator. In 1990, Doe was executed by one of the warring factions vying for control of the government.

After six years of turbulence, during which more than 150,000 Liberians were killed and over half the 2.6 million population was forced to flee to surrounding countries, West African heads of state met in Abuja, Nigeria on August 17, 1996, to choose a ruler of Liberia. This leader was to replace university professor Wilton Sankswulo as president until elections could be held the following year. Ruth Perry was named Chairman of the Council of State, a six-member collective presidency. She told the assemblage that had elected her that she had the "touch of velvet" but could be "as hard as steel."

When peace was finally restored, Perry, who had remained in Liberia throughout the bloody civil war, later credited not only help from outsiders (the Economic Community of West African States) with restoring peace, but also the building of a constituency composed in part of victimized groups such as women.

Elections, originally slated for May 30, 1997, were postponed at the request of 11 of Liberia's 16 political parties on the grounds that more time was needed to ensure stable conditions for free and fair elections. One of the leading candidates was another woman, Harvard-educated Ellen Johnson-Sirleaf, who resigned as head of the United Nations Development Programme's Regional Bureau for Africa to run for the post. She campaigned as being the obvious to continue Ruth Perry's policies of finding non-violent modes for resolving differences. However, when elections were finally held in August, 1997, Charles Taylor was elected.

Three months later, Ruth Perry opened a three-day United Nations inter-agency workshop in Addis Ababa, Ethiopia. The purpose of the meeting, comprised of some 60 African women involved in government or in non-governmental social organizations, was to identify the women's role in "peace-building and non-violent means of conflict resolution."

Suggested Reading:

(1) Reuter Information Service, *Nando Times*, "Africa's First Woman Head of State Pledges to Work for Peace." August 18, 1996. p. 1.
(2) Ghion Hagos, "African Women Seek Role in Peace Building." Panafrican News Agency. *Africa News Online*. November 24, 1997.
(3) Remi Oyo, "Liberia Parties Want Elections Postponed." *Electronic Mail & Guardian*, May 15, 1997) IPS/Misonet.

Pheretima

Queen of Cyrene, or Cyrenaica (ca. A.D. 518)

She was the wife of Battus the Lame, fifth ruler of Cyrene, located in northern Libya. "Battus" was a Libyan word meaning "king." The couple had a son, Arcesilaus. The misfortunes which had befallen the realm prior to Battus' reign (the murder of his father and mother and their son's lameness) had prompted the people to send to Delphi to ask the oracle for advice about changing their luck. The priestess advised them to employ Demonax of Mantinea in Arcadia to make some changes in the kingdom. Once employed, Demonax segregated the people into three groups and gave them many of the privileges previously enjoyed only by the rulers. After Battus died, his son Arcesilaus acceded to the throne with the idea of rescinding Demonax's changes. His demands for a restoration of his ancestral rights led to civil war in which he was defeated. His fled to Samos, while Queen Pheretima went to Salamis in Cyprus. There she asked the ruler Euelthon for an army with which to recapture the throne. Instead of honoring her request, he sent her a golden spindle and distaff with wool on it, saying that he sent her a present which, unlike an army, he thought suitable for her sex. Meanwhile, Arcesilaus was able to raise an army in Samos, and he went back to Cyrene and recovered his throne. But fearing a warning of the oracle, he was afraid to remain in Cyrene, so he went to Barca, leaving Queen Pheretima to represent him, running the government in Cyrene. But her son was assassinated in Barca, and when the queen learned of his death, she fled to Egypt for asylum. Intent on avenging her son's death, she convinced Aryandes to send troops from Egypt to Barca to assist her in laying seige to the town. They called on the citizens to surrender those responsible for Arcesilaus' death, but the people refused, claiming that everyone was equally responsible. The siege then continued for nine months. The Persians, meantime, were interested in mining operations in Barca and were eventually allowed by the Barcans to enter. The Persians then delivered to Queen Pheretima the men responsible for her son's murder. She had them impaled on stakes around the city wall. The wives of the murderers fared no better. She cut off their breasts and stuck them up on stakes, too. She gave the rest of the people, other than those of the house of Bothus, to the Persians, who pillaged their homes and reduced them to slavery. Cyrene and Euesperides were incorporated in a Persian satrapy in ca. 518. According to Herodotus, no sooner had Pheretima returned to Egypt than she died a horrible death, "her body seething with worms while she was still alive."

Suggested Reading:

(1) Herodotus, *The Histories*. tr. Aubrey de Sélincourt. New York: Penguin Books, 1954, 1988. pp. 326-328, 337-339.
(2) Hammond, N.G.L., *A History of Greece to 322 B.C.*). Oxford: Oxford University Press, 1986. p. 178.

Pokou, Aura

See Awura Pokou

Section R

Ranavalona I

Queen, titular ruler of the Kingdom of Madagascar (1828-1861)

The kingdom of Madagascar, which united most of the island, lasted from 1810 to 1896, when Madagascar became a French colony. Of its six rulers four were women. The kingdom was founded by King Radama I (r. 1809-1828), who, in exchange for assistance from the British governor of nearby Mauritius, agreed to cooperate in ending slave trade thoughout his territory. He also allowed into his country European tradesmen and members of the London Missionary Society. He married his cousin, Ranavalona I, a member of the Merina, or Andriana, Dynasty, and the grandniece of Andrianjafy (r. 1760-1783). Ranavalona did not share his romance with the Europeans. The couple had a son, Radama II. When Radama I died prematurely in 1828, she succeeded him and ruled for 33 years. She moved quickly to reverse her late husband's liberal Europeanization policies. Over a number of years she expelled the Europeans, and eventually she had so purged the kingdom of outsiders that the British and French joined forces to unseat her. They were defeated at Tamatave in 1845. She ruled unmolested until her death in 1861. Her son Radama II (r. 1861-1863), who succeeded her, married her niece Rasoherina, a daughter of her sister.

Suggested Reading:

(1) Morby, John E. *Dynasties of the World*. Oxford: Oxford University Press, 1989. p. 237)
(Egan, Edward, et. al., *Kings, Rulers and Statesmen*. New York: Sterling Publishing, 1976. p. 302.

Ranavalona II

Queen of Madagascar (1868-1883)

Madagascar, an island located off the southeastern shore of Africa, is populated by a mixture of African and Indonesian people. Ranavalona II was a member of the Merina, or Andriana, Dynasty and the niece of Queen Ranavalona I (r. 1828-1861), her mother being the queen's sister. The first Ranavalona's son Radama II had succeeded upon his mother's death in 1861, but he was assassinated two years later at the instigation of the Merina oligarchy, tribes of a "higher" pure Indonesian caste. His former army chief, Rainilaiarivony, asserted himself into the position of prime minister, marrying the king's widow Rasoherina (r. 1863-1868), who was another niece of Ranavalona I. When Rasoherina died five years later, Ranavalona II succeeded her, and Rainilaiarivony married her as well. The following year (1869), Christianity was adopted as the official religion of Madagascar, and the traditional Malagasy religion was suppressed. The kingdom soon took on many of the European characteristics once adopted by the queen's uncle and so long fought by her aunt. Ranavalona II's fifteen-year reign was the last peaceful reign of the dynasty. Upon her death leaving no heir in 1883, a distant cousin, Ranavalona III, was found to succeed her.

Suggested Reading:

(1) Morby, John E. *Dynasties of the World*. Oxford: Oxford University Press, 1989. p. 237.
(2) Egan, Edward, et. al., *Kings, Rulers and Statesmen*. New York: Sterling Publishing, 1976. p. 302.

Ranavalona III

Queen of Madagascar (1883-1896)

Ranavalona III was born in 1861, presumably a distant cousin of King Radama II (r. 1861-1863), Queen Rasoaherina (r. 1863-1868), and Queen Tanavalona II (r. 1868-1883). The last ruler of the Merina, or Andriana, Dynasty, she succeeded Queen Ranavalona II upon her death in 1883. In 1883, she married the prime minister, Rainilaiarivony, who had been married to the two preceding queens and who was implicated in the death of Radama II. In 1895 French troops forced her husband into exile. She was forced to sign a treaty allowing Madagascar to become a French protectorate. She was not officially deposed but remained as a figurehead until, in 1916 or 1917, she died. Thereafter, Madagascar was united with the French empire.

Suggested Reading:

(1) Morby, John E. *Dynasties of the World*. Oxford: Oxford University Press, 1989. p,. 237.
(2) Egan, Edward, et. al., *Kings, Rulers and Statesmen*. New York: Sterling Publishing, 1976. p. 302.

Ras Ela Adhana I

Ruler of Axum, or Aksum, Ethiopia (ca. 375-380)

She was succeeded by Ras Ela Adhana II.

Ras Ela Adhana II

Ruler of Axum, or Aksum, Ethiopia (ca. 400)

She ruled for six years.

Ras Ela Giudit

Ruler of Axum or Aksum, Ethiopia (846-885)

Axum, located in northern Ethiopia, was one of the most powerful kingdoms in sub-Saharan Africa. The kingdom of Axum thrived from about A.D. 100 to 800. Ras Ela Giudit was the granddaughter of Ras Demawedem Wechem Asfare, who ruled Aksum from 790 to 820. She was also known as Terdáe Gomaz Yodit.

Rasoherina

Queen of Madagascar (1863-1868)

A member of the Merina, or Andriana Dynasty, she was related to King Andrianjafy (r. 1760-1783) and to Queen Ranavalona I (r. 1828-1861), who was her mother's sister. Rasoherina married her cousin, Radama II, Queen Ranavalona I's son, who ascended to the throne in 1861 but was assassinated only two years later. Rasoherina ruled for five years. Radama II's former army chief, who was implicated in his murder, married Rasoherina, possibly against her will, and rose to become prime minister. On her death she was replaced by another of Ranavalona's nieces, Ranavalona II.

Suggested Reading:

(1) Morby, John E. *Dynasties of the World.* Oxford: Oxford University Press, 1989. p. 237.
(2) Egan, Edward, et. al., *Kings, Rulers and Statesmen.* New York: Sterling Publishing, 1976. p. 302.

Ruete, Emily

Potential queen mother of Zanzibar (fl. 1850s-1880s)

She was born Seyyida Salima, the daughter of Sultan Seyyid Said of Zanzibar, now Tanzania. After Sultan Said died, her brother Majid became Sultan. In 1866, Salima had an affair with Heinrich Reute, a German trader and became pregnant, which was a serious breach of Islamic law and an insult to her family. Sultan Majid threatened to have her killed, but she escaped via a British warship and went to Aden, where Ruete joined her. She was baptized and married Reute, taking the name Emily Reute, the spelling of which was later changed to Ruete. The couple went to Germany where Emily bore two more children before Heinrich died in the 1870s, leaving her penniless. By this time another brother, Barghash, was on the throne of Zanzibar. He was plagued by economic woes and encroaching English and German claims to his territory. Emily, whose son was a candidate for the throne, agreed in 1885 to a plan by German Chancellor Bismarck to board a German warship with her family and return to Zanzibar, hoping to threaten Barghash with usurping the throne if he did not cede the mainland to Germany. But before she reached Zanzibar, Barghash had agreed to German demands. Tanzania was a protectorate of Germany. Barghash watched as Germany and England divided the mainland between them. Barghash then concentrated on solidifying his position on Zanzibar itself, but to appease his sister, he agreed to pay her a small stipend. Emily returned to Germany and wrote her autobiography in 1886. It was translated in 1888 as *Memoirs of an Arabian Princess.*

Suggested Reading:

(1) Coupland, Reginald. *The Exploitation of East Africa.* London: Faber and Faber, 1939.

Rweej

Queen of the Lunda (before 1600)

The Lunda live in the savanna belts of central Africa, specifically the grasslands of Congo-Angola-Zambia. Queen Rweej was from a distinguished family of leaders. Rweej herself was the local Lunda queen when, toward 1600, a handsome Luba (another related people) hunter named Kibinda Ilunga took a band of followers west to the river Kasai. There he met the queen, charmed her, and married her. Thereafter Rweej let Kibinda Ilunga rule. This angered her twin brothers, who left the kingdom for the interior of Angola to establish chiefdoms of their own. Her brother Kinguri was the founding hero of the Imbangala in Angola. Another brother migrated south with a band of followers and formed the Lwena people who today occupy the territory along the headwaters of the Zambezi. Queen Rweej and Kibinda Ilunga had a son, Luseeng, who, along with his son Naweej, built a mighty empire called Lundaland, of which Naweej was the first Mwata Yamvo, or "Lord of the Viper."

Suggested Reading:

(1) Davidson, Basil, *African History.* New York: Collier Books, 1991. pp. 160-161.

(2) Josephy, Jr., Alvin M., ed., *The Horizon History of Africa.* Vansina, Dr. Jan, "Inner Africa". New York: American Heritage Publishing Co., McGraw-Hill, Inc., 1971. p. 267.

(3) Fage, J. D., *A History of Africa.* New York: Alfred A. Knopf, 1978. pp. 137-138.

Section S

Sarraounia

Sorceress-Queen of the Azna Kingdom (fl. 1899)

The Azna occupied the Dallol Mawri, a broad valley in the Hausa country of the present-day Dogondoutchi district of Niger in northwest Africa. Like so many heroes of history, myths have grown about Sarraounia's childhood. She had a Spartan upbringing with adoptive parents. At the age of eighteen she already knew how to lead men into battle, and as a tribal sorceress, she held her warriors and her enemies alike in thrawl. When the Fulani of Sokoto attempted to convert her and her people to Islam, she and her warriors fought bravely to drive them back. She had also successfully resisted invasion by the Tuaregs from the north before the white man appeared.

In January, 1899, French troops—primarily black mercenaries—commanded by captains Voulet and Chanoine left Segou in Mali, crossed the territories of the Zarma and of the Gourma, and entered the dense vegetation of the Dallol Mawri. On April 17, 1899, they laid siege with cannonfire to the village of Lugu, which Queen Sarraounia and her fierce warriors defended valiantly, determined not to let the invaders drive her out: "We won't move a single inch from here . . . . even if he must die to the last person!" But the superior French arms proved too powerful for the natives. Forced to retreat, she took her warriors into the forest, confiding to her adoptive father, " . . . They are many and well-armed . . . . They burn everything along their route . . . ." After her initial defeat, she reorganized and vowed to resist "in spite of hunger. If there is no grain, we will eat vines and roots, but we will resist . . . ." She continued to harass her enemies, so intimidating the mercenaries that many of them abandoned the French. While the French captains, watching her rituals from afar, at first dismissed them as "drunkeness" and "incoherent ramblings of a superstitious woman," the mercenaries came to believe her to be the Nkomo woman, the femme fatale, the Dogoua, or demon-woman. Their abandonment greatly weakened the French forces. However, the Fulani, who, having failed to convert her to Islam, looked upon Sarraounia as a "rebellious, unclean, faithless woman" and her city as "accursed," opted to join forces with the French ultimately to bring about French subjugation of the entire area.

Suggested Reading:

(1) Mamani, Abdoulaye, *Sarraounia, ou "le drame d'une reine magicienne.* Paris: L'Harmattan, 1980.

Schreiner, Olive Emilie Albertina

Political Activist and Early Feminist in South Africa (1883-1920)

She was born in Lesotho in 1855, the daughter of a German missionary and an English woman. Although her younger brother William Phillip Schreiner (1857-1919) trained as a lawyer, Olive received little formal education. She went to work in a remote rural area of Cape Colony as a governess for an Afrikaner family and began writing stories about the harsh life of Afrikaner farmers and their wives. Around 1881 she wrote a novel called *The Story of an African Farm* and felt it had sufficient merit to justify quitting her job and traveling to England in search of a publisher. As was the widely practiced custom, she chose a masculine pen name, Ralph Iron. In 1883 the book was published and became an international success. Meanwhile, her brother William had become active in politics as a liberal opposed to racially discriminatory policies in Cape Colony. Olive returned to South Africa in 1889 and took an interest in her brother's causes. In 1893 William entered the Cape parliament and became attorney general in C. J. Rhodes' administration. Olive married a politician, Samuel Cronwright (1863-1936), who changed his name to Cronwright-Schreiner. Together the couple worked for liberal causes, and following Leander Jameson's (1853-1917) invasion of Ndebele in 1893, Olive wrote a novel condemning Cecil Rhodes's and Jameson's policies in Zimbabwe. It was called *Trooper Peter Halket of Machonaland* (1897). During the South African War, she supported the Afrikaners. In 1898 William's new coalition, the South Africa Party, gained the majority and he became Prime Minister of Cape Colony. In this atmosphere, in 1911 Olive turned her attention to women's causes. She wrote a book condemning men's "sex parasitism" called *Women and Labour.* Two years later she went to Europe, leaving her husband behind. The couple lived apart until 1920, when Olive returned to South Africa and died soon afterward. Two of her works appeared after her death: *Thoughts on South Africa* (1923) and the unfinished *From Man to Man* (1926). Cronwright wrote a biography of her life.

Suggested Reading:

(1) Meintjes, Johannes. *Olive Schreiner.* Johannesburg: H. Keartland, 1965.

Sebekkare

See Nefrusobek

Sebeknefru

See Nefrusobek

Shajar Al Durr (Shajarat al-Durr, Spray or Tree of Pearls)

Queen, regent of Egypt (1250, officially for 80 days)

She was Turkish, or possibly Armenian, and was the devoted slave-wife of Sultan Al Salih Ayyub, Ayyubid Sultan of Egypt from 1240 to 1249. After she bore him a son, he gave her her freedom. During a campaign against the French Crusaders under King Louis in Africa, the sultan died in his tent in Mansoora in 1249. With the Crusaders on the way, Shajar Al Durr kept his death a secret. Daily she assured the officers that the sultan was much better, and she issued orders under the sultan's forged signature. Faced with a major battle against a well-armed force, this extraordinary woman commanded the army and at the same time ruled the land, all under cover, concealing a rotting corpse. The Crusaders were beaten by dysentary and starvation when the Muslims cut off their supply route. Early the next year, the sultan's oldest son, Turan Shah, arrived in Cairo from Syria to be proclaimed Sultan. But in May, 1250, the Mamluks murdered him and hailed Spray of Pearls, to whom they were devoted, as queen of Egypt. She assumed sovereign power and ruled for 80 days, striking her own coins and having herself mentioned in Friday prayers as Sultan of Egypt. But Syria refused to recognize the accession of Spray of Pearls: the Abbasid Khalif wrote, quoting the Prophet, "Unhappy is the nation which is governed by a woman," adding with sarcasm, "If you have no men, I will send you one." As a result, Spray of Pearls was deposed in favor of a Mamluk general of late sultan, Aybak, her commander-in-chief. Shajar Al Durr, who was endowed with both intelligence and beauty, immediately set out to marry Aybak. Some sources say she married him before he became sultan, and then her Egyptian emirs nominated him as sultan. Whatever the scenario, it was through Shajar Al Durr that Aybak, who divorced his former wife, Umm 'Ali, to marry her, became the first Mamluk sultan (r. 1250-1257). In order not to be confined once more to a harem, Shajar Al Durr saw to it that the *khutba* (Friday prayer) was said in both her husband's and her name in every mosque in Cairo, and that every official document bore both their signatures.

However, it was not a happy marriage. In 1257, when she learned that her husband intended to marry the daughter of the atabeg of Mosul, Badr al-Din Lu'lu, she was both humiliated and enraged. With her husband's servants, she devised an elaborate plan to murder Aybak. On April 12, 1257, when Aybak entered the *hammam*, or Turkish bath, at Citadel del Cairo, his servants surrounded and killed him.

The sultan's assassination threw the troops in an uproar. Some remained loyal to Shajar Al Durr, but a few days later Aybak's supporters retaliated. She was brought to the Burj al-Ahmar (Red Fort) and "battered to death with wooden shoes by the slave women of Aybak's first wife . . . ." They threw her half-nude body off the battlements of the citadel of Cairo overhanging a cliff. Her body lay in a ditch for several days before it was buried in the courtyard of a school that she founded. It is known today as Jami' Shajarat al-Durr, the mosque of Shajar Al Durr.

Suggested Reading:

(1) Hitti, Philip K. *The Arabs*. London: Macmillan, 1937. p. 672.
(2) Mernissi, Fatima. *The Forgotten Queens of Islam*. Minneapolis: University of Minnesota Press, 1993. pp. 14, 28-29, 86, 89, 90-93, 97-99, 110.
(3) Glubb, Sir John. *A Short History of the Arab Peoples*. New York: Dorset Press, 1969. pp. 202-205, 210.
(4) Chahin, M. *The Kingdom of Armenia*. New York: Dorset press, 1987, 1991. p. 286.

Sheba

See *Makeda*

Sinqobile Bahle Mabhena

Chief of the Ndebele tribe in Zimbabwe (1997)

Her name means "we have conquered." She was born in 1974, the oldest of four daughters of the clan chief. She had no brothers and no male cousins to inherit the chiefdom. She attended college at the University of Zimbabwe. When her father died, Mabhena, age 23, was elected chief of the Ndebele. Her election was met by hostility by other chiefs, among them Khayisa Ndiweni, who claimed that even talking about "this girl" caused his blood pressure to go up. Despite threats that were made to harm her and to use black magic against her, Mabhena expressed determination to continue in office, voicing puzzlement as to why "men and other chiefs" were opposed to her election. She promised to do her best for her people. Her college friends supported her, dubbing her the "Iron Lady of Matabeleland."

Suggested Reading:

(1) Shelby, Barry. "Iron Lady of Matabele." *World Press Review*. March, 1997. p. 23.

Sitoe, Aline

See Aline Sitoe

Sitre-meryetamun Tawosret

See Twosret

Sitt al-Mulk

Fatamid Queen of Cairo, Regent (1020-1024)

Sitt al-Mulk ("Lady of Power") was born ca. 970, the daughter of the caliph, al-'Aziz (r. 975-996). Her mother was a Christian. By all accounts, she was one of the most beautiful Fatimid princesses. She was 16 years older than her brother, al-Hakim, who was to be the next caliph. When her father died in a freak accident at the age of 42, al-Hakim, who had constantly tormented his sister, became caliph.

Al-Hakim's reign was characterized by oppression. He continued to harass his sister, whom he accused of having lovers. Hordered all dogs killed. He forbade laughing, weeping, and singing in the kingdom. Walking along the banks of the Nile, taking a pleasure boat ride, or even opening one's doors or windows onto a pleasant view were all forbidden. He put a ban on many food items and on the sale of wine. Grapes and raisins were dumped into the Nile. He forbade women to go into the streets, ordered shoemakers to cease making shoes for women, and closed women's bath houses. Women were prisoners in their own homes for seven years and seven months. When women objected to this treatment, he simply had them put to death. He next focused his attention on the Jews and Christians, destroying their places of worship and subjecting them to public humiliation and persecution. Then another fanatic, Hamza Ibn 'Ali, convinced al-Hakim that he was actually God, and the caliph compelled the Muslims to worship him. The majority of the populace was enraged.

Eventually al-Hakim disappeared, and for four months during his "absence" Sitt al-Mulk simply assumed power, an unheard-of occurrence. Eventually the caliph's body was found, and she moved quickly to have his young son named caliph with herself as regent, although normally the caliph was required to be an adult. She immediately organized her regency and began to put the country's economy in order.

Now historians reveal that Sitt al-Mulk conspired with a general, Ibn Daws, to have her brother killed, promising to share power with him after the caliph was dead. After she gained the regency, it was necessary to remove Daws as well. She had some guards point him out as the murderer and he was killed on the spot.

Although she ruled for four years, she did not ask that the *khutba* (ritual Friday prayers affirming the ruler's right to rule) be said in her name. The *khutba* was preached in the name of her nephew, al-Dhahir. It was said that she showed "exceptional ability, especially in legal matters" and that she "made herself loved by the people."

Suggested Reading:

(1) Mernissi, Fatima. *The Forgotten Queens of Islam.* tr. Mary Jo Lakeland. Minneapolis: University of Minnesota Press, 1993. pp. 159-178.

Skemiophris

See Nefrusobek

Sobekneferu

See Nefrusobek

Spray of Pearls

See Shajar Al Durr

Section T

Taitu (or Taytu Betul)

Empress, defacto ruler of Ethiopia (1906-1913)

Taitu was born c. 1844. She married several times and had several affairs. In 1883 she became the fourth wife of King Sahle Mariam of Shoa, and helped him rise to become Emperor Menelik II, ruling all of Ethiopia from 1889 to 1913. It was Taitu who persuaded her husband to construct a home near a warm springs and to grant parcels of land surrounding it to families of the nobility. From this beginning, the new capital city of Ethiopia was founded in 1887. Empress Taitu named it Addis Ababa, meaning "New Flower."

In 1902 Taitu personally led a successful military campaign to quell a revolt in Tigre. In 1906 Menelik suffered the first of a series of strokes which over the years would debilitate him completely. Empress Taitu, who had always been a strong woman with great influence, then exercised her ruling power. She attempted to have her step-daughter, Zauditu, named as her husband's successor, but he named his grandson, Lij Iyasu V, to succeed him. Even after 1908, when Ras Tesemma was named regent for Iyasu, Empress Taitu's authority remained supreme. Ras Tessama died in 1911, and Lij Iyasu was proclaimed emperor; however, he proved to be inept at governing. Empress Taitu's influence waned after her bedridden husband died in 1913. She retired from court but returned in 1916 after Iyasu's government was toppled. Again she supported Zauditu's candidacy, and this time Zauditu was crowned empress. However, Taitu was unable to gain the position of regent. Tafari Makonnen (Haile Selassie) was named instead. Again she returned to her mountain home, where she died in 1918.

Suggested Reading:

(1) Lipschutz, Mark R., and R. Kent Rasmussen. *Dictionary of African Historical Biography*. Berkeley: University of California Press, 1989. p. 230.
(2) Langer, William L., ed. *World History*. Boston: Houghton Mifflin, 1940, 1980. p. 872.

Tausert

See *Twosret*

Tiy

Queen, defacto regent-ruler of Egypt (c. 1370 B.C)

Tiy was a commoner, possibly of Asiatic blood, and possibly from a military family. Her father was Yuya of Akhmin, an officer in the Chariotry and Master of the Stud Farms and possibly also the father of the queen-mother Mutemwia. Tiy's mother's name was Tuya. The couple was eventually able to promote one of their sons, the divine father Ay, to succeed to the throne following Tutankhamun. Tiy married Amenophis (or Amenhotep) III, ruler of Egypt from c. 1405 to 1370 B.C. The king, having departed from the God's Wife concept of marrying the royal heiress (usually one's sister) who would become the chief queen, bestowed upon his commoner wife the august title of "Great Royal Wife." They married during the second year of his reign. Variously described as "formidable," "a woman of long-suffering character," possessing "compelling physical appeal," she maintained her influence over him despite his many other feminine distractions. The king enjoyed sailing with Tiy on the artificial lake outside the palace, while Tiy enjoyed unusual power within the palace. In the ceremonies held renewing kingly power, Queen Tiy participated as well. She bore the king six children. The first died without reigning. The second was Akhenaton (Amenophis IV), who ruled from ca. 1370 to 1352. Of her four daughters, two (Satamun and Isis) were given the title of queen. Tiy stood alongside her husband as the personification of Maat and was therefore afforded certain royal privileges such as participation in the various festivals. She played an important part in formulating foreign policy. The king's last years were spent in illness, and it is possible that during those years Tiy's son was already elevated to ruler or co-ruler. In the early years of her son's reign, she acted as regent. Her father had elevated her brother Inen to the important post of Second Prophet of Amon (Amun). Given the amount of evidence remaining of Tiy's influence and participation, it is safe to assume that during the waning years of her husband's life, this influence and participation increased, especially on behalf of her son. She died in the eighth year of her son's reign. As an indication of her exalted position, she was allowed to have herself represented in the form of a sphinx and a temple was dedicated to her at the Nubian site of Sedeinga.

Suggested Reading:

(1) Grimal, Nicolas. *A History of Ancient Egypt*. New York: Barnes & Noble Books, 1997. pp. 214, 221-222, 226-227, 234, 237, 271.
(2) White, J. S. *Ancient Egypt*. New York: Dover Publishing, 1970. pp. 169, 172, 173.
(3) West, John Anthony. *The Traveler's Key to Ancient Egypt*. New York: Alfred A. Knopf, 1985. pp. 226, 235, 338, 378.

Turunku Bakwa (or Bazao)

Queen, founder and ruler of Zaria (1536-?)

She was the mother of Amina and Zaria, both of whom ruled Zaria after her. She was an immigrant, a Fulani who moved into Macina, the eastern Niger region. Some argue that she might have come from the south because she had acquired guns from traders on the coast. She belonged to a matriarchal clan. In 1536 she founded the city of Zaria in north central Nigeria, naming it for her younger daughter.

Suggested Reading:

(1) Panikker, K. Madhu. *The Serpent and the Crescent: A History of the Negro Empires of West Africa*. Bombay: Asia Publishing House, 1963. pp. 112-113.

Twosret (or Tausert or Twosre)

King, last ruler of Nineteenth Dynasty, Egypt (c. 1202-1200 B.C.).

She was probably the daughter of Merneptah, who ruled c. 1236 to 1223 B.C. She was the wife and probably also the sister of Sethos II (Seti II), ruler from c. 1216 to 1210 B.C. Sethos married three queens, the first of whom, Takhat II, apparently did not provide him with an heir. Twosret was his second wife; she bore a son named Sethos Merneptah, but he died young. The third queen provided the heir, Ramesses Siptah. Apparently Sethos II died or was murdered in 1210. A Syrian officer, Bay, who had become powerful as chancellor of Egypt brought Siptah to the throne. Because Siptah was too young, Twosret, his step-mother and matrilineal link to the throne, acted as regent and married him. Both Bay and Twosret acquired evil reputations. When Siptah died in 1202 (by one dating 1196), possibly at her hand, Twosret herself ruled as "King," appropriating her husband's regnal years and restoring her first husband's name over his. Supposedly Bay seduced her and had free access to the treasury. The throne was probably usurped by Selnakht in 1200 B.C.

Suggested Reading:

(1) West, John Anthony. *The Traveler's Key to Ancient Egypt*. New York: Alfred A. Knopf, 1985. pp. 142, 162.
(2) Grimal, Nicolas. *A History of Ancient Egypt*. New York: Barnes & Noble Books, 1997. pp. 204, 270-271.

Section U

Uwilingiyimana, Agathe

Prime Minister of Rwanda (1993-1994)

Rwanda, located in east central Africa, has long been the scene of conflict between the Hutu agricultural peasants and the Tutsi, a pastoral group that arrived in the fifteenth century and gained dominance over the Hutu. Throughout Africa the number of women in politics has been small, with only the most outstanding women managing to reach the upper tiers of power. Agathe Uwilingiyimana was such a woman, having been born of educated and influential Kigali parents, and having received an outstanding education herself. Uwilingiyama entered politics because she was interested in health and education reform as well as in the general betterment of the status of women. In 1993 she became the first woman ever nominated to head her party and the first to serve as chief executive of Rwanda. She worked hand-in-glove with neighboring Burundi's Prime Minister, Sylvie Kinigi, and together they planned extensive social reforms. However, her leadership was not welcomed even by a substantial faction within her own party. In April of 1994 she was assassinated, thus effectively ending any meaningful reform in Rwanda.

Suggested Reading:

(1) Humarau, Beatrice. "Women on the Run". *World Press Review*. February 1996: 38-39.

Section V

Van Meerhoff, Eva

Broke South African color barriers by marrying a European in a Christian ceremony (1664)

Called "Eva the Hottentot," she was born c. 1642 into a Khoikhoi tribe near present day Cape Town. When she was about ten years old, the Dutch East India Company established its first station in Cape Town and the commandant, Jan Van Riebeeck, took Eva into his household as a domestic servant. Over time she became fluent in Dutch and learned some Portuguese as well so that as she grew older, she was often called upon to act as interpreter between the company officials and Khoikhoi chiefs. Her prominence in the Dutch community led to the insistence that she become a Christian, and in 1664 she was baptized. As she continued to interact with traders and locals, she was thrown more and more into white company. She met and married an explorer, Pieter van Meerhoff, in 1666. Van Meerhoff died in 1667 leaving Eva, neither fish nor fowl, with little money for which to care for at least two children. According to Dutch account, she fell into a dissolute life, so offending the white community that her children were removed from her custody. She died in 1674, having given Europeans a stereotypal reason to discriminate further against the "immoral" Khoikhoi people.

Suggested Reading:

(1) *Dictionary of South African Biography,* 4 vols. Cape Town, Durban: Human Sciences Council, 1968-1981.

Section W

Waizero

See Zauditu

Wakana

Queen Regnant of Ethiopia (Ca. 216)

She ruled for only two days before she was deposed.

Section Y

Yaa Akyaa

Asantehemaa, Queen Mother of the West African Asante (Ashanti) Empire (ca. 1883-1896)

Ya Akyaa was born ca. 1837 of the royal matriclan Oyoko. She was selected from among the women of the royal Oyoko dynasty to succeed Queen Afua Kobi as *asantehemaa*. "*Asantehemaa*," meaning "Queen Mother," does not carry the same connotation as it does in Europe. Each district or group had its own chief and queen mother, but there was one grand chief and one grand Queen Mother, who might not be the mother of anyone, who ruled over all. It was the asantehemaa, in many ways the most vital person in the tribe, who nominated the chief and who made many of the diplomatic decisions. The *asantehemaa* was completely in charge during the long periods, stretching sometimes into years, when no one occupied the Golden Stool.

Yaa Akyaa was married to the Akyebiakyerehene Kwasi Gyambibi. The *akyebiakyerehene* was a secretary or advisor to the chief and the council. The couple had 13 children, several of whom in their turn were to be nominated to sit upon the Golden Stool. Even prior to her election as *asantehemaa*, as Queen Mother of her own tribe or district, she wielded considerable power. In 1883 two factions were vying for supremacy and the right to name the next *asantehene*, or chief of the chiefs. The duty of the *asantehene* was to act as judge. He decided cases of extreme seriousness which could not be solved within the individual districts. The *mamponhene*, or leader of the Mampone district, sent word that he was coming to intercede in the dispute. Yaa Akyaa sent several messages instructing him to withdraw and to remove his guns from Kumase because the two factions were going to fight. The *mamponhene* did as he was told. The battle took place, and the Kumasi people headed by Yaa Akyaa were victorious (1883). Her son Kwaka Dua II was placed on the Golden Stool and another son, Agyemon Badu, became heir apparent.

Following the premature death of Kwaka Dua II of smallpox only a few months later, and apparently the death of the heir as well, and the subsequent death of his predecessor and rival, the kingdom was plunged into confusion. As the Asante attempted to recover from the devastation caused by the outbreak of this strange disease, a lawless people, the Adansis, took advantage of the confusion to rob and plunder travellers enroute to and from the coast. When the Asante retaliated, the Adansis sent false reports to the British, requesting aid to defeat the Asante. For a while, until they bothered to investigate the matter, the British intervened on behalf of the marauders. Meanwhile, Yaa Akyaa called a third son, Agyeman Prempe, to the stool, but a contender from another district had emerged, contesting Prempe's right since he was not the so-named heir apparent. Yaa Akyaa, in despair at the indecision, saw that there was imminent danger of the collapse of the empire and sent an urgent message to the chiefs requesting that they meet together and elect a king.

Still reeling from the unwarranted attacks by the British troops, the chiefs consented to come only if the British government would agree to support the man chosen. She then dispatched an embassy to the local British government requesting that a representative be present at the election so as to observe who was the duly elected ruler. The British took no notice of the message for two years, and it was yet another two years beyond that before the British deigned to comply. This unconscionable delay culminated in the appearance, in 1888, of the long-awaited British representative.

Yaa Akyaa, by this time age 50, short, white-haired, characterized as proud, tenacious, energetic, cunning and intelligent, in a dramatic bit of political maneuvering, demanded that the chief sponsor of the rival candidate return the 3200 ounces of gold which a deposed chief had "deposited" in Saawua. In fact, he had sewn it into a mattress. She was thus able to prevail over the Council of Kumase and Agyeman Prempe was duly elected.

In 1890 she sent envoys to the British about the refugee problem: many Asante had been lured to the British colony on the coast with promises of riches as servants and laborers, and they had acquired undesirable habits from the white men. She requested that the British instruct all Asante citizens residing in the colony to return to Asante in order to "make Asante as it was in the olden days." In exchange, the Asante would affirm its policy of "peace, trade and open roads."

In 1894 she led the more traditional councillors among the West African peoples in insisting that the British desist from interfering with their system of domestic slavery which was integral to the Asante social structure and national plantation economy. The British colonial governor, Maxwell, believed that the arrest and detention of the *asantehene* would precipitate the collapse of the Asante government, and to that end, in 1890, the British government surrounded the town of Kumase and, in a surprise coup, took Yaa Akyaa, her son and others in charge under British "protection." Two days later they were formally arrested.

Her son, who was wrongly accused of killing people but knew that he would be proven innocent, allowed himself to be taken away without struggle, providing that the Queen Mother would go with him. She agreed to go. The two told the British and their people that there was no need to fight; they did not want their nation destroyed. The Asante people, instructed to be proud and not to react, nevertheless all cried. As one Asante wrote, "Kumase was a sea of tears." Agyeman told his people that he and Yaa Akyaa would return, so, in the words of another reporter, "We went to our villages quietly and waited." They would wait for a very long time, for in 1896 the two leaders, never tried but only held in captivity, were deported to Sierra Leone and in 1900 they were exiled to the remote Seychelles Islands.

Ironically, Agyeman's and Yaa Akyaa's submission failed to save the sovereignty of the Asante kindom. Agyeman was not allowed to return (as a "private citizen") until 1924; apparently Yaa Akyaa had died on Seychelles in the interim. On the surface, the British succeeded in "neutralizing" the Asante nation, but in the villages the chant never ceased: "This nation is not yours,/It belongs to Nana Yaa,/This nation is not yours!/It belongs to Yaa Akyaa./This nation is not your nation!/It belongs to Nana Prempe./Nana Prempe is away, and you are occupying his office."

Suggested Reading:

(1) Lewin, Thomas J., *Asante Before the British*. Lawrence, KS: Regents Press of Kansas, 1978. pp. 69-206.
(2) Balmer, W. T., *A History of the Akan People*. New York: Atlantis Press, 1925. pp. 168-185.

Yaa Asantewaa

Edwesohemaa, Queen Mother of the Edweso tribe of the Asante and symbolic leader of the Asante War for Independence (1900-1901)

Yaa Asantewaa was born ca. 1850 and had been elected Queen Mother, or *edwesohemaa*, of the Edweso tribe. Following the arrest by the British of her son, Edwesohene (chief of the Edweso) Kwasi Afrane, the queen mother and two others ran the local administration. The Edweso was one tribe of the Asante Empire. The British reported that under the new leaders, "Edweso appears to be flourishing."

Following the British arrest in 1896 of Asantehene Agyeman Prempe and Asantehemaa Yaa Akyaa, the people hid the Golden Stool, symbol of Asante political sovereignty. The British levied stiff taxes to help recoup the cost of their campaigns against the Asante, and to meet costs of building a fort to house British troops and to build the resident's office and home. In addition, the Europeans had taken over the state-owned "secret" gold mines, which had provided the capital for operating the Asante government.

By 1897, 13 Basel and six Wesleyan missionary schools had been established. But soon the missionaries were interfering in local political and domestic affairs, intruding upon the private lives of the citizens. These conditions and more led to widespread Asante unrest which the British sought to quell one way or another. The British governor then made the shocking demand that the Asante surrender the Golden Stool, and he sent a military attache, Capt. C.H. Armitage, to force the people to tell him where the stool was hidden.

Armitage went to Edweso and confronted Yaa Asantewaa, but the *edwesohemaa* told him that she did not have the Golden Stool. The captain went from village to village demanding the stool. At the village of Bare, Armitage lost patience. By one citizen's account, when the people of Bare learned that Armitage was on the way, they left the village, leaving only the children on the streets. The children told the captain their fathers were gone hunting, and that they knew nothing about the Golden Stool. The captain ordered the children beaten, and the elderly came out of hiding to defend the children. The citizens were bound hand and foot and beaten.

This brutality sparked the beginning of the Yaa Asantewaa War for Independence, so named because the outraged queen mother of the Edweso, described as feisty and gallant, inspired and directed it. But the Asante were no match for the British, who not only killed the citizens, but plundered and pillaged their farms and plantations and confiscated their lands so that the Asante were left completely dependent upon their victors for survival. The queen mother and her close companions were deported as political prisoners, along with the exiled *Asantehene* Agyeman and the Queen Mother of Asante, Yaa Akyaa, to the Seychelles Islands.

Suggested Reading:

(1) Lewin, Thomas J., *Asante Before the British*. Lawrence, KS: Regents Press of Kansas, 1978. pp. 221-222.

Yehudit

Queen of the Falasha Agaw of Abyssinia. See Judith

Yoko, Madame

Ruler of the Kpa Mende Confederacy in Sierra Leone (1878/85-1905/6)

Yoko was born c. 1849 and married three times. She divorced her first husband and was widowed by her second. A charming and personable woman, she then became the head wife of a powerful chief in western Mendeland, taking an active diplomatic role in his government. In 1878, when the chief was near death, he named her as his successor.

Madame Yoko immediately set out to form alliances with her neighbors, building one of the largest political confereracies in Sierra Leone's hinterland. She allied herself with the British, whose influence was expanding into the country's interior. The British stationed a police unit at her capital to help her keep peace and even deported a rival chief after she complained about him.

She started her own Sande Bush (female initiation society to train women leaders), which became so renown in Mendeland that mothers vied to get their daughters accepted. She selected only the most promising young women for her Bush and, according to Sierra Leone historian M. C. F. Easmon, to enter her Bush was like being "Presented At Court." When the young women graduated, she married them off to "leading men who would help her won advancement." (p. 167)

In 1898 war broke out against the British, who two years earlier had declared a protectorate and imposed a porperty tax on its subjects. Yoko remained loyal to the British during this uprising and, as a reward, she was allowed to expand the territory under her jurisdiction and to exercise more control over the Kpa chiefs. She took liberties with her expanded power, engaging in acts of aggression to bring other tribes into her realm of influence. Her territory became so large and unwieldy that at her death the Kpa Mende Confederacy had to be divided into fifteen separate chiefdoms. According to some accounts, fearing old age, she took her own life in 1906.

Suggested Reading:

(1) Rosaldo, M. and L. Lamphere, eds. *Women, Culture and Society.* "Madam Yoko: Ruler of the Kpa Mende Confederacy" by C. P. Hoffer. Stanford: Stanford University Press, 1974.

(2) "Madame Yoko, Ruler of the Mende Confederacy" by M. C. F. Easmon. *Sierra Leone Studies.* December 1958. pp. 166-167.

(3) Lipschutz, Mark R. and R. Kent Rasmussen, *Dictionary of African Historical Biography.* Berkeley, University of California Press, 1989. p. 253.

Section Z

Zainab al-Nafzawiyya

Berber queen of Morocco who shared power with her husband (1061 or 1071-1106)

Zainab was married to Yusuf Ibn Tashfeen (or Tashfin), Prince of the Murabits, the famed founder of the Tashufinid Dynasty and Almoravid empire in Spain and North Africa, as well as the city of Marrakesh. Yusuf was independent ruler in Marrakesh until 1073, when he assumed the title of *amir al-muslimin*. Although it was common knowledge that Zainab shared the power with her husband, she did not have the right to have the *khutba* (a sermon preached in the mosques which gives the sovereign the right to rule) said in her name. Zainab's power was not the only indication of the liberal nature of Yusuf's dynasty. A theologian from another Berber sect, Muhammad Ibn Toumert, was returning to the Maghrib from Baghdad when he saw their daughter riding through Marrakesh among a party of girls, all with their faces unveiled. Outraged, he beat their mules so violently that the young ladies fell off. Zainab's power came to an end in 1106 when the king died and their son 'Ali assumed the throne.

Suggested Reading:

(1) Glubb, Sir John, *A Short History of the Arab Peoples*. New York: Dorset Press, 1969, p. 192.
(2) Morby, John E., *Dynasties of the World*. Oxford: Oxford University Press, 1989., p. 181.
(3) Mernissi, Fatima, *The Forgotten Queens of Islam*. tr. Mary Jo Lakeland. Minneapolis: University of Minnesoya Press, 1993. pp. 14, 205.

Zaela Ahyawa

Queen Regnant, of Ethiopia (ca. 325-334)

When her husband died, Zaela Ahyawa, also known as Ahyawa Sefya or Eguala Anbasa, ruled Ethiopia. In 327 she converted to Christianity.

Zauditu (Also called Zawditu, Zewditu, Waizero or Judith)

Empress, titular ruler of Ethiopia (1916-1930)

Zauditu was born in 1916, the daughter of Emperor Menelik II, ruler of Ethiopia from 1889 to 1913. Her step-mother was Empress Taitu. In 1902 she married Ras Gugsa (Gugsa Wolie). Because he had no sons and was reluctant to name a woman to succeed him, Menelik had named his grandson, Lij Iyasu, as his heir, but the heir apparent refused to ready himself for the position. He refused all schooling after the age of 15. When Menelik died in 1913, despite Taitu's objections in favor of her step-daughter, Iyasu V became emperor. Three years later, he announced his conversion to Islam (1916). As he had not yet been officially crowned, the Ethiopian Church and the local chiefs removed him and, with Taitu as her champion, named Menelik's daughter Zauditu as empress, with Ras Tafari Makonnen (later to be known as Haile Selassie) as her regent and heir. Her appointment was contingent upon her divorcing her husband.

Gradually, Zauditu became concerned about Ras Tafari's usurping more and more power. Her reign was marked by turmoil between the conservative pro-Church group, led by war minister Hapta Giorgis, and liberal, pro-Western group, led by Ras Tafari. In 1923 Ethiopia joined the League of Nations, which later authorized an Ethiopian protest against Britain's plan for division. In 1924 slavery was abolished in Ethiopia. Eventually the country regained access to the sea that had been lost along both the Red Sea coast and the Gulf of Aden. After the death of his old rival Giorgis in 1928, Ras Tafari, not daring to usurp the throne from the empress, nevertheless staged a palace coup and had Zauditu name him "king". Two years later, Zaudita's estranged husband Ras Gugsa, who had been made governor-general of the northern provinces, organized a revolt. Ras Gugsa was killed and the revolt was squelched by Ras Tafari's forces with great effort.

On the day that she heard the news of Ras Gugsa's death, Empress Zauditu died (1930), and Ras Tafari was immediately crowned emperor with the title of Haile Selassi I. Twenty-five years later he enacted a law barring females from becoming monarchs in Ethiopia.

Suggested Reading:

(1) Langer, William L., *World History*. Boston: Houghton Mifflin, 1980. pp. 872, 1078-1079.
(2) Lipschutz, Mark R. and R. Kent Rasmussen, *Dictionary of African Historical Biography*. Berkeley: University of California Press, 1989. p. 255.

Zungu, Dr. Sibongile

Chief of the South African Madlebe tribe (1993)

She was born in Durban and educated as a medical doctor. She married the Madelebe chief, who died in an automobile accident in 1993. After his death, she was chosen to succeed him, officiating over the rural South African tribe of 70,000. Of her election, she said, "People are waiting to see if I fall flat on my face. I'm going to make sure that doesn't happen."

Natal Province, where she is located, has been noted for its violent acts of bloodshed. Dr. Zungu vowed not to "get involved in politics" but gave the opinion that violence was "nature's way of changing this country—her way of cleansing away all the man-made suffering."

Suggested Reading:

(1) "Hail To The Chief" *World Press Review* March 1993: 50.

PART II

*Women Leaders of Asia, India,
Middle East, and Pacific*

Introduction

In 1997 the extremist mullahs of Iran were provoked to promise internal vendettas by news of President Muhammad Khatami's appointment of a woman as one of Iran's seven vice presidents. Massoumeh Ebtekar, a 36-year-old feminist, was made head of the government's environmental organization. A specialist in immunology, Ebtekar, the first woman to hold the position of vice president in Iran, set about attacking the country's pollution problems, while the religious conservatives ranted their outrage. (1)

The situation that caused such concern to the mullahs is puzzling in light of Iran's history: There were several queens, or sultanas, in old Islamic Persia: Kutlugh Khatun, Padishah Khatun, Absh Khatun, Dawlat Khatun, Sati Bek, Tindu, and the country—or the virtue of its men—was apparently none the worse for the experience. Make no mistake; it is woman's sexuality that is behind objections to her ruling in Islam. Alhaj Maulavi Qalamuddin, head of Afghanistan's General Department for the Preservation of Virtue and the Prevention of Vice, voiced the concern for all of Islam in 1997 when he said, "If we consider sex to be as dangerous as a loaded Kalashnikov, it is because it is the source of all immorality." (2)

It is difficult to separate fact from myth surrounding leaders, and it is even more difficult when the leader is a woman from an Islamic nation. Often scribes most easily downplayed the significance of a woman's position in power by alluding to her sexuality and thus her weak morals. Information comes down through the pens of historians with their own biases, sensibilities and tastes such that, for example, acknowledged poor treatment of women in power at the hands of successors may seem to have been either by choice or else best overlooked. Thus we have one historian's account: "Sihasura made Mi Co U . . . his own, a move usually reserved for succeeding monarchs . . ." which another historian records as: "A-san-ge-ye also forced the new king's mother to have sex with him." (3)

An East Java tradition tells of Ratna Jumilah, a princess of Madiun, who was left behind to defend the realm by her fleeing father when King

Senapati of Central Java (Sutawijaya Sahidin Panatagam, d. 1601) invaded the palace. She fought valiantly against the invader, firing pistols, thrusting both spear and daggar (*keri*) at him, and finally attacking him with a razor. At last, we are told, she fell in love with him and submitted to his advances. This story falls into the same category as that from the Finnish *Kalevala* wherein the hero Lemminkäinen sets off on a wooing expedition, intent upon impregnating every woman he encounters. When one maiden spurns him, he drags her away and ties her to the slatted bottom of his sleigh, behavior that so charms her that she immediately consents to become his wife. We might add to this category tales from the Old South about the happy, contented slaves on the U.S. plantations.

Other kinds of myth attach themselves to prominent persons from history. Leaders were often given divine ancestors or a miraculous birth as proof of their right to rule and to exact tribute. Legends about super-human strength or stamina such as those surrounding Queen Pao Ssû of Chou convey vaunted heroic qualities in a much revered monarch. These apochryphal tales in no way suggest that the ruler was fictitious. They can be likened to the story of Washington chopping down the cherry tree; they persist as illustrative of the leader's character, not because we believe they are factual. Many such legends survive about ruling queens, who were often either saintly or else uncommonly evil.

Not so among the most ancient people of the Indo-European culture of record, the Hittites, who invaded Central Asia Minor c. 2000 B.C. and established the Hittite kingdoms (1640-1380 and 1380-1200). Following the model of an older culture of the Middle Minoan III-Late Minoan II at Knossos, Phaistos, and Hagia Triada, in which women held a privileged position in society, (4) the queen occupied a strong central position in this Hittite culture (Tawannanna). (5) The ruler of the feudal state was chosen by the predecessor, and after death the ruler was deified. Deifying of rulers, as was common in ancient Egypt, prevailed from every corner of Africa to Celtic Europe and across Asia, all the way to Japan. Thus we can infer that even certain legendary diety/rulers probably indeed lived, albeit more prosaically than depicted.

Some ancient regimes did in fact leave thorough records. It is recorded that in Lagash in c. 2350 King Lugalanda seized control of the temples and appointed his wife Baranamtarra as administrator, along with other relatives. Baranamtarra managed her own private estates and those of the temple of the goddess Bau. She bought and sold slaves and sent diplomatic missions to neighboring states. (6)

Hundreds of years after the Hittites, a battling queen (Tomyrus) ended the life of Cyrus the Great, founder of the Persian Empire. Herodotus sang the praises of four outstanding women rulers (Artemisia, Semiramis, Pheretima and Nitrocris), but he recounted the berating Darius' son Masistes gave General Artayntes: "He abused him roundly, and, to crown all, told him his leadership was worse than a woman's . . . to call a man 'worse than a woman' is, of course, the greatest insult one can offer to a Persian." (7)

Although there were other Arabian queens who acquitted themselves handily, we have the final word from the Prophet, quoted to the Mameluks by the khalif Mutawakkil when they proclaimed Shajarat al-Durr Queen of Egypt: "Unhappy is the nation who is governed by a woman." This, after the queen had directed all activities, including guiding the army to victory, from within the tent concealing the rotting body of the supposed ruler. (8)

Not all leaders were rulers. Ghaliyya al-Wahhabiyya was a Bedouin *amira al-umara* (generalissimo) in the early 18th c. She was an Arab tribeswoman from Tarba, which is near Ta'if, just southeast of Mecca in Saudi Arabia. At the beginning of the century, foreign Muslims attempted to take control of Mecca. Ghaliyya al-Wahhabiyya formed and led a military resistance movement to defend Mecca. Legend grew among her battlefield adversaries that she possessed the magical ability to render Wahhabi forces invisible. (9) Assigning a woman powers of witchcraft afforded her enemies a face-saving excuse for their defeat by an inferior.

As a measure of progress even in the Arab world, it was suggested in 1991 that Palestine Liberation Organization Chairman Yasser Arafat should be replaced by someone more in touch with the times. Ibrahim Sa'dah, editor in chief of *Akhbar al-Yom*, placed the likeness of a Palestinian woman, Dr. Hanan Ashrawi, on the cover of his magazine, proposing her as Arafat's successor and claiming that Ashrawi would "achieve in one year what Arafat could not achieve in 20." He named as some of her attributes her culture, skill, and forceful defense of her people's rights. Ashrawi, a West Bank academician, was the Palestinian delegation's spokeswoman at the Madrid peace conference. She became better known in the West when later she traveled to Washington, D.C., for more talks. (10)

But the fundamentalist Islamic world is no better prepared to accept a woman as leader than is fundamentalist United States, and not much has changed in six centuries. That devout fundamentalist Muslim Ibn Battuta expressed utter dismay at the behavior of women at court during his visit to Central Asia in 1334. In Mongol states, he found women sharing openly in governing, being awarded apanages, or landed properties, just as were their male siblings. These royal princesses, *khatuns* in their own right, ruled and taxed their own fiefs separately from the state domain. Completely independent of the *khan*, they signed decrees and made major administrative decisions, a situation which Ibn Battuta considered not only scandalous but ungodly. (11)

In India, much the same attitude existed. Concerning Raziyya, the first Moslem woman to rule in what is now Pakistan, an ancient historian named all the virtures which made her such an outstanding ruler, then added, "She was endowed with all the qualities befitting a king, but she was not born of the right sex, and so, in the estimation of men, all these virtues are worthless." (12) However, Islamic law does not delineate the role of Muslim women in politics; in fact, in early Islamic times, according to Professor Ann Elizabeth Mayer, "women played central active roles in political affairs. Only later, as Islamic doctrines combined with local customs that subjugated women, did a consensus develop that in Islam women should be barred from politics." (13)

The religions which preceded Islam in India were no kinder; still, women continued to emerge in Indian history. Megasthenes recorded that a daughter of Herakles founded the Pandyan kingdom in south India (14), and an ancient Ceylonese queen was called to the throne three times. Among all classes, the preference for a son emphasized the inferior status of women, but exceptional women, usually of the upper class, sometimes grabbed the reins of government intended for their husbands or sons. Nur Jahan issued her edicts and even fired her rifle without ever leaving the confines of purdah; Durgavati, during the time of the great Moghuls, and Lakshmi Bai and Hazrat Mahal, during the Sepoy War, were not quite so circumspect. In the aftermath of the Sepoy War, at least one outraged ex-leader's wife turned outlaw: the Rani of Tulsipur, apparently a widow who had escaped with her life and described only as bloodstained, joined a band headed by Babu Ram Babhsh, the Taluqdor of Dhundiakhera, who took advantage of the power vacuum to rustle and plunder everything in sight (1858). She was among those who escaped capture by the British only to die of exposure or disease in the wilds of northern Oudh or southern Nepal. (15)

Hindu women were nevertheless indebted to the British for their attempt at reforms, such as Dalhousie's Hindu Widow's Remarriage Act of 1856 and the British Age of Consent (Sarda) Act of 1891 which raised the age of statutory rape for "consenting" brides from age ten to twelve. (However, the British made no concerted attempt to enforce the laws.) It is noteworthy that in the Punjab under John Lawrence's leadership, incidents of *suttee* (the custom of a Hindu widow being burned upon her late husband's funeral pyre) and infanticide of female children decreased. (16)

Restraints notwithstanding, Hindu India gave us the area's most famous prime minister (Gandhi), but Buddhist Sri Lanka gave us the world's first woman prime minister—twice (Bandaranaike). Bangladesh has had two (Zia and Wajed), and in Pakistan Benazir Bhutto, a Muslim, was twice elected prime minister. Even after she was ousted, Bhutto remained a strong voice in Pakistani politics.

But followers of her political rival, Mian Nawaz Sharif, pointed out that she is from Sind, looked down on as primitive by people in the rich province of Punjab. Punjabis would never follow a leader from Sind, they said, "let alone a Sindi woman." (17) Too, fundamentalists challenged the right or even the ability of a woman to lead. "We will never accept her in power," one said. "How can a woman deal with unemployment?" (18)

In most recent years, state and local governments in India have seen an influx of women, many of whom come directly from Bollywood, India's burgeoning film industry.

Islam has gone through spurts alternately of encouraging its women and "protecting" them. Writers in tenth century Baghdad recounted women who had become lawyers, doctors, university professors and public officials. However, the complete breakdown in law and order which followed made it inadvisable for women to go out unescorted. (19) In these somewhat calmer times, a courageous Benazir Bhutto tried again, aware of danger to her safety. Pakistani businessmen are worldlier, and they know their own history. One businessman explained to reporter Ian Buruma that the election of Benazir Bhutto was not such a break with tradition: "In feudal societies for hundreds of years, when there was no male heir, the mother or wife would take over. So it is no revolution at all. It shows the power of tradition and custom." (20)

This is precisely the model by which many women have come to power in Europe, in Turko-Mongolia, in China, as well as in the Middle East. Even excluding Byzantium, several other Middle East kingdoms which frequently fell into the hands of women were actually European anomalies. The Kingdoms of Jerusalem and Cyprus and the Principality of Antioch were guided by European Crusaders but frequently were governed by women, usually a titular heir whose ruling consort had died, or the mother of a minor legal heir. But such a woman was seldom dignified with title other than regent, even if she was the legal heir. A few women who were never officially named regent, usually mothers of weak sons or wives of ineffectual husbands, simply usurped the power of acquiescent kings and ruled in their stead. Fortunately, few would go to the lengths of Byzantine Empress Irene, who, after her own abdication, still lusted for power to the degree that she finally had her own son blinded and deposed so that she could be sole ruler, or of Athaliah, who seized the throne of Judah and tried to put to death all her own grandsons. In fact, quite the opposite has usually been the case. As a matter of practice around the world, women appear to have attempted to make their husbands and sons look good. Much beautiful Chola art survives today to attest to that principle: several Chola kings, including Rajaraja I (985-1014), have been credited with building many beautiful temples, which actually were the work of the pious Queen Sembiyan Mahadevi, widow of King Gandaraditya (949-957), but never a ruler herself. Through the reigns of Gandaraditya's two successors and well into the reign of a third, her great-nephew Rajaraja I, the queen constructed magnificent temples—many from 970 onward. She lived until A.D. 1001. (21)

Although women have built temples, monuments, churches and monasteries, in the business of ruling, as in all else, it has most frequently been woman's task to keep the home fires stoked while man charged off into battle, and, when he failed to make it back, to mop up and hold things together until the next generation could take over. Usually the latter chore entailed fighting off greedy neighbors or relatives anxious to usurp the throne. As a typical case in point, in the four years following the murder of Persian King Chosroes Parwiz (628), all the male heirs were killed off. Nine claimants, including several women, ascended the throne only to be deposed. (22)

The names of some of the most colorful women did not survive. When Mo-ki-lien, Turkish khan who ruled Mongolia (716-734), was poisoned by his minister, he was succeeded first by his son Yi-jan and then by his brother Tangri khagan (d. 741). During this seven-year period covering two reigns, Mo-ki-lien's widow actually ruled, but no one bothered to record her name. Another crusty Turko-Mongol dowager regent whose name did not survive, the widow of A-pao-ki (d. 926), supposedly ruled "with" her son but in fact held sole power. Her way of dealing with recalcitrant ministers was to send them to the land of the departed "to take news of her to her late husband." The story goes that when one wily old Chinese suggested that such a high honor should go to her instead, she expressed regrets that she couldn't oblige, but lopped off one of her own hands and sent it along with the old gentleman to be buried in her husband's tomb. (23)

Even though the exploits of his own mother Oelun-eke set for him an example of strong womanhood, Jenghiz-khan (whose idea of supreme joy was "to cut my enemies to pieces . . . seize their possessions, witness the tears of those dear to them, and embrace their wives and daughters!") (24) probably did not envision how soon his empire would fall into the hands of his daughters—and granddaughters-in-law. Nor would he have sanctioned the overbearing influence upon their men of other of his progeny's wives: Sorghaqtani, for example, was called the directing spirit of the house of Tolui (Jenghiz-khan's fourth son). Hulägu married a Kerayit princess, Doquz-khatum, who was a Nestorian Christian. When he sacked Baghdad, she interceded to save the lives of all the Christians. The great khan Mongka also respected her wisdom and advised Hulägu that he would do well to consult her in all his affairs. To please his queen, Hulägu heaped favors upon the Christians, and all over his realm, new churches sprang up. (25) The history of the rule of later descendents of Jenghiz-khan is rife with Nestorian wives and mothers making Christians of their men. Jenghiz-khan owes to another queen, Manduqhai, twice at the head of the Mongol army, the fifteenth century renaissance of his all-but-defunct empire.

Burmese women have enjoyed rare equality throughout history. In Pagan, temple inscriptions refer not only to female writers, scholars, even musicians, but also to female chiefs. (26) These women obviously had and administered their own property, for there is more than one inscription alluding to grand donations made by the queen. One commoner, sometimes referred to as Queen Saw, rose to the position of Chief Queen of her second husband but in fact made not only his decisions but his chief minister's as well.

In the late 20th century in Myanmar (formerly Burma), the world's most celebrated political prisoner was Daw Aung San Suu Kyi, leader of the National League for Democracy (NLD). Her party won a landslide election victory in 1990 while she was in detention, although the ruling junta, the State Law and Order Restoration Council (SLORC), refused to honor the results. (27)

In neighboring Thailand women have traditionally held a high position, and acts of courage recounted in Thai history are not confined to men. In 1549 one brave Thai queen, Suriyothai, struck out for the frontlines of a Thai-Burmese battlefield to rescue her husband, King Maka Chakkraphat (1548-1569). The king survived, but she lost her life in saving his. More recently, although bravery was not called for, the beautiful and charismatic Queen Sirikit has governed as regent during her husband's withdrawals to perform his duties as a Bhuddist monk. Queen Sirikit is known for her work in encouraging native crafts and in establishing markets for their sale.

In Indonesia, again the chief challenger to the military government has been a woman. Megawati Sukarno-putri (b. 1947), daughter of the late founding president Dr. Mohammed Achmad Sukarno (r. 1949-1967), headed the Indonesian Democratic Party and established herself for a time as a powerful and vocal populist leader challenging General Raden Suharto, president since 1968.

In Chinese Confucian times women were generally subordinate to fathers, husbands, then sons. In times of famine, baby girls were sacrificed. A woman had no property rights except for a dowery. But once she had become a mother-in-law, all the rules changed: she could—and did—become autocratic and domineering. Nowhere is this principle more apparent than with dowager empresses. During the middle years of the Eastern Han Dynasty, the rebellion of the "yellow turbans" (A.D. 184) was triggered by the power of dowager empresses and their eunuchs. (28) For sheer wanton bloodthirsty mayhem, few could equal Empress Wu Chao, who began by having two of her rivals killed and followed it quickly by killing her own baby almost at birth—and those were only the mild examples. (29)

Some of the strongest women rulers on record were in China, but equally strong were some of the concubines who never cared to rule. Yang Kuei-fei, a buxom concubine of the sexagenarian Emperor Ming Huang, not only had her brother installed as prime minister and infested the court with hundreds of her clansmen, but spent the empire's money lavishly: she sent relays of horsemen nearly 1000 miles to procure litchis for her breakfast, and she ordered a new summer palace built complete with 16 marble bathing pools. But when she took a Tatar general as a lover, she went too far. This ambitious ingrate used her as she had used her emperor: he mounted an insurrection and drove the entire court from the capital. But the palace escort had had enough of the concubine's demands. They murdered her sister, fed her brother's head to the vultures and, in royal fashion, strangled her with a silver cord. (30)

A change in the status of women in China occurred in the late T'ang and Sung periods. With the movement of the upper classes to the city, women became little more than playthings. Secondary wives were forbidden to talk in public, and widows were not allowed to remarry. During the Sung, the fashion of binding the feet of women—breaking the arches and turning the toes under—became a status symbol among upper class men, showing that they could afford a completely useless appendage. (31)

In the 20th century, the People's Republic of China, generally known for its poor record on human rights, had a more enlightened idea of the value of women in public life than did its Tang and Sung predecessors. Madame Soong Ch'ing-ling, widow of revolutionary leader Sun Yat-sen, was even made Acting Head of State for two years in the late 1970's.

The Chinese, whose historic records are generally considered more reliable than early Japanese ones, recorded the earliest Japanese ruling queen in the third century; in fact, in the Chinese Wei accounts Japan is described as Queen Country and a list is given of the countries (within Japan) over which she ruled. Later Japanese records show that between A.D. 592 and 770, half the rulers of Japan were women. Since that time there have been only two. During the Ashikaga period of shoguns (1338-1573), a strictly military society existed. Women were then excluded from any inheritance and relegated to the socially and legally inferior status in which they remained until this century. (32)

We know of a few Polynesian queens, such as Salote Tupou, Hinematioro, Liliuokalani, and Vaekehu, but there had been no women rulers (discounting the queen of England) of either Australia or New Zealand until the 1990 appointment of Dame Catherine Tizard to the post of governor-general of New Zealand, and, more significantly, the election in 1997 of Jenny Shipley as New Zealand's prime minister.

One measure of the increased importance of women in political life is the length to which their opponents will go to silence them. Aung San Suu Kyi's twenty-year imprisonment is one example. The 1998 assassination of 52-year-old Russian legislator Galina Starovoitova is another. Starovoitova, a psychologist and ethnographer who helped found Russia's democratic movement, and who was known for her common sense and her fierce defense of democracy, had recently declared herself a candidate for governor of the region outside St. Petersburg. Officials agreed that it was a politically motivated, contract killing. It was common knowledge that her political enemies had tried in vain to find compromising material against her. "But she was blameless," colleague Victor Krivulin said. "So they hated her even more, and they were afraid of her." (33)

It is appropriate to speculate not only who assassinated former Pakistani Prime Minister Benazir Bhutto, but why. Called out of exile in London after having been pardoned by a reluctant President Pervez Musharraf—no doubt at the urging of the United States in an effort to maintain the uneasy peace in a nuclear power nation—Bhutto's popularity was obviously feared by someone enough to do her in. Her death dismayed the Bush administration, which saw in Bhutto its best hope for keeping nuclear weapons out of the hands of terrorists. This one death of a woman leader may have more long-term consequences for the Middle East than all the preemptive strikes put together.

Notes:

(1) Margaret Bald. "Feminist Among the Ayatollahs." *World Press Review*. December 1997: 37

(2) "Clippings." from *Jeune Afrique*, Paris. *World Press Review*. December 1997: 37.

(3) Michael A. Aung-Thwin. *Myth and History in the Historiography of Early Burma*. (Athens: Ohio University Center for International Studies, 1998), 103, 191.

(4) Hermann Kinder and Werner Hilgemann. *The Anchor Atlas of World History*. 2 vols. tr. Ernest A. Menze. (Garden City, NY: Anchor/ Doubleday,1974), vol. 1, 33.

(5) Ibid., 35.

(6) Gerda Lerner. *The Creation of Patriarchy*. (New York: Oxford University Press, 1986), 62.

(7) Herodotus. *The Histories*. tr. Aubrey de Sélincourt. (New York: Viking Penguin, 1988), 619.

(8) Sir John Glubb. *A Short History of the Arab People*. (New York: Dorset Press, 1969), 204.

(9) Mernissi, Fatima. *The Forgotten Queens of Islam*. tr. Mary Jo Lakeland. (Minneapolis: University of Minnesota Press,1993), 20.

(10) Vera Azar. "A Woman for the PLO?" *World Press Review*. February 1992: 37.

(11) Ibn Battuta. *Travels of Ibn Battuta AD 1325-1354*. tr. H. A. R. Gibb from French translation of C. Defremery and B. B. Sanguinetti (Cambridge: Cambridge University Press, vol. 1, 1958), 168.

(12) Romila Thapar. *A History of India* (London: Penguin Books, 1987), vol. 1, 269

(13) Ann Elizabeth Mayer, "Benazir Bhutto and Islamic Law." *The Christian Science Monitor*. 6 February 1989: 18.

(14) Thapar, *A History of India*, vol. 1, 103.

(15) John Pemble. *The Raj, the Indian Mutiny, and the Kingdom of Oudh 1801-1859*. (Rutherford: Farleigh Dickinson University Press, 1977), 237

(16) Percival Spear. *A History of India*. (London: Penguin Books, Ltd., 1987). vol. 2, 151.

(17) Ian Buruna, "A Nation Divided." *The New York Times Magazine*. 15 January 1989: 26-40, particularly 29.

(18) Sheila Tefft, "Restlessness among Pakistan's Youth." *The Christian Science Monitor*. 3 March 1989: 4.

(19) Glubb, *A Short History of the Arab People*, 284.

(20) Baruna, "A Nation Divided," 27-28.

(21) Basil Gray, ed. *The Arts of India*. (Ithaca, NY: Cornell University Press, 1981), 77.

(22) Glubb, *A Short History of the Arab People*, 46.

(23) René Grousset. *The Empire of the Steppes, a History of Central Asia.* tr. Naomi Walford. (New Brunswick: Rutgers University Press, 1970), 129.

(24) Ibid., 249.

(25) Ibid., 356-357.

(26) W. E. Garrett, "Pagan, on the Road to Mandalay," *National Geographic*, 139. March 1971: 343-365, especially 362.

(27) Aung San Suu Kyi. *Letters from Burma*. (London: Penguin Books, 1997)

(28) Kinder, et. al. *Anchor Atlas of World History*, vol. 1, 33.

(29) Dennis Bloodworth and Ching Ping Bloodworth. *The Chinese Machiavelli, 3000 Years of Chinese Statecraft.* (New York: Farrar, Straus and Giroux, Inc., 1976), 214-215.

(30) Dennis Bloodworth. *The Chinese Looking Glass.* (New York: Farrar, Straus and Giroux, Inc., 1967), 77-78.

(31) Edwin O. Reischauer and John K. Fairbank. *East Asia: The Great Tradition.* (Boston: Houghton Mifflin, 1958, 1960), 224-225.

(32) Ibid., 556.

(33) Celestine Bohlen. "Russian Lawmaker's Killing Stirs Anger." *The New York Times International.* 22 November 1998: 14; Celestine Bohlen. "Illusions Shattered in St. Petersburg." *The New York Times International.* 29 November 1998: 14

Asian, Middle East, and Pacific Section A

Absh Khatun

Queen of Persia (1263-1287)

She was the daughter of Bibi Khatun, one of the daughters of Kirman Queen Turkhan Khatun, and niece of Padishah Khatun, ruler of Kirman from 1291 to 1295. She was married very young to Manku Timur, one of the sons of the great Turko-Mongolian Khan Hulagu. They were living in Urdu, the Ilkhan capital, when Hulagu, displeased at the way things were going in his Persian realm, sent an army to kill Seljuk Shah. He then dispatched his daughter-in-law, Absh Khatun, to Shiraz, the capital of her native country, to become head of state in 1263. She was received with great pomp and coins were stuck in her name. She was the ninth and last sovereign of the Persian dynasty of Atabeks, which was known as the Sulghurid dynasty after the Turkoman chief Sulghur who migrated with his tribe to Iran a century earlier. She reigned until 1287.

Suggested Reading:

(1) Mernissi, Fatima. *The Forgotten Queens of Islam*. tr. Mary Jo Lakeland. Minneapolis: University of Minnesota Press, 1993. p. 104.
(2) Ucok Un, Badriye. *Al-nisa' al-hakimat fi tarikh*. tr. I. Daquqi. Baghdad: Matba'a al-Sa'dun, 1973. pp. 101ff.

Ada

Queen of Caria (344-341 B.C. and 334-? B.C.)

Caria was a separate Persian satrapy belonging to the Delian League. It was located in southern Turkey. Ada was the wife-sister of Idrieus (or Hidreus), who ruled from 351 to 344 B.C. After his death, Ada ruled Halicarnassus (modernday Bodrum) for three years until her younger brother, Pixadarus (or Pixodarus, r. 341-335 B.C.), expelled her. She moved to the strong fortress of Alinda, southwest of Alabanda, where she held out for several years. When her brother Pixadarus died in 335 B.C., his son-in-law Orontobates claimed the throne, but Ada quickly disputed his claim. On the road she had met Alexander (the Great), who was preparing to attack Halicarnassus. She made him her adopted son, thus assuring him her throne. Alexander soon destroyed Halicarnassus and left three thousand mercenaries to garrison Caria, which he granted to Ada with the title of queen (c. 334 B.C.). Soon after, Ada brought about the surrender of the Persians in the citadel of Myndus, which Alexander had been unable to accomplish earlier.

Suggested Reading:

(1) Hammond, N. G. L. *A History of Greece to 322 B.C.* Oxford: Clarendon Press, 1986. pp. 607, 621.
(2) Olmstead, A. R. *History of the Persian Empire.* Chicago: University of Chicago Press, 1948. pp. 436, 483, 499.
(3) Peters, F. E. *The Harvest of Hellenism.* New York: Barnes & Noble Books, 1996. p. 48.

Addagoppe of Harran (Adda-Guppi, possible misnomer Nitrocris)

Priestess, probable regent of Babylon (c. 522 B.C.)

Addagoppe was born in 445 B.C. in Harran and became a priestess of the god Sin. Nitrocris is a possible misnomer for this queen. According to Herodotus, writing of Nitrocris, she was married to an Assyrian king named Labynetus and had a son of the same name. According to Olmstead, based on datable historical facts in Herodotus' account, the son Labynetus corresponds to the ruler Nabonidus, or Nabu-naid. The true history of Addagoppe is known from a stele found (1956) preserved in a paving stone inscription side down in the Great Mosque at Harran. Her remarkable career spanned the whole Neo-Babylonian Dynasty down to the ninth year of its last king. She came to Babylon from Harran and managed to obtain a responsible position for her son at court. Nabu-naid eventually became king of Babylon (r. 556-539 B.C.), although he spent little actual time in Babylon. Herodotus refers to the king's mother as "Queen Nitrocris" and says that in order to strengthen the security of Babylon, she altered the course of the Euphrates, constructed tall embankments on each side, and built a foot bridge across the river that could be removed at night. In great but erroneous detail, Herodotus describes her "grim practical joke": she placed her own tomb above one of the main gates of the city and inscribed on it: "If any king of Babylon hereafter is short of money, let him open my tomb and take as much as he likes. But this must be done only in case of need. Whoever opens my tomb under any other circumstances will get no good of it." The tomb was untouched until the reign of Darius, who opened it to find only the queen's body and the message: "If you had not been insatiably greedy and eager to get money by the most despicable means, you would never have opened the tomb of the dead." Legends abound about illustrious persons, especially those who were particularly long-lived. There is no historical verification of Herodotus' tales, but it is a historical fact that when Addagoppe died (c. 543/7 B.C.) at the age of 104, she was buried in Harran with all the honors reserved for a queen. It is possible that, when Nabu-naid left Babylon in c. 552 to reside in Taima (northeastern Asia), leaving his son Bel-shar-usur (Belshazzar in the book of Daniel) in charge, he also left his mother. It is even likely that, during Belshazzar's absences, Addagoppe would serve as regent, which would explain her being honored as a queen at death. Nabu-naid did not return to Babylon until 542, so she may have been honored by her grandson and not her son, or her death might have been the occasion of her son's belated return. After his mother's death, Nabu-naid named his daughter high priestess of the god Sin.

Suggested Reading:

(1) Herodotus, *The Histories*. tr. Aubrey de Sélincourt. New York: Viking Penguin, 1988. pp. 115-117.

(2) Olmstead, A. T., *History of the Persian Empire*. Chicago: University of Chicago Press, 1948. pp. 55, 115, 321-322.

Alaghai-bäki

Mongolian queen of the Öngüt, Northern China (fl 13th c.)

Alaghai-bäki was a daughter of Jenghiz Khan (Genghis Khan, r. 1206-1227), who rewarded the Turkish Öngüts who helped him overcome the Kins (Chins or Juchens) by giving her in marriage to

Po-yao-ho, son of assassinated Öngüt chief Alaqush-tigin. Young Po-yao-ho had gone with Jenghiz Khan on his campaign against the Khwarizm to restore the Alaqush family to the leadership of the Öngüt. Alaghai-bäki had no children of her own, but Po-yao-ho had three sons by a concubine. When he died, Alaghai-bäki ruled the Öngüt country with "a forceful hand." Described as "a woman of energy," her father's daughter, she treated her late husband's sons as her own, allowing each to marry into the clan.

Suggested Reading:

(1) Grousset, René, *The Empire of the Steppes*. tr. Naomi Walford. New Brunswick, NJ: Rutgers University Press, 1970.

Alam al-Malika

Al-hurra, ruled in Zubayd (c. 1120-1130)

Zubayd (Zabīd) was a principality and city in western Yemen near San'a, with whom it was in a perpetual state of war. During the period from 1022 to 1158 Zubayd was ruled by a Muslim dynasty of Ethiopian Mamluks (slaves). The title *al-hurra* was bestowed on women in Yemen who were active in the political arena, but it did not denote queenship. Alam al-Malika al-hurra was a *jarya*, or singer slave of Zubayd's king, Mansur Ibn Najah (r. c. 1111-1123). Her political astuteness, learning, and intelligence so impressed the king that he ultimately placed her in charge of the realm's management and "made no decision concerning it without consulting her." In 1123 King Mansur Ibn Najah was poisoned by his vizier, Mann Allah. After his death, Alam al-Malika al-hurra continued to govern, and it was written of her that "she discharged her task with distinction." However, she was denied the privilege of having the *khutba* proclaimed in her name. The *khutba*, the privilege reserved for the sovereign, was preached at Friday night prayer, affirming the sovereign's right to rule.

Suggested Reading:

(1) Mernissa, Fatima. *The Forgotten Queens of Islam*. tr. Mary Jo Lakeland. Minneapolis: University of Minnesota Press, 1993. p. 140.

Alexandra (Salome Alexandra or Alexandra Salome)

King of the Maccabees (Judaea) (76-67 B.C.)

She was the wife of King Alexander Jannaeus of the Asmonean, or Hasmonean, dynasty, Syria, who ruled from 103 to 76 B.C., during one of the brief periods of Judaean independence. The couple had two sons, John Hyrcanus II and Aristobulus II. Before he died in 76 B.C., Alexander Jannaeus, realizing that strong religious support would be necessary for his successor, persuaded Alexandra Salome to assume the throne, thus restoring the Pharisees to a position of leadership. She became king, not queen, and her eldest son was appointed high priest, since as a woman, she could not become the high priest herself. She reversed the earlier policy of Hyrcanus I and elevated the Pharisees, who reinforced their temple regulations and resumed their powition of power. Alexandra Salome's brother, Simon bar Shetah, held an important role in the new regime. She died in 67 B.C. and was succeeded by her son Hyrcanus II, who only three months later was driven from power, briefly, by her other son Aristobulus II. On the advice of Antipater the Idumaean, Hyrcanus petitioned Aretas, king of the Nabataean Arabs, for help and eventually regained the throne; however, he was a puppet in the hands of various Roman factions.

Suggested Reading:

(3)　Cooke, Jean, et. al. *History's Timeline*. New York: Crescent Books, 1981. p. 33.
(2)　Langer, William L., ed. *World History*. Boston: Houghton Mifflin, 1948, 1980. p. 94.
(3)　Peters, E. E. *The Harvest of Hellenism*. New York: Barnes & Noble Books, 1996. pp. 294-295, 321-323.

Alexandra

Empress of Russia, absolute ruler in her husband's absence (1915-1917)

She was born in 1872 in Darmstadt, the daughter of Alice, Queen Victoria's daughter, and Louis IV, duke of Hesse-Darmstadt. Darmstadt was located in present day West Germany. Alexandra was often unbending and firm-willed with a strong amd proud appreciation of her Teutonic blood. She married Nicholas II of Russia in 1894 and dominated their entire married life. She was not popular with the Russian people, who considered her a German interloper. As consolation, she immersed herself in religion; however, her interest in religion did not preven her from exerting her influence to undo the 1905 reforms which limited the powers of the monarchy. The couple had four daughters before their son Alexis, a hemophiliac, was born. The boy's perilous health also put the future of the dynasty in peril. Alexandra turned for advice to Grigory Yefimovich Rasputin, a self—proclaimed holy man, upon whom she came to rely so heavily that her conduct became a public scandal. In August of 1915, when Nicholas left for the front to assume command of Russian troops, Alexandra moved quickly to consolidate her own power. She dismissed valuable ministers and replaced them with puppets, choices of Rasputin. The government soon became paralyzed, and Alexandra was further alienated from an already suspicious and mistrusting public. Alexandra apparently believed that she was safely beyond justice, and even when Rasputin was murdered, she continued her despotic rule, paying no heed to public opinion. After the October Bolshevik Revolution, the entire family was imprisoned. On July 29, 1918, she was shot to death at Yekaterinburg, now Sverdlovsk, Russia. It might be concluded that she alone precipitated the collapse of the military government in March of 1911, hastening the advent of the Bolshevik Revolution.

Suggested Reading:

(1)   Thompson, John M., *Revolutionary Russia, 1917*. New York: John Scribner's Sons, 1981. pp. 14-23.

Alice

Princess, regent of Antioch (1130 and 1135-1136)

Born c. 1106, the second daughter of Jerusalem's King Baldwin II and Queen Morphia of Melitene, Alice married tall, fair-haired, handsome Prince Bohemond II of Antioch in 1126. They had a daughter, Constance, who was only two years old when her father died in 1130. Without waiting for her father King Baldwin II to appoint a regent, Alice at once assumed the regency for her daughter. But her ambition to rule, not as a regent, but as a reigning sovereign, drove her to rash measures. When she heard that her father was on the way to Antioch to claim a regency, she sent an envoy to the atabeg Zengi, offering to pay him homage if he would guarantee her possession of the throne of Antioch. But Baldwin intercepted the envoy and had him hanged. When he reached Antioch, he found the gates locked. After three days of negotiations, he entered the city where Alice had barricaded herself in a tower, waiting for guarantees of her safety. When she and her father finally met, she knelt in terror and begged his forgiveness, which she received. However, Baldwin removed her from the regency, assumed it himself, and banished her to her dower lands of Lattakieh and Jabala. After Baldwin's death (1131), Alice reasserted her claims for the regency. She gathered a sizeable following against her brother-in-law, King Fulk, who sailed from Jerusalem to claim the regency. Alice's revolt was put down (1132), but she remained safe at Lattakieh. In 1135, the Latin Bishop of Mamistra, Radulph of Domfront, assumed the Patriarchal throne without canonical election. Not wishing to be dominated by Jerusalem, he opened negotiations with Alice, who saw opportunity to regain power in Antioch. She appealed to her sister, Queen Melisende, Fulk's wife, who arranged Alice's return to Antioch. Although Fulk retained the title of regent, the governing power was actually shared by Alice and Radulph in what was characterized as an uneasy alliance. However, Radulph soon quarreled with his clergy, and Alice seized the opportunity to govern Antioch alone. She endeavored to strengthen her rather tentative position by offering the hand of her nine-year-old daughter, the heir Princess Constance, to the Byzantine Emperor's son Manuel. Radulph, fearing he would be replaced as Patriarch by a Greek if such a union occurred, sent an urgent secret message to King Fulk advising him to find a suitable husband for Constance at once. Fulk, keeping both Alice and his wife Melisende uninformed, chose as Constance's consort Raymond of Poiters. Patriarch Radulph then requested audience with Alice to say her that a handsome stranger had offered himself as a candidate for marriage to Alice. She was most receptive to the proposal, but while Alice waited for the arrival of her future husband, Constance was kidnapped and taken to the cathedral, where Radulph quickly performed the ceremony uniting the child and Raymond. Alice, seething at the betrayal and having no more claim to the rule of Antioch, retired again to Lattakieh. At the time, she was still under 30 years old.

Suggested Reading:

(1) Runciman, Steven, *History of the Crusades*. Cambridge: Cambridge University Press, 1952, 1987. vol. 2, *The Kingdom of Jerusalem*. pp. 176-177, 183-184, 188-190, 198-200.

Anchimaa-Toka, Khertek

Chairman of the Presidium of the Little Khural, Tuva (1940-1944)

Khertek Amyrbitovna Anchimaa-Toka has been the first at many things in her life. She was born to the poor peasant family Anchimaa on January 1, 1912 in what is now Bay-Tayginsky kozhuun (district) in Tuva, which is a part of Siberia once claimed by China, now a Russian republic. Tuva's capital Kyzyl is the geographical center of Asia.

Both her father and older brother died of smallpox when she was young. Although her remaining parent, Mrs. Anchimaa, could not read or write, in a place where few females ever learned to read, Khertek somehow learned Mongolese. When she was 18, the first national alphabet in Tuvinian was introduced, and she quickly learned that as well, being among the first to do so.

That same year she was inducted into Revsomol, the youth arm of the Tuvan People's Revolutionary Party, and was charged with teaching reading and writing to peasants in her district. Her accomplishments in that area led to her induction in 1931 into the party proper and to being one of seventy chosen to go to Far East University, also called Communist University of the Toilers of the East, which, in addition to its headquarters in Moscow, also had regional branches in Baku in Azerbaijan, Irkutsk, and Tashkent in Uzbekistan. While a student, Khertek met and was greatly impressed by Nadezhda Krupskaya, a Marxist revolutionary and the wife of Vladimir Lenin.

Khertek graduated in 1935, one of eleven of the original seventy. She returned to Tuva and was placed in charge of the propaganda department of Revsomol. In 1938 she was appointed director of the Tuvan Zhenotdel, which was, like its earlier Russian counterpart, an organization that sought to improve the conditions of women's lives, eradicating illiteracy and educating women about the new marriage, education, and working laws put in place by the Revolutionary Soviet government.

During the late 1930s she was said to have been a member of a troika which sentenced to death Tuvan Prime Minister Churmit Dazhy and other high-ranking officials accused of being Japanese spies. However, she was never legally prosecuted; in fact the case has never even been properly investigated

By 1940 she had risen to the Chairmanship of Little Khural (parliament), the highest-ranking woman at that time. The same year she married Tuvan

People's Revolutionary Party general secretary Salchak Toka, retaining her maiden name until Toka's death.

As head of state, she put Tuva's assets at the disposal of Russia in its fight against Nazi Germany in World War II and was influential in Tuva's inclusion in the USSR in 1944. Her mandate as Chairman of the Presidium ended November 10, 1944.

Following her term as Chairman, she became Vice-Chairman of the Regional Executive Committee, and then Vice-Chairman of Tuvan Council of Ministers, being responsible for social welfare, culture, sports and propaganda. She retired in 1972.

A year later her husband died and she took the surname of Anchimaa-Toka.

With the dissolution of the Soviet Union, Khertek Anchimaa-Toka found herself living under a cloud in modern Tuva due to her alleged involvement in the troika that sentenced the several high-ranking officials to death.

Suggested Reading:

(1)   www.tuvaonline.ru/2006/03/04/anchima.html.

Anga

See Maham Anga

Anna Anachoutlou

Queen of Trebizond (Trabzon, Trapezus) (1341 and 1341-1342)

The Empire of Trebizond was located in what is now northeastern Turkey. With the help of Georgian Queen Thamar (r. 1184-1212), Trebizond was captured by grandsons of Andronicus I, East Roman emperor, David and Alexius Comnena, who established the Empire of Trebizond with Alexius I as its first ruler. Anna was one of three queens who ruled this empire, which lasted from 1204 until its capture by the Turks in 1461. She was the daughter of King Alexius II (r. 1297-1330). She was brought to the throne twice in 1341, first following the deposition of Irene Palaeologina (r. 1340-1341). She was briefly deposed in favor of Michael, son of former King John II (r. 1280-1284), but was restored that same year and ruled until 1342, when Michael's son John III was brought to the throne.

Suggested Reading:

(1) Morby, John. *Dynasties of the World.* Oxford: Oxford University Press, 1989. p. 56.
(2) Ostrogorsky, George. *History of the Byzantine State.* New Brunswick, NJ: Rutgers University Press, 1969. pp. 425-426.

Anna Dalassena

Acting regent of Byzantine Empire (c. 1081-1082)

She was the formidable wife of John Comnenus, who was the brother of Isaac I (r. 1057-1059). With her help and the support of her son Isaac and the powerful Ducas family, her third son, Alexius, seized the Byzantine throne from Nicephorus III and founded the Comnenian dynasty as Emperor Alexius I (r. 1081-1118). She exercised great influence over Alexius and served as regent during his absence from Constantinople at the time of the war against invading Italian Normans headed by Robert Guiscard.

Suggested Reading:

(1) Ostrogorsky, George, *History of the Byzantine State.* New Brunswick, NJ: Rutgers University Press, 1969. p. 376.

Anna Leopoldovna

Regent of Russia (1740-1741)

Born in 1718, she was a niece of Anne (Anna), Empress of Russia. In 1739 she married Prince Anton Ulrich, nephew of Charles VI, Holy Roman Emperor. They had a son, Ivan, born in 1740, the year Empress Anne died. Empress Anne had named the retarded two-month-old boy heir to the throne and made her lover Biren (Biron) his regent. However, the unpopular Biren was arrested a few weeks later by members of his own ruling German coalition, who then named Anna Leopoldovna regent. The Germans expected to play important roles in Anna's government; however, they were unpopular with the people and unable to maintain order even among themselves. In 1741, a palace favorite, Elizabeth I, Peter the Great's daughter, who also aspired to the throne, took advantage of the disorder in Anna's administration to mount a palace revolt, in which she donned a guard's uniform and marched with palace guards into the winter palace, personally woke Anna and her sleeping family and had them imprisoned. In 1744 she exiled them to Kholmogory. Anna died two years later in childbirth.

Suggested Reading:

(1) Asprey, Robert B., *Frederick the Great: The Magnificent Enigma*. New York: Ticknor and Fields, 1986. pp. 160, 230, 275.

(2) Riasanovsky, Nicholas, *A History of Russia*. New York: Oxford University Press, 1963, 1993. p. 245.

Anne (or Anna Ivanova)

Empress of Russia (1730-1740)

She was born in 1693, the daughter of Ivan V, nominal Tsar of Russia, a chronic invalid. She was the niece of Peter the Great. She married the Duke of Courland, but he died on their wedding trip (1710) to Courland. After the death of Peter II (at age fifteen, of smallpox), Anne was offered the throne by the Privy Council, which, conceiving of her as weak, expected her to act as figurehead while it continued to govern. However, when she came to the throne, she tore up the conditions she had previously accepted, dismissed the Council, and made herself absolute ruler. She brought from Courland a cadre of favorites, and in general patronized not only Germans but other foreigners in preference to Russian nobility.

Criticized for her excesses in office, Anne was also responsible for beginning some social reform. In 1731 she repealed Peter the Great's law that only one son could inherit his father's estate. She gave away state lands to her gentry supporters, the peasants on the land becoming serfs. Also in 1731, she opened a cadet school in St. Petersburg where graduates could become officers without first serving in the lower ranks, a practice Peter the Great had opposed. In 1736 the law requiring gentry to serve the state for an unlimited amount of time was altered to specify a term of no more than 25 years. Furthermore, one son would be exempt from service to manage the estates.

Soon the tedium of her office began to pall; she lost interest in governing, for which she was untrained. She left it in the hands of her ruthless lover, Ernst Johann Biren (or Biron), who brought in his German friends as advisers. They exploited the country while Anne held extravagant court in St. Petersburg. On the day before she died in 1740, she named her two-month-old nephew Ivan as her successor and Biren as regent. But within a month Biren was overthrown and Ivan's mother, Anna Leopoldovna, became regent for one year. Then late in 1741, Ivan, his mother, and the entire cabinet were ousted in a *coup* led by Peter the Great's daughter Elizabeth, who ascended the throne.

Suggested Reading:

(1) Asprey, Robert B., *Frederick the Great: The Magnificent Enigma*. New York: Ticknor and Fields, 1986. pp. 119, 160.
(2) Langer, William L., ed., *World History*. Boston: Houghton Mifflin, 1940, 1980. pp. 515-516.
(3) Riasanovsky, Nicholas V., *A History of Russia*. New York: Oxford University Press, 1963, 1993. pp. 243, 245, 249, 250.

Anula

Queen of Sri Lanka (Ceylon) (47-42 B.C.)

She was the wife of King Darubhatika Tissa, whose death in B.C. 47 threw the country into a period of great turmoil. For short periods during that year, three people, Siva, Vatuka, and Niliya tried briefly to rule. Eventually Queen Anula was called upon to restore order. She ruled for five years and was succeeded by her son, King Kutakanna Tissa in 42 B.C.

Suggested Reading:

(1) Codrington, H. W., *A Short History of Ceylon*. Cambridge: Cambridge University Press, 1947.
(2) Egan, Edward et. al., *Kings, Rulers, and Statesmen*. New York: Sterling Publishing, 1976. p. 438.

Aquino, Maria Corazon (Cory)

President of Republic of the Philippines (1986-1992)

She was born in 1933, the daughter of Jose Cojuangco Sr., the wealthiest man in Tarlac Province, and Demetria Sumulong Sojuangco. She was educated at elite girls' schools in Manila, Philadelphia and New York before attending Mt. Vernon College in New York. She married Benigno S. Aquino, Jr. in 1954 and became his political helpmate. They had five children: Elena, Aurora, Benigno S. III, Victoria, and Kristina. Her husband entered politics and rose to become the most popular opponent of President Ferdinand Marcos, who declared martial law in 1972 to prolong his presidency. Marcos jailed Benigno Aquino, whom he considered his greatest threat. When Aquino was released, the family sought refuge in the United States, where they lived in exile from 1980 to 1983. In August, 1983, Aquino attempted to return to The Philippines but was assassinated in the Manila airport. This assassination was the rallying point which united the opposition and which forced Corazon Aquino to choose a political career. She led the dissidents calling for Marcos' resignation. In the meantime, she returned to school for postgraduate work in law, receiving an LLD degree from the University of the Philippines in 1986. In 1986 she ran for President on the Unido party ticket, and abandoning the speeches which had been prepared for her, she spoke simply of her own victimization by Marcos. She was elected President and immediately attempted to forge unity, bring about order and commence economic reform, all the while fending off attacks by political foes. She immediately appointed a constitution commission to replace the 1973 charter that had been passed by a show of hands shortly after former President Ferdinand E. Marcos declared martial law. In September, 1986, she traveled to the U.S. seeking support for her government and for the country. Although President Reagan refused to give her an audience, she received assurance that the U.S. would retain its two military bases in The Philippines. Following her speech to the joint session of Congress, which Speaker Thomas P. (Tip) O'Neill, Jr. labeled "the finest speech" he had heard in his congressional career, Congress approved $200 million additional aid to her country. Although she instituted an economic growth program, much of her presidency was marked by unrest among citizens who wanted quicker results. In 1988 her land redistribution law was criticized by the press as not going far enough. Her detractors charged her with downgrading human rights as a trade-off for military support. On one occasion her palace troops opened fire and killed twenty demonstrators. In 1989 she took on one of the most powerful groups in the Philippines, the big-industry loggers, citing environmental devastation caused by "the greed of commerce, the corruption of officials and the ignorance of men." She weathered numerous crises, including several coup attempts. Although untrained in politics, she was a member of the class of wealthy "oligarchs" who had long ruled The Philippines. She spoke English, French, Spanish, Japanese and Tagalog, the native language. Eschewing Marcos' elaborate Malacanang Palace was too opulent in a country where wealth had too long been kept in the hands of a few, she lived in a more modest home/office nearby. She repeatedly denied Marcos permission to return to The Philippines in an effort to still opposition before it developed, buying time for her economic programs to work. In 1992, although her popularity was on the wane, her choice of president, Fidel Ramos, won the presidential election to succeed her. However, he won with only twenty-three per cent of the vote in an election that was so close, the ballots had to be counted by hand.

Suggested Reading:

(1) Jones, Clayton, "Aquino Plans Cabinet Shifts." *The Christian Science Monitor.* November 10, 1986: 11.
(2) Jones, Clayton, "Aquino Joins Bid to Protect Forests." *The Christian Science Monitor.* March 22, 1989: 4.
(3) Kosimar, Lucy, *Corazon Aquino: The Story of a Revolution.* New York: George Braziller, 1987.
(4) Mydans, Seth, "Aquino Is Working on Some Laws to Rule By". *The New York Times.* 1 June 1986: 3.
(5) Sheehy, Gail, "The Passage of Corazon Aquino." *Parade Magazine.* June 8, 1986: 4-9.
(6) "The Stalled Revolution." *World Press Review.* August 1988: 40.

Arroyo, Gloria Macapagal

Fourteenth President of the Philippines (2001-)

Gloria Macapagal was born April 5, 1947, the daughter of former Philippine President Diosdado Macagapal and his wife, Dr. Evangelina Macaraeg-Macagapal. She was valedictorian of her high school class at Assumption Convent, was consistently on the Dean's List in Georgetown University in Washington DC, and graduated magna cum laude at Assumption College in Makati. She obtained a Master's degree in Economics from the Ateneo de Manila University and a doctorate degree in Economics from the University of the Philippines.

In 1986 she entered government service as Undersecretary of Trade and Industry. 1992 she entered politics for the first time and was elected as Senator, then reelected in 1995 with the highest number of votes ever recorded for that office. During her service in the Senate, she authored 55 laws dealing with social and economic reform. In 1998 she was elected Vice President, again with the highest number of votes ever recorded for President or Vice President. During her tenure as Vice President, she also held the post of Secretary of Social Welfare and Development. In anticipation of assuming her new duties, she resigned from the Cabinet on October 12, 2000. After the position of President was declared officially vacant by the Supreme Court, she was sworn in to the highest office in the land on January 20, 2001, the second woman to come into power through peaceful means. In 2004 she ran for reelection and won by a million votes over her closest opponent.

Suggested Reading:

(1) *Current Biography International Yearbook 2004*. The H. W. Wilson Company.
(2) *President Gloria Macapagal-Arroyo Biography*. Office of the President, June 30, 2008.

Arsinoë II

Queen of Thrace, Macedonia, Egypt, co-ruler of Egypt. See Arsinoë II in African section.

Artemisia I

Queen, ruler of Halicarnassus and Cos (c. 480 B.C.)

Halicarnassus was a Greek city-state in southwestern Anatolia and Cos was an island off the coast. As a tribute-payer to Xerxes, king of Persia, Artemisia participated in his war of invasion against the Greeks in 480 B.C. She ably commanded five ships during the naval battle off the island of Salamis. Herodotus, a great admirer of her accomplishments, claimed that Xerxes, who was badly defeated, had sought Artemisia's advice. She advised him to retreat, which he did.

Suggested Reading:

(1) Bowder, Diana, *Who Was Who in the Greek World*. Ithaca, NY: Cornell University Press, 1982. p. 106.
(2) Hammond, N. G. L., *History of Greece*. Oxford: Clarendon Press, 1986. p. 239.
(3) Herodotus, *The Histories*. tr. Aubrey de Sèlincourt. New York: Penguin Books, 1954, 1988. pp. 8, 11, 14, 474, 545-546, 552-558.
(4) Olmstead, A. T., *History of the Persian Empire*. Chicago: University of Chicago Press, 1948. pp. 253,269,433-434.

Artemisia II

Ruler of Caria (353/2-351/0 B.C.)

Caria was located in southwestern Anatolia. Artemisia was the daughter of King Hecatomnos of Caria and wife and sister of King Mausolus, who succeeded him. In her own right, she was a botanist and medical researcher. A plant genus, a sagebrush, is named for her. Artemisia and her husband were extremely devoted. When he died (353 or 352 B.C.), Artemisia succeeded him as sole ruler. During her approximately three-year reign, the Rhodians, believing that a woman's rule offered them excellent opportunity to rid themselves of Caria's dominion, charged the capital. Artemisia, apprised of their approach, ordered the citizens to pretend surrender. Even as the Rhodians landed and began plundering the marketplace, the hidden Carian fleet emerged from a man-made channel connected to a hidden harbor and seized the empty Rhodian ships. Soldiers hiding along the city walls shot down the plunderers. Then Artemisia wreathed the captured ships in laurel, signifying victory, and with her own forces aboard, sailed the Rhodian ships back to the island. Before her ruse was discovered, the Carians had entered the Rhodian harbor. The Rhodian leaders were executed and Artemisia erected two monuments in Rhodes commemorating her conquest of the island. In the capital of Halicarnassus (modern day Bodrum, Turkey), she had erected for her late husband a magnificent tomb for which all subsequent tombs which are splendid edifices are named. It was called the Mausoleum of Halicarnassus, one of the Seven Wonders of the World. Tradition holds that she never recovered from his death and died of grief (c. 350 B.C.). A statue of Artemisia in Museo Archeologico Nazionale, Naples, shows her as a beautiful woman with a purposeful stride and an aura of strength.

Suggested Reading:

(1) Bowder, Diana, *Who Was Who in the Greek World*. Ithaca, NY: Cornell University Press, 1982. pp. 299-300.
(2) Durant, Will, *The Story of Civilization*. vol. 2., *The Life of Greece*. New York: Simon & Schuster, 1939, 1966. pp. 586, 593.
(3) Olmstead, A. T. *History of the Persian Empire*. Chicago: University of Chicago, 1948. pp. 426, 429, 432-435.

'Arwa

Shi'ite Malika (queen) and ruler of Yemen (1091-1138)

She was the wife of al-Mukarram Ahmad, ruler of Yemen from 1067 to 1084, who carried on his father's tradition of allowing his wife to share his power. Al-Mukarram came to power while his parents took a pilgrimmage to Mecca. But his father 'Ali al-Sulayhi was murdered on the trip by the Banu Najah family and his mother Asma was taken prisoner by them. When Asma was released, she directed her son's rule until her death, along with 'Arma. The unquestioned criterion of a head of state in the Muslim world was the right to have the *khutba* (sermon) pronounced in his name. The *khutba*, the privilege of the sovereign, was preached at Friday prayers and it affirmed the sovereign's right to rule. Ordinarily it was not to be said in the name of a woman; however, 'Arwa had the right to have the *khutba* pronounced in her name. She bore the royal title, *al-sayyida al-hurra,* meaning, "The noble lady who is free and independent; the woman sovereign who bows to no superior authority." By late in his rule, the king saw the kingdom that his father had established threatened on the north by the Najabids and on the south by the Zuray'ids. Beset by illness, he transferred control of the principality to 'Arwa. The exact wording of her *khutba* was, "May Allah prolong the days of al-Hurra the perfect, the sovereign who carefully manages the affairs of the faithful." Although many Islamic scholars have swept under the table any mention of rule by women as if it were a shameful thing, Yemeni historians, both ancient and modern, point with pride to their women rulers. Of 'Arwa, contemporary historian 'Abdallah al-Thawr says she "held fast to her principles, loved her people, and was faithful to them." He notes that she left more monuments, buildings, roads, and mosques than the imams who governed San'a (the capital city) from 1591 to 1925. She ruled until her death in 1138.

Suggested Reading:

(1) Al-Dahbi, *Siyar a'lam al-nubala'*. Cairo: Dar al-Ma'arif, 1958. This reference contains a biography of 'Arwa.

(2) 'Abdallah Ahmad Muhammad al-Thawr, *Hadhihi hiyya al-Yaman*. Beirut: Dar al-'Awda, 1979, p. 331.

(* al-Zarkali, Khayr al-Din, *Al-a'lam, qamus ash'ar al-rijal wa al-nisa' min al-'arab wa al-musta'rabin wa al-mustashraqin*. Beirut: Dar al-'Ilm li al-Malayin, 1983, 8 vols., vol. 1.)

Asma Bint Shihab al-Sulayhiyya

Shi'ite Malika, (Queen) and co-ruler of Yemen (1047-1067)

She was married to 'Ali Ibn Muhammad al-Sulayhi, Shi'ite imam who founded of the Sulayhid dynasty and consolidated the principality of Yemen, who reigned from 1047 to 1067. 'Ali al-Sulayhi imposed his rule and his beliefs so easily upon Yemen because he was descended from the older culture as a member of the Yam clan of the Hamdan tribe from the realm of Sheba. Historians note that Asma "attended councils with her 'face uncovered'" and that "the *khutba* (a sermon affirming a sovereign's right to rule) was proclaimed from the pulpits of the mosques of Yemen in her husband's name and in her name." She bore the title of *al-sayyida al-hurra*, "The noble lady who is free and independent; the woman sovereign who bows to no superior authority." In 1066 'Ali decided to undertake a pilgrimmage to Mecca. He and Asma took a splendid caravan of a thousand horsemen, a military force of five thousand Ethiopians, and all of the Yemeni princes whom he had conquered over the years, plus Asma's whole court entourage. 'Ali had designated their son al-Mukarram, married to 'Arma, to govern in his stead during his absence. But the caravan was attacked by the Ethiopian Banu Najah family in retribution for 'Ali's murder of their father. 'Ali was among the people killed, and Asma was taken prisoner. When she was finally freed and sent back to San'a, her son continued to take orders from his mother. She died in 1097.

Suggested Reading:

(1) al-Thawr, 'Abdallah Ahmad Muhammad, *Hadhihi hiyya al-Yaman*. Beirut: Dar al-'Awda, 1979. pp. 275, 281.

(2)   al-Zarkali, Khayr al-Din, *Al-a'lam, qamus ash'ar al-rijal wa al-nisa' min al-'arab wa al-musta'rabin wa al-mustashraqin* vol 1. Beirut: Dar al-'Ilm li al-Malayin, 1983. p. 299.

Athaliah

Ruler of Judah (c. 844/5-837/9 B.C.)

She was the daughter of Queen Jezebel and King Ahab, seventh King of the northern kingdom of Israel, according to the Old Testament. She married Jeham (or Joram or Jehoram), King of Judah. Their son, Ahaziah, became the sixth king of Judah upon his father's death in 841. Athaliah served as queen mother in court, a position of honor, while her son went off to war. After a reign of only one year, Ahaziah was killed in battle by Jehu. Athaliah seized the throne and tried to put to death all her own grandsons, heirs to the throne, in order to destroy the line of David and keep the throne for herself. One of the infants, Joash, was hidden away by followers loyal to Ahaziah. Athaliah reigned tyrannically for seven years. She eliminated the Omrites from Judah and eradicated the House of David. She also introduced the worship of Baal. When Joash was of age, he came out of hiding and in the revolution which followed, Athaliah was overthrown. She was executed ca. 839 or 837 B.C.

Suggested Reading:

(1)   Langer, William L., ed., *World History*. Boston: Houghton Mifflin, 1980. p. 45.
(2)   Wilson, Robert Dick, *A Scientific Investigation of the Old Testament*. revised by Edward J. Young. Chicago: Moody Press, 1959. p. 71.
(3)   Wright, Ernest, *Biblical Archaeology*. Philadelphia: Westminster Press, 1957. p. 162.

Aung San Suu Kyi

Prime Minister-elect, pro-democracy leader of Myanmar (Burma), (1900-2010)

She was born June 19, 1945 in Rangoon, the daughter of the martyred military hero and father of his country, Gen. Aung San, who was assassinated in 1947 on the eve of Burma's independence. Until 1988 she had lived most of her life abroad as part of a diplomatic family. In 1972 she married an Oxford classmate and Tibet specialist, Michael Aris, and had two sons. Following this, she earned a Ph.D. in Oriental and African Studies from the University of London.

In 1988 she returned to Myanmar when Burmese citizens, who had taken to the streets to protest authoritarian rule, were massacred. Aung San Suu Kyi founded the National League for Democracy and spoke publicly despite military threats against her. In July 1989, the junta had placed her under house arrest and held her for six years. With her tucked away out of sight, the generals pitted their popularity against hers in an election in 1990 and lost overwhelmingly, but they still refused to release their grip on power. Although her party won the election, she was never allowed to take office.

In 1991, still a prisoner, Aung San Suu Kyi won the Nobel Peace Prize for her attempts to bring democracy to Myanmar, which had been controlled by the military since 1962.

When she was again allowed partial freedom, she immediately began campaigning for democracy and for the right to govern which the election results should have afforded her. Her greatest sacrifice, she told interviewers, was being deprived of watching her sons grow up.

In 1996, during a brief period of freedom from house arrest, Daw Aung San Suu Kyi again publicly challenged the military junta in a speech as thousands of supporters stood cheering in the rain. "Why are you so afraid of us?" she called out, again taunting the captors who have kept her under house arrest for the better part of twenty years.

The junta, which has jailed its opponents and crushed popular uprisings by force, has been afraid of Mrs. Aung San Suu Kyi, 63, the pro-democracy opposition leader in the country formerly known as Burma, and of the continuing undercurrent of support she commands among the people.

"Her achievement has been to concentrate the values that are associated with democracy and freedom into one person," said David Steinberg of Georgetown University, an expert on Myanmar.

Her husband Michael died of cancer in 1999, separated from his wife because the junta refused him permission to re-enter the country.

The junta experimented with lifting her house arrest in 2002, but locked her up again a year later after ecstatic crowds gathered to cheer wherever she went. Since her detention in May 2003, she has rarely been allowed to see visitors outside her gated, guarded compound in downtown Yangon.

In September 2008 her lawyer, U Kyi Win, reported that Daw Aung San Suu Kyi was malnourished after refusing for a month to accept food supplies that had been regularly left at her gate. "She was eating little because she hasn't accepted food supplies since August 16," he said, but added that since the junta had decided to ease the restrictions on her, she would resume accepting food deliveries.

In May of 2009 the generals demonstrated their continuing fear of this lone challenger by charging Mrs. Aung San Suu Kyi with violating the terms of her most recent, six-year term of house arrest and locking her inside what it calls a prison "guesthouse."

She faced a trial hearing on charges that resulted in a prison term of up to five years, a harsher form of the isolation she has endured for 13 of the past 19 years.

"They are trying their best to put her out of the minds of the population," said her lawyer, U Kyi Win. "But the more they do that, the more they are highlighting her. That is the reverse effect that it is having."

The circumstances of the latest charges against her border on the ridiculous. They stem from the capture of an American adventurer, John Yettaw, 53, who twice swam across a lake to her house where, according to her lawyer, he delivered her a Bible, although she is a Theravada Buddhist.

Mrs. Aung San Suu Kyi faced trial for violating the terms of her house arrest, though her lawyer described the American as an intruder, not a guest. She was charged along with two housekeepers and her doctor, who treated her for low blood pressure and dehydration shortly after Mr. Yettaw swam away May 5.

The housekeepers and the doctor were among the only people she was allowed to talk to over the past half-dozen years. She was unable to participate in the pro-democracy uprising led by monks in late 2007.

And yet, like a silent ghost, she shadows the country's military leaders, who have sought without success to exorcise her with propaganda and repression.

Today, the generals are on the verge of achieving a goal that in their eyes would justify their harsh rule and crown them as saviors of the country: an election scheduled for 2010 that would legitimize the continued dominance of the military. And they appear to be afraid that this woman could ruin it all if she were allowed a voice that could rally opposition against them.

Thirteen years ago, when Mrs. Aung San Suu Kyi was addressing her ecstatic supporters in the rain, a Western diplomat predicted that her confrontation with the generals could not last much longer. "She is under a lot of pressure," he said, speaking on condition of anonymity. "She has to keep the momentum up, but fatigue is setting in. Some of her leaders are old. Some are in prison. Some have died. She knows she will lose a waiting game."

Suggested Reading:

(1) Aung San Suu Kyi. *The Voice of Hope* with Alan Clements. 1998, reissued by Rider Books, 2008.
(2) "Myanmar's Junta Eases Restrictions on Opposition Leader Under House Arrest" by Seth Mydans, *The New York Times*, September 15, 2008.
(3) "Myanmar Junta Charges Democracy Leader," May 15, 2009.
(4) "After Years of Isolation, a Dissident Still Torments Her Tormentors," by Seth Mydans, *The New York Times*, May 15, 2009)

Azarmedukht

Sasanid queen of Persia (631-632)

The younger daughter of King Khusrau II, who ruled Persia from 590 to 628, she succeeded her sister Boran on the throne. Her reign was marred by pretenders and rival kings in various parts of the empire. She was succeeded by her nephew, Yazdgard III. Sasanid monarchs used the oriental title Shahanshah, or king of kings.

Suggested Reading:

(1) Morby, John E., *Dynasties of the World*. Oxford: Oxford University Press, 1989. p. 49.

Section B

Bai

See Lakshmi Bai, Tara Bai, and Udham Bai

Balkis (or Balqis or Bilqis)

Legendary queen of Sheba

See African section for this queen, for whom an Arabian tradition also exists.

Bandaranaike, Sirimavo Ratevatte Dias

Prime Minister of Sri Lanka (1960-1965 and 1970-1977, 1994-2000)

She was born Sirimavo Ratwatte on April 17, 1916 to a prominent family in Ratnapura, Balangoda, in southern Ceylon (now Sri Lanka). Although she received a Catholic education at St. Bridget's Convent in Colombo, she remained a Bhuddist. In 1940 she married Solomon West Ridgeway Dias Bandaranaike, an Oxford-educated attorney already committed to a life in politics, which Sirimavo loved as well. The couple had three children: a daughter Sunethra, who became a philanthropist but did not get involved in politics, a daughter Chandrika Kumaratunga, who became Sri Lanka's third president, and a son Anura Bandaranaike, who became a minister, and leader of the opposition, the United National Party.

In 1956, as leader of the People's United Front, a coalition of four nationalist-socialist parties, Solomon Bandaranaike was appointed prime minister. Three years later he was assassinated by a Buddhist monk. Sirimavo became president of the Sri Lanka Freedom Party which her husband had founded in 1952. In 1960, with no previous political experience, she became the world's first female prime minister, elected with the understanding that she would continue her husband's socialist policies. She followed a neutral policy with both communists and non-communists. She attempted to stabalize the economy by extending the government into various businesses, but worsening economic conditions and racial and religious clashes led to her party's ouster in 1965. Sirimavo did not retire from politics, however, and in 1970 her party again regained power. During her second term as prime minister she took more radical steps to bring the country's economic and ideological difficulties under control. Much of the turmoil of her administration had to do with ethnic problems which she failed to address adequately. These problems continue into the 1990s. The dominant population is Sinhalese. The minority Tamil group, Indian in origin, has agitated for years for a separate state. When Sirimavo nationalized key industries, a court determined that she had gone too far. It expelled her from Parliament and stripped her of her civil rights (1977). The election of 1977 decimated her power base. The United National Party, under President Junius R. Jayewardene, was no more successful than she in solving the island's worsening problems.

Her daughter Chandrika Kumaratunga followed in her mother's footsteps and in 1994 the People's Alliance which she headed narrowly defeated the ruling United National Party, making Chandrika the new Prime Minister. A year later, Chandrika became President. Sirimavo had reentered the political arena to run for president in November of 1994 but served as Prime Minister under her daughter. With the new laws in effect since the new constitution of 1978, this time she was subservient to the President. She served until 2000 and resigned her post in August of that year, retaining her seat in Parliament. She died on October 10, 2000 at the age of 84.

Suggested Reading:

(1) Seneviratne, Maureen, *Sirimavo Bandaranaike: The World's First Woman Prime Minister.* Sri Lanka: Colombo, 1975.
(2) "Sri Lanka's Racial Riots Could Cost Us Dearly." *U. S. News & World Report.* 8 August 1983: 8.
(3) "A Family Affair?" *World Press Review.* October 1994: 24.
(4) "Sirimavo Bandaranaike of Sri Lanka Dies at 84; First Woman Premier" by Celia W. Dugger. *The New York Times,* October 11, 2000.

Beatrice

Countess, regent of Edessa (1150)

Edessa was a Crusader state in northern Syria. Beatrice was the wife of Joscelin II (r. 1131-1150). In April 1150 Count Joscelin was captured by the invading Moslems. Countess Beatrice sold what remained of the land to Byzantium in the summer of that year, thus ending the county's fifty-year history.

Suggested Reading:

(1) Carpenter, Clive. *The Guinness Book of Kings, Rulers, & Statesmen.* Enfield, Middlesex: Guinness Superlatives Ltd., 1978. p. 55.

Berenice (or Julia Berenice)

Co-ruler of Caesarea Paneas and Tiberias in Judaea (fl c. A.D.52)

She was born Julia Berenice in A.D. 28, the daughter of King Herod Agrippa I (10 B.C.-A.D. 44). who ruled Judaea from A.D. 37 to A.D. 44. She was the older sister of Drusilla, who was linked both to Aziz, Arab ruler of Emesa, and Feliz, the Roman Procurator of Judaea. However, Berenice was much more active than her sister. She first reputedly married, or was sleeping with, Marcus, a nephew of Philo Judaeus of Alexandra, and lived in Alexandria, Egypt. After his premature death, she married her father's brother, Herod, who was given rule over Chalcis in Greece. To Herod, Berenice bore two sons, Berenicianus and Hyrcanus. Herod died in A.D. 48 while she was still in her twenties. In ca. 52, she shared the Chalcis throne and the business of the kingdom, in Batanala and Trachonites in southern Syria, with her brother, Agrippa II, who had succeeded as King of Judaea when their father died in A.D. 44. The couple was popularly believed to be cohabiting in Caesarea before and after Berenice's brief marriage to Polemon II, king of Olba in Cilicia (in present-day Turkey and Armenia). Her powers of persuasion were such that she convinced Polemon, a non-Jew, to be circumcised before she would consent to marry him. This marriage was also cut short by the husband's death.

From the historian Josephus's account of the Jewish revolt against Florus, Nero's chosen procurator of Judaea, Agrippa relied heavily upon

Berenice. At one point, to dissuade the Jewish people from revolting against Rome, he placed Berenice conspicuously on the roof of the palace where she could be seen by the crowd while he pleaded for peace. At the end of his impassioned speech, both he and his sister burst out in tears, moving the crowd to accompany the couple to repair the temple which had been damaged in the uprising. Thus they were able to postpone a confrontation which would cost many Jewish lives.

When the Caesarean palace was burned down and Jerusalem sacked, Agrippa and Berenice became Flavian sympathizers. Commander-in-chief Titus (A.D. 41-81), a 28-year-old widower, fell under the charms of the 41-year-old widow and for 13 years made her his mistress. But after Titus became emperor in A.D. 79, his intention to make her his empress—a Jewish princess 13 years his senior—caused such an uproar among the court in Rome that he was compelled to banish her to Gaul, where she is thought to have lived until age 72. Titus reigned barely two years before he died in A.D. 81.

Suggested Reading:

(1) Bowder, Diana, *Who Was Who in the Roman World*. New York: Washington Square Press, 1984, p. 70.

(2) Josephus, *The Jewish War*. tr. G. A. Williamson. London: Penguin Books, 1959, 1970. pp. 143, 152-153, 155-156, 162, 166, 192-193.

(3) Mommsen, Theodor. *The Provinces of the Roman Empire*. tr. Wm. P. Dickson. Chicago: Ares Publishers, 1974, vol. 2 pp. 201, 219.

(4) Peters, F. E., *The Harvest of Hellenism*. New York: Barnes & Noble Books, 1996. p. 513n.

(5) Wright, Ernest, *Biblical Archaeology*. Philadelphia: Westminster Press, 1957. p. 162.

Bhutto, Benazir

Prime Minister of Pakistan (1988-1990, 1993-1996)

She was born in 1953, the eldest child of Zulfiqar Ali Bhutto, a Berkeley and Oxford trained Pakistani lawyer, and his number two wife Nusrat, an Iranian. Ali Bhutto became a cabinet member at the age of 32, when Benazir was five years old, thus she and her younger siblings were reared in proximity to power. When she was 16 she entered Radcliffe, graduating cum laude with a BA degree. From there she went to Oxford, where she was elected president of the Oxford Union and received another BA cum laude. Her father became leader of the new truncated state of Pakistan in 1971. In 1979, in a U.S. supported coup, Ali's rival, General Zia ul-Haq, sent tanks to surround the prime minister's house. Ali was dragged away before his family's eyes and sentenced to be hanged by a court rigged by Zia. Ali immediately became a national martyr and his wife and daughter became symbols of resistance to Zia's military dictatorship. They were imprisoned and mistreated until their health failed.

In 1983 Benazir received permission to be sent abroad for medical treatment. In 1984 Indira Gandhi personally intervened in behalf of Nusrat, believed to be suffering from cancer. The family was reunited in London, where Benazir began to organize her supporters. Zia lifted martial law in 1985 and Benazir returned the next year to a tumultuous welcome. She was promptly imprisoned and some of her supporters shot.

But Zia's popularity was waning: his generals had grown wealthy from heroin money, and the whole country was weakened by heroin. She was released only a month later, when Zia realized that public sentiment was in her favor. In 1987 she consented to an arranged marriage with Asif Ali Zardari, of a wealthy landed family like her own. Ultimately the couple would have two children, Bilawal and Bakhtawar. In 1988, Benazir was several months pregnant when the plane upon which Zia and most of his high command were traveling exploded and crashed. Her People's Party won the election which followed despite discriminatory practices which prevented women and the poor from voting. Benazir was sworn in as prime minister of Pakistan at the age of 35. It was widely reported by Islamic news sources at the time that Bhutto was the first woman to lead an Islamic state; however, research has uncovered more than a dozen other women Islamic rulers, in Yemen, Egypt, Kirman, and the Maldive islands. Her mother Nusrat became a member of the Parliament. Benazir faced enormous problems of a bankrupt economy, which included huge debts to the International Monetary Fund; a heroin mafia; 1.35 million heroin addicts; and thousands of Afghan refugees. In an interview with David Frost about her long political struggle, she said, "You can never survive on your fears. Only on your hopes." Meanwhile violence had erupted in the provinces of Sind and Baluchistan, forcing Bhutto to consider opposing central rule.

Bhutto governed Pakistan from 1988 to 1990, but her government, the first democracy after a decade of military rule, was thrown out on corruption charges that were never substantiated. Under this government, her mother,

Nusrat Bhutto, was a senior cabinet minister and her husband, Asif Ali Zardari, was a visible presence in government circles. However, after her downfall, Zardari, charged with taking kickbacks, spent more than two years in prison, although the charges were never proved. From 1990 to 1993 her Pakistan People's Party led the opposition, during which time she built a coalition of minor parties.

In October, 1993, her party won a slim margin in the national elections and the National Assembly named her prime minister for a second time. This time her husband was kept at a distance during the elections, and her aides reported that none of her family would be included in her new cabinet.

In 1994 she was able to facilitate the sale of Pakistan Telecom shares abroad, raising $1 billion, and the signing of deals with local industrialists by American investors in the amount of $4 billion. However, although she had cut the budget deficit, privatized public utilities, and instituted an austerity drive, her success as judged by the International Monetary Fund did not translate to help for the common citizen. In September, 1994, her long-time political opponent Nawaz Sharif, leader of Pakistan Muslim League, called for a general strike. Another opponent to both factions, Zahid Sarfaraz, a member of a group of right-wing policians and retired generals, called for the army to step in and save the country, while yet another faction, led by Mir Zafarullah Jamali, to avert a military takeover, called for the military to back a vote of no-confidence against Bhutto.

During that same month Benazir attended the United Nations Population Conference in Cairo, where she spoke against abortion. Norwegian Prime Minister Gro Harlem Brundtland spoke in favor of abortion at the same conference.

In 1995 Owais Aslam Ali, with the Pakistan Press Foundation, reported that, after a decade of trends toward a freer press, Bhutto's government, as well as other political groups and terrorists, had turned against the media, particularly the newspapers in Karachi. Bhutto's officials complained that the papers sensationalized the violence that had gripped Karachi. In June the government of Karachi's Sind province banned six mass-circulation newspapers for 60 days. However, when a nationwide newspaper strike was threatened, the government rescinded the order. Journalists in other towns reported being harassed and physically assaulted by law-enforcement officials and political groups. A prominent journalist in Lahore was arrested because his campaign against child labor was "against the national interest."

That same year, Ms. Bhutto's three-year-old government was dismissed amid accusations of mismanagement and corruption. Her brother, Murtaza, tried to claim leadership of the Pakistan People's Party, which had been founded by their father. In 1996, Murtaza was shot and killed, and Bhutto's husband, Asif Ali Zardari, was accused of the murder and jailed, but the case was never proven. Bhutto said that Pakistani intelligence had planned the killing to divide and weaken her family dynasty. She suffered a resounding defeat in elections. While she says the balloting was rigged, the polls also reflected the disillusion and anger of Pakistanis over a deteriorating economy, rising violence and a leadership that many here felt was concerned only with itself.

Although Bhutto's party was voted out in favor of Nawaz Sharif, she remained a formidable and popular spokesperson for her party and for her country in the international arena. Threatened with arrest, Bhutto and her family went into voluntary exile for eight years in Dubai and London. During that time, her former chief of military operations, General Musharraf, seized power in a coup in October of 1999, taking control from Sharif. Later President Musharraf was compelled to hold an election but he was widely criticized for continuing to hold a military title. His first term as an elected president was marked by unrest and a continual slide away from democratic government and U.S. Intelligence showed that Al-Qaeda was strengthening in Pakistan's tribal areas. As time approached for another election, which must occur before the end of 2007, Musharraf announced that he would renounce his general's title, but his popularity had waned to such an extent that rumors circulated that he might drop charges against Bhutto and allow her to return as prime minister, sharing power with him as president. U.S. Secretary of State Condoleezza Rice discussed the idea of a power-sharing arrangement in a telephone conversation with Musharraf in which she also warned him not to declare emergency powers. Both the U.S. and Pakistani governments confirmed the content of the call.

In October of 2007, Musharraf announced amnesty for Bhutto, clearing the way for her triumphal return on October 18. During a homecoming procession in Karachi on that date, she narrowly escaped a suicide bombing that killed 140 people. Everywhere she went, Bhutto was greeted by throngs of enthusiastic supporters. On December 1 she officially launched her election campaign for a third time as prime minister, urging resistance against Islamic militancy and a return to democratic principles. On December 27, 2007, she was assassinated at a campaign rally in Rawalpindi, Pakistan. Her death set off widespread violence and worldwide unease. Al-Qaida, tribal insurgents, and local terrorists were among the suspects, while the government put out a spurious account, quickly discredited, of her death's being caused by a bump on the head.

Never has the loss of a leader left the Middle East in a more unstable condition, as her country's slide toward anarchy caused increased worries about Pakistan's nuclear weapon vulnerability to terrorist takeover.

Suggested Reading:

(1) Bhutto, Benazir, *Daughter of Destiny*. New York: Simon & Schuster, 1989. Or see Bhutto, Benazir, Daughter of the East. London: Hamish Hamilton, 1988.

(2) Ali, Tarik, "Dynasty's Daughter." *Interview*, February 1989: 68-71.

(3) Mayer, Ann Elizabeth, "Benazir Bhutto and Islamic Law". *Christian Science Monitor*. 6 February 1989: 18.

(4) Brody, James, "In Step with David Frost". *Parade*. February 18, 1989: 18.

(5) Bokhari, Farhan. "Pakistan's Benazir Bhutto Gets a Second Chance". *Christian Science Monitor*. 20 October 1993: 2.

(6) Ali, Owais Aslam. "Regression in Pakistan" from "IPI Report". *World Press Review*. April 1996: 17-18.

(7) "The 'Strongwomen' of South Asia" *World Press Review* December 1994: 18-20.

(8) "U.S. Is Prodding Pakistan Leader to Share Power" by Mark Mazzetti and Helene Cooper from Washington and Carlotta Gall from Islamabad. *New York Times*. August 16, 2007)

(9) "Musharraf-Bhutto Accord Sets Stage for Vote" by Carlotta Gall. By Carlotta Gall. *New York Times*. October 5, 2007.

(10) "The Bhutto Assassination: Pakistan Deep in Chaos; U.S. Policy in Tatters" by Salman Masood and Carlotta Gall. *New York Times*. December 28, 2007.

(11) "Deadly Events Show How Little Influence America Has in Islamabad's Politics." By Helene Cooper and Steven Lee Myers. *New York Times*. December 28, 2007

(12) "Charisma, Controversy Marked Ex-Premier's Life" by Pamela Constable. *Washington Post*. December 28, 2007.

(13) "Frantic Mourners Rush Hospital" by Griff White. *Washington Post*. December 28, 2007

(14) "Identifying the Killers: Number of Groups Wanted Her Dead" by Kathy Gannon from Islamabad. Associated Press, *Houston Chronicle*. December 28, 2007.

(15) "Pakistan Blames Militant Tied to Al-Qaida for Death" by Carlotta Gall from Islamabad. *New York Times*. December 29, 2007.

Boran

Sasanid queen of Persia (630-631)

Boran was the daughter of King Khusrau II the Victorious, ruler of Persia from 590 to 628. During two chaotic years following his death, two of her brothers, Kavad II and Ardashir II, and a usurper, Shahrbaraz, each held the throne briefly. Boran was then placed on the throne, but the following year her sister, Azarmedukht, succeeded her.

Suggested Reading:

(1) Morby, John E., *Dynasties of the World*. Oxford: Oxford University Press, 1989. p. 49.

Boraqchin, Khatum

Regent of the Mongolian khanate of Kipchak (1255-1257)

She was the wife of Batu, khan of Kipchak from 1227. When he died in 1255, his son and heir Sartaq had gone to pay court to Grand Khan Mongka, his father's friend. But before Sartaq could return home and be crowned, he died. Mongka nominated a young prince Ulaqchi, either Sartaq's younger brother or his son, to succeed to the throne of Kipchak, and he made the widow Boraqchin regent. She served until Ulaqchi died in 1257.

Suggested Reading:

(1) Grousset, Rene, *The Empire of the Steppes*. tr. Naomi Walford. New Brunswick, NJ: Rutgers University Press, 1970. p. 397.

Section C

Catherine I (or Ekaterina I Alekseyevna)

Empress of Russia (1725-1727)

She was born Marta Skowronska, the daughter of Lithuanian peasants, in ca. 1683 in Marienburg, now Malbork, Poland. Orphaned when she was three years old, she was reared by a Lutheran minister who later made her his servant, an inauspicious beginning for a future empress. Her chief attribute was her beauty, and that alone, plus a misfortune of war, changed her fortunes. However, her more durable attributes were her intelligence, her diplomacy and her ambition, and these would prove to be more valuable as she rose to prominence. During the Great Northern War, Russian troops swept through Marienburg and Marta was taken prisoner by Marshal Boris Sheremetev, who made her his mistress. When he tired of her, she was handed over to a close advisor to Peter I, Prince Aleksandr Menshikov. Peter had put aside his wife Eudoxia, banishing her to a nunnery, and it was not long before he took notice of Marta. She became his mistress in 1702 and the following year bore a son. The tzar set about making his heir more palatable to the court by having Marta received into the Orthodox Church and rechristened Catherine Alekseyevna. For the next nine years Catherine was Peter's companion, bearing many children, only two of whom, Elizabeth and Anna, survived past infancy. Peter, already having a legitimate heir in Alexis, his son by Eudoxia, and having no sons by Catherine, felt no need to marry her. In addition, his first wife still loomed in the background, having first taken vows and then rescinded them. However, in 1712, after some pressure from the outside, Peter and Catherine were married. In 1718 Alexis was implicated in a conspiracy against the crown, and Peter had him condemned to death, possibly by torturing. When Peter was well past 50, he consented to allow Catherine to be crowned empress consort of Russia (1724). When he died nine months later without naming an heir, Menshikov and his other advisors, whose cases she had often supported before Peter, now supported her candidacy. She was declared sovereign of Russia "according to the desires of Peter the Great" by the Senate and the Holy Synod, which had controlled the government during her husband's reign. She soon began to transfer control into a new governing body of her own design, the Supreme Privy Council, which effectively robbed the Synod of its power. This council, formed to deal with "matters of exceptional significance", was comprised of six members, chiefly Menshikov, her former lover, and five others. During her reign, which lasted only two years and three months, Menshikov remained the most influential member of the government. Shortly before her death, urged by her advisors, she named Peter's 12-year-old grandson, Pyotr (Peter) Alekseyevich, as heir to the throne and sanctioned his marriage to Menshikov's daughter. She died in 1727 in St. Petersburg. Her daughter Elizabeth would later become empress and Anna's son, Peter III, would later become tzar.

Suggested Reading:

(1) Riasnovsky, Nicholas V. *A History of Russia*. Oxford: Oxford University Press, 1963, 1993. pp. 238-239, 243.

(2) Dvornik, Francis. *The Slavs in European History and Civilization*. New Brunswick, NJ: Rutgers University Press, 1962. pp. 517, 533-534, 542.

Catherine II the Great (or Ekaterina II Alekseyevna)

Tsaritsa or Empress of Russia (1762-1796)

She was born Princess Sophia Augusta Frederica in 1729 in Stettin, Anhalt-Zerbst, a small kingdom in Prussia. She was the daughter of Prince Karl Augustus and Joanna Elizabeth, an indifferent mother, who, being vain and envious of the bond between father and daughter, convinced Sophia that she was far homlier than she actually was. Smart, astute, self-disciplined and energetic, she concentrated on other interests besides attracting suitors. Elizabeth I of Russia, looking for a suitable mate for her scrawny, pocked 15-year-old nephew/heir Peter, chose Sophia when she was only 14 and not the beauty she was later to become. In the winter of 1743, Sophia, ambitious but ill-prepared to become a tzarina by education or possessions (three shabby dresses in a half-filled trunk), traveled secretly with her mother to meet her future husband. At the Russian border, the party was met with a welcoming escort which paraded all the way to Moscow with much fanfare. In the beautiful Elizabeth, Sophia found the kindness which her own mother had never shown; the young girl idolized the empress and from the very first day tried to emulate her. Taking the name Catherine, she converted to Russian Orthodoxy and threw herself zealously into preparing for her role, studying and mastering Russian, a language her future husband never bothered to learn.

The couple was married a year later and Elizabeth personally escorted them to the marriage chamber and dressed the bride for bed. But the groom did not respond to the challenge, then or for years to come; desultory and immature, he spent much of his time playing with toy soldiers. Catherine became a tall and slender beauty but was still an untouched maiden eight years later. Elizabeth, convinced that Peter was impotent, arranged for a clandestine lover for Catherine. However, once she had become pregnant and delivered a son, Catherine was again ignored. For years she could only see her child by appointment. At 30, she took a lover, Gregory Orlov, a handsome war hero five years her junior, an officer in the imperial guard. Eventually she bore a child by him.

Upon Elizabeth's death, Peter, who refused to observe a period of mourning, began a disastrous reign of six months, during which he ended the war against his beloved Prussia and forced France and Austria to do likewise, restoring to Frederick the Great the lands he had lost. Still obsessed by his toy soldiers, he dressed his guards in Prussian-like uniforms. During Orthodox Church services he would stick his tongue out at the priests. He then decided to have Catherine arrested, and to divorce her so that he could marry his mistress, Elizabeth Woronotsov.

Catherine, near to term with Orlov's child, delivered in secret while a servant distracted Peter, who loved fires, by setting fire to his own cottage. Word spread of Peter's intentions, so Orlov spirited her away to an army barracks, where Catherine begged for protection. The soldiers rushed to kiss her hands, calling her savior. She was sworn in as empress on the spot. Peter was arrested and killed by a brother of Orlov.

Catherine II assembled more than 500 leaders and scholars, gave them each extracts from Montesquieu's *The Spirit of Laws*, and charged them with reform of the government. However, she later disbanded the commission and actually increased her own power. Her action was probably the direct cause of the 1917 revolution, although in later years of her reign she was to become more lenient. During her reign Russia became a world power. As a result of two wars with Turkey, Russia gained the Crimea and an outlet to the Black Sea. Its image as a barbaric state receded further as she established the Russian Academy and encouraged the arts, belatedly bringing the Renaissance to Russia. She became the protectoress of the philosopher Diderot, chief editor of the *encyclopedie*, the most important publishing enterprise of the century. She had Voltaire to visit in Russia; he had, in fact, advised her to take up arms and drive the Turks from Europe.

During the time of the Turkish wars, Catherine took a Crimean general, Gregory Potemkin, as lover. Well into old age, she took yet another lover, Platon Zubov, who was 40 years younger than she. She ruled for 34 years. Her son Paul I, who should have been Peter's successor, did not come to the throne until he was 44 years old and ruled only five years. The other rightful heir, Ivan VI, who held the crown briefly as an infant before Elizabeth's rule, was imprisoned, never knowing his real identity. Catherine gave orders that if he became ill, he was not to be given medical treatment. He was eventually stabbed by a jailor during an escape attempt. She died in 1796 of a stroke at the age of 67. Among her papers was found her credo: "Be gentle, humane, accessible, compassionate and liberal-minded. Do not let your grandeur prevent you from being condescending with kindness toward the small and putting yourself in their place . . . . Behave so that the kind love you, the evil fear you, and all respect you."

Suggested Reading:

(1) Oldenbourg, Zoe. *Catherine the Great*. New York: Pantheon Books, 1965.
(2) Coughlan, Robert. *Elizabeth and Catherine*. New York: G.P. Putnam's Sons, 1974.
(3) Durant, Will and Ariel. *The Age of Voltaire*. New York: Simon & Schuster, 1965. pp. 216, 360, 477479, 510, 516, 575, 606, 644, 646, 665, 675, 679, 730, 733, 744, 774, 776, 779, 785.

Catherine Cornaro

Regent ruler of Jerusalem (on Cyprus) (1473-1489)

She was a Venetian noblewoman married to James II, bastard of the house of Lusignon, who ruled Cyprus from 1460 to 1473, and who had also become archbishop of Nicosia. When Jerusalem's ruling Lusignon family was driven from the mainland in 1291, it had retreated to Cyprus, but it still claimed to be rulers of the kingdom of Jerusalem. Catherine and James had a son, James III, who was too young to rule when his father died in 1473. Catherine and her son remained in Venice, from whence she ruled for her son, who died only a year later. She continued to rule in the queen's name from Venice until 1489, when, partly by gift and partly by extortion, she deeded Cyprus to Venice and abdicated. Cyprus remained a Venetian possession until 1570.

Suggested Reading:

(1) Langer, William L., ed. *World History*. Boston: Houghton Mifflin, 1980. p. 279.

Catherine of Valois

Titular Byzantine empress (1313-1346, sole ruler from 1331)

She was the daughter of Emperor Charles of Valois and Catherine of Courtenay. As a child, in 1313, she was given in marriage to Philip of Tarentum (or Tarento). They became co-rulers upon Charles' death in 1313. Catherine gave birth to three sons. Philip died in 1331 and Catherine ruled alone. In 1337, she also became ruler of the principality of Antioch. At her instigation, the governor of Dyrrachium stirred up a revolt in favor of the deposed Despot Nicrophoros. Upon her death in 1346, her second son, Robert II, succeeded her.

Suggested Reading:

(1) Langer, William L., ed. *World History*. Boston: Houghton Mifflin, 1980. p. 282.
(2) Ostrogorsky, George. *History of the Byzantine State*. New Brunswick, NJ: Rutgers University Press, 1969. pp. 497, 508, 510.

Chan, Anson

Chief Secretary, No. 2 Official, of Hong Kong (1997-2001)

Anson Maria Elizabeth Chan Fang On Sang and a twin sister were born in Shanghai on January 17, 1940 to a textile manufacturer father and a well-known painter-mother, Fang Zhaoling. Her grandfather, Fang Zhenwu, was a Kuomintang general who fought against Japanese occupation. Her uncle, Sir Harry Fang, is a well-known doctor in Hong Kong. When the twins were ten years old, their father died, leaving their mother with eight young children. She took the two sons and moved to England to study. Chan and her other five siblings stayed in Hong Kong with their grandmother and uncle. Chan was educated at Italian Convent School and Sacred Heart School in Hong Kong, now the Sacred Heart Canossian College. In 1959 she entered the University of Hong Kong to study English literature, working as a private tutor on the side. Later she attended to Tufts University in Medford, Massachusetts. In 1962 she joined the Civil Service.

During the ensuing years, in an effort to better working conditions for women, she helped set up the Association of Female Senior Government Officers. By 1970 she had worked her way up to a senior administrative officer.

By the 1980s she was Director of Social Welfare, and in 1986 she came under sharp media criticism for her handling of a child custody case infamously known as the "Daughter of Kwok-A Incident."

From 1987 to 1993, she was Secretary for Economic Services, becoming the thirtieth and last Chief Secretary in 1993. She was often referred to as the "Iron Lady" with "an iron fist in a velvet glove" As the deputy of British Governor Chris Patten and, after Hong Kong's handover on July 1, 1977, to the People's Republic of China, as deputy to the Chief Executive Tung Chee-hwa, Chan was cited as the most powerful woman in Asia. Her public pronouncements calling for faster democratization have sometimes put her at odds with her more conservative superior, but they have also earned her the reputation as "Hong Kong's Conscience."

In 2001, she criticized a senior Mainland Chinese official for his views against Hong Kong media reports on Taiwan. Bejing began to perceive her as being part of a "Dump Tung" campaign. She announced that she would quit if asked to support policies that were against her principles. In April of that year, she stepped down.

She was the first woman and the first Chinese to hold the second-highest government position in Hong Kong.

In recognition of her 34 years of public service to the British Crown, in 2002, Chan was appointed by Queen Elizabeth II to be an honorary Dame Grand Cross of the Most Distinguished Order of St. Michael and St. George. Such award is usually given only to Governors of Hong Kong before the return of sovereignty.

After her retirement, Chan kept a somewhat lower profile, although many believe Chan now harbours political ambitions. Such assertions were said by some to have been proved by her participation in the protest against her successor Donald Tsang's constitutional reform package. Shortly thereafter, she called on Tsang to demand from Bejing greater democracy in the media. However, on September 23, 2006, she announced in a news conference that she will not run in 2007. Instead, she announced that she was forming a group to push for universal suffrage.

Suggested Reading:

(1) "Shaping Hong Kong's Future." on "Conversations with History." Institute of International Studies, U.C. Berkeley, January 27, 1997.
(2) Vanessa Gould, "The Iron Lady with a Soft Centre." *The Standard*, January 13, 2001.
(3) "Anson Chan, the Best Bellwether in Hong Kong." *Business Week*, August, 1997.

Charlotte

Queen of kingdom of Jerusalem (Cyprus) (1458-1464)

She was the elder daughter of John II, who ruled the remnants of the kingdom of Jerusalem, located on Cyprus, from 1432 to 1458. She married Louis of Savoy. When her father died in 1458 she ruled alone for two years and then shared the rule with her younger brother, James II. In 1464 she was deposed, when James came of age. James died in 1473, and his wife Catherine Cornaro ruled from Italy until her abdication in 1489, but Charlotte continued to exercise authority until her death in 1487.

Suggested Reading:

(1) Langer, William L,. ed. *World History*. Boston: Houghton Mifflin, 1980. p. 279.

Cheng-Chun (Also Wang Cheng-Chun)

Empress, defacto co-ruler of China (48 B.C. to A.D. 13)

She was a member of the Wang family which had come to dominate the 200-year-old Han Dynasty. She was married to Emperor Yuan Ti and came to the throne in 48. BC. The couple had a son, Ch'eng Ti. When Yuan Ti died in 32 B.C., she was given the title of empress dowager, which carried much power and influence. She exercised her powers not only through her own office, but also through those of her relatives. Ch'eng Ti reigned from 32 to 7 B.C., during which time the empress dowager appointed four of her relatives as his regents. She had eight brothers or half-brothers, five of whom were appointed in succession to the equivalent of prime minister. She also bestowed titles of nobility upon a number of other relatives. She introduced changes in the state religious cults in an effort to secure blessings from various spiritual powers. Ch'eng Ti had several wives, and to please his favorite, he had his two sons by two other wives put to death. Therefore, he had no heir at the time of his own untimely death—probably murder—in 7 B.C. With her son's death, Cheng-Chun's influence waned, for Ai Ti, who succeeded him, was not of the Wang family. He tried to appease other families, primarily the Ting and Fu families, by assigning them court appointments against Cheng-Chun's judgment. The influence of the Wang family was thus diluted but was saved from further dilution by Ai Ti's death in 1 B.C. after only a five-year reign.

Following Ai Ti's death, the empress summoned her nephew Wang Mang to the capital. A young boy, Ping Ti, had been chosen to become emperor, and the empress dowager chose Wang Mang to serve as regent. Wang Mang was an astute politician and, when Ping died five years later—probably from poisoning—he selected, from more than 50 possible candidates, all legal heirs, a one-year-old baby so that he could be named acting emperor. Three years later he made himself emperor, declaring that Heaven had mandated that he establish a new dynasty, the Hsin Dynasty.

Empress Cheng-Chun died in A.D. 13, distressed to see what she believed to be the end of the Han Dynasty, but confident that the Wang family name and influence would live on.

Suggested Reading:

(1) Morton, W. Scott, *China: Its History and Culture*. New York: McGraw-Hill, 1982. p. 57.
(2) Reischauer, Edwin O. and John K. Fairbank, *East Asia: The Great Tradition*. Boston: Houghton Mifflin, 1960. p. 117.
(3) Latourette, Kenneth Scott, *The Chinese: Their History and Culture*. New York: Macmillan, 1934.

(4)   Langer, William L., ed., *World History*. Boston: Houghton Mifflin, 1940, 1980. p.146.

Chindók Yówang

Queen of the Kingdom of Silla (647-654)

Silla, established in the 3rd. or 4th century, was originally located in South Korea. By the 7th century, it encompassed the entire Korean peninsula. Chindók was a cousin of Queen Sondok (r. 632-647), who came to the throne upon Sondok's death to perpetuate the "hallowed-bone" lineage. This term refers to the institution which existed in Silla called "bone rank", or hereditary bloodlines, of which there were two. The "hallowed-bone" status was reserved for those in the royal house of Kim who possessed the qualifications to rule. The "true-bone" rank was held by members of the Kim royal house who lacked (originally) qualifications to rule.

Chindók continued her predecessor's alliance with China, whose influence was felt throughout the kingdom. During her reign, she adopted not only the literary culture of the T'ang Dynasty, but it clothing fashions as well. She also began to use the Chinese calendar. Her state minister was Chukjvrang, a member if the organization of warriors called Hwarang. Considered uniquely competent, he continued as state minister under the three kings who followed her.

Chindók was the last of the "hallowed-bone" rulers, and the last to preside over a divided Korean peninsula. Her successor, T'aejong, King Muyol Wang, of "true-bone" lineage, came to the throne after suppressing a rebellion of the head of the Council of Nobles and prevailing over his closest rival for kingship. During his reign, he consolidated the Korean peninsula under Silla's rule (668).

Suggested Reading:

(1)   Lee, Ki-baik. *A New History of Korea*. tr. Edward W. Wanger, with Edward J. Schulz. Cambridge, Massachusetts: Harvard University Press, 1984. pp. 49-50, 74, 390.

(2)   Lee, Peter, tr. "Samguk Sagi" 47:437-438. *Sourcebook of Korean Civilization VI*. New York: Columbia University Press, 1993. pp. 105-106.

Chinsong Yowang

Queen of Silla (887-897)

Silla, first established in South Korea in the 3rd or 4th Century, had, by Queen Chinsong's time, grown to encompass the entire Korean peninsula. Chinsong was the daughter of Hon'gang Wang (r. 875-886) and the sister of Chonggang Wang, who succeeded his father but died after ruling only one year. Chinsong presided over a Silla in decline. Her attempts to collect taxes were hampered by local warlords, who ignored her emissaries.

In addition, there was cautious growing unrest about the outdated entrenched class system. Confucianists made veiled criticisms of Silla's antiquated ranking system for royalty. One such protestor, Wang Ko-in, was arrested and charged with having criticized the government by using language with hidden meaning. Another, Ch'oe Ch'i-won, a reknown scholar, submitted a detailed proposal to the queen, suggesting changes aimed at dealing with problems besetting the realm. When his proposals were rejected out-of-hand, he went into self-imposed exile away from the capital.

Queen Chinsong is remembered for having commissioned the monk Taegu and the high courtier Wishong to compile an anthology of *hyangga*, a poetic genre with themes having to do with religious practices in general and Buddhism in particular. The resulting collection, "Samdae mok" ("Collection of Hyangga from the Three Periods of Silla History"), has not survived.

One of the disgruntled warlords managed a successful rebellion against Chinsong. She was succeeded by a cousin, Hyongong Wang (r. 897-912).

Suggested Reading:

(1) Lee, Ki-baik. *A New History of Korea*. tr. Edward W. Wagner, with Edward J. Schulz. Cambridge, Massachusetts: Harvard University Press, 1984. pp. 85-86, 94, 106, 391.

Ciller, Tansu

Prime Minister of Turkey (1993-1996)

She was born in Istanbul, Turkey in 1946. She studied economics at Roberts College (Bosphorus University in Istanbul) and the University of New Hampshire, received a PhD from the University of Connecticut, and did postdoctoral work at Yale. She married Ozer Ucuran Ciller and they had two children. She returned to Roberts College where she headed the department of economics from 1976 to 1979. She entered politics in 1990 and in 1991 became the minister of state for economy. In that post, she proposed privatizing mismanaged state enterprises, restricting public spending, and lowering interest rates. Whenever her reforms were criticized, she blamed her opponents within Prime Minister Demirel's administration. Her strong free-market approach gained her the support of the business sector. She served as minister of economy until 1993. With only three years of political experience, in a surprising upset she defeated two long-serving cabinet members at the True Path Party (DYP) convention June, 1993, and was appointed prime minister. As an English-speaking economist, a woman, and a devout secularist, she seemed the ideal person to counteract the Muslim fundamentalist movement and lead Turkey into the next century. However, in June 1996 the Welfare Party, an Islamic group, came into power in coalition with Ciller's party, forcing her resignation. In 1997 questions were raised as to the source of her wealth. Investigators examined her claim that she inherited more than $1 million in cash and gold from her mother, whom former neighbors described as a penniless pensioner, and also examined the 1992 purchase by Mr. Ciller's company of $1.5 million in New Hampshire properties. Five coalitions attempted to govern in the next two years, but Ciller maintained strong rightist support, preventing their success.

Suggested Reading:

(1) "Turkey's Reform-Minded Premier Faces Stiff Opposition" by Sami Kohen. *The Christian Science Monitor*. 17 June 1993: p. 7.
(2) Stephen Kinzer. "Once the Hope of Secular Turks, Ex-Leader is Now Widely Reviled". *New York Times* 6 April 1997: 2, 6.
(3) *Who's Who in the World*. New Providence: Marquis, 1997. p. 267.

Cixi (or Tz'u-hsi)

Empress of China (1862-1873, 1875-1889, 1898-1908)

She was born in Peking in 1835 and first came to court as a minor concubine to Emperor Xian Feng, who reigned from 1851 to 1862. In 1856 she bore his only son, Tong Zhi, and contrived, with the emperor's senior consort,

Tz'u-an, to become Tong's co-regent when Xian Feng died in 1862. Cixi immediately assumed the dominant role, setting the groundwork for a remarkable career which brought China under her control for 50 years. Ruthless, politically astute, and power hungry, she continued, even after her son attained his maturity, to wield her power over affairs of state. The young emperor was completely dominated by her. He led a dissolute life, which she probably encouraged so as to have a freer rein herself. He died at the age of 19, the victim of his own excesses.

Cixi engineered the ascension of her four-year-old nephew Guang Xu by adopting him and naming him heir. The tradition of ancestor worship dictated that the next emperor should be of the next generation, which her nephew quite obviously was not, but this fact did not deter Cixi. The two empresses again served as regents until Tz'u-an's sudden death in 1881, possibly by poisoning.

Prince Gong, the principal court official, had instituted some crucial governmental reform measures which Cixi sabotaged whenever she could. In 1884 she dismissed him in favor of Li Hongzhang, who would cooperate with her more fully.

She was particularly fond of the theater and attended often accompanied by one or both of her two favorite palace eunuchs who, with her patronage, soon became wealthy and powerful in their own rights, to the disgust of Prince Gong in particular.

In the late 1880s, urged on by her favorite eunuch and with the help of Li Hongzhang, Cixi appropriated funds from the navy to construct a magnificent summer palace northwest of Peking. There she retired, briefly, in 1889. The only new ship constructed during that time was a marble one which was placed at the edge of an ornamental lake. Thus the Chinese navy was ill-prepared when Japan struck Korea in 1894. China went to the aid of its ally but suffered a humiliating defeat. In 1895 Li Hongzhang was forced to sue for peace.

In 1898 the new young emperor Guang Xu was prevailed upon to institute the far-reaching Hundred Days of Reform. Opposition to the reform rallied around Cixi and in 1898 she came out of retirement as head of a military coup, had the emperor seized and six of the reformers put to death. She confined the emperor to his quarters for good and again assumed the regency. By 1900 the Boxer Rebellion had reached its peak, and when foreign troops invaded Peking, the court was forced to flee west to Xian. Before she left, out of pure spite, Cixi arranged for one of the emperor's favorites, the Pearl Concubine, to be drowned in a well. She was forced to accept heavy peace terms before she was allowed to return to Peking two years later. Although the emperor Guang was not allowed to participate in the government, Cixi continued to rule, belatedly attempting to implement some of the preposed reforms in an attempt to salvage a crumbling dynasty. The day before she died in 1908, she issued an order for Guang's poisoning and from her deathbed named three-year-old Pu Yi as the new emperor, unable to relinquish the reigns of power even at the end.

Suggested Reading:

(1)   Warner, Marina, *The Dragon Empress: Life and Times of Tz'u-hsi (1835-1908)*. New York: Atheneum Press, 1986.
(2)   Morton, W. Scott, *China: Its History and Culture*. New York: McGraw-Hill, 1982. pp. 168-175.

Cleopatra Thea

Ruler of Mesopotamia (125-120 B.C.)

She married Demetrius II Nicator who ruled the Seleucid Empire and the kingdom of Pergamum in Mesopotamia from 145 to 139 B.C., when he was captured by Mithridates by treachery. Cleopatra Thea and Demetrius had two sons, Seleucus V and Antiochus VIII Epiphanes Philomater Callinicus Grypus. She also had at least one son by Antiochus VII Euergetes Eusebes Soter Sidates, who ruled while Demetrius was held prisoner. That son was Antiochus IX Philopater Cyzicenus. In 129 B.C. Demetrius II was released and sent back to Syria, to rule for four more years, but he was murdered by Alexander Zabinas, a pretender to the throne. Cleopatra and her son Seleucus V assumed the throne, but she soon had him put to death. She ruled with her second son, Antiochus III Epiphanes, until her death in 120 B.C. Three years later, her youngest son Antiochis IX, forced his brother to abdicate, and he ruled briefly. Later the two half-brothers divided the realm.

Suggested Reading:

(1)   Peters, E. E. *The Harvest of Hellenism*. New York: Barnes & Noble Books, 1996. pp. 271-272, 274.

Constance

Co-ruler of Antioch (1130-1163)

Constance was born in 1127, the daughter of Bohemund II, ruler of Antioch (1126-1130) and Alice of Jerusalem. When her father died, Constance was only two years old. Instead of waiting for King Baldwin, Alice's father, to appoint a regent, Alice assumed the regency for Constance at once. But rumors spread that Alice planned to immure Constance in a convent so that she could rule, not as regent, but as reigning sovereign. When Baldwin arrived, he removed Alice from the regency and banished her to Lattakieh. He placed Constance under the guardianship of Joscelin. A year later Joscelin died, and Alice reasserted her claim to be her daughter's regent. Late in 1135 Alice, who had been allowed to return to Antioch and rule the city in her daughter's name but who did not have the regency, thought of a plan to enhance her own power. She offered the hand of the eight-year-old Constance to the Byzantine emperor's younger son, Manuel. Quickly the Patriarch Radulph notified King Fulk that he must find a husband for Constance. In 1136 Fulk decided on handsome 37-year-old Raymond of Poiters, son of Duke William IX of Aquitaine. In a disguise, Raymond reached Antioch, while Constance was kidnapped and brought to the church for a quick wedding, and while Alice, deceived into believing Raymond was coming to ask for her hand, waited at the palace. Constance, once married, was then considered a legitimate ruler. The couple had at least three children: Bohemund III, Maria, and Philippa. Raymond died in 1149 when Constance was only 22.

The throne was Constance's by right, but it was thought, since Moslems threatened and times were treacherous, that a man was needed at the head of government. Her elder son Bohemund III was only five. King Baldwin of Jerusalem, her nearest male relative, tried to find her a husband and offered her what he considered three suitable choices. Constance was not interested in any of them. Baldwin had no choice but to return to Jerusalem and leave Constance in charge of the government. Constance then sent word to Constantinople to ask the overlord, Emperor Manuel, to find her a suitable mate. Manuel chose his middle-aged brother-in-law John Roger, but Constance, whose first husband had been dashing and handsome, sent the older man packing. Her own choice was a young knight named Reynald of Chatillon. She married him in 1153, probably before she asked permission of King Baldwin. She did not ask Emperor Manuel's permission at all.

The choice was not a popular one, since it was generally believed that she had married beneath her station. Reynald, ambitious but lacking in funds, embarked on an unpopular expedition against Cyprus, while Constance stayed at home and bore at least one child, Agnes (who later married Bela III, king of Hungary). Reynald, after a humiliating groveling in the dirt at the feet of Emperor Manuel for his brash attack on Cyprus, never gained the prestige he longed for. In 1160 he made a raid into the Euphratesian valley and was taken prisoner by Nur el-Din. He was bound and sent on camelback to Aleppo, where he remained in gaol for 16 years, for neither King Baldwin nor Emperor Manuel was in any mood to ransom him.

Constance claimed the power to rule Antioch which was hers, but public opinion leaned toward her son Bohemund, age 15. King Baldwin came back to Antioch, declared Bohemund III king and appointed the Patriarch Aimery as regent. Constance was immensely displeased, and the overlord, Emperor Manuel, was displeased that Baldwin had taken the decision into his own hands without consulting him. Constance appealed to Emperor Manuel to restore her and in addition proposed her daughter Maria as wife for the widowed emperor. Baldwin, fearing a closer tie between Manuel and Antioch would diminish his own authority over Antioch, suggested Melisende of Triploi as Manuel's wife instead. Miffed by Baldwin's affrontery in appointing Constance's son as ruler and acting amid rumors of Melisende's illegitimacy, Emperor Manuel chose Constance's daughter Maria as his wife and sent his emmissaries to Antioch to establish Constance as ruler.

Again, when Bohemund III reached 18, he wanted to take over the throne from his mother. Constance felt the throne should be hers until she died. She appealed to General Constantine Coloman for military aid to protect herself from being bodily removed from office by her son. The rumors of her actions provoked a riot in Antioch. She was exiled and died soon after, ca. 1163.

Suggested Reading:

(1) Runciman, Steven A., *A History of the Crusades, v. 3: The Kingdom of Jerusalem*. Cambridge: Cambridge University Press, 1987. pp. 183-184, 198-200, 305-306, 330-333, 345-349, 352, 358-360.

(2) Egan, Edward et. al., *Kings, Rulers and Statesmen*. New York: Sterling Publishing, 1976. p. 16.

Section D

Dawlat Khatun

Ruler of Luristan (1316)

Luristan is located in southwestern Persia. Dawlat, who was married to 'Izz al-Din Muhammad, thirteenth sovereign of the Mongol Bani Khurshid dynasty, succeeded to the throne when he died in 1316. But she proved to be a poor administrator, "who was not successful in managing the affairs of state," and she abdicated after a short period of time in favor of her brother-in-law, 'Izz al-Din Hasan.

Suggested Reading:

(1)   Mernissi, Fatima. *The Forgotten Queens of Islam.* tr. Mary jo Lakeland. Minneapolis: University of Minnesota Press, 1993. pp. 104-105.

Deborah

Judge, ruler of Israel (c. 1224-1184 B.C.)

Deborah lived in a time when Israel was ruled by judges, (as was Sardinia 2500 years later), but the term carried a broader meaning than simply legal advisors. Judges were local and national leaders, chieftains and battle commanders as well. Deborah was also a prophetess. She was the wife of Lapidoth, about whom nothing is known. She lived in the hill country of Ephraim, on the road between Ramah and Beth-el. She obviously possessed wisdom, because she became a counselor to passersby. She was also a keeper of the tabernacle lamps. Eventually she was elevated to judgeship, Israel's only woman judge. Although Athaliah is mentioned in the Bible as a ruler of Judah, Deborah is the only woman listed in the Bible who was raised to political power by the common consent of the people. Her chief concern became dealing with marauders. For 20 years the king of neighboring Canaan, Jabin, had raided the camps of Israel using iron Chariots, pillaging homes and vineyards and raping and murdering women and children. (The Canaanites are believed to have been a Celtic tribe.) Deborah sent a message to neighboring Kedesh, where lived Barak, a man noted for his military skill. Jabin's army, under the command of Sisera, was said to possess 900 iron chariots, a formidable force for a people to face who still fought on foot, using arrows, slings, and swords. Deborah commanded Barak to raise an army and go to meet Sisera's forces near mount Tabor, which rises 1000 feet above the Plain of Jezreel. General Barak announced that unless Deborah accompanied him, he would not go. Deborah consented to accompany him, and they led the troops to the foot of mount Tabor, near the Kishon River. They arrived in a cloudburst of hail, sleet, and rain which changed the Kishon into a raging torrent. Sisera's iron chariots became mired in the mud, making the charioteers easy marks for the foot soldiers. Sisera escaped and fled on foot. A woman named Jael, wife of Heber the Kenite, saw him and invited him to hide in her tent. Since the Kenites were at peace with the Canaanites, this tent seemed to offer safe refuge. After Sisera fell asleep, Jael drove a tent stake through his temple. When Barak arrived, searching for the retreating general, he found him dead. Without a commander, the Canaanites were defeated and retreated in disarray. To celebrate the victory, Deborah and Barak sang a duet, the Ode of Deborah, one of the most ancient pieces of writing in the Old Testament, and certainly the lengthiest: it runs through 31 verses in the fifth chapter of Judges. It was also one of the earliest military songs in history. Her story and song are recorded in the fourth and fifth chapters of the book of Judges in the Old Testament.

Suggested Reading:

(1) Josephus Flavius, *Life and Works*. tr. William Whiston. Philadelphia: Winston Company, n.d. p. 150.

(2) Deen, Edith. *All the Women of the Bible*. New York: Harper and Brothers, 1955. pp. 69-74)

(* Alexander, David and Patricia Alexander, eds. *Eerdman's Handbook to the Bible*. Berkhamsted, Herts, England: Lion Publishing Co., 1973. pp. 219-222.

(3) Packer, J. I. et. al. *The Bible Almanac*. Nashville: Thomas Nelson, 1980. pp. 44-52, 204, 427, 429.

Didda

Queen, regent, later sole ruler of Kashmir (980-1003)

The *damaras*, or feudal landlords, having defeated the powerful Tantrins, had in turn become so powerful that they had been a threat to several rulers. Didda was the daughter of Simharaja of Lohara. She.was married to King Kshemagupta, ruler of Kashmir. The couple had at least one son, Abhimanyu, who was underaged when his father died in 980 A.D. When Queen Didda assumed the regency for her son, the landlords saw opportunity to refuse payment of tribute and to assert their independence. The era was rife with feudatories vying for power and Turks threatening the borders. In spite of much opposition, Queen Didda, who was not only comely and clever, but also aggressive and ruthless, ably conducted affairs of state. After the death of her son, she ruled in her own right until 1003, when she placed Samgramaraja, her brother's son, on the throne, thus beginning the Lohara dynasty.

Suggested Reading:

(1) Thapar, Romila. *A History of India*. London: Penguin Books, 1987. vol. 1, p. 226.

Durgavati (or Durgawati)

Rani, queen of Gondwana (c. 1545-1564)

Gondwana (also called Garha-Kalanga), outside of the southern boundary of the Indian Mughal Empire at the time, had been ruled by independent and tributary chiefs. Fed by the Mahandi River, Gondwana lay on the east-central side of India north of the Deccan. The Gonds were a group of Dravidian tribes, aboriginal (pre-Aryan) people of India. To this day the Raj Gonds still remain outside the Hindu caste system, neither acknowledging the superiority of Brahmins nor being bound by Hindu rules. Queen Durgavati was a member of the Gond Chandels, the remnants of which are now in Bundelkhand in north central India. She was the daughter of Kirat Rai, chandella king of Mahoba and Kalanjar, who was king when Sher Shah besieged the fort in 1545. She married Raja Dalpat Sa Garha Mandala of Gondwana, ca. 1545, but was soon left a widow to rule the kingdom in behalf of her infant son, Bir Narayan. With magnificent courage she maintained its sovereignty for the better part of two decades in the face of repeated threats of both Baj Bahador of Malwa and the Afghans of Bengal. Historians have termed her one of the most female leaders in Indian history. In 1564 the Moghul Akbar, intent upon enlarging his empire, sent general Asaf Khan with an army of 50,000 men to make an unprovoked invasion of Gondwana. Queen Durgavati and her son, now about 18, met the Moghul army with a seasoned force of their own at a bloody two-day pitched battle at Narhi. On the second day, her son was wounded and had to be escorted to safety by a large contingent of the Rani's troops. Withdrawal of the escort so weakened her army that it was quickly overpowered. Durgavati, wounded by two arrows, stabbed herself to death to escape the disgrace of capture. Akbar then annexed her kingdom

Suggested Reading:

(1) Bhahacharya, Sachchinananda. *A Dictionary of Indian History*. New York: George Braziller, 1967. pp. 321-322.
(2) Gasciogne, Bamber. *The Great Moghuls*. New York: Dorset Press, 1971. p. 88.
(3) Langer, William L., ed. *World History*. Boston: Houghton Mifflin, 1940, 1980. pp. 356-358, 569.

Section E

Ebuskun

Khatun, regent of Turkestan (1242-1246)

She was the wife of Mutugen, eldest son of Jagatai. Jagatai was one of the four sons of Jenghiz-khan who shared in their father's empire, and Mutugen would then inherit the land of Jagatai when he died. However, Mutugen preceded his father; he was killed in 1221 at the siege of Bamian, leaving his wife Ebuskun and their son Qara-Hulagu. So upon Jagatai's death in 1242, the throne went to his grandson, Qara-Hulagu, under the regency of his mother. Ebuskun served as regent for four years, when the new grand khan Guyuk intervened and replaced Qara-Hulago with a personal friend, Jagatai's younger brother, Prince Yissu-Mangu (Mongka).

Notes;

(1) Grousset, René, *The Empire of the Steppes: A History of Central Asia.* tr. Naomi Walford. New Brunswick: Rutgers University Press, 1970. p. 329.

Erato

Queen of the ancient Kingdom of Armenia (?-A.D.14)

Erato was the last ruler of the House of Artashes (Artaxias). In the first century B.C. Tigranes I, a descendant of the founder Artaxias, had deposed Artanes, the last king of Armenia Minor, and united the two countries under his rule. In 69 B.C. he was defeated by Lucullus and stripped of his other professions such as Syria but allowed to continue to rule over Armenia as a vassal of Rome. But after the first year, Artaxias paid tribute to no one, ruling for 29 years and outlasting his overlord Antiochus by five years. Technically,

Armenia remained at war with Rome, but in fact Armenia appeared to be a buffer state between the two greater warring factions of Rome and Parthia. However, when Tigranes' fourth-born son Artavsd-Artavasdes II came to the throne (55 B.C.), Armenia still managed to thrive as an independent state. Artavsd, although outwardly a Parthian ally since 53 B.C., appeared to submit when Mark Antony appeared on the scene. He guided Antony to his battle with Parthia, which Antony lost. Pretending friendship, Antony invited Artavsd and his family to his tent, where he seized them and took them off to Alexandria to be paraded as captors and to be turned over to Cleopatra. She tortured them unmercifully in an attempt to find the whereabouts of the Armenian crown jewels. But the entire family died in 33 B.C., with the exception of Artavsd's eldest son Artashes, who only two years later recaptured the Armenian throne and had all the Roman traders killed. Armenian disobedience continued despite Roman intimidation under Queen Erato, presumably Artashes' widow, who was herself twice dethroned by the Romans, the second time in A.D. 14.

Suggested Reading:

(1) Chahin, M. *The Kingdom of Armenia*. New York: Dorset Press, 1987, 1991, p. 245.

Eschiva of Ibelin, Lady

Queen of Beirut (1282-ca.1284)

She was the younger daughter of John II of Beirut and Alice de la Roche of Athens. Her older sister Isabella became queen of Beirut following their father's death in 1264. Eschiva married Humphrey of Montfort, younger son of Philip of Montfort, lord of Toron and Tyre. The couple had a son, Roupen. When her sister Isabella died in 1282, the fief of Beirut passed to Eschiva. When Humphrey's brother John of Montfort died ca. 1283 leaving no issue, Humphrey inherited Tyre. But he died ca. 1284, so Tyre then went to John's widow, Margaret. After a suitable interval, Eschiva was married (by King Hugh III of Cyprus and Jerusalem) to King Hugh's youngest son, Guy. When the Mameluk sultan Qalawun was preparing to attack those of the Franks who were not protected by the truce of 1283, Eschiva hastened to ask him for a truce, which was granted. (Mameluks were former slaves from Russia and Central Asia who founded a dynasty in Egypt and Syria in

1250 that lasted almost 300 years. Mameluks made up an important part of Islamic armies from 833 forward.) However, in 1291, the truce did not keep the Mameluks under a later leader, Shujai, from tearing down, not only the walls of Beirut, but the Castle of the Ibelins as well, and turning the cathedral into a mosque.

Suggested Reading:

(1) Runciman, Steven, *A History of the Crusades*, 3 vols. Cambridge: Cambridge University Press, 1952, 1987. Vol. 3, pp. 329, 343, 393-395, 422.

Eudocia Macrembolitissa

Empress, regent of the Byzantine Empire (1067), co-ruler (1071)

She was born in 1021, the daughter of John Macrembolites. She was also the niece of the patriarch of Constantinople, Michael Cerularius. She married Emperor Constantine X Ducas. They had three sons, Michael VII, Andronicus and Constantine, and two daughters, Zoe and Theodora Anna (also called Arete). When Constantine died in 1067, by Michael Psellus' own account, Eudocia succeeded him as supreme ruler in accordance to the wishes of her late husband. She assumed control of the administration in person, instructing her two sons (Andronicus had died earlier) in the nature of political affairs. Psellus said, "I do not know whether any other woman ever set such an example of wisdom or lived a life to hers up to this point." After a series of set-backs from the Turks who threatened along the frontier, Eudocia was convinced of the need for a strong military government. Psellus recalled praying aloud that she might enjoy power as long as she lived and Eudocia's calling the prayer a curse: "I hope it will not be my fate to enjoy power so long that I die an empress," she told him. Despite the opposition of her advisers, Psellus and Caesar John, her brother-in-law, Eudocia married General Romanus IV Diogenes, who became ruler in 1068. He was an unpopular choice with the people. He fought the Turks with valor but was defeated in 1071 and taken prisoner. Again the throne was vacant. Some preferred that Michael succeed his step-father, while others favored the complete restoration of Eudocia's rule to the exclusion of her sons. It was Psellus' suggestion that Eudocia and her son Michael assume joint and equal rule, which they did for a while. Meanwhile, Romanus concluded a treaty with the Turks that freed him if he paid an annual tribute to them. Romanus, intent on regaining the throne, wrote to Eudocia that he was free and wished to return. Eudocia, caught in an embarrassing situation, did not know what to do. Michael did not want to lose his reign, so he decided to cut himself off from his mother and assume sole control. His advisors decreed that Eudocia should leave the city and live in a convent which she herself had founded. Michael refused to ratify such a decree. But with Romanus threatening, a constant stream of propaganda was directed against Eudocia. It was feared that she would allow Romanus to return and assume the throne. At length a second decree was issued stating that she must take the veil of a nun. In 1071 she was immured in a nunnery and Michael was declared sole ruler. When Romanus returned, before he ever reached Constantinople, he was set upon by agents of Psellus and his eyes were put out with hot irons. He died soon after, in 1072, as a result of his horrible injuries. Eudocia died in the nunnery in 1096, having been granted her wish not to die an empress.

Suggested Reading:

(1) Ostrogorsky, George, *History of the Byzantine State*. New Brunswick: Rutgers University Press, 1969. pp. 344-345.

(2) Psellus, Michael, *Fourteen Byzantine Rulers*. tr. E. R. A. Sewter. Harmondsworth, Middlesex: Penguin Books, 1982. pp. 339-360 *passim*.

Eudoxia (or Eudocia)

Augusta, defacto co-ruler of Eastern Roman Empire (A.D. 400-404)

She was the daughter of a mercenary general, the Frankish chief Bauto. In 395 she married Arcadus, emperor of the Byzantine Empire from 383 to 408. The marriage was engineered by a corrupt court eunuch Eutropius in an effort to weaken the status of a political rival. Eudoxia soon found that she was married to a weak and ineffectual ruler who let Eutropius dominate him. In time she decided to join Eutropius' opposition in order to bring about his ouster (399). Eudoxia and Arcadus had four children: Theodocius II, who, like his father, was weak; Pulcheria, who, like her mother, was strong; and two other daughters. Despite the fact that she was frequently pregnant, Eudoxia exercised enormous influence over her husband's affairs. The period of her greatest influence dates from her designation as Augusta in January, A.D. 400. The patriarch of Constantinople, John Chrysotom, openly criticized her and her court and publicly reproached her and her court. She retaliated, after several bitter quarrels, by appealing to a rival archbishop for help in expelling him from his see (403) and permanently exiling him (404). She died shortly afterward of a miscarriage (A.D. 404).

Suggested Reading:

(1) Previté-Orton, C. W., *The Shorter Cambridge Medieval History*. 2 vols. Cambridge: Cambridge University Press, 1952, 1982. vol. 1, pp. 77-83.
(2) Ostrogorsky, George, *History of the Byzantine State*. New Brunswick: Rutgers University Press, 1969. p. 54.
(3) Langer, William L., ed., *World History* Boston: Houghton Mifflin Company, 1940. p. 683.

Euphrosyne

Empress, defacto co-ruler of the Byzantine Empire (1195-1203)

She was the wife of Byzantine Emperor Alexius III Angelus, who wanted to rule so badly that he blinded and deposed his own brother in 1195. Alexius, a weakling with a lust for power, adopted the name Comnenus after the great Comneni emperors, because he thought Angelus didn't sound distinguished enough. The couple had three children: Irene, whose grandson became Michael VIII Palaeologus; Anna, whose husband became Throdore I Lascaris; and Eudocia, or Eudokia, whose second husband became Alexius IV. Alexius III busied himself with diplomatic affairs, at which he showed some aptitude, but home affairs were left to Euphrosyne. She proved to be extravagant and as corrupt as her brother-in-law Isaac had been.

Suggested Reading:

(1) Vasiliev, A. A., *History of the Byzantine Empire*. Madison: University of Wisconsin Press, 1952. pp. 440-445, 487.
(2) Ostrogorsky, George, *History of the Byzantine State*. New Brunswick: Rutgers University Press, 1969. pp. 408, 410-416, 577.
(3) Previté-Orton, C. W., *The Shorter Cambridge Medieval History*, 2 vols. Cambridge: Cambridge University Press, 1952, 1982. vol. 2, p. 112.

Section F

Fatima

Sultana, ruler of the Maldive Islands (1383-1388)

The Maldive Islands are located in the Indian Ocean, southwest of India's southern tip. When Islam was adopted in the 12th Century, the islands begame a sultinate. For forty years, Muslim women ruled the Maldive Islands. Fatima's aunt, Sultana Rehendi Kabadi Kilege, called Khadija, had begun the dynasty, ruling from 1347 to 1379. The Muslim traveler Ibn Battuta spent a long period in Queen Khadija's kingdom and even married four times while there, one of them being Sultana Khadija's step-mother. He describes the kingdom in his own work, called the *Rihla* or *Rehla*.

Fatima was the daughter of Khadija's sister, Sultana Myriam, who had succeeded upon Khadija's death and reigned from 1379 to 1383. Upon her mother's death, Fatima ascended the throne and ruled until her death in 1388.

Suggested Reading:

(1) Dunn, Ross E., *The Adventures of Ibn Battuta*. Berkeley: University of California Press, 1986. pp. 230-235, 245.
(2) Mernissi, Fatima, *The Forgotten Queens of Islam*. tr. Mary Jo Lakeland. Minneapolis: University of Minnesota Press, 1993. p. 108.

Section G

Gandhi, Indira

Prime minister of India (1966-1977) and (1980-1984)

Born Priyadarshini Nehru in 1917, she was the only child of Jawaharlal Nehru, India's first prime minister, and his wife Kamala. As leaders of the movement for India's independence, her parents were frequently imprisoned by the British during her childhood, but Nehru wrote his daughter many letters which inspired her to follow in his footsteps. As a girl of 12, she organized the Monkey Brigade, an association of thousands of children who assisted the National Congress Party. Sporadically she attended boarding schools in India and Switzerland, then college in West Bengal and Oxford. At 21 she joined the National Congress Party and became actively involved in the revolution. Against her father's advice, she married a childhood friend, Feroze Gandhi, lawyer, economist and member of Parliament—and Parsi. The mixed marriage raised a public fruor. The couple had two sons, Rajiv and Sanjay, in the ten years before they separated. In 1947 India was free to choose her own leader, and Nehru was the obvious choice. Since his wife had died in 1936, his daughter Indira served as "First Lady." In 1959 she was elected president of the Congress Party, the second highest political position in India. In 1960 her husband died, but she never remarried. Her father died in 1964. His successor Lal Badahur Shastri brought her into his cabinet as minister of information and broadcasting. In 1966 Shastra died and Gandhi was elected prime minister, the first woman ever to lead a democracy, the world's largest democracy. In the 1967 election, her win was less than an absolute majority and she had to accept a right wing deputy prime minister. In 1971 India annexed the kingdom of Sikkim, exploded its first nuclear device and put a satelite into orbit. Gandhi then called for another election and won handily, running on the slogan, "Abolish poverty." Her party won two-thirds of the seats in parliament. At that point she was probably the most popular leader in the world. U.S. Secretary of State Henry

Kissinger said of her at that time, "The lady is cold-blooded and tough", although Indians called her *Mataji,* "respected mother." However, she could not both abolish poverty and please the rich, to whom she owed her power. A voluntary sterilization program she had instituted was attacked by her right wing opponents as being a compulsory program. In 1975, amid riots and protests, she declared a state of emergency and severely limited personal freedoms with new laws and with prison terms for political opponents. In effect, she suspended the democratic process in which she professed to believe. Two years later, having restored democratic practices, she was voted out of office and replaced by the right wing Janata party. She was charged with abuse of office by the new administration and even spent a week in jail. In December of 1979 she was reelected by a large plurality with the help of her younger son Sanjay, who was her heir-designate. When he died in a plane crash in 1960, there was speculation about the future of the Congress Party and Indira's rule, but her popular support remained strong for a long time. She began to groom her other son, Rajiv, to be her successor. In 1983 she told the World Energy Conference, "We are opposed to nuclear weapons and do not have any," but that India was developing a nuclear program for peaceful purposes. Gandhi could not begin to solve India's economic, social, religious, linguistic and cultural problems and contend with a devastating drought that affected 2.7 million Indians. She said in a 1982 interview, "Can democracy solve such vast problems, especially when we have this constant opposition in the way? People are hitting at our feet and still saying, 'You must go further, you must go faster.' But we believe in democracy; we were brought up with those ideals. And in India we simply cannot have another way . . . Only a democracy will allow our great diversity . . . . The only danger to democracy is if the people feel it is not solving their problems." Her chief detractors were the right wing and the two Communist parties. In 1984, after she had again placed restraints on personal freedoms and ordered a raid on a Sikh temple, she was assassinated. Her son Rajiv Gandhi became the new prime minister of India. In her autobiography, Indira Gandhi, the most powerful woman India has ever known, wrote simply, "To a woman, motherhood is the highest fulfilment."

Suggested Reading:

(1) Bhatin, Krishan, *A Biography of Prime Minister Gandhi.* New York: Praeger, 1974.
(2) Gandhi, Indira, *My Truth.* New York: Grove Press, 1980.

(3) Szulc, Tad, "What Indira Gandhi Wants You To Know". *Parade* 25 July 1982. pp. 6-8.
(4) "Gandhi on Atomic Power". *Houston Post*. 18 September 1983. p. A 3.
(5) "Clouds Over India Dim Gandhi's Global Star". *U.S. News & World Report*. 21 March 1983.
(6) Tefft, Sheila, "Gandhi Murder Inquiry Released". *Christian Science Monitor*. 29 March 1989. p. 4.

Gandhi, Sonia

Leader of India's Congress Party, Elected Prime Minister (2004)

Sonia was born Sonia Maino on December 9, 1940 in Ovassanjo, Italy, to Paola and Stafaco Maino, a building contractor. She and her two sisters were raised and educated Roman Catholic. In the 1960s, Sonia went to Cambridge to study English. There she met the grandson of India's first Prime Minister Jawarhlal Nehru, and son of former Prime Minister Indira Gandhi, Rajiv Gandhi, who had come to Cambridge to study mechanical engineering at Trinity College. The couple married in 1968 and returned to India, where Sonia immersed herself in Indian culture and eventually became a naturalized citizen (1983). They had two children: son Rahul, born ca. 1971, and daughter Priyanka, born ca. 1972. Rajiv joined the New Delhi flying club and became a pilot for Indian Airlines. Sonia developed a close relationship with her mother-in-law, Prime Minisdter Indira Gandhi, becoming a sort of personal assistant, often traveling with her on business. She professed to be glad that her husband had chosen not to enter politics.

However, in 1980 Rajiv's brother Sanjay, who had chosen the political path, died in a plane crash. Out of a sense of duty to carry on the family name in India's political history, Rajiv entered the political arena, and soon thereafter won his brother's parliamentary seat. Sonia abandoned wearing Western designer clothes in favor of saris; and eschewed beef barbecues and disco music in an effort to become a more traditional Hindu wife. In 1984 when Indira Gandhi was shot in the garden of her New Delhi residence by her own Sikh security guards, Sonia was one of the first people on the scene and she cradled the dying prime minister in her lap as they sped to the hospital.

In an emergency session, Rajiv was elevated to fill his mother's position as Prime Minister, an office he held until 1989, when when his party was defeated following a scandal involving kickbacks deposited into Swiss bank accounts as part of a weapons procurement deal. Rajiv Gandhi swore his family played no role in the operation. In 1991, as Rajiv Gandhi was campaigning to win back the prime minister's post, he was killed by a suicide bomber.

As the last surviving member of India's most famous political family which had furnished Prime Ministers for 37 of the country's first 47 years, Sonia was urged to take up her husband's mantle as leader of the Congress Party, but she refused. Then, in December 1997, Sonia Gandhi had a change of heart. She announced her intention to campaign on behalf of the Congress Party, hoping to revive its image and establish its position as a favorable alternative to the right—wing Hindu—nationalist Bharatiya Janata Party (BJP). The Gandhi family had represented the Congress Party for years—it was the party the family lived and died for and Sonia Gandhi could not stand to see it falling apart. In her first campaign speech, Sonia Gandhi explained her change of heart. Her words are found in Paul Dettman's book *India Changes Course:* "In the years since Rajiv Gandhi left us, I had chosen to remain a private person and live a life away from the political arena. My grief and loss have been deeply personal. But a time has come when I feel compelled to put aside my own inclinations and step forward. The tradition of duty before personal considerations has been the deepest conviction of the family to which I belong."

By the spring of 1998, Sonia Gandhi had risen to become president of the Congress Party. She told crowds the Congress Party would restore the ideal of secularism to government. She lured Muslim voters to the party's ranks. The opposition continued to make her foreignness an issue; however, her foreign-born status did not seem to hurt the party. People flocked to see the Italian woman wearing an Indian sari who spoke Hindi with a foreign accent. She drew crowds of more than 200,000 people, boosting the morale of party members and injecting enthusiasm into their campaigns. In 1999 she won a seat in parliament.

As the 2004 election approached, Sonia Gandhi was still president of the Congress Party and still its most outgoing speaker. Many assumed that if her party won the election, she would become prime minister, though she never campaigned as a candidate. The campaign turned nasty. Once again, the Bharatiya Janata Party (BJP) used Sonia Gandhi's birthplace as a point of contention. She had been an Indian citizen for 20 years, yet opposition leaders questioned her Indian loyalty. Her party did indeed win the election, but Sonia Gandhi stunned supporters by announcing that her "inner voice" had urged her to turn down the post of prime minister.

Instead, she nominated former finance minister Manmohan Singh for the post. Her fear was that the question of her nationality would tear apart the nation the Gandhi family had sacrificed so much for. The opposition BJP politicians, declaring that having a foreign-born woman as Prime Minister would constitute a threat to national security, threatened to walk out of parliament and boycott her swearing-in ceremony if Sonia Gandhi became Prime Minister.

After Singh was sworn in, opposition leaders charged that Sonia Gandhi was still calling the shots, even though she was not prime minister. Maneka Gandhi, widow of Sanjay Gandhi and a parliament member of the right-wing opposition BJP, said that by stepping down Sonia Gandhi had outsmarted her opponents. "I think she's the power in front of the throne," Maneka Gandhi told the *Los Angeles Times*. "I don't think she makes any bones about the fact that she has avoided the flak that would have gone with the position, but she has no intention of relinquishing any of the power of the position."

Others speculate that Sonia Gandhi was trying to hold the door open for her son, Rahul Gandhi, to become prime minister. As of 2004, he was representing Amethi in parliament, the same seat his father, mother and uncle once held. Though she turned down the post of Prime Minister, Sonia Gandhi remained president of the Congress Party, thus in a position to groom her son, Rahul Gandhi, to become Prime Minister, continuing the Gandhi family's dynasty.

Suggested Reading:

(1) Dettman, Paul R., *India Changes Course: Golden Jubilee to Millennium,* Praeger, 2001.

(2) Mehta, Ved, *Rajiv Gandhi and Rama's Kingdom,* Yale University Press, 1994.

(3) *Commonweal,* June 18, 2004.

(4) *Far Eastern Economic Review,* February 16, 1995.

(5) *Los Angeles Times,* June 22, 2004.

(6) *Ms.,* Fall 2004.

(7) *National Review,* June 24, 2004.

(8) *New York Times,* February 6, 1998.

(9) *Time,* June 3, 1991.

(10) *"Sonia Gandhi: Indian National Congress Party Chairman,"* Sonia Gandhi website, *http://www.soniagandhi.org/* December 20, 2004.

Gemmei-tennō

Empress of Japan (708-714)

Originally named Abe, she was born in A.D. 662, the daughter of Emperor Tenchi, who ruled Japan from 662 to 673. Following his abdication in 673, two other rulers, his brother Temmu (673-686) and Tenchi's daughter and Temmu's consort Jitō (687-696), followed before Gemmei's son Mommu, Jitō's nephew, became emperor. He had been born in 682 and was 20 years old when he ascended to the imperial throne. He ruled for 11 years. At his death, Abe became Empress Gemmei-tennō at the age of 46. She proved to be an exceptionally able ruler. It is due to her foresight that the early traditions of Japan have survived. At her instruction, the *Kojiki* (712) and the *Fudoki* (713) were written to preserve the ancient traditions. In keeping with the ancient belief that a dwelling place was polluted by death, it was customary upon the demise of a sovereign for the successor to move into a new palace. Emperor Tenchi had enacted an edict to regulate the capital in 646, but the edict was not carried out until 710, when Empress Gemmei moved the court from Asuka to Nara, or Heijo, as it was called then, in the province of Yamato in central Japan. She also ordered the coinage of the first copper money. She abdicated in 714 in favor of her daughter, Hitaka (Genshō-tennō). She died in A.D. 723 at the age of 61.

Suggested Reading:

(1) Papinot, E., *Historical and Geological Dictionary of Japan*. Rutland, VT: Charles E. Tuttle Company, 1972. p. 115.
(2) Sansom, George, *A History of Japan to 1334*. Stanford: Stanford University Press, 1958. p. 82.
(3) Reischauer, Edwin O., *East Asia: The Great Tradition*. Boston: Houghton Mifflin, 1960. p. 480.

Genshō-tennō

Empress of Japan (715-723)

She was born Princess Hitaka in 779, the daughter of Empress Gemmei-tennō and the older sister of Emperor Mommu. She encouraged the work of her mother by encouraging the arts, letters, science and agriculture. The

Nihongi, chronicles of Japan to the year A.D. 697, were completed and published during her reign (720). When her nephew Shōmu reached age 25, she abdicated, at the age of 45, in favor of him. She died in 748 at the age of 69.

Suggested Reading:

(1) Papinot, E., *Historical and Geographical Diction of Japan*. Rutland, VT: Charles E. Tuttle Company, 1972. p. 117.

Go-Sakuramachi-tennō

Empress of Japan (1763-1770)

She was born Princess Toshi-ko in 1741, the daughter of Emperor Sakuramachi-tennō, who after a reign of 11 years during which the Shōgun Yoshemune had held actual power, had abdicated in favor of his 11-year-old son Momosono. During the boy's reign, power rested with the Shōgun Ieshige. When her brother died in 1763, Go-Sakuramachi-tennō, two years his junior, succeeded to the ceremonial position and permitted Ieshige to continue his government. She abdicated at the age of 30 in favor of her nephew Hidehito. She died in 1814 at the age of 73.

Suggested Reading:

(1) Papinot, E., *Historical and Geographical Diction of Japan*. Rutland, VT: Charles E. Tuttle Company, 1972. pp. 127, 399, 535.

Section H

Hasina Wazed, Sheikh

Prime Minister of Bangladesh (1996-2001)

Hasina was born September 28, 1947 in Gopalganj, East Bengal, the eldest of five children of Sheikh Mujibur Rahman, Bangladesh's first president. In the 1960s she studied at Government Intermediate College, where she was vice president of the College Students Union (1966-1967). She was a student activist at Eden College. Later she attended Dhaka University, where she was a member of the Chhatra League, the student wing of the Awami League, one of Bangladesh's major political parties, and secretary of the Rokeya Hall unit. However, she was mostly under the shadow of her father, mother and three brothers were killed in a coupd'état on August 15, 1975, while she and her sister Sheikh Rehana were on a good will mission to West Germany. Hasina sought refuge in the United Kingdom and later, in India. She was exiled to New Delhi, India, until May 17, 1981, when she was allowed to return to Bangladesh.

During her self-exile in India, Sheikh Hasina was elected the president of Bangladesh Awami League, a position she holds to the present. After she returned to the country, the erstwhile president Ziaur Rahman was assassinated in yet another coup in May, 1981. The following year, General Hossain Mohammad Ershad gained power through a bloodless coup and declared martial law.

In 1983, Hasina formed the 15-party alliance to launch a movement to oust Ershad from power. She was in and out of prison throughout the 80's. Her party along with the Bangladesh Nationalist Party led by Khaleda Zia, widow of slain president Zia, were instrumental in the movement against the military rule. In 1984, Hasina was put under house arrest in February and again in November. In March 1985, she was put under house arrest for three months at a stretch.

In 1990, Hasina's 8 party alliance was instrumental along with another BNP-led alliance in finally overthrowing the Ershad regime.

Interestingly, her opponent was the leftist student leader Motiya Chowdhury, who eventually joined Awami League and became a minister in Hasina's cabinet.

During the liberation war in 1971, Hasina, then a young mother, was under house arrest with her mother, brothers, sister and her son. Sheikh Mujibur Rahman was imprisoned in West Pakistan During this period. After liberation, Hasina's involvement in politics was minimal as Sheikh Kamal, her brother, was touted as Mujib's successor.

Suggested Reading:

(1) Ahmed, Moudud. *Democracy and the Challenge of Development: Study of Politics and Military* Intervention *in Bangladesh*. New Delhi: Vikas, 1995.
Baxter, Craig. *Bangladesh from a Nation to a State*. Boulder, CO: Westview, 1997.

Hazrat Mahal, Begam

Regent of Oudh (1856-1858)

Until 1856 the kingdom of Oudh in northern India, with its capital of Lucknow, had been ruled by a nominally independent king. But the exile of King Wajid Ali Shah and the annexation in 1856 of his kingdom were two of the causes of the Sepoy War or Indian Mutiny of 1857. Hazrat Mahal, a concubine of the harem, was the only one in the harem willing to commit herself to the rebellion. Raja Jai Lal visited her and made a bargain: he would present her young son, Birjis Qadr, to the army as the son and rightful heir of the deposed king if she, as new queen regent, would appoint him as military leader. Hazrat Mahal agreed, although it was common gossip in Lucknow that the boy was really the son of her paramour, Mammu Khan. Birgis Qadr was accepted by the army and enthroned in 1857. Hazrat Mahal appointed her lover chief of the high court. The new queen fought valiantly against the British, and worked hard to retain the leadership of the revolt by fiery personal speeches to the troops, but during the final assault by the British in 1858, she could sense that she was losing control. People were leaving Lucknow in search of safety. She considered suing for a compromise peace, but the British were having none. As the British advanced on Lucknow, the rebels escaped; Hazrat Mahal, her ailing son, and her court went northeast to Bithavli, where they attempted to regroup for a pitched defense. The British demanded surrender, but Hazrat and her party refused and tried to escape to Nepal. Among her party were the Rani of Tulsipur, Raja of Gonda, and Beni Madho. By that time Hazrat had come to realize that she and her son had been virtual prisoners of the sepoys; she berated them, saying they had made goats of her and her son, although the queen had never sought their support. The British tried to prevent the retreat of the rebels. Many were killed or captured. Hazrat and her party did escape capture but it was presumed that they all died of exposure or disease soon after. Reporters at the time likened her to Penthesilea, queen of the Amazons, who in post-Homeric legends fought for Troy; hence, a strong commanding woman.

Suggested Reading:

(1) Pemble, John, *The Raj, the Indian Mutiny and the Kingdom of Oudh, 1801-1859.* Rutherford, NJ: Farleigh Dickinson University Press, 1977. pp. 4, 210-211, 213, 222-223, 229, 234, 245-247.

Helen Glinski

See Yelena Glinskaya

Helena Lecapena

Co-ruler of Eastern Roman Empire (945-959)

She was the daughter of the regent of the Roman Empire, Romanus Lecapenus. In 919 she married the young Emperor Constantine VII Porphyrogenitus, who wore the crown from 913 to 959, and who raised her father to the rank of caesar and the status of co-emperor of the Eastern Roman Empire. The father-in-law dominated Constantine and became one of the most important rulers in Byzantine history. But in 944, as he began to age noticeably, two of his sons, Helena's brothers, anxious that Constantine VII not gain control upon Romanus' death, staged a *coup d'etat* and sent their father to a monastary. However, the *coup* did not have popular support. The brothers were executed and Constantine VII was left in reluctant control of his throne. Helena and Constantine had at least six children, one of whom was Romanus II, who became emperor of the Eastern Empire from 959 to 963, and another of whom was Theodora, who married John I Tzimisces, emperor of the Western Empire from 969 to 976. Constantine VII, a scholarly man who was more interested in intellectual pursuits, did not come into his full rights as sole ruler until he was nearly 40 (945). By that time he had worn the crown for 33 years, most of his life. During the period of his sole rule, he was most apt to follow the lead of Helena, who had inherited her father's strong leadership abilities. Of great historical importance was the visit of the Russian Princess Olga, who came to Constantinople to cement Byzantine and Russian relations. As a measure of her esteem, Olga, a Christian, took at her baptism the name of the Byzantine Empress Helena. This honor by the regent of the Kievan state and her stay with Helena and Constantine at the Imperial Palace at Constantinople ushered in a new era between the two nations and gave fresh impetus to the missionaries of the Byzantine church in Russia. In 959 Constantine VII died and their son Romanus assumed the throne. He had married the beautiful and ambitious Theophano and was completely under her spell. To please Theophano, Helena had to retire from court, and her five daughters were forcibly removed to convents.

Suggested Reading:

(1) Psellus, Michael, *Fourteen Byzantine Rulers*. tr. E. R. A. Sewter. Harmondsworth, Middlesex: Penguin Books, 1982. pp. 63, 308.

(2) Ostrogorsky, George, *History of the Byzantine State*. New Brunswick: Rutgers University Press, 1969. pp. 262, 264, 279, 283-284.

Himiko

See Pimiku

Hind al-Hirah

Queen, regent of the kingdom of Lakhm in Syrian Desert (554-?)

She was a Christian princess of either Ghassan or Kindah who married Mundhir, al Mundhir III, whose mother was Mariyah or Mawiya. Al

Mundhir III, the most illustrious ruler of the Lakhmids, ruled ca. A.D. 503 to 554. He raided Byzantine Syria and challenged the kingdom of Ghassan, possibly the homeland of Queen Hind. They had a son, Amr ibn-Hind, who inherited the throne in A.D. 554 when his father died and ruled until A.D. 569. Queen Hind, an independent and resourceful queen, served as regent for her son. Although she has been described bloodthirsty, she founded a convent in the north Arabian capital which survived. She reared her son Amr ibn-Hind to appreciate the finer things of life; he became a patron of the poet Tarafah and other practitioners of the art of Mu'allaqat, or suspended odes.

Suggested Reading:

(1)   Hitti, Philip K., *History of the Arabs.* New York: St. Martin's Press, 1968. p. 83.

Hinematioro

Paramount chieftainess of the Ngati Porou (17th or 18th c)

The Ngati Pirou is a Maori group of some 40 tribes in New Zealand. The Maori are a Polynesian people which migrated to New Zealand in two waves, ca. the ninth and fourteenth centuries. The largest social division is the tribe, based on common ancestry. The subtribes are the principal land owners. Unlike other tribes, the Ngati Pirou have retained most of their ancestral lands and the *mana*—prestige and power—that comes with it. Hinematioro was one of the rare women who attained lofty status, due in part to the prestige of her ancestors. The Maori not only record their ancestors in the "treasured book," but also memorize these genealogies and the most skilled orators relate them to guests. All that remains that attests to Hinematioro's ferocity and her status are ornately carved wooden openwork prows and figureheads outfitting her 100-foot long war canoe.

Suggested Reading:

(1)   Newton, Douglas, "The Maoris: Treasures of the Tradition." *National Geographic* 166, October 1984. pp. 542-553, particularly 546.

(2)   Momatiuk, Yva and John Eastcott, "Maoris: At Home in Two Worlds."
National Geographic 166, October 1984. pp. 522-542.

Hodierna of Jerusalem

Countess, regent of Tripoli (1152-1164)

She was one of the four popular daughters of King Baldwin II of Jerusalem
(ruled 1118-1131) and Queen Morphia. Her sisters were Melisende, who
married King Fulk of Anjou and bore King Baldwin III; Alice, who married
King Bohemond IIII of Antioch; and Joveta, who, because she had been
captured by Turks as a child, was considered too tainted to make a suitable
marriage and was sent off to become abess of Bethany. Hodierna was married
in 1133 to Count Raymond of Tripoli, a man of strong passions who was
jealously devoted to her. In 1140 their son Raymond III was born. They also
had a daughter of great beauty, Melisende. The marriage was not entirely
happy; gossip was circulated concerning the legitimacy of Hodierna's daughter
Melisende. Raymond, wildly jealous, attempted to keep his wife in a state of
seclusion. Early in 1152 their relationship was so bad that Hodierna's sister,
Queen Melisende, felt it her duty to intervene. She persuaded her son, King
Baldwin III, to accompany her to Triploi to try to achieve reconciliation
between the two. Raymond and Hodierna agreed to call off their quarrel,
but it was decided that Hodierna should take a long cooling-down holiday in
Jerusalem. Queen Melisende and Hodierna set off southward for Jerusalem,
accompanied for the first mile or so by Raymond. As he returned to the
capital, he was attacked by a band of assassins as he entered the south gate
and stabbed to death. King Baldwin III, who had remained behind at the
castle playing dice, marshalled the garrison which rushed out and killed every
Moslem in sight, but did not find the assassins. Baldwin sent messengers to
bring back Queen Melisende and Hodierna and tell them the grim news.
Hodierna then assumed the regency in the name of her 12-year-old son
Raymond III. Since the Turks were a constant threat, it was thought that
a man was also needed as guardian of the government. Baldwin, as nearest
male relative, obliged. The Turks attacked Tortosa and were driven out, but
with Hodierna's consent, Baldwin gave Tortosa to the Knights of the Temple
and returned to Jerusalem. In 1164 King Amalric assumed the regency for
Raymond III. Hodierna's daughter's questionable parentage cost her the
opportunity to become the bride of Byzantine Emperor Manual.

Suggested Reading:

(1) Runciman, Steven, *A History of the Crusades*. Cambridge: Cambridge University Press, 1952, 1987. vol. 2, *The Kingdom of Jerusalem and the Frankish East*. pp. 280, 332, 333, 335.

Homāy (or Chehrzād or Sheherezade)

Traditional Queen of Persia

Homay appears in the first version of Persian traditional history, the Yashts, retold in the Persian epic *Shah-Nama* by Firdausi. She was the daughter of Ardashir (Bahman) and the sister of Sāsān, a lion hunter. She was "endowed with wisdom and perspicuous judgment" as well as beauty. According to the custom (called Pahlavi), her father married her, and she became pregnant. On his deathbed, Ardashir passed the crown to her, and after her, to her unborn child, bypassing his son Sāsān. Dismayed at being shunned, Sāsān left Iran and married in Nishapur. Homāy succeeded to the throne, establishing a new practice and a new order. She distributed money from her treasury to her troops and was said to surpass her father in judgment and equity. She gave birth to a boy, Dārāb, but kept his birth a secret so that she could continue to rule. She had an elaborate casket constructed and placed the baby in it, launching it in the Euphrates River, accompanied by two attendants who were to report back that the casket had traveled and arrived safely. A fuller (clothes washer) and his wife found the casket and raised the baby. When he was grown and joined the army, his commander wrote to Queen Homāy, informing her of his history. She summoned Dārāb to the capital and had him enthroned.

Suggested Reading:

(1) Firdausi. *Shah-Nama, The Epic of Kings*. tr. Reuben Levy. Chicago: University of Chicago Press, 1967. pp. 219-228.

Hsiao-shih

Queen, regent of Khita (A.D. 983-?)

She was the wife of the Khitan khan Ye-lu Hsien, who died in A.D. 983. Their son Ye-lu Lung-su, born in A.D. 971, acceded to the throne upon his father's death with Hsiao-shih as regent. The appearance of a minor ruler under the guardianship of a female regent generally sparked an attempt by neighboring foes to attempt to usurp the throne. In 986 the kingdom was attacked by the army of the second Chinese Sung emperor T'ai-tsung, but Khitan general Ye-lu Hiou-ko defeated the Chinese, then threw the retreating troops into the Sha river to drown. In 989 the Chinese tried again to overcome the Khitans but were defeated near Paoting Pao Ting.

Suggested Reading:

(1)   Grousset, René, *The Empire of the Steppes: A History of Central Asia*. tr. Naomi Walford. New Brunswick: Rutgers University Press, 1970. pp. 131-132.

Hu (Ling Tai Hu)

Dowager Queen Regent, ruler of the Toba Wei in Northern China, Central Asia (A.D. 515-520, 525-528)

She was the wife of King Toba K'iao, who ruled Toba (or Touba) from A.D. 499 to 515. Upon his death his widow reigned for 13 years. A descendant of the old Tabatch dynasty, she was a forceful leader and the last member of the Tabatch to display the ancient strength. Described as a woman of exceptional energy, even bloodthirsty on occasion (she executed her own son, Yuan Xu, Emperor Xiao Mingdi), with a passion for power, nevertheless, she was a devout Buddhist. She added to the elaborate adornment of the Lungmen sanctuaries and dispatched the Buddhist pilgrim Sung Yun on a mission to northwest India (518-521). He returned bringing expensive Buddhist documents which she prized. But her extravagant spending brought on a revolt, and she fled to a Buddhist nunnery. She and her son were captured and tossed into the Yellow River, and some 1000 of her courtiers were slain. Eventually various warlords divided the Northern Wei Empire among themselves.

Suggested Reading:

(1)   Grousset, René, *The Empire of the Steppes: A History of Central Asia*. tr. Naomi Walford. New Brunswick: Rutgers University Press, 1970. pp. 64-65.

Section I

'Inayat Shah Zakiyyat al-Din Shah

Sultana of Atjeh in Indonesia (1678-1688)

Atjeh, a small Muslim sultanate on the northern tip of Sumatra, was at one time a bustling trade center, dominating the world pepper market. 'Inayat was the third in a succession of four Muslim queens who ruled Atjeh for a total of forty years. She is listed in H. Djajadiningrat's article on "Atjeh" in the *Encyclopedia of Islam* as being the sixteenth sovereign of the dynasty. She came into power at the death of Sultana Nur al-'Alam Nakiyyat al-Din Shah in 1678 and ruled for ten years, until 1688. She was succeeded by Kamalat Shah, possibly her daughter. The fact that the political enemies of these four sultanas had brought a *fatwa* from Mecca forbidding by law that a woman rule suggests that each woman wielded considerable power and was popular with her subjects.

Suggested Reading:

(1) Mernissi, Fatima, *The Forgotten Queens of Islam*. tr. Mary Jo Lakeland. Minneapolis: University of Minnesota Press, 1993. pp. 30, 110.

Irene

Empress, co-ruler of Byzantine Empire (780-790 and 792-797), "Emperor" (797-802)

Irene was born c. 752, the daughter of Athenian parents. In c. 769 she married Leo IV, surnamed the Chazar (or Kahzar) for his barbarian mother. Leo ruled the Byzantine Empire from 775 to 780. They had a son, Constantine VI, in 770. The following year, the infant was crowned co-emperor to prevent Leo's stepbrother Nicephorus from claiming the throne. When Leo IV died prematurely in 780, Irene became co-emperor with her ten-year-old son. A concealed iconodule with a lust for power, Irene could justify all her actions because she believed she was the chosen instrument of God. Her efforts were focused on gaining and keeping power, not on improving the welfare of the state.

Her first test came immediately, when Caesar Nicephorus, supported by the iconoclasts, attempted to overthrow her regime. She rapidly suppressed the rebellion and made it known that she was firmly in control. With cunning, diplomacy and intrigue, she was instrumental in restoring the use of icons in the Eastern Roman Empire when the Seventh Ecumenical Council met in Nicea in 787. This action earned her the devotion of the Greek Church, and all her actions to follow could not deny her eventual sainthood.

She forced a wife, Maria, on her son Constantine VI who, as he matured, grew resentful of his mother's power. A first attempt to wrest control from her was quelled, Constantine was flogged, and Irene demanded to be recognized as senior ruler, with her name placed above Constantine's. Finally, in 790, the army, with whom she was unpopular, rejected the ambitious demands of Irene and proclaimed Constantine sole ruler. She abdicated and was banished from the court.

But Constantine VI proved disappointingly weak. In 792 he allowed his mother and her faithful lieutenant, the eunuch Stauracius, to return, and Irene was even allowed to resume the position of co-ruler. She incited her son to blind the general, Alexius, who had led the attack against her on Constantine's behalf, and to mutilate his uncles who had plotted against her. In 795 she encouraged him in his lust for his mistress Theodote and persuaded him to divorce his wife, Maria. In marrying Theodote, he violated all ecclesiastical laws, outraging public opinion. With Constantine in such general disfavor, she was free to have him arrested, blinded and deposed. In 797 she proclaimed herself sole reigning Emperor, not Empress. She was the first wonam to control the empire as an independent ruler in her own right and not as a regent for a minor or an emperor unfit to rule.

The monks praised their benefactress, who bestowed large gifts upon them. She lowered taxes while raising endowments, making everyone happy, but ruining the finances of the Byzantine state. In 798 she opened diplomatic relations with Charlemagne. In 802 he was said to be contemplating marriage to Irene, but the plan never reached fruition.

In 802 a conspiracy led by the Logothete-General Nicephorus seized the throne, and Irene was exiled to the island of Principio, then to Lesbos, where she died in 803. She is a saint of the Greek Orthodox Church.

Suggested Reading:

(1) Ostrogorsky, George, *History of the Byzantine State*. New Brunswick, NJ: Rutgers University Press, 1969. pp. 175-182, 186-188, 192-197, 220-225.
(2) Previté-Orton, C. W., *The Shorter Cambridge Medieval History*, 2 vols. Cambridge: Cambridge University Press, 1952, 1982. vol. 1, *The Later Roman Empire to the Twelfth Century*. p. 249.

Irene Palaeologina, Empress

Ruler of the Empire of Trebizond (1340-1341)

Trebizond, now Trabzon, located in northeastern Turkey on the Black Sea, was a Greek state founded after the fall of Constantinople, by two grandsons of Byzantine Emperor Andronicus I Comnenus. The first ruler was one of these two men, Alexius I (r. 1204-1222). The Commenian Dynasty remained in power in Trebizond, remote from the struggle for the restoration of Byzantium, for over 250 years, longer than any other Byzantine family. By the 14th. century, Trebizond had been defeated by the Mongols and became their tributary vassal. Irene was the wife of Basil (r. 1332-1340). After his death, Irene ruled for about a year and was deposed in favor of another woman, Anna Anachoutlou, daughter of King Alexius II (r. 1297-1330).

Suggested Reading:

(1) Morby, John E. *Dynasties of the World*. Oxford: Oxford University Press, 1989. p. 56.
(2) Ostrogorsky, George. *History of the Byzantine State*. New Brunswick, N.J.: Rutgers University Press, 1969. pp. 426fl-439.

Isabella

See Zabel

Isabella

Queen of Beirut (1264-1282)

She was the daughter of John II of Beirut, who died in 1264, and the sister of Eschiva of Ibelin, queen of Cyprus. Isabella remained a figurehead all of her life. She was first married to the child king of Cyprus, Hugh II, who died in 1267 before the marriage could be consummated. She then married an Englishman, Hamo (Edmund) L'Etranger (the Foreigner), who soon died, leaving her under the protection of the Sultan Baibar. King Hugh of Cyprus tried to carry her off and remarry her to the candidate of her choice, but the Sultan Baibar, citing the pact that her late husband had made with him, demanded that she be sent back to Beirut, where a Mameluk guard "protected" her. She married twice more, to Nicholas L'Aleman and William Barlais. When she died in 1282, Beirut passed to her sister, Eschiva.

Suggested Reading:

(1)   Runciman, Steven, *A History of the Crusades*, 3 vols. Cambridge: Cambridge University Press, 1952, 1987. vol. 3, *The Kingdom of Acre*. pp. 329, 342.

Isabella of Cyprus

Regent of Jerusalem (1263)

She was the eldest sister of King Henry of Cyprus. She married Henry of Antioch, youngest son of Bohemond IV. In 1253 the couple had a son, Hugh II of Cyprus. Isabella also reared her late sister's son, also named Hugh (of Brienne). Much information that remains about Isabella concerns her efforts to attain her rightful regency. When Queen Plaisance of Cyprus died in 1261, a new regent was required for Cyprus and Jerusalem, as Isabella's son, Hugh II, was only eight years old. Plaisance's late husband was Isabella's brother, and thus Isabella was the next in the line of succession as regent. The High Court of Cyprus refused Isabella as regent in favor of her young son, but the High Court of Jerusalem, in 1263, named her regent de facto, refusing to administer the oath of allegiance because King Conradin was not present. Isabella appointed her husband Henry as *bailli*. In the thirteenth century the *bailli* was much more powerful than the English bailiff. The *bailli* had authority to act for the monarch in collecting and dispensing funds, raising an army, defending the area, maintaining order, holding court, and overseeing minor officials.

Isabella died in 1264 and her son, who was by then 11, became regent, although her nephew Hugh of Brienne put in a counter claim. But as Isabella had been accepted as the last regent, the vote was unanimous that her son should succeed her.

Suggested Reading:

(1) Runciman, Steven, *A History of the Crusades*, 3 vols. Cambridge: Cambridge University Press, 1952, 1987. vol. 3, *The Kingdom of Acre*. pp. 206, 288-289.

Section J

Jayaram, Jayalalitha

Chief of Tamil Nadu (1995-1996)

She was born in India in 1947. In the 1960's she became an actress, starring in many Tamil-language films that established her reputation as a romantic heroine. She married M. G. Ramachandran, who was an even bigger star than she. Ramachandran was elected Chief Minister of Tamil Nadu State, located on the southeastern tip of the Indian peninsula and having a population of 55 million people. However, when he died while in office, Jayalalitha was elected by a landslide vote from poor villagers. She won the admiration of some villagers for projects such as improving irrigation, providing a local burial ground, aiding orphans and the disabled. However, she was mocked for having 85-foot plywood cutouts painted with her image erected at various intersections in Madras, the capital, as well as elsewhere throughout the land.

By mid 1995, local newspapers and magazines had printed lengthy exposes detailing governmental corruption said to have spread through every level, as well as political ties to criminal gangs. She was accused of reinforcing her rule with hired thugs. In September of that year she staged a wedding of maharajah-like opulence for her "foster son," the nephew of her closest friend, Sasikala Natarajan. The bride was a granddaughter Shivaji Gansean, considered the Madras studio's greatest star ever. The wedding drew more than 100,000 people, many of whom were bused in from faraway villages. Thousands of guests received invitations inscribed on silver salvers. At least 12,000 of the guests were served a wedding lunch by 3,500 cooks and waiters. A leading film designer was commissioned to construct a tableau of Tamil mythology running for miles between Jayalalitha's official residence and the wedding site. At least 20,000 special-duty policemen provided crowd control.

Minister Jayaram, stating, "My conscience is clear," filed more than 200 lawsuits against opponents, and publicly accused Governor Channa Reddy, in his late seventies, of "misbehaving" toward her in their private meetings.

Suggested Reading:

(1)   Burns, John F. "For Indian Politician, An Opulent Wedding Means Political Bliss". *The New York Times International.* 10 September 1995: 6.

Jindan

Rani, regent of the Sikh kingdom of the Punjab (c.1843-1846)

Jindan was the daughter of a chieftain of the Kanhayas and of the domineering Sada Kaur. In 1795 she became the first wife of Ranjit Singh, age 15, who had been chief of the Sukerchakias since he was 12. For the first few years of their marriage, the Rani's mother directed all of Ranjit's affairs. In 1801 he proclaimed himself maharajah of the Punjab. In 1838 the British viceroy persuaded him to assist in placing a British choice on the throne of Kabul in Afghanistan. Following the victory in Afghanistan, Ranjit fell ill and died (1843). He was succeeded by his youngest son, Dalip or Dulop Singh, with his widow, Jindan, as regent. In 1845 British encroachment on the Punjab made it necessary for the rani, the chief minister and the commander in chief of the army to agree to attack the British. Their defeat in 1846 led to the Treaty of Lahore whereby they lost a number of territories, including Kashmir. Jindan was deposed as regent and a council was appointed to govern. But a second Sikh revolt erupted in 1848, which the new government was powerless to stop was put down by the British. This time the British deposed the young king and sent him and Rani Jindan to England. He became a Christian and a land owner in Norfolk. A final bloody encounter in 1849 between the Sikhs and the British ended with British annexation of the Punjab.

Suggested Reading:

(1)   Bhahacharya, Sachchidananda. *A Dictionary of Indian History.* New York: George Braziller, 1967. pp. 321-322.

Jingō-kōgū (or Kōgō)

Empress, regent of Japan (c. A.D. 200-269)

She was born c. 169, the daughter of Prince Okinaga no Sukune and Katsuraki no Taka-nuka-hime. She married Chūai-tennō (Tarashi-Naka-tsu-hiko), fourteenth Emperor of Japan, who ruled from 192 to 200. The emperor had planned an expedition to conquer Korea but died in A.D. 200 before he could undertake it. The empress, although pregnant with their son at the time, conducted the expedition to Korea and brought the kings of Koryo, Pekche, and Silla (Kōrae, Hakusai, and Shinra) under her suzerainty. (Some descrepancy can be seen between Japanese and Korean dating of the expedition. According to Korean records, the expedition occurred in A.D. 346.) She returned to Japan in time to give birth to Homuda, the future Emperor Ōjin. Two sons of one of her husband's concubines revolted, claiming succession by right of primogeniture. Jingō sent General Taki-shiuchi no Sukune to put them to death, thus ending all threat to her reign. She refused to ascend to the throne but ruled as regent for 69 years. She died in 269 at the age of 100 and was honored with the name Kashi-dai-myōjin. (According to Korean histories, the empress died in 380.)

Suggested Reading:

(1) Aston, W. G., trans., *Nihongi: Chronicles of Japan from the Earliest Times to A.D. 697.* Rutland, VT: Charles E. Tuttle Company, 1972. pp. 224-253.
(2) Reischauer, Edwin O. and John K. Fairbank, *East Asia: The Great Tradition.* Boston: Houghton Mifflin, 1960. pp. 468-469.
(3) Sansom, George A., *A History of Japan to 1334.* Stanford: Stanford University Press, 1958. pp. 16-17.
(* Papinot, E., *Historical and Geographical Dictionary of Japan.* Rutland, VT: Charles E. Tuttle Company, 1972. pp. 229-230)

Jitō-tennō

Empress, ruler of Japan (686-697)

She was born in A.D. 625, named Hironu hime, or Uno no Sasara, a daughter of the emperor Tenchi, who ruled Japan from 662 to 671, and a sister of Kōbun-tennō, who ruled from 671 to 672. When their father fell ill, he shaved his head and retired to Yoshino-zan. Kōbun-tennō assumed the throne, but a civil war broke out. Tenchi's brother, Ō-ama no Ōji, revolted and claimed the succession. Ō-ama defeated the imperial troops, so Kōbun-tennōo killed himself after a reign of only eight months. Ō-ama ascended the throne and ruled for 14 years as Temmu-tennō. He married his niece, Jitō. When he died in 687, Jitō succeeded him, at the age of 42. During her reign she made important administrative reforms, encouraged the development of agriculture, and had the first silver coin struck. Sensitive to the religious plurality over which she reigned, she endeavored to remain impartial in her religious devotions and contributed to both Buddhist and Shintō temples. After a reign of 11 years, she abdicated in favor of her nephew (and grandson) Mommu. Upon her retirement she was the first to take the honorary title for past emperors, Dajō-tennō. She was also the first monarch to be cremated. She died in A.D. 701.

Suggested Reading:

(1) Aston, W. G., trans., *Nihongi: Chronicles of Japan*. Rutland, VT: Charles E. Tuttle Company, 1972. pp. 382-423.
(2) Sansom, George A., *A History of Japan to 1334*. Stanford: Stanford University Press, 1958. p. 65.
(3) Papinot, E., *Historical and Geographical Dictionary of Japan*. Rutland, VT: Charles E. Tuttle Company, 1972. pp. 70, 232.

Joya, Malalai

Afghani MP (2003-)

She was born April 25, 1978, the daughter of a former medical student who lost a foot while fighting the during the Soviet invasion of Afghanistan. In 1982 the family fled Afghanistan for a refugee camp in Iran. Later they moved on to Pakistan. When she was twenty, Malalai Joya returned to Afghanistan, during the reign of the Taliban. She worked in the western provinces of Farah and Herat as a social activist and was named a director of the non-governmental group, *Organisation of Promoting Afghan Women's Capabilities (OPAWC)*. She is married.

She was elected to the Loya Jirga (Parliament) from Farah province in 2003, convened for the purpose of ratifying a new Constitution, and gained international attention in Kabul on December 17, 2003 when she spoke out publicly against the domination by the warlords, a word few people in Afghanistan were brave enough to utter. Her criticism of the fundamentalist leaders and clergy who were war criminals caused an uproar of disbelief. In response, Assembly Chairman of the Loya Jirga Sibghatullah Mojaddedi labeled her a "communist" and "infidel" and demanded that she apologize. She refused. Male mujahideen, many of whom were carrying guns, threw things at her and lunged toward her, so that she had to be protected by sympathetic colleagues.

Since that time she has survived at least four assassination attempts, and travels in Afghanistan under a burqa and with armed guards.

Joya's controversial stance against other members of the Loya Jirga has earned her much popularity as well as heavy criticism from her political opponents. In September of 2005 she was elected to the 249-seat National Assembly, Wolesi Jirga, with the second highest number of votes in Farah Province.

On May 7, 2006, she was physically and verbally attacked by fellow members of parliament after accusing several colleagues of being "warlords" and unfit for service in the new Afghan government. "I said there are two kinds of mujahedeen in Afghanistan," Joya told the Associated Press. "One kind fought for independence, which I respect, but the other kind destroyed the country and killed 60,000 people."

In response to such threats, Joya continues to speak out against inclusion of those she believes to be former mujahedeen in the current government of Afghanistan, stating: "Never again will I whisper in the shadows of intimidation. I am but a symbol of my people's struggle and a servant to their cause. And if I were to be killed for what I believe in, then let my blood be the beacon for emancipation and my words a revolutionary paradigm for generations to come."

During 2006 and 2007 she traveled more than once to Canada and Australia speaking out about the injustices, particularly against women, in her country.

At one interview, she said, "My voice tears apart the lies of the Western media about so-called democracy and liberation in Afghanistan."

She also criticized the United States policy: "While we hate the war mongering and criminal-fostering policies of the U.S. government, we feel, acknowledge and thank the sympathies and support of the U.S. people and learn from their humanism and dedication."

In a January 27, 2007 interview with BBC News Joya commented on her personal political mission amid continuous death threats: "They will kill me but they will not kill my voice, because it will be the voice of all Afghan women. You can cut the flower, but you cannot stop the coming of spring."

On May 21, 2007, fellow members of the Wolesi Jirga voted to suspend Malalai Joya for three years from the legislature, citing that she had broken Article 70 of the Parliament, which had banned Wolesi Jirga members from openly criticizing each other. Joya had compared the Wolesi Jirga to a "stable or zoo" on a recent TV interview.

Joya said the vote was a "political conspiracy" and that she had been told Article 70 was written specifically for her saying "since I've started my struggle for human rights in Afghanistan, for women's rights, these criminals, these drug smugglers, they've stood against me from the first time I raised my voice at the Loya Jirga."

People in her province of Farah, and some other provinces staged protests against her suspension. On June 21, 2007, one month after she was suspended, her supporters in Melbourne staged protests against the Afghan government in her support. In November 2007, an international letter with a number of prominent signatories called for her reinstatement to the Afghan Parliament. She addressed the European Parliament in May 2008.

Suggested Reading:

(1) "Delegate lashes out at Afghan Council." Associated Press, December 17, 2003.
(2) "The Woman Who Defies Warlords." *World Pulse Magazine*, Issue 1, 2005.
(3) "Malalai Joya: courage under fire." *Telegraph Magazine*, September 29, 2007.
(4) "The woman vs. the warlords: a post 9/11 story." *The Ottawa Citizen*, September 11, 2007.
(5) "Canada should change its policy on Afghanistan," by Malalai Joya. *Rabble News*, March 3, 2008.
(6) "Because Someone Had to Do It." *The American Prospect Magazine*, June 25, 2007.
(7) Afghan parliament suspends outspoken female lawmaker after critical TV interview." *The Associated Press*, May 21, 2007.

Julia Berenice

Co-ruler of Judaea (c. A.D. 52) See Berenice

Section K

Kaahumanu, Queen

Co-ruler of Hawaii (1823-1832)

She was the wife of Kamehameha I (r. 1795-1819), first ruler over the entire Hawaiian archipelago, whose greed almost ruined the islands. Under his rule, every sandalwood tree on the islands was chopped down and sold to Canton. Queen Kaahumanu had at least three children, one of whom, Liholiho, ascended the throne upon his father's death in 1819, just in time to play host to an influx from the West. He ruled as Kamehameha II (r. 1819-1823 or 1824).

In 1820, the first foreign whalers reached the islands. That same year, two Christian Congregationalist missionaries arrived from America. They made no inroads in converting the populace until the royal family agreed to be baptized. This conversion was eventually to have an impact on the sexual conduct of young Hawaiian girls upon whom, until that time, there had been no sexual taboos. The whalers had immediately taken advantage of the native girls and as a result, venereal diseases swept the island.

In 1823 or 1824, Kamehameha II and his wife both died while in England on an official visit. His younger brother, Kauikeaouli, succeeded him and ruled, under his mother Queen Kaahumanu's supervision as Kamehameha II (r. 1825-1854).

Queen Kaahumanu endeavored to raise the sexual moral standards of her subjects, an effort not appreciated by the foreign sailors. Her policy, called "stupid morality" by the whalers, was praised by United States President Andrew Jackson in 1829. However, after her death in 1832, the young king reverted to "lacivious ways", although otherwise, he was considered a strong king. When he died in 1854, Queen Kaahumanu's daughter Kinau's son succeeded as Kamehameha IV (r. 1854-1863), followed by his brother Lut as Kamehameha V (r. 1863-1872).

Suggested Reading:

(1) Knappert, Jan, *Pacific Mythology*. London: Diamond Books, 1995. p. 109.
(2) Suggs, Robert C., *Island Civilizations of Polynesia*. New York: Mentor, 1960, p. 144.
(3) Morby, John E., *Dynasties of the World*. Oxford: Oxford University Press, 1989. p. 243.

Kalyanavati

Queen of Sri Lanka (1202-1208)

Kalyanavati was a member of the non-Sinhalese faction of the Kalinga dynasty. She ruled during a chaotic period in Ceylonese history which followed the reign of Parakramabahu I, who for the first time had united the island under one rule (1153-1186). Following his death, the country was ruled by a succession of relatives of his Kalingan wife, none of whom ruled for very long. Queen Kalyanavati was the fifth ruler to take the throne in 16 years. She succeeded King Sahassamalla, who had ruled for only two years. Following her six-year reign, she was succeeded by another relative, King Dharmasaka, who ruled for only one year.

Suggested Reading:

(1) Egan, Edward, et. al., eds. *Kings, Rulers and Statesmen*. New York: Sterling Publishing Company, 1976. p. 438.

Kamalat Shah, Zaynt al-Din

Sultana of Atjeh in Indonesia (1688-1699)

Atjeh, a small Muslim sultanate on the northern tip of Sumatra, was once a busy trade center, dominating the world pepper market. Kamalat was the fourth in a succession of Muslim sultanas who ruled Atjeh for a total of forty years. She succeeded Sultana 'Inayat Shah Zakiyyat al-Din Shah, possibly her mother, who ruled from 1678 to 1688. In his article on "Atjeh" in the *Encyclopedia of Islam*, H. Djajadiningrat lists Kamalat Shah as the seventeenth sovereign of the dynasty. She ruled from 1688 to

1699. Despite decrees from Mecca and opposition from the caliphs, the sultanas were apparently popular enough to override the *fatwa* forbidding a woman to rule.

Suggested Reading:

(1)   Mernissi, Fatima, *The Forgotten Queens of Islam*. tr. Mary Jo Lakeland. Minneapolis: University of Minnesota Press, 1993. pp. 30, 86, 110.

Khadija

Sultana of the Maldives (1347-1379)

She was one of three daughters of Sultan Salah al-Din Salih Albendjaly. When her father died, her brother Shihab-ud-din became king at a very young age. The vezier, 'Abdallah, son od Muhammad al-Hazrami, married the young king's mother and overpowered him and had him put to death. Meanwhile, Khadija had married Jamal-ud-din, who managed to take over the reins of power for his wife. As vizier, he issued orders in his Sultana Khadija's name. The orders were written on palm leaves with a bent piece of iron, because paper was not used except for writing the Koran and books of learning. She for thirty-three years, during which time Ibn Battuta traveled to the Maldives. He wrote: "one of the wonders of these islands is that its ruler (*sultana*) is a woman named Khadija . . . ." She died in 1379 and was succeeded by her sister Myriam.

Suggested Reading:

(1)   Ibn Battuta, *Travels of Ibn Battuta AD 1325-1354*. vol. 2. tr. H. A. R. Gibb from the French translation of C. Defremery and B. B. Sanguinetti. Cambridge: Cambridge University Press, vol. 1, 1958, vol. 2, 1962.

Kirum

Queen, mayor of Khaya-Sumu's city in Ilansura (c. 1790-1745 B.C.)

Kirum was one of many daughters of King Zimri-Lim, who ruled Mari in the mid-1700's B.C. The king arranged her marriage to Khaya-Sumu, who ruled Ilansura, and also appointed her mayor of Khaya-Sumu's city. She presided over the city, A high-spirited woman, she not only administered the city, writing her father for advice, but also dispensed political advice to her father. Her independence and her seeking her father's political opinion about Khaya-Sumu's realm displeased her husband. He also married her sister or half-sister, Shimatum, creating a bitter rivalry. Kirum eventually asked her father for permission to return home. She quoted her husband as saying, "You exercise the mayorship here. (But) since I will (surely) kill you, let him come . . . and take you back." Apparently her father did not reply, for she wrote again, threatening, "If my lord does not bring me back, I will head toward Mari (and) jump (fall) from the roof." This time the king instructed his wife, Queen Shibtu, to bring Kirum home.

Suggested Reading:

(1) Lerner, Gerda. *The Creation of Patriarchy*. New York and Oxford: Oxford University Press, 1986. pp. 70-74.

Kogyku-tenno

Empress, twice ruler of Japan (642-645) and, as *Saimei-tenno*, (655-ca 662)

She was born in A.D. 594, the daughter of Prince Chinu no Oji and Princess Kibi, and the grandaughter of Shotoku-taishi, a Japanese regent from 593 to 621. Her birth name was Ame-toyo-takara-ikashi-hitarashi hime, or Hitarashi-hime, or Tarashi for short. She first married Emperor Yomei-tenno, who ruled from 586 to 587, and bore the Imperial Prince Aya. After her first husband died in 587, she then married her uncle, Emperor Jomei-tenno, who ruled from 629 to 641. She bore two more sons and a daughter. She succeeded her husband, at the age of 48, upon his death in 642, having been chosen by the Soga clan, which planned to wrest the ultimate control. During her first reign, she was influenced by two powerful Soga ministers, Iruku and Emishi, who, at the instigation of her younger brother, Kotoku, were assassinated in her presence in ca. 644. The next morning she abdicated in his favor. When he died ten years later, she reascended the throne at the age of 62. This time she did not allow herself to be influenced by her ministers. She built a palace at Yamato, the first to be covered with tiles. The feast of the dead was first celebrated during her second reign. She sent a force to Ezo to subdue the Ebisu. In 660 China attacked the two Korean kingdoms of Koma and Kudara, which asked for Japan's help. The empress prepared to lead personally an army bound for Korea but died unexpectedly on the way, at the palace at Asakura, at the age of 68. For her second term as empress, she received the posthumous name of Saimei-tenno.

Suggested Reading:

(1) Aston, W. G., trans., *Nihongi: Chronicles of Japan*. Rutland, VT: Charles E. Tuttle Company, 1972. pp. 171, 248-273.
(2) Papinot, E., *Historical and Geographical Dictionary of Japan*. Rutland: Charles E. Tuttle Company, 1972. pp. 296, 527-528.
(3) Sansom, George, *A History of Japan to 1334*. Stanford: Stanford University Press, 1958. p. 54.

Koken-tenno

Empress, twice ruler of Japan (749-758) and, as *Shotoku-tenno*, (764-770)

She was born Abe-naishinno in 716, the daughter of Shomu-tenno, who ruled Japan from 724 to 748. In 749 he shaved his head and abdicated in favor of his unmaarried daughter, Koken, then age 33. An ardent Buddhist like her father, she assembled some 5000 bonzes (priests) in the To-daiji temple, the Eastern Great Monastary, to read the sacred books. She exacted severe penalties for the killing of any living things. More interested in religion than government, she was eventually persuaded by an advisor, Nakamaro, to abdicate in favor of a kinsman, Junnin, whom Nakamaro then dominated completely. Koken shaved her head and took the name of Takano-tenno. She allowed herself to be dominated by the bonze (Buddhist priest), Dokyo, who may also have been her lover. Dokyo was a bitter rival of Nakamaro. In 764 the latter raised an army and marched against Dokyo, but Nakamaro was killed in the fighting. Dokyo persuaded Koken, now age 48, to return to the throne, while Junnin-tenno was bannished to the island of Awaji, where he died a year later. The empress bestowed favors and titles upon Dokyo, but he aspired for more: he wanted to be emperor, and in 768 he tried to persuade the empress to abdicate in his favor. However, the throne had been held by the same lineage for 14 centuries, and before the empress could bring herself to step down in favor of an usurper, she consulted an oracle. The oracle brought an answer from the god Hachiman to the effect that a subject should never become emperor. She kept the throne but died the following year. Because of her second term, she received the posthumous name of Shotoku-tenno. Her amorous abandon with the ambitious Dokyo prompted Japanese nobles to vow that no more women would rule. Since her time, only two women have ruled.

Suggested Reading:

(1) Papinot, E., *Historical and Geographical Dictionary of Japan*. Rutland: Charles E. Tuttle Company, 1972. pp. 237, 299-301.

(2) Sansom, George, *A History of Japan to 1334*. Stanford: Stanford University Press, 1958. p. 89.

(3) Reischauer, Edwin O. and John K. Fairbank, *East Asia: The Great Tradition*. Boston: Houghton Mifflin, 1960. p. 484.

Kollontai, Alexandra Mikhaylovna

Russian revolutionary, USSR diplomat, Ambassador to Norway, Mexico, Sweden (1923-1943)

She was born Alexandra Mikhaylovna Domontovich on March 31 (O.S. March 19), 1872 in St. Petersburg to Mikhail Domontovich, a general in the Russo-Turkish War of 1877-1878 and head of the Russian chancellery in Bulgaria (1878-1879). Her mother was Alexandra Masalin-Mravinsky, the daughter of a wealthy Finnish timber merchant.

As a member of the aristocracy, she married Tsarist General Kollontai and had one child. But her leanings were to the left. As early as 1909 she was writing the feminist tract, *The social basis of the woman question*.

She was 31 years old when the two communist revolutionary factions of the Russian Social Democratic Labor Party split into Martov's Mensheviks and Lenin's Bolsheviks. She eventually opted to join the Mensheviks. For her beliefs and poilitical activities, she spent a period of exile in Sweden and America. However, in 1914 she joined the Bolsheviks and returned to Russia. She had left her husband and child in 1898 to become a Bolshevik.

Following the Bolshevik revolution in 1917, she was appointed People's Commissar for Social Welfare, the most prominent woman in the Soviet administration. In 1919 she founded the Zhenotdel, or Women's Department, which sought to improve conditions of women's lives by eliminating illiteracy and educating women in the new work, marriage and education laws put in place by the new administration. In 1920 her treatise, *Towards a history of the working woman's movement in Russia,* appeared.

She viewed marriage and traditional families as legacies of the oppressive, property-rights-based past. Under Communism, both men and women would work for, and be supported by, society, not their families. Their children would be wards of, and reared basically by society. Kollontai admonished men and women to discard their nostalgia for traditional family life. "The worker-mother must learn not to differentiate between yours and mine; she must remember that there are only our children, the children of Russia's communist workers," she wrote in a treatise called "Communism and Family."

She had an affair with Pavel Dybenko, a Ukrainian seventeen years younger, who later became commissar for the navy. Eventually he became so powerful that Trotsky had him court-martialed for overruling Trotsky's decisions. The prosecutor only released Dybenko after Kollontai promised to marry Dybenko, which she did. But later she left him.

Increasingly she became an internal critic of the Communist party and joined with her friend, Alexander Shlyapnikov, to form a left-wing faction known as the Workers' Opposition. However, Lenin managed to dissolve the Workers' Opposition, after which Kollontai was more or less politically sidelined. Lacking political influence, she was appointed by the Party to various diplomatic positions from the early 1920s, keeping her from playing a leading role in the politics of women's policy in the USSR. In 1923, she was appointed Soviet Ambassador to Norway, becoming the world's first female ambassador. She was also a member of the Soviet delegation to the League of Nations. Meanwhile, in 1930 the Women's Department closed. In 1933 she was awarded the Order of Lenin for her long service. She later served as Ambassador to Mexico and Sweden (1943). In 1945 she received the Order of the Red Banner of Labour. (1945). She was also awarded the Knights Grand Cross of the Royal Norwegian Order of St. Olav, Norway's highest honor at that time.

She died on March 9, 1952.

Twice she has been portrayed onscreen, first by Greta Garbo in the 1930s film Ninotchka, then in a 1994 TV film, "A Wave of Passion: The Life of Alexandra Kollontai" in which Glenda Jackson provided the voice of Kollontai.

Suggested Reading:

(1) A. Kollontai, "Communism and the Family. Text Kommunistka, 1920.

(2) A. Kollontai, "Theses on Communist Morality in the Sphere of Marital Relations." Kommunistka No 12-13 (May) 1921, pp.28-34.

(3) A. Kollontai. "Memoirs" (Letopis mojei zizni) 1946, Progress Publishers, 1990.

(4) Stalin and his Hangmen, by Donald Rayfield, published in 2004 by Random House, pages 267-270.

Kossamak

Queen, joint ruler of Cambodia. (1955-1960)

She was born Kossamak Nearirath, the daughter of King Sisowath, who ruled from 1904 to 1927, and the sister of King Monivong, who ruled Cambodia from 1927 to 1941. She married Prince Norodom Suramarit, and they had a son, Sihanouk, born in 1922. When Monivong died in 1941, Sihanouk was placed on the throne by the French governor general of Indochina, Admiral Jean Decoux. In 1952 Sihanouk dissolved the cabinet, declared martial law and went into voluntary exile to dramatize Cambodian demands for complete independence from France. In 1954 the Geneva Conference confirmed complete independence. A referendum the following year approved King Sihanouk's rule, but he abdicated in favor of his father and became prime minister. According to Egan, et. al., Queen Kossamak ruled jointly with her husband until his death in 1960, when her son Sihanouk reassumed the position of head of state.

Suggested Reading:

(1) Egan, Edward W. et. al., eds. *Kings, Rulers and Statesmen*. New York: Sterling Publishing, 1976. p. 69.

(2) For an account of the times, see Abercrombie, Thomas J., "Cambodia: Indochina's 'Neutral Corner'. *National Geographic 126*. October 1964, pp. 514-551.

Ku-Baba

Queen, founder of the dynasty of Kish in Sumeria (c. 2350 B.C.)

According to the king list, Queen Ku-Baba, founder of the Third Dynasty, appears to have reigned a hundred years, for she is the only ruler listed for the period. According to earliest Sumerian records, Ku-Baba, formerly a tavern-keeper, holds the distinction of being the only woman listed in the king list as reigning in her own right. She led Kish's war for independence from Uruk. Later she was deified—not an uncommon occurrence at the time—and worshipped in Northern Mesopotamia as the goddess Kubaba.

Suggested Reading:

(1) Edwards, I. E. S. et. al., eds. *Cambridge Ancient History*. Cambridge: Cambridge University Press, 1970. vol. 1, pt. 2. p. 115.

(2) Carpenter, Clive. *The Guinnes Book of Kings, Rulers, & Statesmen*. Enfield, Middlesex: Guinness Superlatives Ltd., 1978. p. 15.

(3) Oppenheim, A. Leo. *Ancient Mesopotamia*. Chicago: The University of Chicago Press, 1977. p. 151.

(4) For chronological list of Mesopotamian rulers: Roux, Georges. *Ancient Iraq*. Harmondsworth, Middlesex: Penguin, 1980. p. 459.

Kumaratunga, Chandrika

President of Sri Lanka (1995-1996), Prime Minister (1994-1995)

Born in 1945, she was the daughter of Solomon Bandaranaike, Prime Minister from 1956 to 1959, and Sirimavo Bandaranaiko, who succeeded her husband as the island nation's first woman Prime Minister in 1959. Chandrika had a brother, Anura, and a sister, Sunethra. When Chandrika was 13, her father was assassinated before her eyes by a fanatical Buddhist monk. His widow was elected to succeed him, becoming the first woman to be elected prime minister anywhere in the world, and instituting some economically devastating socialist experiments. Chandrika was educated in Paris, studying political science, and embracing the radical socialism of Mao Zedong and North Korea. She married Vijaya Kumaratunga, the country's most popular movie star, and the couple had two children. But Vijaya, who was one of the country's most radical left-wing politicians as well, was shot by Sinhalese fascists, again before Chandrika's eyes. Following the assassination, she and her family fled abroad for three years. Meanwhile, her younger brother Anura had been his mother's first choice as heir to the political dynasty, but he declined. Chandrika was her mother's next choice, but Chandrika had cast off her socialist leanings and embraced the free-market policies which had resulted in improved economic conditions. She announced that she sought "capitalism with a human face." In 1993 she became the first woman to head a provincial government in Sri Lanka. In the spring of 1994, she defeated the long-governing United National Party in its home territory, the south. In elections of August, 1994, she headed a nine-party parliamentary alliance which was able to put an end to the 17-year reign of the UNP to become the new Prime Minister.

In 1995 she was elected President on the promise of striking a "peace deal" with the separatist Liberation "Tigers" of Tamil Eelam, led by Vellupillai Prabhakaran. Prior to her election, the country had been involved in a civil war between the government and the separatist forces of Prabhakaran, who has been labeled "one of the century's most vicious and treacherous leaders" by Lindsay Murdoch of the Sydney Morning Herald. In January, 1995, she persuaded both sides to agree to a 100-day cease-fire; however, when the cease-fire expired, guerrilla activity resumed.

By then the country had been gripped for twelve years by civil war in which more than 50,000 people had been killed. Kumaratunga then offered to grant broad new autonomy to the Tamil minority in hopes that the Tamil "Tigers" would lay down their arms. However, although her message received a good reception among the Tamil population, the "Tigers" rejected her peace offer which would have caused the guerrillas to lose their iron grip on the region.

Suggested Reading:

(1) "A Family Affair?" *World Press Review* October 1994, p. 24.
(2) "The 'Strongwomen' of South Asia" *World Press Review* December 1994, pp. 18-20.
(3) "Return of the Tigers" *World Press Review* August 1995, pp. 28-29.
(4) "Peace at Hand?" *World Press Review* November 1995, p. 26.

Kutlugh Khatun (or Turkan Khatun or Kutlugh Turkhan)

Queen of Kirman (1257-1282)

Since there are many women on the political scene of that era with the name of Turkan Khatun, in order to avoid confusion, she will be referred to here as Kutlugh Khaten. She was the daughter of Barak Hajib, ruler of Kirman as Kutlugh Khan and later, Kutlugh Sultan. She was married to her father's cousin, Qutb al-Din. After her father's death in 1234, her brother, Rukn al-Din, acceded to the throne. His reign was followed by that of his cousin, Qutb al-Din, Kutlugh's husband, in 1252. When Qutb al-Din died in 1257, their son Hajjaj was under-age, so the officials at Kirman requested the Mongol court to allow his widow to reign, which she did for 26 years.

She did so by sending her son Hajjaj to fight in Mongolian ruler Hulagu's army and by marrying her daughter Padishah Khatun to Hulagu's son, Abaka Khan. This union was most unusual in that Padishah was Muslim and Abaka was Bhuddist. In addition, in order to save her daughter from an obligatory marriage, Kutlugh Turkhan had reared her daughter as a boy. Officially Hulagu confirmed Kutlugh Turkhan's title seven years later, in 1264. Her title was *'Ismat al-dunya wa al-din,* and she had the right to have the *khutba* proclaimed in her name in all the mosques.

Her reign was marked by prosperity, and her power and popularity were at their peak when one of her stepsons, Suyurghatamish, appeared to contest her reign. To appease him, she had his name added to hers in the *khutba,* but she complained to her daughter Padishah, who used her influence to obtain a *yarligh* forbidding Suyurghatamish from interfering in the affairs of Kirman.

Toward the end of her life, her son-in-law Abaka died. He was replaced by his brother who converted to Islam and took the name of Ahmad Teguder. Ahmad had Kutlugh Khatun removed and installed her stepson Suyurghatamish on the throne of Kirman. Although she traveled to the Mongol court at Tabriz to plead her case, Ahmad refused to rescind his order. She died a year later without having regained her throne or having witnessed the unanticipated reign of her daughter Padishah Khatun.

Suggested Reading:

(1) Mernissi, Fatima, *The Forgotten Queens of Islam* tr. Mary Jo Lakeland. Minneapolis: University of Minnesota Press, 1993. pp.29, 100-101.
(2) Grousset, René, *The Empire of the Steppes.* tr. Naomi Walford. New Brunswick: Rutgers University Press, 1970. p. 237.

Section L

Lakshmi Bai

Rani, regent ruler of Jhansi (1853 and 1857-1858)

Jhansi is located in Uttar Pradesh state in Northern India. Lakshmi Bai, originally named Manukarnika, was born c. 1833 in Benares, the daughter of Moropant Tambe, a Brahmin official. She married Ganyadhar Rao and on her wedding day took the name of Lakshmi, the wife of the god Vishnu. The couple had one son who died at the age of three months. When Ganyadhar Rao became seriously ill in 1853, to assure the continuation of his line, the couple adopted five-year-old Damodar Rao, a descendant of Rao's grandfather. Rao died the same year, and by his will Lakshmi assumed the reign for their adopted son.

At this point, the British saw the opportunity to annex Jhansi and declared that Damodar was not a legal heir. For over a year Lakshmi battled in the courts, but ultimately she was deposed by the British East India Company. But in 1857, when the Indian Mutiny escalated into a Jh_nsian uprising against the British, Lakshmi was hastily recalled by the same people who had deposed her and was requested to restore order: "We suggest that you take your kingdom and hold it, along with the adjoining territory, until the British authority is established. We shall be eternally grateful if you will also protect our lives." Lakshmi resumed the reins of government with her father as minister. Later in 1857 the British moved to recapture Jhansi, and Lakshmi's forces, with Lakshmi at their head dressed in male attire, resisted.

The rebel leader Ramchandra Panduranga, who called himself Tantia Topi, rode to assist her, but the British defeated their combined forces. Lakshmi and her father escaped and were welcomed by Topi at Kalpi. They all proceeded to Gwalior and recaptured it from the British, but in 1858, the British again took Gwalior, and Lakshmi's father was captured and hanged. The rani, who was still leading her troops, died a soldier's death on the battlefield.

Suggested Reading:

(1) Bhahacharya, Sachchinananda. *A Dictionary of Indian History*. New York: George Braziller, 1967. p. 538.
(2) Premble, John. *The Raj, the Indian Mutiny, and the Kingdom of Oudh 1801-1859)*. Rutherford, NJ: Farleigh Dickinson University Press, 1977. p. 192.
(3) Spear, Percival. *A History of India*. (London: Penguin Books, 1987. vol. 2, p. 142.

Laodicé (or Nysa)

Queen of Cappadocia (c. 131/0 B.C.-c. 126 B.C.)

Cappadocia was a small kingdom in eastern Anatolia. Laodicé was the wife of Ariarathes V, king of Cappadocia (r. c. 163-c. 131/0 B.C.) The couple had six sons. When Ariathes was killed in battle, Laodicé poisoned five of her sons before they were old enough to assume the throne so as to be able to rule in her own right. One son, the youngest, was saved and, after Laodicé was removed by an outraged public and assassinated, he ascended the throne as Ariarathes VI.

Suggested Reading:

(1) Rawlinson, George. *Ancient History*. New York: Barnes & Noble Books, 1993. p. 247.
(2) Carpenter, Clive. *The Guinness Book of Kings, Rulers & Statesmen*. Enfield, Middlesex: Guinness Superlatives Ltd., 1978. p. 40.

Laodike III

Sovereign Lady of Propontis (253), Regent of Syria (247-246)

She was born ca. 287/284. She was married to her husband/brother or cousin, King Antiochiaos II of Syria (267/266) and was politically active during his reign prior to their divorce. Then she was named Lady of Propontis, which is in Turkey. She had a son, Seleukos II Kallinikos, for whom she acted as regent until he came of age in 246. She continued to take an active part in politics until her murder in ca. 237/236.

Liang

Empress, regent in China (A.D. 144-150)

Following the reign on Emperor Ho-Ti (r. A. D. 88-105), there were civil wars and anarchy, as many local warlords managed to establish their independence. Liang was the first of six powerful empresses from three great families who, with court eunuchs, managed to keep the court's wealth and power in their hands by seeing to it that infants and young children were appointed to the throne. Of the twelve emperors of the Eastern Han Dynasty, eight were between the ages of three months and 15 years. In A.D. 132, Empress Liang secured influence for her father, and the Liang family captured control of the court. Empress Liang's father held power for 12 years until he died in 144. Beginning with the year 144, three young emperors were appointed for whom Empress Liang served as regent. One was her brother, Liang Chi. She died in 150, to be replaced by another young empress. In 159 Emperor Huan Ti put Liang Chi to death and wiped out the last of the Liangs.

Suggested Reading:

(1) Morton, W. Scott, *China: Its History and Culture*. New York: McGraw-Hill, 1980. p. 63.
(2) Reischauer, Edwin O. and John K. Fairbank. *East Asia: The Great Tradition*. Boston: Houghton Mifflin, 1960. pp. 125-126.
(3) Langer, William L., ed. *World History*. Boston: Houghton Mifflin, 1940, 1980. pp. 148-149.

Lilavati

Queen, ruler of Sri Lanka (1197-1200, 1209-1210, 1211-1212)

During a period of political instability in Sri Lanka, Queen Lilavati was called to the throne on three separate occasions. Frequent incursions from South India kept the island in turmoil. In addition, political factions would frequently break away to form a separate feudal state.

Lilavati, a Kalingan, married Parakramabahu I (r. c. 1153-1186). Following his death, her brother Nissankamalla reigned for approximately ten years. Briefly the island fell into the hands of Codaganga before Queen

Lilavati came to the throne on her own in 1197. She ruled for three years and was deposed. Her first reign was followed by the two-year reign of King Sahassamalla, the six-year reign of Queen Kalyanavati, and the one-year reigns each of King Dharmasoka and King Anikanga. In 1209 Queen Lilavati was restored for one year and again deposed; in 1210 she was replaced by King Lokesvara, but she was reinstated for another brief reign the following year. In 1212 she was again deposed in favor of King Parakráma Pandu.

This frequent unseating of the monarch is an indication of the general anarchy that existed which allowed a ruthless South Indian fortune-seeker named Magha to invade in 1215, seize power, and rule dictatorially for over two decades.

Suggested Reading:

(1) Carpenter, Clive. *The Guinness Book of Kings, Rulers & Statesmen.* Enfield, Middlesex: Guinness Superlatives Ltd., 1978. p. 228.

Liliuokalani

Queen, ruler of Hawaii (1891-1895)

She was born Lydia Paki Kamekeha Liliuokalani in 1838. Her mother was Keohokalole, an adviser to King Kamehameha III, who ruled from 1825 to 1854. Before his death in 1824, the king adopted his nephew, who ruled as Kamekameha IV from 1855 to 1862. When King Kamekameha IV's only son died, he withdrew from public office, grief-stricken. He was replaced by Lunalilo, who had the support of the ex-king and his wife, Queen Emma. Lunalilo died in 1874 without appointing a successor. The contest that followed pitted the partisans of Dowager Queen Emma against the supporters of the lineage of Keohokalole, Lydia's mother. The latter faction was victorious. Lydia's brother, David Kalakaua, reigned from 1874 to 1891. In 1877 her younger brother, Prince Regent W.P. Leleiohoku, died and Lydia was named heir presumptive. She succeeded to the throne at the age of 53 upon the king's death (1891). Shortly after her succession, her husband John Owen Dominis, whom she had married in 1862, died. American colonists led by Sanford Dole, who controlled most of Hawaii's economy, revolted when the queen attempted to restore some of the monarchy's power dissipated during her brother's reign. Dole's faction asked for her abdication in 1893, and she had to appeal to U.S. President Grover Cleveland for reinstatement. Dole's defied the president's orders and set up a republic of his own. The royalists revolted, but Dole's forces squelched the revolt and jailed the queen's supporters. She abdicated in 1895 in order to win pardons for them. In 1898, the year the islands were formally transferred to the United States, she composed "Aloha Oe," which quickly became the farewell song for her country. She died in 1917.

Suggested Reading:

(1) James, Edward T., ed. *Notable American Women 1607-1950.* Cambridge: Belknap Press of Harvard University Press, 1971. vol. 2, pp. 403-404.
(2) Langer, William L., ed. *World History.* Boston: Houghton Mifflin, 1940, 1980. p. 938.

Livni, Tzipi

Israeli Foreign Minister, Leader of the Kadima Party (2009)

Tzipi Livni was born Tzipora Malka Livni in Tel Aviv on July 7, 1958, the daughter of Irgun members Eitan Livni and Sara Rosenberg, Jewish activists. She was a former Mossad agent although her exact role has been shrouded in mystery for political reasons. She attained the rank of lieutenant in the IDF. After leaving Mossad she graduated from Bar Ilan University with a degree in Law. She is married with two children.

Her political career took off when she left the right wing Likud party in the mass exodus initiated by hawkish Ariel Sharon to form the Kadima party. She served as Minister of Justice, Minister of Regional Cooperation, Minister of Agriculture and Rural Development, Minister without Portfolio, Minister of Immigrant Absorption, Minister of Housing & Construction, and Foreign Minister.

When Ariel Sharon suffered a stroke, Ehud Olmert took over the reins as party leader and Prime Minister. However, following a disastrous incursion into Lebanon in 2006 and a perceived military miscalculation by Olmert, there were calls for him to stand down as Prime Minister. Olmert held on until he became mired in bribery allegations from his time as mayor of Jerusalem. From within Kadima, Livni, as Foreign Minister, was the first to speak out against Olmert. She went on to win the party's nomination as leader in September of 2008, while Olmert took on an interim leadership role. Her inability to form a government meant that she had to call elections in February, 2009. She was resolved not to be held hostage by the ultra orthodox religious parties whose demands she could not live with. With Likud's Binyamin Netanyahu surging in the polls, Livni, flanked by Labor's Barak and Olmert, unleashed an assault on the Gaza Strip. The fallout from this assault may determine who becomes the next Prime Minister of Israel. For now Tzipi Livni remains Israel's Foreign Minister. Were she to win the elections on February 10, 2009, she would be Israel's second female Prime Minister after Golda Meir.

Suggested Reading:

(1) "Israel's Foreign Minister Wins in Party Election," by Ethan Bronner. *Yahoo News*, September 17, 2008.
(2) "Olmert Quite Post, and Political Maneuvering Begins," by Ethan Bronner. *The New York Times*, September 21, 2008.

Lucia of Antioch (Lucy)

Princess of Antioch and Countess, titular ruler of Tripoli (1288-1289)

This Tripoli is located in Lebanon, not to be confused with Triploi, Libya. During the time of the latter Crusades, it became part of the kingdom of Acre.

Lucia was the daughter of Bohemond III (Tripoli) and VI (Antioch), prince of Antioch and count Tripoli (r. 1252-1275), during whose reign Antioch was captured by the Mamluks. She was the younger sister of Bohemond IV (Tripoli) and VII (Antioch), titular prince of Antioch and count of Triploi (1275-1287). She married Narjot of Toucy, the former Grand Admiral under Charles of Anjou, and went to live in Apula. Her brother died childless in 1287, naming Lucia as his heir. Her mother, Dowager Princess Sibylla of Armenia, fought bitterly to obtain the rule; meanwhile, a Commune was established which was to be the real sovereign authority. But with help and maneuvering, Lucia was able to garner acceptance by opposing factions of Tripoli and was given supreme authority by the nobles and the Commune. Foes had traveled to Cairo to ask the Sultan Qalawun to intervene against Lucia's reign. In 1289, the Sultan brought a huge army and launched a general assault on Tripoli. Countess Lucia was able to escape to Cyprus, but the majority of the men were massacred and the women and children captured as slaves. Tripoli officially fell to the Moslems on April 26, 1289.

Suggested Reading:

(1) Runciman, Steven. *A History of the Crusades.* Cambridge: Cambridge University Press, 1952, 1987. vol. 3, *The Kingdom of Acre.* pp. 343, 403-407.

Lucienne

Princess, regent of Antioch (c. 1252)

She was born Lucienne of Segui, a great-niece of Pope Innocent III and a cousin of Pope Gregory IX. When Prince Bohemond V of Antioch and Tripoli divorced Alice of Cyprus by reason of consanguity and began looking for a second wife, he asked Pope Gregory to choose her. Gregory chose his kinswoman Lucienne. This choice pleased Bohemond, for he could thus claim fortuous ties with the Papacy; however, the number of her Roman relatives and friends which flocked to visit Tripoli at her invitation irritated both Bohemond and the local barons. The couple took little interest in Antioch, but held court at Triploi. Lucienne had two children: Plaisance, who married King Henry of Cyprus; and Bohemond VI, who was 15 years old when his father died in 1252. Lucienne assumed the regency for her son. She was described as a feckless woman who never left Tripoli and who left the governing of Antioch to her Roman relatives. In c. 1258 members of the Embriaco family gained control of Triploi. Lucienne was removed from the regency but managed to keep many of her Roman relatives in high places. The irate local barons, who had long resented interference by foreigners, marched upon Tripoli and actually wounded Bohemond in an effort to rid the city of Lucienne's relatives. Later Bohemond arranged for the murder of Bertrand, head of the younger branch of the Embriaco, and the rebels withdrew. This murder precipitated a long blood feud between the houses of Antioch and Embriaco.

Suggested Reading:

(1) Runciman, Steven. *A History of the Crusades.* Cambridge: Cambridge University Press, 1952, 1987. vol. 3, *The Kingdom of Acre.* pp. 207, 230-231, 233, 278, 288, 343.

Lü Hou

Empress, regent of China (188-179 B.C., or 195-180 B.C.)

She was married to a former peasant named Gao Zu (or Kao Tsu), whom she had goaded into power and who ruled as first emperor of the Han dynasty from 206 or 202 to 195 B.C. Over the centuries, it became the custom that, when the child of an emperor was made heir apparent, the mother was then recognized as empress, and on accession of her son, she, as dowager empress, often became the real ruler. This tradition began with Lu. Having ambitions of her own, she saw to it that her son, Hui Ti, was formally named heir apparent. After her husband's death, the child Hui Ti ascended, and Lu was able to ignore the more important members of the imperial clan who were located in various kingdoms and marquisates some distance from the seat of government. She dominated the palace by replacing her husband's relatives with members of her own family in all positions of power. When her son died, Empress Lu designated another young child to succeed him. When the new young emperor began to question her authority, she simply had him imprisoned, seized absolute power, and designated a third child as emperor. Her efforts to usurp the throne for her family posed a serious threat to the central government, which the late emperor's kinsmen eventually recognized. His loyal ministers put her to death in 180, massacred the whole Lu clan, and placed Wen Ti, Gao Zu's son by another wife, on the throne. Lü Hou has been compared with a later Chinese strongwoman, Mme. Mao.

Suggested Reading:

(1) Bloodworth, Dennis and Ching Ping Bloodworth. *The Chinese Machiavelli: 3,000 Years of Chinese Statecraft.* New York: Dell, 1976. pp. 143, 148.

(2) Reischauer, Edwin O. and John K. Fairbank. East Asia: The Great Tradition. Boston: Houghton Mifflin, 1960. pp. 94, 117.

(3) Morton, W. Scott. *China: Its History and Culture.* New York: McGraw-Hill, 1980. p. 50.

Section M

Maham Anga

Defacto regent of Mughal Empire (1560-1562)

She was Akbar's chief nurse prior to his enthronement at age thirteen as emperor (Kalanaur, 1556). Her own son, Adham Khan, as Akbar's foster brother, was regarded as almost one of the family. Maham Anga, shrewd and ambitious and very much in charge of the household and the harem, sought to advance her own authority and that of her son. In 1560 the two tricked Akbar into coming to India without his chief minister and guardian Bairam, and they were able to convince Akbar that now that he was seventeen, he didn't need Bairam. Akbar dismissed his minister and sent him on a pilgrimmage to Mecca. Months later Bairam was murdered by an Afghan, and much of his former power passed to Maham Anga. Her son was sent to invade Malwa, but his conduct following his victory was reprehensible. He kept tha treasure and the harem for himself and had the other captives butchered while he and his fellow officer sat jesting. Akbar, enraged when he heard of the outrage, set off for Malwa at such speed that Maham Anga had no chance to send a warning to her son. Adham Khan, chastened but not dismissed, handed over the booty to Akbar and was forgiven, but he secretly kept back two young girls for himself. When Akbar heard rumors of this last treachery, Maham Anga had the girls murdered before they could testify against her son. Her power began to wane in 1561, however, when Akbar appointed Atkah Khan, a man outside her sphere of influence, as his new chief minister. Five months later (1562), her son attempted to assassinate the new minister and was thrown off the parapet—twice—as execution. Akbar himself informed Maham Anga of her son's death, and she died shortly afterward. The emperor, age 19, was then able to rule without interference.

Suggested Reading:

(1) Gascoigne, Bamber. *The Great Moghuls.* New York: Dorset Press, 1971. pp. 79-81.
(2) Spear, Percival. *History of India.* vol. 2. London: Penguin Books, Ltd. 1987. pp. 29-30.

Mandughai

Khatun, regent of Mongolia (1470-c. 1492)

She was the very young widow of Grand Khan Mandaghol, Jenghiz—khan's 27th successor, who died in 1467 of war wounds. His great-nephew and heir, Bolkho, succeeded him, but was assassinated in 1470 before he could be proclaimed khan. The mother of Bolkho's five-year-old son Dayan had deserted the child, so Mandughai took him under her protection, proclaimed him khan, and became his regent. She assumed command of the Mongol troops and defeated their enemy, the Oirat. In 1481 she married Dayan, who was then 16. In 1491-1492 she again led the army to fend off the Oirat. History gives Mandughai credit for abolishing Oirat supremacy and restoring that of the eastern Mongols. She, and after her, Dayan, infused new life into the Jenghiz-khanate's fading authority.

Suggested Reading:

(1) Grousset, René, *The Empire of the Steppes.* tr. Naomi Walford. New Brunswick, NJ: Rutgers University Press, 1970. p. 509.

Margaret of Antioch-Lusignan

Regent of Tyre (1283-1291)

Called "the loveliest girl of her generation", she was the daughter of Henry of Antioch and Isabella of Cyprus and the sister of King Hugh III, ruler of Cyprus and Jerusalem. She married John of Montfort, lord of Tyre, who died ca. 1283. When Sultan Qalawun was preparing to attack those Franks not protected by the truce of 1283, Lady Margaret asked him for a truce, which was granted. She renewed the truce in 1290 after Qalawun invaded Tripoli. Early in 1291 she handed Tyre over to her nephew Amalric, brother of King Henry II of Cyprus.

Suggested Reading:

(1) Runciman, Steven, *A History of the Crusades*. Cambridge: Cambridge University Press, 1952, 1987. vol. 3, *The Kingdom of Acre and the Later Crusades*. pp. 329, 394-395, 408, 421.

Marie (also Maria La Marquise or Maria of Montferrat)

Regent of Jerusalem (1205-1212)

She was born ca. 1192, the oldest daughter of Princess Isabella, heiress of the kingdom of Jerusalem, and her second husband, Conrad of Montferrat, who was murdered shortly after Marie was born. In 1198 Isabella and her fourth husband, Amalric II, were crowned king and queen of Jerusalem. In the kingdom of Jerusalem, hereditary right to rule dictated that Maria would inherit the throne, but the High Court preserved its claim to elect a ruler. Isabella died in ca. 1205, as did Amalric. Maria, at age 13, acceded to the throne, and John of Ibelin, lord of Beirut, was appointed egent for three years. In 1208, at age 17, she was married to a penniless knight from Champagne, John of Brienne, who was already 60 years old. In 1212 they had a daughter, Yolanda (also called Yolande or Isabella II). That same year Marie died. Her husband continued to rule for their daughter.

Suggested Reading:

(1) Runciman, Steven, *A History of the Crusades*. Cambridge: Cambridge University Press, 1952, 1987. vol. 3, *The Kingdom of Acre and the Later Crusades*. pp. 32, 66, 84, 94-95, 104, 132-134, 320.

Mary

Queen, regent of Georgia (1027-c. 1036)

Mary was the daughter of Sennacherib-John of Vaspurahan and the wife of George I (Giorgi), Bagratid king of Georgia from 1014 to 1027. They had a son, Bagrat, born in 1018. During George's reign, he determined to restore the lands of David of Tao to Georgia, and when he occupied Tao in 1015-1016, he broke the peace with Byzantium. Eventually, in 1021, King Basil II and his Armenian Bagratid allies swept through Georgia and devastated the land, slaughtering women and children as well. When he invaded again in 1022, King George submitted to the emperor, relinquished all claim to Tao, and gave him his three-year-old son Bagrat as a hostage. Both Georgia and Armenia were left under the Byzantine thumb. George died in 1027, and Bagrat IV succeeded his father as a minor of eight. Queen Mary served as regent during a troubled time in Georgia's history but was able to secure for her son a kingdom that was the major indigenous power in Caucasia.

In 1031 after the *Katholikos* of Iberia, Queen Mary and the minister Melchisedech journeyed to Constantinople on a diplomatic mission on behalf of her son. Peace was concluded, and young Bagrat received the dignity of *Curopalate*, which had been denied his father. Bagrat was able to use his power as *Curopalate* to remove recalcitrant princes holding hereditary possessions, reducing those who opposed him to a lowly status, and to elevate loyal followers into the upper nobility. Mary also made arrangements at the time of her journey to Constantinople for her son to marry the Emperor's niece, Helena. Bagrat IV reigned for forty-five years.

Suggested Reading:

(1) Allen, W.E.D., *A History of the Georgian People from the Beginning Down to the Russian Conquest in the Nineteenth Century*. New York: Barnes & Noble Books, 1971. pp. 87-90.

(2) Suny, Ronald Grigor, *The Making of the Georgian Nation*. Bloomington: Indiana University Press, in association with Hoover Institutions Press, Stanford University., 1988. pp. 33-34.

(3) Hussey, J.M., ed., *The Cambridge Medieval History*. Cambridge: Cambridge University Press, 1966. vol. 4, pt. 1, p. 621.

Mary (or Maria) of Antioch

Empress, regent of Byzantine Empire (1180-1183)

Maria was the daughter of Constance of Antioch and Raymond of Poitiers, and the sister of King Bohemond III. In 1160, in an undeclared contest between Mary and Melisende, daughter of Raymond II of Tripoli, she was chosen by Byzantine Emperor Manuel I (1143-1180) as his second wife. The couple had a son, Alexius II, who acceded to the throne at the age of 11 with his mother as regent. Empress Mary was the first Latin to be ruler of the Empire, and as such, she was resented by the people. Italian opportunistic merchants had all but gained a monopoly on trade in the city. To confound her proplem with her subjects, Mary took as her advisor and, as rumors had it, possibly her lover, her husband's nephew, the Protosebastus Alexius Comnenus, uncle of Maria of Jerusalem. He, too, was unpopular. The Porphyrogennete Maria and her husband, Ranier of Montferrat, plotted to kill her uncle Alexius, but their plot went awry.

In 1182 Empress Maria's cousin-in-law, Andronicus Comnenus, invaded Constantinople; it was the opportunity the people had needed to fall upon all the hated Latins in their midst. The citizens slaughtered the haughty Italian merchants who had controlled the city's trade. Andronicus then eliminated his rivals one by one, beginning with the Porphyrogennete and her husband, whom he murdered. Young Alexius II was forced to sign a warrant condemning his mother Mary to be strangled to death (1182). The boy himself was murdered two months later.

Suggested Reading:

(1) Ostrogorsky, George. *History of the Byzantine State*. New Brunswick, NJ: Rutgers University Press, 1969. pp. 394, 396.
(2) Runciman, Steven. *A History of the Crusades*. Cambridge: Cambridge University Press, 1952, 1987. vol. 2, *The Kingdom of Jerusalem*. pp. 359-360, 427-428.
(3) Previté-Orton, C.W. *The Shorter Cambridge Medieval History*. Cambridge: Cambridge University Press, 1982. vol. 1, p. 536.

Al-Mashhadani, Tayseer

Sunni Arab Lawmaker (—2006—)

Tayseer Najah Awad al-Mashhadani, a Sunni Muslim, trained as an engineer and joined the Iraqi Islamic Party. In December 2005 she was elected to the National Assembly of Iraq as part of the Sunni-Arab-led Iraqi Accord Front. After serving a little more than six months, on July 1, 2006, she and eight of her bodyguards were detained at a checkpoint in the Shiite neighborhood of Shaab in Eastern Baghdad. One of the bodyguards escaped Tayseer and the seven remaining members of the party were abducted. The Iraw Islamic Party accused Shiite militias under the leadership of Muqtada al-Sadr of masterminding the abduction, and Abu Dereh, Sadrist warlord was also implicated.

Vice President Tariq al-Hashimi told reporters that a group claiming to be holding Tayseer al-Mashhadani contacted his Iraqi Islamic Party and made the demands. Al-Hashimi did not say when or how the contact was made and whether the group offered proof to back up their claim to be holding her. But al-Hashimi, a Sunni and the party's leader, said, "We believe she is alive."

Two months later, she was released.

(1) "Sunni Lawmaker, Freed by Captors in Iraq, Describes Her Ordeal" by Damien Cave and Qais Mizher. *The New York Times*. August 27, 2006.
(2) "Lawyer's fate sealed with a judas kiss." *Sydney Morning Herald*, August 23, 2006.

Mayawati, Kumari

Chief minister of Uttar Pradesh in India (2007-)

Kumari Mayawati, a daughter of so-called untouchables, low-caste, of Dalit, has become India's most maverick politician. She was born into a community once relegated to leather work and, according to Hinduism's ritual purity code, forbidden to share tea cups or water wells with upper-caste people.

The daughter of a government worker in Delhi, she became a schoolteacher, earned a law degree and then devoted herself full time to what was then a fledgling party. In 2007 she stunned the nation when she won majority control of India's largest state with an inventive political coalition that fused votes from up and down the ancient Hindu caste pyramid.

By 2008 Ms. Mayawati had emerged as the most important low-caste politician in India's history, and she was asserting herself as a rainbow coalition leader, a woman whom all Indians can trust to be their prime minister one day.

While the advance of so-called low-caste, or Dalit, politicians like Ms. Mayawati has reshaped Indian politics for 20 years, no one from her social rank has so shaken up the country's traditional political order. Dalits represent roughly 16 percent of the population and have traditionally been shunted to the lowest rungs of Indian society.

Ms. Mayawati leads the government of Uttar Pradesh, a sprawling northern state with a population of more than 160 million. Her admirers see the rise and reinvention of this unmarried outcaste woman of 52 as a triumph of India's democracy over its deeply conservative and stratified traditions.

Her detractors see her as a symbol of an increasingly crude and unprincipled politics. She is accused of being ostentatious and corrupt and of striking deals with anyone who will advance her political ambitions.

Even though caste discrimination has been officially banned in India, politics remains one of caste's last bastions, with every caste group looking to its own to advance its interests.

Ms. Mayawati has been especially skillful in forging alliances with upper castes, and as chief minister of Uttar Pradesh, she has promoted an ambitious agenda devised to appeal across caste and class lines. Her main rallying cries are for an eight-lane highway, better policing and private investment as a means to ease poverty.

"I prefer to be known as a leader for all the communities," she said in a rare interview with American journalists. "In every community there are poor and unemployed people."

Her ascent is all the more important today because of the jigsaw puzzle nature of Indian politics. Neither of the national parties—the governing Congress Party or its main opponent, the Bharatiya Janata Party—was expected to win a majority in Parliament on its own in the next election, which was expected within a year.

Ms. Mayawati was positioning herself as a vital ally to whichever party may need her to govern—and if she bargains hard enough, she could even become India's first Dalit prime minister. Uttar Pradesh, her state, has the largest bloc of seats in India's 543-member Parliament.

"She is an original," said Ajoy Bose, author of a largely sympathetic political biography of Ms. Mayawati published recently by Penguin Books India. "She is someone who is obviously going to play a major role in our lives."

Mrinal Pande, chief editor of the Hindi-language daily newspaper Hindustan, predicted that Ms. Mayawati could link arms with any party and in turn exact a high price, calling her a "predator with little ideological baggage."

A few years ago, Ms. Mayawati campaigned on behalf of a radical Hindu nationalist, Narendra Modi; in the summer of 2008, she was seen warming up to Communist leaders in a potential alliance against the coalition government led by the Congress Party.

In a country where caste continues to shape the way people vote, it remains to be seen whether Ms. Mayawati's cross-caste strategy will resonate broadly and whether her Bahujan Samaj Party—in Hindi, the party of the majority of society—will be able to expand nationally.

Asked where she sees herself a few years from now, she demurred, suggesting only that she would aim to do across India what she had done in Uttar Pradesh, commonly known by its initials, U.P.

"Now," she said, "people in the rest of the country are watching."

"We cannot fight just as Dalits," was a message she repeated. "I understand for centuries people have fought each other. It is not easy to bring them together. But we have done this in U.P."

She is affectionately referred to as Behenji, which is a respectful way to address a sister.

Her greatest innovation has been to lift a page from the Congress Party's playbook, and flip it. She has gone after Congress's traditional constituents—Dalits, socially privileged Brahmins and Muslims—but while a Brahmin has often led the others under the Congress Party, she insists on being the low-born leader at the helm.

Ms. Mayawati has lately sharpened her attacks on Congress Party leaders. As Rahul Gandhi, scion of the upper-caste Nehru-Gandhi dynasty, went on a widely publicized tour of the Uttar Pradesh countryside, eating and sleeping in low-caste homes, Ms. Mayawati accused him of having to purify himself afterward with a "special soap."

Ms. Mayawati's governing of Uttar Pradesh has been characterized by supersize acts of political symbolism. She has ordered the arrests of notorious organized crime bosses, along with a handful of known criminals in her own party, and in so doing, sought to send a message that the police would be free to do their job. She is famous for lording over civil servants in her state and transferring them at the drop of a hat. She has put up giant statues of Dalit icons, including herself, in the heart of this capital.

Her big-ticket plank today is a nearly 600-mile, $7.5 billion highway stretching across the state and promising to sprout several private townships along the way. It is financed with private money, and observers of Uttar Pradesh politics say it could become an inviting source of graft.

Corruption is in fact the most serious criticism against Ms. Mayawati. The latest accusations surfaced in July, 2008, in selected leaks to the news media. The Central Bureau of Investigation, the nation's highest law enforcement agency, accused Ms. Mayawati and her relatives of having illegally accumulated $2.4 million in property, including a villa in the elite diplomatic enclave of New Delhi, and $1.2 million in bank accounts. Ms. Mayawati promptly denounced the charges as politically motivated.

Among her Dalit loyalists, Ms. Mayawati is sometimes called "a goddess." In interviews across the state, many readily said they felt proud that a Dalit's daughter was governing the state. They also said her ascent had emboldened them to report crimes or seek benefits from the state.

In Agrona village, on the western edge of the state, Rakesh Kumar, 34, a factory worker who belongs to one of the lowest castes, offered his own example. For years, his family had tried to retrieve a small patch of land, about 170 square yards, that had been occupied by middle-caste villagers called Gujjars.

Every time the Kumars went to the local authorities for redress, they got a runaround. Then, last summer, shortly after Ms. Mayawati took office, Mr. Kumar, with the aid of a local worker from the Bahujan Samaj Party, tried once more. "Behenji became chief minister," he said. "That's what gave me strength."

This time, the officials responded. They warned the Gujjars and threatened to call the police if they did not vacate the Kumars' land. After 12 years of trying, Mr. Kumar put a fence around his land. He plans to build a house there. (A Gujjar leader in the village confirmed the story.)

"The chief minister is our own kind," marveled Rajpal, who said that he was around 50 and that he was a sweeper by caste. "Now we are not afraid of the police. We are not afraid of the Gujjars. We are not afraid of anyone."

Suggested Reading:

(1) "Daughter of India's Underclass Rises on Votes That Cross Caste Lines" by Somini Sengupta. *The New York Times,* July 18, 2008.

Mehr-on-Nesa (or Mehrunissa)

See Nur Jahan

Meir, Golda

Premier of Israel (1969-1974)

She was born Goldie Mabovitch in 1898 in Kiev, Russia, to Moshe Mabovitz and his wife. To escape persecution, the family migrated in 1906 to Milwaukee, Wisconsin, where Golda's father became a railroad worker and her mother a grocery clerk. Golda attended Milwaukee Teachers Training College. She joined the Poale Zion, a faction of the Labor Zionists Party. In 1917 she married Morris Myerson, a sign painter she had met while visiting her sister in Denver. In 1921 she persuaded her husband to move to Palestine and live in a kibbutz. In 1924, after their first child was born, they moved to Jerusalem where Morris worked as a bookeeper and Golda took in laundry. They had another child, born in Jerusalem. By 1929 Golda had immersed herself in the Zionist movement, quickly becoming a leader. During World War II she emerged as a forceful spokesperson to the British in behalf of Zionism. Her husband hated his life in Israel, but Golda was possessed by her mission. In 1945 he and Golda divorced. He died in Tel Aviv in 1951. Golda was a signer of Israel's Proclamation of Independence, and in 1948, during the war for independence, Golda traveled to the United States to raise 50 million dollars for the cause. In 1949 she was elected to the legislature, where she served for 25 years; Ben Gurion called her "the only man in the cabinet." In 1956, at Ben Gurion's suggestion, she Hebraized her name to Golda Meir. In 1969 she became Israel's fourth prime minister. Meir faced hostility of Israel's neighbors, necessitating a huge defense budget in a struggling economy, and mass disunity, not only within her own Labor party, but in the country as a whole, which was a mixture of occidental and oriental Jews. In 1974, after the outbreak of the fourth Arab-Israeli War late the year before, she was forced to resign, although she continued to work in politics. Her private life and her political career had been ones of constant struggle, but her ability to see humor in the bitterest of moments helped her to keep her perspective. She once said, "Can you imagine Moses dragging us forty years through the desert to bring us to the one place in the Middle East where there is no oil?" When she died in 1978 at the age of 80, it was discovered that she had had leukemia for 12 years.

Suggested Reading:

(1) Meir, Golda, *My Life*. New York: G.P. Putnam's Sons, 1975.
(2) Avallone, Michael, *A Woman Called Golda*. New York: Norton Publications, 1982.

Mei

Queen of Cambodia (1835-1847)

Mei, the daughter, of King Ang Chan (r. 1797-1835), came to the throne upon her father's death. At the time Cambodia was a vassel of Vietnam, so she exercised very little power during her 12-year reign. In 1847 she was deposed in favor of Ang Duang, son of former King Ang Eng. She died in 1875.

Suggested Reading:

(1) Morby, John E. *Dynasties of the World*. Oxford: Oxford University Press, 1989. p. 231.

Melisende (or Melissande)

Queen of Jerusalem (1131-1152)

She was the eldest of four d daughters of Queen Morphia (the daughter of Gabriel of Melitene) and King Baldwin II, ruler of Jerusalem from 1118 to 1131. Before her marriage, her chief companion was Hugh of Le Puiset, lord of Jaffy, a tall, handsome man who had lived in the court as a boy. In 1129 her parents married her to Fulk V, who was short, wiry, red-faced and middle-aged, for whom she never cared. After she and Fulk ascended to the throne following her father's death in 1131, she continued her intimate friendship with Hugh, now married to an older woman, Emma, widow of Eustace I of Sidon. Fulk grew jealous and soon the court was divided between Count Hugh and the king. Emma's son, to protect his mother's honor, challenged Hugh to a duel. Hugh did not appear for the duel, a sign of his cowardice and his guilt. Sometime soon afterward, supporters of either Fulk or Emma, the aggrieved parties, stabbed Hugh, but he did not die. Because Fulk was suspected of being behind the plot to kill Hugh, when the would-be assassin was caught, Fulk arranged for a public execution. The assassin had his limbs cut off one by one, but while his head remained, he was to continue to repeat his confession. Melisende was still so angry over the incident that for many months afterward, Hugh's enemies and even Fulk himself feared for their lives. Melisende had several children by Fulk, but only two survived: Baldwin III, born in 1130, who ruled from 1143 to 1162, and Amalric I, born in 1136, who ruled from 1162 to 1174. In 1143 Fulk died, thrown from a horse while on a family picnic. Melisende appointed her older son, Baldwin, as her colleague and assumed the government herself. When Baldwin reached the age of 22, he wanted to rule alone, but Melisende, conscious of her own hereditary right, declined to hand over the power to him completely. She made arrangement for his coronation with the stipulation that she would be crowned again by his side so that her joint authority would be specifically honored. However, Baldwin secretly changed the date of the coronation and was crowned without her. The act created dissention between supporters of each side, but Melisende, striken at her own son's perfidy, yielded to him and retired from politics. She died in 1161.

Suggested Reading:

(1) Runciman, Steven, *A History of the Crusades*. Cambridge: Cambridge University Press, 1952, 1987. vol. 2, *The Kingdom of Jerusalem*. pp. 177-178, 185-187, 191-193, 231-236, 247, 279-283, 311, 333-337, 360-161.

Min (or Bin)

Queen, twenty-fifth regent ruler of Yi Dynasty in Choson (Korea) (1873-1882 and 1882-1895)

The Yi Dynasty, with 26 monarchs, ruled Korea until the Japanese annexation in 1910. During the first ten years of the reign of King Kojong, usually known as Yi T'aeWang, power was in the hands of his father, Taewon-gun, who was first driven out in 1873 by Confucian officials whom he had antagonized and by the powerful Min family. Although Taewon-gun had arranged for Kojong's marriage to a member of the Yohung Min clan, Queen Min used the occasion of a public denunciation of Taewon-gun to end his regency. Power then passed to Min, who at first opposed all efforts at modernizing or westernizing Korea. But after an expedition to Japan resulted in the adoption of a policy of enlightenment that would establish ties with Japan and Western powers, which the Confucian literati opposed, Taewon-gun's popularity began to rise again. He made plans to return to power, and in 1881 he determined to put his eldest son Yi Chae-son, born of a secondary wife, on Kojong's throne. He also planned to eliminate the advocates of enlightenment. The plot was uncovered, however, and, although Taewon-gun was not prosecuted, Yi Chae-son and more than thirty of his followers were put to death. Taewon-gun was now pitted against Queen Min as the country reacted violently to the expansion of Japanese influence in Korea. In 1882 a mutiny by old line soldiers resulted in an attack on the Japanese legation, and the building was burned to the ground. The soldiers next invaded the palace and Queen Min escaped assassination by hiding. To quell the violence, King Kojong had no choice but to re-call

Taewon-gun to power. His return was a vote for a policy of exclusion, but now both Japan and China vied for power over Korean affairs. When Taewon-gun paid a courtesy call to Chinese headquarters, he was kidnapped (1882) and taken to Tientsin in China. A *coup* in 1884 resulted in the progressives pressing for his return, not because they favored his policies, but because they needed his help in overcoming the entrenched influence of Queen Min's family. Eventually, Kojong and the Min oligarchs could only maintain power by enlisting foreign support. Min was characterized as "the one vital ruling spark in the effete Korean court." She was assassinated in 1895 in a plot engineered with the connivance of the Japanese resident, Viscount Miura, because she was suspected of being the mastermind behind the anti-Japanese attitude of the Korean government.

Suggested Reading:

(1) Bergamini, David, *Japan's Imperial Conspiracy*. New York: William Morrow, 1972. pp. 282-283.
(2) Langer, William L., ed., *World History*. Boston: Houghton Mifflin, 1940, 1980. pp. 916-917, 922.
(3) Lee, Ki-baik, *A New History of Korea*. tr. Edward W. Wagner with Edward J. Shultz. Cambridge: Harvard University Press, 1984. pp. 268, 273-274, 278, 281.

Mo-ki-lien, Khatun of

Regent of Mongolia (A.D.734-741)

Although the name of this Turkish queen did not survive, we know that she was married to Turkish khan Mo-ki-lien, who ruled in Mongolia from A.D. 716 and who was poisoned by his minister in 724. The couple had a son, Yi-jan, who succeeded his father and for whom the khatun served as regent. When Yi-jan died, Mo-ki-lien's younger brother, Tangri khagan, took the throne, also as a minor, and Mo-ki-lien's widow continued to serve as regent and advisor until Tangri khagan's death in 741.

Suggested Reading:

(1) Grousset, René, *The Empire of the Steppes*. tr. Naomi Walford. New Brunswich, NJ: Rutgers University Press, 1970. p. 69.

Munjong, Queen Dowager

Regent of Choson Dynasty in Korea (1545-(?)

Munjong was the strong-willed wife of King Chungjong (r. 1506-1544), who was succeeded by his eldest son, Imjong, by a different wife. Imjong was favored by the Neo-Confucian literati. However, in a purge by a rival, more traditional political faction, the "Meritorius Elite", the new king was killed and Queen Munjong's eleven-year-old son Myongjong (r. 1545-1567) was brought to the throne with the Queen Dowager as regent. Her intention was to re-establish the country's traditional social and religious practices.

During her regency the famous monk Pou was given important responsibilities in encouraging and revitalizing Buddhist, which had been declining as Confucianism had become more influential. The temple Pongun-sa was made the main temple of the Son (Zen) School of Buddhism, and Pongson-sa became the main temple of the Textual School. In 1552 the "monk examination" was re-instituted.

But with Munjong's death, Buddhism again went into decline and bacame a faith practiced primarily by women.

Suggested Reading:

(1) Lee, Ki-baik, *A New History of Korea.* tr. Edward W. Wagner with Edward J. Schulz. Cambridge, Massachusetts: Harvard University Press, 1984. pp. 199-200, 206, 394.

Myojo-tenno (or Myosho)

Empress of Japan (1630-1643)

Myosho was born in 1623, the daughter of Emperor Go-Mi-no-o, who ruled Japan from 1612 to 1629, and his consort Tofuku-mon-in (Tokugawa Kazu-ko), who was the sister of the Shogun Iemitsu. Myojo's father abdicated when she reached the age of six, and she succeeded him. During her reign of 15 years, the power was primarily in the hands of her uncle, Shogun Iemetsu. She abdicated in 1643 in favor of her brother, Go-Komyo, and lived in retirement for 53 years. She died in 1696.

Suggested Reading:

(1) Papinot, E., *Historical and Geographical Dictionary of Japan*. Rutland, VT: Charles E. Tuttle Company, 1972. pp. 124, 417.

Myosho

See Myojo-tenno

Myriam

Sultana of the Maldive Islands (1379 to 1383)

The Maldive Islands are located in the Indian Ocean, southwest of the southern tip of India. Myriam was the middle daughter of Sultan Salah al-Din Salih Albendjaly, ruler of the Maldives. When the father died, Myriam's young brother Shihab-ud-din became king. But their mother married the vizier 'Abdallah, who overpowered the young king and took over the reins of government. Later 'Abdallah married Myriam's older sister, Khadija, after her first husband died. Khadija then reigned for 33 years and died in 1379. Myriam succeeded her sister to the throne, where she remained until 1383. Her husband occupied the post as vizier. The couple had a daughter, Fatima, who succeeded her mother in 1383.

Suggested Reading:

(1) Mernissi, Fatima, *The Forgotten Queens of Islam*. tr. Mary Jo Lakeland. Minneapolis: University of Minnesota Press, 1993.

Section N

Naqi'a (also called Nitrocris)

Regent of Assyria (c. 689 B.C.)

Confusion exists over the identity of the builder queen whom Herodotus called "Nitrocris." Because of the building activity associated with Naqi'a, she has mistakenly been identified as the Nitrocris of whom Herodotus writes. However, that "queen" was probably either Addagoppe, who was never a queen at all, or Sammuramat. Naqi'a was the wife of Sennacherib, who ruled Assyria from 705 to 681 B.C., when he was murdered in Babylon, according to the biblical account (II Kings 19:37), by two of his sons. One of these sons, called Adrammelech in the bible, has now been identified as Arad-Mulissi. Naqi'a's name indicates that she was probably either Jewish or Armaean.

In c. 700 B.C. Sennacherib and Naqi'a transformed the capital city of Nineveh into a city of unparalleled splendor, building for themselves an 80-room palace to overlook it. To water the botanical gardens and orchards surrounding the palace, the king constructed major irrigation works. In 689, after having defended the city of Babylon several times, Sennacherib sacked it. Naqi'a may have served as regent during his absences on military campaign, for in the old Assyrian capital Ashur, among the steles devoted to kings, one of three devoted to women was for a "lady of Seeeacherib". Presumably this refers to his queen, although the title is now lost.

One of her sons—not one of the patricides—was a younger son, Esarhaddon, who had been picked by his father to succeed him. Esarhaddon ruled c. 680 to 669/70 B.C. When Sennacherib was murdered, Esarhaddon was far away on the field of battle, possibly so that presumably with Naqi'a's help, Esarhaddon rebuilt the city of Babylon which his father had destroyed and placed it under the rule of his son, Shamash-shum-ukin. In 670 Esarhaddon was killed while on campaign to Egypt, and his other son Ashurbanipal ascended (669).

Suggested Reading:

(1) Fairservis, Walter A., Jr., *The Ancient Kingdoms of the Nile*. New York: Mentor/NAL, 1962. pp. 182-187.
(2) Saggs, H.W.F., *The Might That Was Assyria*. London: Sidgwick and Jackson Ltd., 1984. p. 79, 98-99.
(3) White, J. E. Manchip, *Ancient Egypt*. New York: Dover Publications, 1970. pp. 188, 192.

Naryshkina, Natalya Kirillovna (Nathalie)

Queen-mother, de-facto ruler of Russia (1689-1694)

A member of the influential Naryshkin family, she was educated by a guardian, Artamon Sergeyevich Matveyev, in Western ways. She had a powerful brother, the boyar, Leo Naryshkin. She became the second wife of Tsar Alexis and had a son, Peter (Peter I the Great). Tsar Alexis died in 1676 when Peter was only four years old. The tsar was succeeded by Peter's half-brother, Fyodor III, although Fyodor's mother's relatives, the Miloslavsky's, held ultimate power. After Fyodor died without leaving an heir in 1682, Peter was first named tsar over his feeble-minded half-brother Ivan, but after a revolt by the Miloslavsky faction, the two brothers were proclaimed co-tsars, with Peter's 25-year-old half-sister Sofya as regent. Sofya went to great lengths to keep Peter and Natalya at a distance from power; in fact, they lived in some fear for Peter's safety in the village of Preobrazhenskoye. There, Peter received a much more liberal education than he would have received in the confines of the palace. In 1689, in an attempt to show the world that Peter was old enough to govern, Queen Natalya arranged a political marriage for her 17-year-old son with Yevdokiya Fyodorovna Lopukhina (Eudoxia). However, Peter had no interest in his wife and later banished her to a convent. When an attempted *coup* by Sofya's adherents was uncovered, Peter and the Narynshkins removed Sofya as regent and sent her to a Moscow convent. When the *coup* failed, Peter was at last acknowledged. Ivan V was still nominally a joint ruler, and Peter, at seventeen, showed no inclination to take personal charge of the government. the direction of the state fell into the hands of Natalya, her brother Leo, and Patriarch Joachim. After Joachim's death in 1690, Patriarch Hadrian also assumed some power. During this time, with Natalya assuming a role as acting regent, Muscovite isolationism and suspicion of anything foreign again flourished. But when Natalya died in 1694, Peter I, at age twenty-two, finally assumed the reigns of government.

Suggested Reading:

(1) Riasnovsky, Nicholas V., *A History of Russia*. Oxford: Oxford University Press, 1863, 1993. pp. 213-216.

Nitrocris

Possible misnomer of Addagoppe, or Adda-Guppi, of Haran). See Addagoppe.

Nur al-'Alam Nakiyyat al-Din Shah

Sultana of Atjeh in Indonesia (1675-1678)

Atjeh was a small Muslim sultanate on the northern tip of Sumatra which was a center of trade, dominating the world supply of pepper. Nur al-'Alam is listed by H. Djajadiningrat in his article on "Atjeh" in the *Encyclopedia of Islam* as the fifteenth sovereign of the dynasty. She succeeded another woman, probably her mother, Sultana Tadj al-'Alam Safiyyat al-Din Shah, who had reigned from 1641 to 1675. Nur al-'Alam ruled for only three years. She was also followed by another woman, probably a sister or daughter, 'Inayat Shah Zakiyyat al-Din Shah. The fact that their political enemies had brought from Mecca a *fatwa* forbidding by law that a woman rule further suggests that the women wielded considerable power.

Suggested Reading:

(1) Jones, Russell,tr. *Hikayat Sultan Ibrahim Ibn Adham*, Lanham, MD: University Press of America, 1985.

(2) Mernissi, Fatima, *The Forgotten Queens of Islam*. tr. Mary Jo Lakeland. Minneapolis: University of Minnesota Press, 1993. pp. 30, 110.

Nur Jahan (also called Mehr-n-Nesa, Mihn-un-Nisa, or Mehrunissa)

Empress, defacto ruler of India (1611-1627 intermittently)

Originally called Mehrunissa, she was born in 1577, the daughter of a Persian, Sher Alkun (or I'timad-ud-Dawlah), who was in the service of the

Moghul Jahangir, who ruled from 1605 to 1627. Mehrunissa married a Persian, Sher Afkun, whom Jahangir posted to Bengal. She had a daughter, Ladili Begam, who married Prince Shahiryar, a son of Jahangir. Sher Afkun died in 1607, possibly at Jahangir's instigation. The widow Mehrunissa was brought to court as lady-in-waiting to Salima, a widow of the previous Moghul, Akbar.

Jahangir married Mehrunissa four years later and gave her the name Nur Mahal, "Light of the Palace." Her brother, Asaf Khan, was given a high ranking position second only to that of her father, who was promoted to chief minister. Mehrunissa soon made herself indispensable to the dependent, alcoholic king, who gave her a new name, Nur Jahan, "Light of the World." Her mother discovered attar of roses and was rewarded with a pearl necklace. The family had clearly taken over the palace. Nur Jahan, her brother, and her father dominated the politics of the realm, with Nur Jahan making the decisions and the others carrying them out. British Ambassador Sir Thomas Roe wrote home to the future King Charles I that Nur Jahan "governs him and wynds him up at her pleasure." Jahangir fell ill in 1620, and from then on his poor health, conpounded by alcohol, opium and asthma, made it imperative for Nur Jahan to exercise control. Her father died and her brother was occupied elsewhere during the final five years of Jahangir's life, and Nur Jahan ruled alone, from inside the harem. There is no evidence that she ever broke purdah. She even hunted tigers from a closed howdah on top of an elephant with only the barrel of her musket exposed between the curtains. In 1626 she even rode into battle in an elephant litter, dispensing her orders through her eunuch. She also carried on a business, specializing in indigo and cloth trades.

After her daughter married Shahiryar, Nur Jahan began actively to work against Shah Jahan, Jahangir's appointed heir to the throne. After her husband died in 1628, Shah Jahan was able to sieze control, and Nur Jahan quickly accepted retirement and a pension of 200,000 rupees a year. She died in 1646.

Suggested Reading:

(1) Gascoigne, Bamber, *The Great Moghuls*. New York: Dorset Press, 1971. pp. 136-137, 141, 154, 158-160, 165-172, 178-179, 181.

Nysa

Queen of Cappadocia. See **Laodicé**

Section O

Oghul Qamish

Empress, regent of Karakorum (1248-1251)

Karakorum was the capital of the Mongol empire. It was located on the Orhon Gol river in the Arhangay province of present-day Mongolian People's Republic. Oghul Qamish was the wife of Güyük, great khan of the Mongols, who ruled from 1246 to 1248. She was believed to be of Markit birth. She had three young sons, Qucha, Naqu, and Qughu, for whom she acted as regent when their father died in 1248. Jenghiz-khan had given each of his four sons a khanate over which to rule. The four khans then elected a supreme or great khan who was head of the entire empire. Since her husband had been great khan, Oghul was not only regent of the land of the house of Ogödäi, but regent for the empire as well. In 1250, in the patrimonial lands of the house of Ogödäi, she received three envoys of Louis IX of France, who arrived by way of Persia. As an example of her avarice, she accepted their presents from King Louis as tribute and demanded that the king of France make more explicit submission to her. It would later be claimed by her rival that during her regency she was given to the practice of sorcery. Oghul Qaimish wanted the throne of the great khan to pass to a member of the house of Ogödäi, either to Güyük's nephew Shiramon, whom the former khan, his grandfather Ogödäi, had groomed for succession, or better still, to her own son Qucha. However, although Qucha was the eldest of her sons, he was too young. The head of the Jenghiz-khanite family, Batu, wanted to set the Ogödäi line aside and was persuaded to nominate as supreme khan a member of the Tolui family, Mongka, at an assembly not attended by representatives of the house of Ogödäi and their supporters from the house of Jagatai. The Ogödäis obviously refused to ratify such a nomination, and Mongka was elected by default. The relegation of the house of Ogödäi was a violation of legitimacy, and Shiramon and his cousins did not intend to let the election stand. They plotted to surprise Mongka and his supporters during the drunken feast following the inauguration ceremony, overpower them and depose Mongka. The plot miscarried and a civil war erupted, the houses of Ogodai and Jagatai on one side and the houses of Jochi and Tolui on the other. After a year of bloodshed, Mongka triumphed over all his rivals. He had the sons of Oghul Qamish exiled and saved his venom for their mother. She was stripped of her clothes for questioning, convicted of sorcery, sewn up in a sack and drowned (May-July, 1252).

Suggested Reading:

(1) Grousset, René, *The Empire of the Steppes: A History of Central Asia*. tr. Naomi Walford. New Brunswick, NJ: Rutgers University Press, 1970. pp. 272-274, 330, 349, 596.

(2) Runciman, Steven, *A History of the Crusades*. Cambridge: Cambridge University Press, 1952, 1987. vol. 3, *The Kingdom of Acre*. pp. 260, 293-294.

Olga, Saint

Princess, regent of Kiev (945-964)

Olga was born ca. 890 in Russia and became the wife of Grand Prince Igor I and the mother of a son, Svyatoslav. In 945 Igor was assassinated for exorting huge sums from his subjects to pay for his campaigns against the Byzantines. Olga became regent of the grand principality of Kiev until her son reached his majority. She hunted down Igor's murderers and ordered them scalded to death. In ca. 955 to 957 she became an Orthodox Christian and shortly afterward ushered in a new era in Byzantine-Kievian relations by visiting Constantinople. There she was baptised, or rebaptised, taking as her Christian name Helena, in honor of the Byzantine empress. It was through her efforts and those of her grandson Vladimir that Christianity was brought to Russia. However, during her lifetime she did not see her conversion affect the pagan faith of her subjects; in fact, during the first part of Vladimir's reign there was even a strong pagan revival. She died in 969 and was canonized by the Orthodox Church; her feast day is July 11.

Suggested Reading:

(1) Langer, William L., ed., *World History*. Boston: Houghton Mifflin, 1948, 1980. pp. 195, 259, 260.

(2)   Ostrogorsky, George, *History of the Byzantine State*. New Brunswick, NJ: Rutgers University Press, 1969. pp. 283, 292.

(3)   Previté-Orton, C. W., *The Shorter Cambridge Medieval History*. Cambridge: Cambridge University Press, 1952, 1982. vol. 1, p. 265.

(4)   Riasanovsky, Nicholas V., *A History of Russia*. Oxford: Oxford University Press, 1963, 1993. pp. 31, 34, 53.

Orghana

Princess, regent of the Mongolian khanate of Jagatai (1252-1261)

Orghana was first the wife of Qara-Hulagu, a grandson of Jenghiz-khan's son Jagatai and the ruler of the Turkestan khanate from 1242 to 1246. She had two sons, Buri and Mobarak Sha. In 1246 the new great khan Güyük replaced Qara-Hulägu with Jagatai's younger brother, Yissu-Mangu, but in 1252, with the election of a new great khan, Mongka, Yissu-Mangu was deposed and Qara-Hulägu was reinstated and ordered to execute Yissu-Mangu. However, Qara-Hulägu died on the way to reclaim his throne, and it was up to Princess Orghana as regent to have Yissu-Mangu executed. Her husband's former minister Habash 'Amid took care of the matter without waiting for the executioner. She took over control of the khanate and held it for nine years. She was described as beautiful, wise and discerning. Upon the great khan Mongka's death, one of his sons, Hulägu, became khan of Persia, while the other two, Kublai and Ariq-bögä, vied to become the supreme khan. Kublai outwitted his brother and became grand khan, but Ariq-bögä planned to dethrone him. To keep his other brother from sending reinforcements from Persia to Kublai, he decided to take over the khanate of Jagatai, sending Prince Alghu to remove Orghana from power and become regent himself. But Alghu had ambitions of his own: to make the Jagatai khanate independent. He seized Ariq-bögä's tax collectors and executed them, keeping the wealth for himself. In the war that followed, Ariq-bögä suffered severe losses. After two years, he tried to make peace with Alghun. At the time, he had with him Princess Orghana, who had come to protest her removal from the khanate. He sent her and Mas'ud Yalavach to Alghun's camp in Samarkaland with peace proposals. But on her arrival, Alghu married her and made Mas'ud his finance minister. With the money Mas'ud raised, Alghun and Orghana raised another large army. In 1264, Ariq-bögä was forced to surrender to Kublai. Alghun died in 1255 or 1266 and Orghana placed on the throne her son by her first marriage, Mobarek-shah, who became the first Jagataite to be converted to Islam.

Suggested Reading:

(1) Grousset, René, *The Empire of the Steppes.* tr. Naomi Walford. New Brunswick, NJ: Rutgers University Press, 1970. pp. 274-275, 286, 329-332.
(2) Runciman, Steven, *A History of the Crusades.* Cambridge: Cambridge University Press, 1952, 1987. vol. 3, *The Kingdom of Acre.* p. 309, and Appendix III.

Section P

Padishah Khatun

Queen of Kirman (1291-1295)

Padishah was the daughter of Kutlugh Turkhan, or Turkan Khatun, Queen of Kirman from 1257 to 1282. At that time, the Mongols subjected the princesses of their "colonies" to obligatory marriages. To escape this fate, she was reared as a boy among the boys. Nevertheless, Padishah, a beautiful and gifted poet, was eventually married to Abaka Khan, son of the great Mongolian Khan Hulagu. Ultimately Abaka inherited the Ilkhan court of his father, but when he died in 1282, his successor-brother converted to Islam and took the name of Ahmad Teguder. He was dethroned two years later by Abaka's son Arghun, a strong Buddhist. Meanwhile, Ahmad Teguder had removed Padishah's mother from the throne of Kirman and replaced her with her stepson Suyurghatamish. Eventually, she charmed the fifth ruler of the Ilkhan dynasty, Gaykhatu, who was one of the sons of her former husband. When he succeeded to power in 1291, Padishah asked that as proof of his love, he give her the throne of Kirman, which he did. As soon as she came to power as head of state, she had her step-brother Suyurghatamish arrested and thrown in prison. After an escape attempt, she ordered him strangled and took the title of *Safwat al-dunya wa al-din*, meaning Purity of the Earthly World and of the Faith and became the sixth sovereign of the Kutlugh-Khanid dynasty. Some of the gold and silver coins she had minted in her name still exist. She ruled until the death of her husband in 694/1295, at which time his successor Baydu, on advice of the leader of Suyurghatamish's clan, who happened to be his widow Khurdudjin, a descendant of Hulagu, had Padishah put to death.

Suggested Reading:

(1) Mernissi, Fatima, *The Forgotten Queens of Islam*. tr. Mary Jo Lakeland. Minneapolis: University of Minnesota Press, 1993. pp. 21, 99, 100, 101-2.

Pandit, Vijaya Lakshmi

President of United Nations General Assembly (1953)

Vijaya was born Swarup Kumari Nehru in 1900, the daughter of Sarup Rani Nehru and Motilal Nehru, a Kashmiri Brahmin, prominent lawyer and one of Mahatma Gandhi's lieutenants. She was the sister of Jawaharlal Nehru, who became the first prime minister of independent India; and the aunt of Indira Gandhi, first woman prime minister of India. She was privately educated in India and abroad and, along with the rest of her family, worked for Indian independence. In 1921 she married Ranjit S. Pandit, a co-worker. In connection with her efforts for India's independence, the British imprisoned her for one year (1931). Her husband died in 1944, three years before India achieved independence from Britain. Madame Pandit embarked on a distinguished political career, heading the Indian delegation to the United Nations from 1946 to 1948 and again from 1952 to 1953. She served as ambassador to Moscow from 1947 to 1949 and afterwards to the United States and Mexico until 1951. In 1953 she became the first woman to serve as president of the United Nations General Assembly. From 1954 to 1961 she served as ambassador in England and Ireland. During that time, she wrote *The Evolution of India* (1953).She became the governor of the state of Maharashtra in 1962, and two years later she accepted the seat in India's parliament formerly held by her brother Jawaharlal Nehru. In 1978 she became the Indian representative to the Human Rights Committee. In 1977 she left the Congress Party to join the Congress for Democracy. In 1977 she wrote her memoirs, *The Scope of Happiness*. She was placed on the Board of the Mountbatten Memorial Trust in 1980.

Notes;

(1) *International Who's Who, 1987-1988*. London: Europa Publishing, 1987. pp. xvi, 1130.

(2)   Mehta, Ved, *The New India*. Harmondsworth, Middlesex: Penguin Books, 1978. pp. 154-155.

Pandyan Queen

Ruler in South India (2nd. c. B.C.)

The Pandya was a Tamil dynasty in the extreme south of India first mentioned by Greek authors in the fourth century. Megasthenes mentions that the Pandyan kingdom was ruled by a daughter of Herakles. If poetry and heroic ballads which survive are any indication, the Cheras, the Cholas and the Pandyas were in constant conflict with one another. The Pandyan queen is credited by Megasthenes with having an army of 4000 cavalry, 13,000 infantry and 500 elephants with which to fight her wars.

Suggested Reading:

(1)   Thapar, Romila, *A History of India*. London: Penguin Books, 1987. vol. 1, p. 103.

Pao-Ssu

Queen, possible co-ruler of Chou, or Zhou (c. 1st or 2nd. millennium B.C.)

The Chou, Chow, or Zhou Dynasty in China lasted from 1122 B.C. to 221 B. C. Although the Chinese tradition contains a Chou genealogy, no dates can definitely be assigned to the reigns. Legend surrounding Pao-Ssu's infancy claims that attempts were made to destroy her but proved fruitless. Such legends abounded about larger-than-life heroes such as King Cyrus the Great, Queen Semiramis, Moses, King Gilgamish. This would suggest that Queen Pao-Ssu was a heroic, well-revered queen.

Suggested Reading:

(1)   Waley, Arthur, tr. *The Book of Songs*. New York: Grove Press, 1960. p. 239.

Pratibha Patil

First Woman President of India (2007-)

Pratibha was born December 19, 1934 in Jalgaon district of India. She studied law and practiced as a lawyer before entering politics. She married Devi Singh and had a son, Rajinder, and a daughter, Jyoti. The Congress loyalist held several posts in Maharashtra besides being Deputy Chairperson of the Rajya Sabha and Governor of Rajasthan. She was a member of the Maharashtra assembly from 1962 to 1985, and served as a minister holding portfolios like urban development and housing, education, tourism, parliamentary affairs, public health and social welfare and cultural affairs. She worked her way up from the rank of deputy minister to the cabinet and also in the Congressional hierarchy. Nearly eight years after her tenure as a Lok Sabha member ended in 1996, Patil, a staunch supporter of the Nehru-Gandhi family, went into a virtual political wilderness before she was brought in as Rajasthan's Governor in November 2004. At the age of 72, Patil was brought out of the relative obscurity of the Raj Bhawan in Jaipur to become the choice of the UPA-Left combine, and she created history by becoming the country's first woman President. She took the oath of office in the historic Central Hall of Parliament in the presence of her highly popular predecessor A P J Abdul Kalam, Prime Minister Manmohan Singh and Congress President Sonia Gandhi. Unlike her predecessor, Kalam, who was a bachelor and stayed alone in Rashtrapati Bhavan, Patil immediately moved herself and nine family members into the presidential palace. Leaders from several parties voiced hope that the elevation of a woman to the nation's highest office would go well for the nation. RJD chief Lalu Prasad said the UPA-Left combine had installed a woman on the highest constitutional post and "we are hopeful that she will fulfil all our aspirations." Union Minister Renuka Chowdhury said that Patil's appointment was "a proud moment for all women in the country'.'

Suggested Reading:

(1) NDTV.com, July 25, 2007.

Parysatis

Queen, Regent of Persia (424-404 B.C.)

Parysatis was the daughter of Xerxes I, who ruled Persia from 486 to 466 B.C. He was murdered by his chamberlain, Aspamitres, and the captain of his guard, Artabanus, the latter choosing Xerxes's youngest son and Parasatis's brother, Artaxerxes I, to succeed him. Artaxerxes I reigned for nearly forty years, dying in 425 B.C. His son, Parysatis's nephew, Xerxes II, succeeded him but was assassinated after only 45 days by his half-brother, Secydianus (or Sogdianus), who was in turn murdered after only 6 1/2 months by Ochus, another brother. Ochus, who became known as Darius Nothus, was married to his aunt, Parysatis. Under her tutelage, he reigned for 19 years (424-404 B.C.) The couple had at least two sons. When Darius Northus died, Parysatis attempted to put her younger son, Cyrus, on the throne—possibly so that she could control his affairs, but the older son, Arsaces (Artaxerxes II), was named to succeed his father. Parysatis urged Cyrus to take up arms against his brother in an attempt to overthrow him, which Cyrus did. But Cyrus was killed in battle at Cunaxa, thus ending Parysatis's influence.

Suggested Reading:

(1) Peters, F. E., *The Harvest of Hellenism*. New York: Barnes & Noble Books, 1996. p. 29.
(2) Rawlinson, George, *Ancient History*. New York: Barnes & Noble Books, 1993. pp. 88-90.

Pimiku (or Himiko, Pimisho, Pimiho, Yametsu-hime, or Yamato-hime-mikoto)

Queen, first known ruler of Japan (c. A.D. 190-247)

Chinese and Korean histories call her Pimiho, a corruption of Hime-ko. She was reputed to be the daughter of Suinin, who entrusted her with the sacred mirror, symbol of the sun goddess. In archaic Japanese, "Pimiko" meant "Sun Daughter." She was said to have built the Great Shrine of Ise, the most important Shinto shrine in Japan. She remained unmarried and, according to the *Wei chih*, ancient Chinese records considered more accurate than Japanese records, she ruled in Yamatai, which may have been Yamato. Other research indicates her realm was in western Japan. She seems also to have been a priestess. The *Wei* records say that she bewitched her subjects with magic and sorcery. A list survives of the names of the lands over which she presided. In 234 she had a daughter, Iyo-hime. After she conquered the savage tribes in southern Tsukushi, Chinese Emperor Ming-ti awarded her with a golden seal inscribed with the title of "king" of the country of Wo (A.D. 238). At her death in A.D. 247, over 100 of her servants buried themselves alive around her tomb.

Suggested Reading:

(1) Reischauer, Edwin O. and John K. Fairbank, *East Asia: The Great Tradition*. Boston: Houghton Mifflin, 1960. p. 463.
(2) Sansom, George, *A History of Japan to 1334*. Stanford: Stanford University Press, 1958. vol. 1, pp. 22, 45.

Plaisance of Antioch

Queen, regent of Cyprus and Jerusalem (1253-1261)

Plaisance was the daughter of Bohemond V, prince of Antioch from 1233 to 1252, and his second wife Lucienne of Segni. Her brother was Bohemond VI, prince of Antioch from 1252 to 1287. In 1251 she became the third wife of King Henry I, ruler of Jerusalem and Cyprus, and a year later bore him a son, Hugh II. King Henry died in January, 1253. As their son was only a few months old, Queen Plaisance claimed the regency of Cyprus and the titular regency of Jerusalem. The High Courts of Cyprus confirmed her position there immediately, but the Jerusalem barons required her attendance in person before they would recognize her. She was formally recognized as regent of Jerusalem upon her visit to Acre in 1258. An efficient ruler of high integrity, she was deeply mourned when she died in 1261, leaving her son Hugh II an orphan at age eight.

Suggested Reading:

(1) Runciman, Steven, *A History of the Crusades*. Cambridge: Cambridge University Press, 1952, 1987. vol. 3, *The Kingdom of Acre*. pp. 278, 281, 284-286, 288-289.

Pomare IV

Queen, ruler on Tonga (c. 19th c.)

According to Knappert, Pomare is the name of a series of queens on the island of Tonga. One, Queen Pomare IV, is "credited" with inadvertantly inviting Western diseases to her island by lifting the ban on marriages with non-Polynesians.

Suggested Reading:

(1) Knappert, Jan. *Pacific Mythology*. London: Diamond Books, 1992. p. 232.

Pomare V

Queen, ruler on Tahiti (fl. 1836-1836)

Pomare is a family name that appears throughout the South Pacific. It was the name of several kings of Tahiti, but it was also the name of at least one queen. Queen Pomare V is remembered for having expelled two French Roman Catholic missionary priests from the Protestant island in ca. 1835 or 1836. As a result of this action, France demanded reparations from the Tahitians. In 1842 the Tahitians asked for a protectorate, which was granted in 1843. Eventually, Tahiti would become a colony. (1880)

Suggested Reading:

(1) Langer, William L., ed. *World History*. Boston: Houghton Mifflin, 1980. p. 925.

Prabhavati Gupta

Regent of the kingdom of the Vakatakas (c. 390-410)

Prabhavati was the daughter of Chandra Gupta II, who ruled Northern India from A.D. 380 to 415. To strengthen his southern boundaries, Emperor Chandra married his daughter to King Rudrasena II, ruler of the Vakatakas (c. 385-390). The Vakataka kingdom was based on what remained of the earlier Satavahana kingdom and was located in the central Deccan region of Indian. When Rudrasena died c. 390 after a reign of only five years, his sons were infants. His widow Prabhavati served as regent from c. 390

to 410. During her unusually lengthy regency, she made, with her Gupta culture and her ties to the northern Indian kingdom, a significant impact on Vakatakas culture.

Suggested Reading:

(1) Thaper, Romila, *A History of India*. London: Penguin Books, 1987. vol. 1, pp. 139-140.

Pu-abi (or Puabi, formerly Shubad)

Queen, co-ruler of Ur (c. 2500 B.C.)

The Sumerian Dynasty of Ur was located on the Euphrates River. There are several surviving indications of Pu-abi's importance. Her name is one of only two with the title "nim" (meaning queen) inscribed on a cylinder-seal of lapis lazuli in the Royal Cemetery of Ur. She was the wife of an unknown king. Her body, along with several other bodies of presumed attendants, was found in a stone chamber. The queen's body was on a bier. She wore a head-dress of gold, lapis lazuli and carnelian, and she held a gold cup in her hand. Her burial place showed signs of human sacrifice, an indication that more than kingship was being honored. This would indicate that she was considered a god as well, or at least that she represented a god on earth and thus was entitled to take her court with her into the next life. Apparently at this early period, the royal/divine quality meriting human sacrifice could be possessed by a woman as well as a man.

Suggested Reading:

(1) Glubok, Shirley, ed. *Discovering the Royal Tombs at Ur*. London; Macmillan, 1969. pp. 48-49.
(2) Roux, Georges. *Ancient Iraq*. Harmondsworth, Middlesex: Penguin Books, 1980. pp. 132-133.

Puduhepa (or Pudu-Kheba)

Queen, co-ruler of the Hittites (c. 1275-c. 1250 B.C.), co-regent (c. 1250-? B.C.)

Puduhepa was the daughter of a priest and grew up in Kizzuwatna (or Kizzuwadnian), a town on the coast of what is now Turkey. She was educated in history and literature and became a priestess until she married the man who would become King Hattusilis III (r. c. 1275-c. 1250). He was the younger brother of King Muwatallis (r. c. 1306-1282), who had appointed Hattusilis as viceroy over his northern provinces as a reward for Hattusilis's victories over the Kashas. When Mwatawallis died, his son, Urhi-Teshup (r. c. 1283-1275), succeeded him, but the new king soon began to belittle his uncle. In c. 1275 Hattusilis usurped the throne from his weak nephew. Later, in justifying his actions he wrote that he was following the will of the goddess Ishtar.

Together, the king and queen reconstructed and reoccupied the old capital at Hattusa (present-day Bogazköy, Turkey). The two shared the rule for 24 years. A strong and influential woman, Puduhepa had her own seal, with which she signed the king's international correspondence.

The couple had several children; a surviving self-critical, self-justifying autobiography from her husband says, "God granted us the love of husband and wife, and we had sons and daughters." This document is the first such in recorded history. One of their daughters, Naptera, was given in marriage as chief wife to Pharaoh Ramses II, as part of an "everlasting peace" between the Hittites and the Egyptians. This peace treaty (c. 1269), written in both languages, the oldest written document of its kind, heralded a peace that lasted for some 70 years. Their son Tudhaliyas IV (or Tudkhaliash, r. c. 1250-1220) succeeded Hattusilis upon his death, and because he was a weak ruler, Puduhepa became co-regent with him.

Suggested Reading:

(1) Ceram, C. W. *The Secret of the Hittites*. New York: Alfred A. Knopf, Inc., 1955.

(2) Lehman, Johannes. *The Hittites*. Chicago: The University of Chicago Press, 1975.

Pulcheria

Augusta, regent of the Eastern Empire (A.D. 414-453)

Pulcheria was born in Constantinople in 399, the daughter of Eastern Roman Emperor Flavius Arcadius, ruler from 383 to 408, and his wife Eudoxia. She was the older sister of Theodosius II, born in 401, who ruled from 408 to 450. When her father died in 408, Pulcheria was appointed Augusta and made regent for her brother, although she was only two years his senior. She took her responsibilities very seriously and assumed a personal hand in Theodosius' education. A devout Christian, she maintained her court with great piety and chastity. In 421 she arranged the marriage of her brother to Athenais (Eudocia), who eventually became her rival in court. In 443 friction between the two had mounted to such an extent that Eudocia voluntarily withdrew to Jerusalem. The eunuch chamberlain Chrysaphius gradually worked his way into the emperor's favor and eventually gained dominance over him for a while, but Pulcheria had recovered the initiative before Theodosius' death in 450. She selected a retired soldier, Marcian, as her brother's successor and married him to preserve the dynasty. She died in 453.

Suggested Reading:

(1)   Bowder, Diana, *Who Was Who in the Roman World*. Ithaca, NY: Cornell University Press, 1980. p. 452.

Purea (or Oberea)

Queen of the Landward Teva of Tahiti, self-proclaimed Queen of all of Otaheite, or Tahiti (mid 18th. c.)

Purea and her mate Amo were the leaders of the Landward Teva tribe. She had a son, Teri-i-reree, b. c. 1758/1759. On June 26, 1767, Captain Samuel Wallis, captain of the English ship *Dolphin*, being ill in bed, sent his second lieutenant, Tobias Furneaux, to take possession of Tahiti for the British. Two weeks after the ship's arrival and the rituals of possession, the English had seen a procession of canoes bearing colorful penants passing in review. Ten days later a member of the crew came upon a "palace" where he was entertained by the "queen", who was fed by her "ladies in waiting." In their reports the men of the *Dolphin* invariably used quotation marks when describing the queen or her court, for to their way of thinking, the only "authentic" courts were European. In July the queen made her first visit aboard the ship. The captain treated her royally, but behind her back the Englishmen laughed at her awkward use of Western cutlery and at the tatoos on her rear.

There began a series of social exchanges designed by the English to present to their own government the idea that they had established diplomatic relations with the Tahitians. In reality the English sailors found the Tahitian women's lack of sexual inhibition the most promising coin of social exchange. When Samuel Wallis sailed the *Dolphin* for home, it is recorded that Queen Purea evinced "extravagant sorrow" at its leaving. However, the Englishmen left behind a legacy of veneral diseases.

The Admiralty contracted with Dr. John Hawkesworth, a geographer of sorts, to record in a book the voyages of the various English explorers of the South Pacific. In this account there appears an engraving entitled "A representation of the surrender of the island of Otaheite to Captain Wallis by the supposed Queen Oberea." This depicted a purely fictitious event.

In 1767-1768 Purea and her mate Amo (Suggs omits mention of the mate) built Mahaiatea, a sacred place which was intended to be the ritual center of the island, for their son, Teri-i-reree, in hopes of establishing him as the ruler over all of Tahiti. One account says that when Purea imposed certain prohibitions of food and behavior on the people, her sister and her sister-in-law paid her formal visits, challenging the imposed fast. Ordinarily, formal visits among equals demanded hospitality, thus having the effect of lifting Purea's ban. But, intent upon upholding the fast, Purea refused to acknowledge their equality, and according to one account, this rift precipitated a battle.

Another account of the cause of the uprising says that after Teri-i-reree's investiture and the ceremonial procession of symbols around the island began, Purea and Amo demanded submission of the subjects as the ceremony passed. But the Seaward Teva tribe refused to submit to a new authority, and they evinced their outrage with violence.

Whatever the cause, when Captain James Cook with young Joseph Banks sailed for Tahiti in 1768, they found that Purea and Amo had failed in their attempt to establish Teri-i-reree as the supreme ruler of all of Tahiti. The Seward Teva had massacred many of the people of Papara, destroyed Mahaitea, and would ultimately defeat Purea.

The queen was said to be enamored of young Banks; one account tells of Banks' loss of his waistcoat and pistol while he slept on "Oberea's" canoe. At one point she directed a ritual at the gate of Fort Venus, which Cook observed, of the public colulation of a young man and a girl of ten or twelve. Letters exist in London, one dated 1775, from "Oberea, Queen of Otaheite to Joseph Banks, Esq." as well as one of Banks' replies, written after Cook had returned from his first voyage. Supposedly she also wrote a letter to Wallis. No record of her exists after the time of these documents.

Suggested Reading:

(1) Dening, Greg, *Performances*. Chicago: The University of Chicago Press, 1996. pp. 147, 151, 153-156, 161-167.
(2) Suggs, Robert C. *The Island Civilizations of Polynesia*. New York: Mentor, 1960. pp. 133, 144.

Pu-su-wan

See Ye-lu-Shih

Section R

Radiyya, Sultana (or Raziyya (or Razia) Iltutmish, or Altamsh, or Malika Iltutmish)

Sultana, Muslim queen of Delhi, Northern India (1236-1240); Called "Pillar of Women, Queen of the Times"

Radiyya was the Turkish-born daughter of Shamsudin Iltutmish, a former slave who rose to be the third and greatest Sultan of the Moslam Slave Dynasty in Delhi. Her mother was the daughter of Qutb-ud-Din Aybak, the second Sultan of Delhi. Sultan Shamsudin, originally a Turkish slave, a Mamluk, as General of the Army, had helped found the Muslim state of India in 1229.

Mamluks were Turks from the Asian steppes who were captured as white slaves by slave merchants who sold them to the sultans. They received a military education and then joined the military caste of the palaces. After a period of apprenticeship, the Mamluks were named to important posts in the military hierarchy, thus becoming one of the military elite. Iltutmish's bravery so impressed the sultan, Qutb al-Din Aybak, that he married the young Turk to his daughter. At Aybak's death in 1211, Iltutmish took power and declared himself independent of the Ghaznah masters. He reigned for 26 years, and realizing that his two sons by other wives were both feeble minded, designated his daughter Raziyya as his successor. When he died in 1236, she became the first Moslem woman to rule northern India, but not without opposition. One of the sons, Rukn al-Din, rebelled and killed his half-brother, hoping to intimidate Radiyya into stepping down. Radiyya, adopting a custom instituted by her father, donned a garment dyed to indicate that she was a victim. When her brother emerged from the palace to attend Friday prayers at the mosque, she mounted the balcony and addressed the army saying, "My brother killed his brother and he now wants to kill me." She reminded the people of her father's many good deeds. The crowd became incensed, captured Rukn al-Din and put him to death. The army declared that Radiyya, a spinster, was queen. Thirteenth century historian Amir Khusrau said, "Since there were no worthy sons, worthy opinion turned to Raziyya."

One of her first acts was to unveil. She "cut her hair and dressed like a man and in this fashion mounted the throne," according to an account by Badriye U{c,}ok Un. According to Ibn Battuta's account, "She ruled as an absolute monarch for four years. She mounted horse like men armed with bow and quiver, and she would not cover her face."

Raziyya came to the throne at a difficult time in her country's history. During her reign, the two dominant sects of Islam, the Sunnis (the orthodox sect traditionally favored by the sultanate) and the Shias (a more radical splinter group) were pitted against each other. The Shias, joining some other schismatics, revolted against the sultanate but were roundly put down by Raziyya's forces. After that time, the Shias ceased to be a serious challenge to Sunnis during the history of the sultanate.

However, her subjects turned on her when she began a rapid promotion of Jamal al-Din Yaqat, an Abyssinian Ethiopian slave, who soon became Master of the Horse. It was suspected that she had embarked on a torrid love affair with him. Once, according to Ibn Battuta's account, when she was mounting her horse, "He slid his arms under her armpits in order to hoist her up on to her mount." Word spread rapidly that she had violated ethical behavior by allowing herself to be touched by her slave.

Courageous and intelligent, nevertheless, after 3 1/2 years on the throne, she was toppled in palace *coup*. An army, raised by the governor, Ikhtiyar al-Din Altuniyya, agreed to depose her and have her marry. Radiyya left Delhi with her own army to combat Altuniyya. She lost the battle and was taken prisoner, but her charms proved too much for Altuniyya. He freed her, married her, and took her, wearing men's clothing over her own, and their armies back to Delhi to recapture her throne. But they were defeated, and Radiyya fled.

She wandered into a peasant's cottage and begged for food. The peasant, spying her jeweled gown under her disguise, killed her, drove away her horse, and buried her in his field. The peasant took some of her finery into the market to sell, but the *shihna* (magistrate) became suspicious and forced him into confessing his crime. Her body was disinterred, washed, and shrouded, and given a proper burial. According to Ibn Battuta, "A dome was built over her grave which is now visited, and people obtain blessings from it."

Historian Yahya ibn Ahmad then wrote of the tragic event, "Every head that the celestial globe raises up/It will likewise throw a noose around the neck of that very same." <)6>5<)1>

WOMEN LEADERS OF AFRICA, ASIA, MIDDLE EAST, AND PACIFIC

The historian Siraj (Shams al-din Siraj) said, "Sultana Raziyya was a great monarch. She was wise, just and generous, a benefactor to her kingdom, a dispenser of justice, the protector of her subjects and the leader of her armies. She was endowed with all the qualities befitting a king, but she was not born of the right sex, so, in the estimation of men, all these virtues were worthless."

She was succeeded by a grandchild of her father's.

Suggested Reading:

(1) Ibn Battuta. *The Rehla of Ibn Battuta. India, Maldive Islands and Ceylon*. tr. Mahdi Husain. Baroda, India: Oriental Institute, 1976. pp. 34-35.

(2) Ibn Battuta, *The Travels of Ibn Battuta AD 1325-1354)* tr. H. A. R. Gibb. Cambridge: Cambridge University Press, vol 1., 1958; vol. 2, 1962.

(3) Hardy, Peter, *Historians of Medieval India*. Wesport, CT: Greenwood Press, 1982. pp. 65, 91

(4) Ali, Tariq, "Dynasty's Daughter". *Interview*. February 1989. p. 124

(5) Eliot, H. M. and J. Dowson, *A History of India as Told by Its Own Historians*. Cambridge: Cambridge University Press, 1931. vol. 2, p. 185.

(6) Thapar, Romila, *A History of India*. London: Penguin Books, 1987. vol. 1, pp. 269, 301.

(7) Mernissi, Fatima, *The Forgotten Queens of Islam*. tr. Mary Jo Lakeland. Minneapolis: University of Minnesota Press, 1993, pp. 89-90, 93-97.

Russudan (or Rusudani or Rusudan)

Queen, ruler Georgia, first alone (1223-1234), then jointly with her husband David (1234-1245/7)

She was the daughter of Queen Thamar (Tamara) the Great, who ruled Georgia from 1186 to 1212, and Thamar's cousin and consort, David Soslan, who ruled jointly from 1193 to 1207. Her brother, King George III (Giorgi III Lasha, or the Brilliant, or the Resplendent), co-ruler from 1205 to 1212, then sole ruler until 1223, had many mistresses and even fathered an illegitimate child, but he had no legitimate heir to succeed him other than his sister. In 1221 the Georgian troops had been cut to ribbons at Khunani by Mongol generals of Jenghiz-khan, Jebe and Subotai. Russudan, having something of the same disposition as her brother and little of her mother's Christian piety, described in fact as "an unmarried but not a virgin queen," acceded to the throne when her brother died, and was proclaimed "King of Karthalinia." Karthalinia, or Kartlia, was a section in presentday Soviet Georgia. In 1225 Jelal ad-Din Manguberti (Jalal on-Din), heir to the Khwarizmian empire who had been driven into exile by Jenghiz-khan, invaded Georgia. Queen Russudan sent an army to meet them, but her troops had not regained their strength since their trouncing by Jenghiz-khan: they were defeated at Garnhi on her southern frontier. The invaders, after ravaging Southern Georgia, moved on into Russia. Queen Russudan wrote to the Pope: "A savage people of Tartars (a play on words for the Tatars, "tartar" meaning "hell"), hellish of aspect, as voracious as wolves in their hunger for spoils and brave as lions, have invaded my country . . . The brave knighthood of Georgia has hunted them out of the country, killing 25,000 of the invaders." Learning that nearby Persia had been weakened by Mongol attack, she took advantage of their recent disaster and attacked Persia. But in 1225 Jalal ad-Din swooped down again and attacked the capital of Tiflis. Queen Russudan fled to Kutais while Jelal ad-Din occupied and sacked the capital, destroying all the Christian churches. In 1228 she attempted to regain control of the provinces along the Kur river which Jelal ad-Din held, but she was driven back. In 1231 the Mongol army reappeared to challenge Jelal ad-Din under the leadership of General Chormaqan. Jelal ad-Din, who had been defeated by Mongols before, retreated hastily, to die in Kurdestan in 1231. That year, with the Mongols fighting the Turks, Queen Russudan reoccupied her capital of Tiflis, but five years later Chormaqan invaded Georgia, and she was forced to take refuge once again in Kutais. Around 1241 Chormaqan was stricken with dumbness and was replaced by Baiji. Queen Russudan soon became an irritant to him because of her stubborn refusal to give in to the Mongols. Eventually, however, in 1243 she herself became a vassal of the Mongols with the understanding that the whole kingdom of Georgia would be given to her son David Narin to rule under Mongol suzerainty. However, David Narin was in actuality only given Imeretia, while David Lasha, an heir of Russudan's brother, was given Kartlia.

Suggested Reading:

(1) Suny, Ronald Grigor. *The Making of the Georgian Nation*. Bloomington: Indiana University Press, in association with Hoover Institution Press, Stanford University, 1988. pp. 40-41.

(2) Grousset, René. *The Empire of the Steppes*. tr. Naomi Walford. New Brunswick, NJ: Rutgers University Press, 1970. pp. 260, 263, 272, 350.

(3) Runciman, Steven. *A History of the Crusades*. Cambridge: Cambridge University Press, 1952, 1987. vol. 3, *The Kingdom of Acre*. pp. 249-250.

(4) Hussey, J. M., ed. *The Cambridge Mediecal History*. Vol. 4 pt. 1. Cambridge: Cambridge University Press, 1966. p. 783.

(5) Buchan, John, ed. *The Baltic and Caucasian States*. Boston: Houghton Mifflin, 1923. pp. 173-174.

(6) N.A. *Storm Across Georgia*. London: Cassel, 1981. p. 40.

Section S

Sada Kaur

Rani, de-facto co-ruler of Sukerchakias, Pakistan (1795-c. 1801)

She was the widow a chieftain of the Kanhayas, whose daughter Jindan married 15-year-old Ranjit Singh, chief since the age of 12 of the Sukerchakias, a Sikh group. For many years Sada Kaur directed his affairs. Eventually Ranjit Singh proclaimed himself maharaja of the Punjab, a state which he single-handedly created.

Suggested Reading:

(1) Spear, Percival, *A History of India*. London: Penguin Books, 1987. vol. 2, pp. 2, 76, 104, 107, 117, 132, 135.

Saimei-tenno

See Koyoku-tenno

Salome Alexandra

See Alexandra

Salote Tupou III

Queen, ruler of Tonga (1918-1965)

She was born in 1900, the daughter of King Tupou II, ruler of Tonga from 1893 to 1918, member of a dynasty which had ruled from at least the 10th century. During her father's reign, Tonga became a British protectorate because of financial difficulties. Salote came to the throne at the age of

18, following her father's death. A commanding figure at six feet two inches tall—size and stateliness has characterized the ruling family for generations—the queen guided the islands with wisdom and grace for 47 years, endearing herself to the people of Britain as well to her own. To encourage Tonga's traditional crafts, she organized a women's cooperative which maintains at least one handicraft shop in a local hotel. In 1917 she married Sione (John) Fe'iloakitau Kaho (Prince Viliami Tungi). Their son, Taufa (or Tung, born in 1918), succeeded upon his mother's death (1965) as King Tafua'ahou Tupou IV. The queen who ruled so long and well did not live to see Tonga regain complete independence in 1970.

Suggested Reading:

(1) Egan, Edward W. et. al., eds. *Kings, Rulers, and Statesmen*. New York: Sterling Publishing, 1976. p. 465.
(2) *International Who's Who, 1987-1988*. London: Europa Publishing, 1987. p. xvi.
(3) Candee, Marjorie Dent, ed., *Current Biography 1952*. New York: H. W. Wilson Co., 1954. pp. 552-554.
(4) Marden, Luis, "The Friendly Faces of Tonga". *National Geographic 133*. March 1968. pp. 345-367.
(5) Grosvenor, Melville Belle, "South Seas' Tonga Hails a King". *National Geographic 133*. March 1968, pp. 322-344.

Samsia

Queen, ruler of Southern Arabia (c. 732 B.C.)

In 734 B.C. King Ahaz of Judah asked the help of his suzerain Tiglath-Pileser III, who had taken over the New Assyrian Empire (745-727 B.C.), in defending against a coalition of the forces of Rezen of Damascus and Pekah (Pakaha) of Israel. Tiglath-Pileser obliged by, first, demolishing Israel's forces and then, in 732, marching against Damascus. He turned Damascas and outlying parts of Israel into provinces. In the central part of Israel he devastated the stately gardens outside the city, then swept through the capital and killed King Pekah, replacing him with Hoshea. Two queens of the Arabs sent tribute to him. Records mention that a Queen Samsia, queen of Southern Arabia at the time, was forced to pay tribute to Tiglath-Pileser in return for use of the harbor of Gaza, over which he had gained control.

Another ruler called Zabibê, designated as "Queen of the Arabs", also brought him tribute.

Suggested Reading:

(1) Packer, J. I., et. al., *The Bible Almanac.* Nashville: Thomas Nelson, 1980. pp. 134, 316, 500, 675.
(2) Biblical records: I Chronicles 5:26; II Kings 15 and 16. In biblical accounts, Tiglath-Pileser is called "Pul" or "Pulu."
(3) Roux, Georges. *Ancient Iraq.* Harmondsworth, Middlesex: Penguin Books, 1980. p. 285.
(4) Oppenheim, A. Leo. *Ancient Mesopotamia.* Chicago: University of Chicago Press, 1977. p. 169.

Sati Beg (or Sati Bek)

Il-Khanid sultana of Persia (1338-1339)

The daughter of Mongol Sultan Öljeitü of the Chingizid Dynasty (r. 1304-1316) and the sister of Abu Sa'id (r. 1316-1335), she was one of four to come to the throne in the three years following her brother's death. Her first husband was Amir Tchoban, grandson of one of Hülagü's generals, and commander-in-chief of the armed forces. After he died, she married Sultan Arpa (r. 1335-1336). When he died, two more men accended to the throne briefly before Sati Beg became head of state in her own right. During her reign the *khutba* was proclaimed in her name in the temple, signifying her right to rule. She had coins struck which read, "The just sultana Sati Bek Khan, may Allah perpetuate her reign." She was deposed after only nine months, and she took one of her two successors, Sulayman Amin Yusuf Shah (r. 1339-1343), as her third husband. Following his rule, the Il-Khanid state broke into petty kingdoms. The title il-khan denoted nominal subordination to the great Mongolian khan.

Suggested Reading:

(1) Morby, John E. *Dynasties of the World.* Oxford: Oxford University Press, 1989. p. 200.
(2) Mernissi, Fatima. *The Forgotten Queens of Islam.* Minneapolis: University of Minnesota Press, 1993. p. 105.

Saw (or Mi Co U or Phwa Co)

Chief queen, virtual ruler of Pagan (1255-1287)

Ma Saw was born (c. 1229) in a Burmese village, the beautiful, talented daughter of peasants. She became a "deputy queen" at age c. 16 of a Pagan king who in a fictionalized account is called Usana (r. c. 1211-1254/5). During his reign, Saw showed herself to be wise and diplomatic and so impressed the powerful chief minister that, when the king died, the minister made her chief queen of the king's successor, his bastard son Narathihapade (or Narasihapati, r. 1255-1287). This young man was chosen over the legitimate heir by the chief minister, who wished to maintain his own position. The young king was ignorant and unschooled in matters of the court. Both he and the chief minister came to rely upon Queen Saw's counsel, so that she became the most influential figure in the kingdom of Pagan. Beginning in 1271 Kublai Khan sent missions to Pagan demanding tribute be paid. When their demands were rejected, the Mongols invaded. The king and his family fled the capital to a small town in the south. But he was lured to Prome and taken captive by his younger son, Sihasu, Prome's governor, who offered him a choice of dying by poison or by the sword. The queen advised him that it would be nobler to die by poison than by "thy blood gushing red at point of sword." Following his death, she retired with her retinue to her village.

Suggested Reading:

(1) Aung-Thwin, Michael A. *Myth and History in the Historiography of Early Burma*. Singapore: Institute of Southeast Asia Studies, 1998, pp. 56, 59, 177-178 fn., 186 fn.
(2) Collis, Maurice. *She Was A Queen*. New York: New Directions Books, 1991.

Shagshag

Queen, administrator in Lagash (early 3rd. millennium B.C.)

She was the wife of Urukagina. Her duties included but were not confined to administration of the temple of the goddess Bau, whose area extended over approximately one square mile, and which employed 1000-1200 people. Shagshag also managed the temple devoted to the children of Bau.

As administrator of these two temples, she exercised legal and economic authority over them and in addition functioned as chief priestess.

Suggested Reading:

(1)   Batto, Bernard Frank. *Studies on Women at Mari*. Baltimore: Johns Hopkins University Press, 1974. p. 8.

Shajarat al-Durr (or Shajar Al Durr, Tree of Pearls, or Spray of Pearls)

Muslim Queen of Egypt, (1249-1257, officially for 80 days in 1250)

Of Turkish, or possibly Armenian, lineage, she was the devoted slave-wife of Sultan al-Salih Ayyub, Ayyubid Sultan of Egypt from 1240 to 1249. When she bore him a son, he gave her her freedom. During a campaign against the French Crusaders under King Louis, who were conducting a siege of Egypt, her husband died in his tent in Mansorra (1249). With the Crusaders on the way, Shajarat al-Durr kept his death a secret. Daily she assured the officers that the sultan was much better, and she issued orders under the sultan's forged signature. By another account, she negotiated with the army to keep the sultan's death a secret. Faced with a major battle against a well-armed force, this extraordinary woman commanded the army and at the same time ruled the land, all under cover, concealing a rotting corpse. The Crusaders were beaten by dysentary and starvation when the Muslims cut off their supply route. The sultan's oldest son and heir, Turan Shah, was absent in Syria at the time. Once the battles were won, Shajarat al-Durr sent messengers to inform him of the death of his father. Turan Shah returned to Cairo early the next year to be proclaimed sultan, but he proved incapable of leading the troops, whom he alienated at once. In May, 1250, the Turkish officers assassinated him and hailed Shajarat al-Durr, to whom they were devoted, as queen of Egypt. She assumed sovereign power and ruled officially for 80 days, striking her own coins and having herself mentioned in the Friday prayers as sultan. But the Abbasid Khaliph in Syria refused to recognize the accession of Shajarat al-Durr: he wrote, quoting the Prophet, "Unhappy is the nation which is governed by a woman," adding with sarcasm, "If you have no men, I will send you one." She was deposed and her commander in chief, a Mamluk general, 'Izz al-Din Aybak, was chosen to take her place. Shajarat al-Durr, who was endowed with both great beauty and intelligence, immediately set out to marry the new sultan. Some sources say she married him before he became sultan, and then her Egyptian emirs nominated him as sultan. Whatever the circumstances, it was through Shajarat al-Durr that Aybak became the first Mamluk sultan (1250-1257). The sultan divorced his former wife, Umm 'Ali. In order not to be confined once more to the harem, Shajar al-Durr saw to it that the *khutba* was said in both her husband's and her name in every mosque in Cairo, and that every official document must bear the signatures of them both.

It was not a happy union. Seven years later, when she learned that her husband intended to marry the daughter of the atabeg of Mosul, Badr al-Din Lu'lu, she was both humiliated and enraged. She engineered an elaborate plot with her husband's servants to murder him. On April 12, 1257, when Aybak entered the *hammam*, or Turkish bath, at Citadel del Cairo, he was surrounded by his servants and killed.

Aybak's assassination caused pandemonium among his troops. Although part of the army remained loyal to Shajarat al-Durr, others, loyal to the sultan's former wife, Umm 'Ali, turned on her. She was brought to the Burj al-Ahmar (Red Fort) and "battered to death with wooden shoes by the slave women of Aykab's first wife . . . ." Her half-nude body was thrown from the battlements of the citadel of Cairo. It remained there for several days before it was buried in the courtyard of a school that she founded. It is known today as Jami' Shajarat al-Durr, the mosque of Shajarat al-Durr.

Suggested Reading:

(1) Glubb, Sir John, *A Short History of the Arabs*. New York: Dorset Press, 1969. pp. 202-205, 210.
(2) Mernissi, Fatima. *The Forgotten Queens of Islam*. Minneapolis: University of Minnesota Press, 1993, pp. 28-29, 90-93, 97-99.
(3) Hitti, Philip K. *The Arabs*. London: Macmillan, 1937, p. 672.
(4) Chahin, M. *The Kingdom of Armenia*. New York: Dorset Press, 1987, 1991, p. 286.

Shammu-ramat (Shamiran, Sammuramat, or Semiramis)

Queen, regent of New Assyrian Empire (c. 811-806/9 B.C.)

She was born in Babylonia and married King Shamshi-Adad V, ruler of Assyria (823-811 B.C). Following her husband's death, Shammu-ramat, as capable, energetic regent, ruled for three or five years before passing the reins of government to her son, Adad-nirari III. Proof that she clearly held the real power survives in dedications made in her own name, placed before that of her son. A memorial stele to her was found at Assur along with those of kings and other high officials, a singular honor for a woman then. The historical evidence stops there, but Greek historian Diodorus Siculus (c. 1st. B.C.) credited her with rebuilding Babylon, a task historians attribute in part to a priestess, Addagoppe. Armenian legend attributes to "Queen Semiramis" much of the surviving construction of the kingdom of Urartu, which also belonged to Assyria at the time; however, there is no historical evidence to suggest that Shammu-ramat ever intervened in governing Urartu.

Suggested Reading:

(1)   Oates, Joan, *Babylonia*. London: Thames and Hudson, 1979. p. 111.
(2)   Omstead, A. T., *History of the Persian Empire*. Chicago: University of Chicago Press, 1948. pp. 118, 163, 321-322, 380.
(3)   Langer, William L., ed., World History. Boston: Houghton Mifflin, 1940, 1980. p. 33.
(4)   Herodotus, *The Histories*. tr. Aubrey de Sélincourt. New York: Penguin Books, 1954, 1988. p. 115.
(5)   Chahin, M. *The Kingdom of Armenia*. New York: Dorset Press, 1987, pp. 67-71.
(6)   Oppenheim, A. Leo. *Ancient Mesopotamia*. Chicago: The University of Chicago Press, 1977. p. 104.
(7)   Roux, Georges. *Ancient Iraq*. Harmondsworth, Middlesex: Penguin Books, 1980. p. 279.

Shibtu

Queen, frequent regent of Mari (c. 1790-1745 B.C.)

Mari was a Sumerian and Amorite city near present-day Abu Kamal on the Euphrates River in Syria. Shibtu was the wife of King Zimri-Lim, who ruled Mari in the mid-1700's B.C., and she acted as his deputy during his frequent absences. She had a variety of duties. The governor of Terqa, a neighboring city, addressing her as "his mistress", reported to the queen on business matters and carried out her directives. Governors and vassal kings paid homage to her. She offered sacrifices, supervised oracles, and executed the king's orders.

Suggested Reading:

(1) Batto, Bernard Frank. *Studies on Women at Mari*. Baltimore: Johns Hopkins University Press, 1974. pp. 16, 20.

Shipley, Jenny

Prime Minister of New Zealand (1997-)

Jenny Shipley was born in 1952 in Gore, New Zealand, in the southern reaches of South Island. She was the second daughter in a family that ultimately was to consist of four daughters. She grew up in Wellington, on the southern tip of North Island, and Blenheim, on the northern part of South Island. She graduated from Christchurch Teachers College in 1971 and taught in the primary grades for a number of years. She married Burton Shipley, who was to become a business development manager for a New Zealand bank. The two had a farming partnership for a number of years. After the birth of her children, Anna (b. 1977) and Ben (b. 1978), she became involved in politics at the local level.

In 1987 she entered national politics as a member of the New Zealand National Party and was elected as a legislator. In 1990 she was appointed Minister of Social Welfare and Minister of Women's Affairs, a position she held until 1996. In 1993 she was also appointed Minister of Health, and in 1996 she accepted an appointment to the portfolios of State Services, Transportation, State Owned Enterprises, Accident Rehabilitation Compensation Insurance, and Radio New Zealand. In September of 1997 she again became Minister of Women's Affairs, at which time, she relinquished the portfolio of State Services. As leader of the National Party, she formed a coalition government with Winston Peters, leader of the New Zealand First Party. In November of 1997 she was chosen Prime Minister-elect, and she was sworn in on December 8 as New Zealand's first woman Prime Minister.

During an interview following her inauguration, Shipley said, "I hope I've won this task on my merit. If it means that other young women in New Zealand will aspire to be the best that they can be, I'll feel very pleased." She described New Zealand as "a small but cheeky nation which seems to . . . do most things rather better than our size would suggest."

Speaking to the Auckland Regional Chamber of Commerce, she summed up the philosophy of her governmental style: "I am proud of the Government's determination to be realistic about the balance between what we would like and what we can afford."

Suggested Reading:

(1) Peterson, Kara J. "Ungentle Coup". *World Press Review* February 1998: 20
(2) Shipley, Jenny and Simon Robinson. "A Small but Cheeky Nation". *Time.* 15 December 1997: 50.
(3) Speech to the Auckland Regional Chamber of Commerce. New Zealand Executive Government News Release Archive.

Shotoku-tenno (Also Takano-tenno)

See Koken

Shu-lu shih

Khatum, regent of Turkish Mongolia (A.D.926-?)

Shu-lu shih is not the empress' name. It simply means "of the Shu-lu clan"; unfortunately, although all the other names in this account are known, the empress' name was not preserved. She was the wife of A-pao-ki, chief of the Ye-lu clan of Khitan in the tenth century. The couple had two sons, T'u-yu and To-kuang. When her husband died in A.D. 926, the dowager empress rigged a popularity contest so between her sons so that her favorite second son, To-kuang, would win. She then governed "with" him for the first few years, although she in fact held sole power and had indefatigable staying power. Each time a minister displeased her, she dispatched him to "take news of her to her late husband." Guards at her husband's tomb would then speed him on his way to join the departed. One sage Chinese minister, Chao Ssu-wen, upon being named the next victim, respectfully demurred with true oriental courtesy, deferring such a high honor to the widow, who was far more deserving than he. The khatum (empress) acknowledged that this was so, but much as she would like to go, her presence was essential to the horde. But just to be a sport about it, she lopped off one hand and sent it along to be buried in the tomb.

Suggested Reading:

(1) Grousset, René. *Empire of the Steppes: A History of Central Asia.* tr. Naomi Walford. New Brunswick, NJ: Rutgers University Press, 1970. pp. 128-129.

Sibylla (or Sibyl or Sybil)

Queen of Jerusalem (1186-1190)

She was born in 1160, the daughter of King Amalric I, ruler from 1162 to 1174, and his first wife, Agnes of Courtenay. She was the sister of Baldwin IV, who acceded upon his father's death in 1174 and ruled until 1183. When Baldwin IV was nine years old, his instructor realized he was a leper and might not live to reign. So special care was given to Sibylla's education and choice of a mate, since he might be called upon to act as regent or, if need be, even as king. She first married William of Montferrat, count of Jaffa (1176). They had a son, Baldwin V, born posthumously, his father having died of malaria two months before. In 1180 she took as her lover Guy of Lusignan, of whom her brother the king disapproved on the grounds that he was a weak and foolish boy. When the king discovered this relationship, he wanted to put Guy to death, but at the request of the Templars, he reluctantly allowed Sibylla to marry him. The marriage produced two daughters. Guy was to prove the king's estimation of him was correct. Baldwin IV, from his sickbed, first appointed Guy regent, then rescinded the order, banished him, and proclaimed Sibylla's son Baldwin V as his heir. He died in 1185, but the child died only one year later. Of the two contenders for the throne, Sibylla and Isabella (by Amalric's second wife Maria Comnena), the public favored Sibylla, even though her husband was generally despised. Backers of Sibylla, through subterfuge, managed to trick the other side and to proclaim Sibylla queen. At the coronation, only she was crowned, because of Guy's unpopularity. She was then asked to crown whatever man she thought worthy to serve; she of course crowned her husband. As an indirect result of Guy's foibles, Jerusalem was soon embroiled in a disastrous war with Sultan Saladin. Saladin took Guy prisoner and asked for Ascalon in exchange for his release, but the people, ashamed of Guy's selfishness on numerous occasions, refused to give up Ascalon for the ransom. After Ascalon fell anyway, Queen Sibylla wrote Saladin, asking that he release her husband (1188), and he complied with her request. In 1190 the queen and her two young daughters all died of a disease which swept through the countryside.

Suggested Reading:

(1) Runciman, Steven, *A History of the Crusades*. Cambridge: Cambridge University Press, 1952, 1987. vol. 2, *The Kingdom of Jerusalem and the Frankish East.* pp. 362, 392-393, 404, 407, 423-449. vol. 3, *The Kingdom of Acre.* pp. 19-21, 30.

Sibylle

Princess, ruler of Tripoli (October 1287)

She was the widow of Count Bohemond III and VI (r. 1252-1275) amd the mother of Bohemond IV and VII (r. 1275-1287) When her son died, she ruled briefly in the month of October 1287. In November of that year a republic was established called The Commune of Tripoli which lasted for one year.

Suggested Reading:

(1) Carpenter, Clive. *The Guinnes Book of Kings, Rulers, & Statesmen.* Enfield, Middlesex: Guinness Superlatives Ltd., 1978. p. 55.

Sirikit

Queen, regent of Thailand (1956)

She was born Princess Mom Rajawong Sirikit Kitiyakara in 1932, the daughter of a titled Thai diplomat, H. H. Prince Nakkhatra Mongkol Kitiyakara, and Krommuen Chandaburi Suranat. She was soon noted for her striking beauty. In April 1950 she married Bhumibol Adulyadej, who assumed office June 9, 1946, but was crowned one month after the wedding as King Rama IX, ruler of Thailand. In 1956 she was named regent of Thailand while the king, who is considered holy by his people, performed his meditations and the duties of a Buddhist monk. At that time she took an oath before the National Assembly: "We will reign with righteousness for the benefits and happiness of the Siamese people." Although the constitutional monarchy wields little real political power, the monarch is head of state and commander of the armed forces and a stabilizing and unifying force. Queen Sirikit's special project was promoting the export of handwoven Thai silk. The queen traveled to remote provinces to promote various cottage industries and to encourage rural people to practice their traditional crafts. She then obtained markets for these crafts. In some cases, where knowledge of the crafts had been lost, Queen Sirikit sent instructors to reteach the natives. To achieve those ends she established the Foundation for the Promotion of Supplementary Occupations and Related Techniques which not only provides a chain of shops selling native crafts, but also gives rural women the training and provides materials to set up artisans' cooperatives. She used her organizational skills for the Thai Red Cross, for aid to refugees, orphans, wounded soldiers and flood victims. Of Thai women, she said, "They never had the feeling of being inferior to their menfolk." The royal couple had four children: Princess Ubol Ratana, an M.I.T. graduate who renounced her title and married an American Peter Ladd Jensen; Crown Prince Ma Ha Vajiralongkorn, who, with his two wives and six children, calls himself the family "black sheep;" Princess Maha Chakri Sindhorn, who is president of the Foundation for Development set up by her father to improve the quality of life in Bangkok; and Princess Chulabhorn, a scientist with a doctorate in organic chemistry, married to a Thai commoner. The Crown Prince seemed little interested in civilian pursuits and there was speculation that he might remove himself from succession. In 1979 the popular and brilliant Princess Sirindhorn was accorded a special dynastic title by the National Assembly: Ma Ha Chakri (in effect, making her "Crown Princess"), and in the early 1980s the parliament revised royal law to permit a woman monarch for the first time in Thai history. In 1985 Queen Sirikit abruptly withdrew from public life; in a much later television interview Princess Chulabhorn made the only explanation ever to come from the royal family about the queen's retirement. The princess described her mother as an insomniac who was exhausted and who had been "ordered to rest."

Suggested Reading:

(1) Gray, Denis and Bart McDowell. "Thailand's Working Royalty." *National Geographic 162.* October 1982: 486-499.
(2) *International Who's Who, 1987-1988.* London: Europa Publishing, 1987. p. xvi.

(3) Crossette, Barbara. "King Bhumibol's Reign." *New York Times Magazine*. 21 May 1989: 30-36.

Sirimavo

See Bandaranaike

Sivali

Queen, ruler of (Ceylon) Sri Lanka (A.D. 35)

For a brief period following the death of King Chulabhaya (r. A.D.34-35), Queen Sivali, who was probably his wife, reigned. However, before the year was out, she was succeeded by King Ilanaga, probably a usurper (r. A.D. 35-44).

Suggested Reading:

(1) Egan, Edward W. et. al., eds. *Kings, Rulers, and Statesmen*. New York: Sterling Publishing, 1976. p. 438.
(2) Gray, Denis and Bart McDowell. "Thailand's Working Royalty". *National Geographic 162*. October 1982: p. 23.

Sofya Alekseyevna (or Sophia)

Regent of Russia (1682-1689)

She was born in 1657, the eldest daughter of Tzar Alexis, who ruled Russia from 1645 to 1676, and his first wife, Mariya Miloslavskaya. She was the sister of Fyodor III (Theodore), who acceded to the throne upon his father's death and ruled for six years. When Fyodor died in 1682, Peter (the Great), Sofya's half-brother by Alexis's second wife Natalya Naryshkina, was proclaimed tzar; however, Sofya, indignant that the rights of her younger brother Ivan, sickly and feeble-minded though he was, had been ignored, incited the already discontented palace guard to riot, terrorizing and actually murdering members of Peter's clan. Sofya effected a compromise co-tzarship between Peter I and Ivan V, for which she assumed the regency. With the advice of her favorite (by some accounts lover), Prince Vasily (Basil) V. Golitsyn, who was enlightened and cosmopolitan, Sofya immediately moved

to strengthen her position by arming the frontier and by removing those from positions of authority whom she did not trust. They included Peter, whom she exiled from the Kremlin. Well educated by Russian standards of the day, she invited skilled craftsmen from Europe to settle in Russia. These western Europeans profoundly influenced Peter, who later introduced elements of their style and culture into his reign. With Golitsyn's help, Russia and Poland signed a treaty of "eternal peace" that confirmed Russia's ownership of Kiev and territory east of the Dnieper River. Sofya took Golitsyn's advice and engaged in two costly and disastrous military campaigns against the Tatars in exchange for this peace treaty. Her military failures, as compared with Peter's consuming interest in military skills, led to her unpopularity among the disgruntled military which had supported her originally but which had since suffered loss of face in defeat. By 1689 Sofya had shown signs of her intention to get rid of Peter and to reign as tzaritsa. Theodore Shaklovity, whom she had appointed to command the streltsy, apparently attempted to incite his troops to stage a *coup* which would place Sofya on the throne. The plot was revealed to Peter, who fled in the middle of the night to the Holy Trinity-St. Sergius Monastery. In the days following, the patriarch, much of the populace, and even several regiments of the streltsy, rallied behind Peter. The matter was resolved without open military action while Peter remained sequestered. Following several riots by her supporters, in which Sofya, faced with certain defeat, took no active part, she was tried and sentenced to take the veil. Although Peter, at age seventeen, became the effective ruler, with Ivan retaining his position as so-tzar, the government actually fell into the hands of his Peter's mother Nathalie and her associates. Shaklovity and two of his aides were executed. Golitsyn and several others were exiled. Sofya died in a monastary in 1704.

Suggested Reading:

(1) Riasanovsky, Nicholas V., *A History of Russia*. Oxford: Oxford University Press, 1963, 1993. pp. 214-216, 220-221.

(2) Dvornik, Francis, *The Slavs in European History and Civilization*. New Brunswick, NJ: Rutgers University Press, 1962. pp. 491-492, 510, 526.

(3) Grey, Ian, *Peter the Great: Emperor of All Russia*. Harmondsworth, Middlesex: Penguin Books, 1960. pp. 4-30.

(4) Langer, William L., ed., *World History*. Boston: Houghton Mifflin, 1940, 1980. pp. 514-515.

Sondok Yowang (Sunduk)

Queen of Silla (632-647)

The kingdom of Silla was originally located in South Korea, having its beginnings in the 3rd or 4th century. By the end of the 7th century, it encompassed the entire peninsula. Sondok was the daughter of King Chinp'yong Wang (r. 579-632), who had no sons and bequeathed the throne to his daughter.

The story is told that when she was seven years old, her father received as a gift a box of peony seeds accompanied by a painting of what the flowers would look like. Sondok examined the picture and commented that, while the bloom was pretty, it was unfortunate that it had no odor. She deduced this from the fact that the painting showed no butterflies or bees around the blossom. This astute observation proved her intelligence and her competence for assuming the throne.

Sondok became sole ruler of Silla in 632. As she grew older, she was revered for her facility of anticipating events. She gormed an alliance with China, sending scholars there to study and to bring back knowledge to Silla. Són (Zen) Buddhism is said first to have come to Korea during her reign. She presided over the building of Buddhist temples: the nine-tiered pagoda of Hwanguyongsa was built during her reign and the temples at Punhwangsa and Yongmyosa were completed during her reign. She also presided over the building of the first observatory in the Far East. Called the "Tower of the Moon and Stars," it still stands today in the old Sillan capital, Kyongju.

Sondok's reign was characterized by rebellions and agressions in the kingdom of Paekche, her neighbor to the west, and Koguryo, to the north. Nevertheless, she ruled successfully for fourteen years, choosing a strong and capable general, Kim Yusin, to lead her military forces. She was succeeded by another woman, her cousin Chindok. Sondok's tomb is located in Silla.

Suggested Reading:

(1) Lee, Ki-baik, *A New History of Korea.* tr. Edward W. Wagner with Edward J. Shulz. Cambridge, Massachusetts: Harvard University Press, 1984. pp. 74, 106, 390.

Soong (or Sung) Ch'ing-ling, Madame

Acting Head of State, The People's Republic of China (1976-1978)

She was born c. 1892 in Shanghai, the elder sister of prominent industrialist, financier, and Chinese government official T. V. Soong, and of Soong Mei-ling, also known as Madame Chiang Kai-shek. In 1914 Soong Ch'ing-ling married revolutionary leader Sun Yat-sen, who was 26 years her senior. After his death in 1925, she became an active leader in the left wing of the Nationalist Party which her husband had founded, while her brother-in-law, Chiang Kai-shek, became the leader of the right wing. In 1949 Chiang Kai-shek established the People's Republic of China, or Nationalist China, and moved to Taiwan, while Soong Ch'ing-ling remained on the mainland, where she became an important official in the new government. In 1951 she was awarded the Stalin Peace Prize for her efforts on welfare and peace initiatives. As Chairperson of the Standing Committee of the National People's Congress, she was acting Head of State from July 6, 1976 to March 4, 1978. In 1981, a few months before her death, she was made a member of the Communist Party.

Suggested Reading:

(1) Carpenter, Clive. *The Guinness Book of Kings, Rulers, & Statesmen.* Enfield, Middlesex: Guinness Superlatives Ltd., p. 49.

Spray of Pearls

See Sharajat al-Durr

Sugandha

Queen, regent of Kashmir (A.D. ?-914)

During the tenth century two opposing military factions vied for ascendancy in Kashmir: the Ekangas and the Tantrins, a wild, ungovernable and unpredictable clan. Queen Sugandha allied herself with the Ekangas in order to maintain her control of Kashmir as a whole. In a 914 clash between the two factions, Queen Sugandha's forces were defeated, leaving the Tantrins in complete control. Queen Sugandha was deposed, and none of the succeeding rulers was able to assert his authority over the Tantrins.

Suggested Reading:

(1) Thapar, Romila, *A History of India*. London: Penguin Books, 1987. vol. 1 pp. 225-226.

Suiko-tenno

Empress, ruler of Japan (A.D. 592-628)

She was born Toyo-mike-kashikiya-hime in A.D. 554, the third daughter of Emperor Kimmei-tenno, who reigned from A.D. 548 to 571. Her mother was the daughter of Soga Iname. The Soga was a Samurai family of great distinction. Her half-brother, Bidatsu, acceded to the throne when their father died (571) and reigned until 585. In 576 she married Bidatsu and bore seven sons. Bidatsu died in 585 and was succeeded by his brother Yomei, who died in 587, and his brother Sushun, who was murdered in 592 by Soga Umako, the head of the Soga family. Soga Umake then placed his own niece Suiko on the throne. Although Chinese ancient history records earlier reigning women in Japan, and although Japanese history records the earlier rule of Jingo-kogo as regent for her son Ojin, Suiko is the first reigning empress listed in Japanese recorded history. During her reign the total supremacy of the monarch was established. She encouraged the efforts of her nephew Shotoku-taishi to implant Buddhism in Japan. Through her nephew, the empress invited craftsmen from Korea and China to come to Japan. The Nihongi Chronicles record not only the first embassy to be sent to China (607), but also much intercourse between Japan and the mainland, resulting in the adoption of the Chinese bureaucratic system and even the Chinese calendar. Suiko died in 628 at the age of 75.

Suggested Reading:

(1) Aston, W. G., trans., *Nihongi: Chronicles of Japan*. Rutland, VT: Charles E. Tuttle Company, 1979. vol. 2 pp. 126-156.
(2) Papinot, E., *Historical and Geographical Dictionary of Japan*. Rutland, VT: Charles E. Tuttle Company, 1972. p. 605.

(3) Sansom, George, *A History of Japan to 1334*. Stanford: Stanford University Press, 1958. vol.1 p. 50.

(4) Rauschauer, Edwin O. and John K. Fairbank, *East Asia: The Great Tradition*. Boston: Houghton Mifflin, 1960. p. 475.

Sung

Empress, regent of China (c. 1021-?)

Since her given name is not recorded, she will be referred to as an empress of the Sung dynasty, or Empress Sung. She was the wife of Sung Chen Tsung, (Tseng Tsung), third emperor of the Sung Dynasty, who ruled from 998 to 1022. When her husband became insane, she assumed power. Following his death in 1022, his teen-aged son by a minor concubine of humble rank acceded to the throne with Empress Sung as regent. The dowager empress was frequently at odds with the young emperor, and his young wife sided with her against him as well. After Empress Sung died, the emperor divorced his wife for favoring the dowager empress, causing a scandal in the court which practiced strict Confucian morality.

Suggested Reading:

(1) Grousset, René. *The Empire of the Steppes*. tr. Naomi Walford. New Brunswick, NJ: Rutgers University Press, 1970. p. 132.

Sung

Empress, Regent of China (1274-1276)

Since the name of this empress is not recorded, she will be referred to by the name of her dynasty, Empress Sung. She was the wife of Sung Emperor Tu-Tsung, ruler of China from 1265 to 1274. Following the death of her husband in 1274, she became regent for his son, Kung-Ti, age two, with minister Chia Ssu-tao in charge. The Mongolian general Bayan, under Kublai Khan, invaded the Sung capital city of Hangchow in 1276. The Empress Regent handed over the empire to Kublai Khan, whereupon Bayan sent the young Emperor, now age four, to Kublai, who treated him kindly. How the Empress Sung was treated is not recorded.

Suggested Reading:

(1) Grousset, René. *The Empire of the Steppes.* tr. Naomi Walford. New Brunswick, NJ: Rutgers University Press, 1970. p. 287.

(2) Langer, William L., ed. *World History.* Boston: Houghton Mifflin, 1940, 1980. p. 369.

Section T

Tadj al-'Alam Safiyyat al-Din Shah

Sultana of Atjeh in Indonesia (1641-1675)

Atjeh was a Muslim sultinate on the northern tip of Sumatra. It was a center of trade and at one time dominated the world supply of pepper. Religious scholars noted throughout Southeast Asia were located there. As early as 1514 several small states along the coast were brought under the control of an Atjehnese sultan. The country continued to expand and reached the peak of its power and influence during the reign of Sultan Iskandar Moeda (1607-1636), and it is believed that Sultana Tadj came to the throne as the surviving heir after the death of Moeda's successor. There is mention in an early manuscript of an Atjehnese queen in ca. 1640 making a gift of a four-tusked elephant to Gujerat. She is listed, along with the dates of her reign, as the fourteenth sovereign of the dynasty by H. Djajadiningrat in his article on "Atjeh" in the *Encyclopedia of Islam*. The length of her reign, and the fact that she was succeeded by another woman, Sultana Nur al-Alam Nakiyyat al-Din Shah, probably her daughter, would suggest that she was a popular ruler. The fact that her political enemies had brought from Mecca a *fatwa* forbidding by law that a woman rule further suggests that she wielded considerable power.

Suggested Reading:

(1) Jones, Russell. *Hikayat Sultan Ibrahim Ibn Adham*. Berkeley: University of California Center for South and Southeast Asia Studies, 1985.
(2) Mernissi, Fatima. *The Forgotten Queens of Islam*. tr. Mary Jo Lakeland. Minneapolis: University of Minnesota Press, 1993.

Takano-tenno

See Shotoku-tenno or Koken

Tamara (or Thamar)

Queen, co-ruler (1178-1184), then "king" of Karthalinia (Georgia) (1184-1212)

She was born ca. 1156, the daughter of King George III (Giorgi), who ruled Georgia from 1165 to 1184. Georgia included the ancient countries of Colchis and Iberia in the Caucasus. In 1178, six years before his death, King George had Tamara, "the bright light of his eyes," crowned as co-ruler. He gave her the official name of Mountain of God. The most celebrated monarch of the era, she has been described as being "remarkable for her moderation, humanity, and personal culture." She became sole ruler when he died in 1184, but she was put under the guardianship of her aunt, Rusudani, her father's sister. In 1187 she married George Bogolyuaski of Kiev, but the marriage was still childless after two years. She exiled him and in ca. 1193 married again, a cousin, David Sosland, who was of the house of Bagrationi, as was she. She made him co-ruler from ca. 1193 until 1207. In 1194 they had a son, Giorgi, and in 1195, a daughter, Rusudani. A devout Christian, Queen Tamara requested of Sultan Saladin that he sell her the Holy Cross for 200,000 dinars, but he refused. In 1191 her still disgruntled cast-off first husband, with the help of the Seljuk Sultan of Erzerum, attempted to depose her but failed. In 1200, with the aid of Turkish troops, he tried again. She fought off repeated attacks by Rukn ad-Din; by then she had built an invincible military power. In 1205 she made her son George co-ruler. She helped her nephews Alexius and David Comnenus, grandsons of the Emperor Andronicus, to occupy Trebiz and establish a domain along the Black Sea shores of Asia Minor. David Comnenus was killed in 1206, but Alexius lived to become emperor and to found a dynasty that lasted 250 years. In 1207 her husband David Soslan died. Her son George IV succeeded her when she died in 1212. For her work in furthering the cause of Christianity, she was canonized by the Georgian Church.

Suggested Reading:

(1) Suny, Ronald Grigor, *The Making of the Georgian Nation*. Bloomington:Indiana University Press, 1988. pp. 37-41, 49, 87, 283, 290.

(2) Buchan, John, ed., *The Baltic and Caucasian States*. Boston: Houghton Mifflin, 1923. p. 173.

(3) Runciman, Steven, *A History of the Crusades*. Cambridge: Cambridge University Press, 1952, 1987. vol. 3, *The Kingdom of Acre*. pp. 3, 74, 101, 126, 163, 247.

(4) Hussey, J. M., ed., *The Cambridge Medieval History*. Cambridge University Press, 1966. vol. 4, pt. 1, p. 783.

Ta-pu-yen

Queen, regent of Kara-Kitai Empire (1142-1150)

The Kara-Khitai Empire, located in Eastern Turkestan, was founded by the gur-khan Ye-lü Ta-shih, who ruled ca. 1130 to 1142. This pagan Mongol line in Muslim Turkic territory was looked upon so contemptuously by Arabian/Persian historians that they did not record the names of the rulers; as a result, they are known only by the Chinese transcriptions of their names. After the death of Ye-lü Ta-shih in 1142, his widow Ta-pu-yen became regent of the Empire for their son, Ye-lü Yi-li, who reached his majority in 1150. Their daughter, Pu-su-wan (Ye-lü Shih) also ruled following her brother's death in 1163.

Suggested Reading:

(1) Grousset, René, *The Empire of the Steppes: A History of Central Asia*. tr. Naomi Walford. New Brunswick, NJ: Rutgers University Press, 1970. pp. 165-166.

Tara Bai

Empress, ruler of the Maratha Kingdom of the Deccan (1700-1707)

Tara Bai was the wife of Raja Ram (r. 1687-1700), who succeeded the throne when Mughals hacked to death his brother Sambhaji (or Shambhuji, r. 1680-1687). Raja Ram had escaped the advancing Mughal forces of the fanatical Muslim Aurangzeb and had gone to Jinji, a fort southwest of Madras, at the foot of which a Mughal army was camped off and on for seven years. When Aurangzeb demanded that Mughals finally attack, the Mughal commander arranged for his friend Raja Ram to escape before the fort fell. Raja Ram took up the fight against the Mughals who had long persecuted and threatened to overrun his Hindu kingdom. When Raja Ram was killed, his widow, Tara Bai, took up leadership, not only of the kingdom, but of the military movement against the invaders. When Aurangzeb died of old age (1707), the Mughal threat ended. Sambhaji's son Shahu, who with his clever and talented mother Yesubai, had been held prisoner by the Mughals, escaped and returned to claim the crown. Tara Bai challenged Shahu's succession, and for years he was engaged in internal struggles, leaving the government in the hands of his ministers.

Suggested Reading:

(1) Carpenter, Clive. *The Guinness Book of Kings, Rulers, & Statesmen.* Enfield, Middlesex: Guinness Superlatives Ltd., pp. 130-131.
(2) Gasciogne, Bamber. *The Great Moghuls.* New York: Dorset Press, 1971. p. 236.

Teng

Empress, regent of China (A.D. 105-121)

During the Later or Eastern Han Dynasty, following the death of Emperor Ho Ti, ruler from A.D. 88 to 105, Teng ruled as dowager queen regent for her infant son until her own death in A.D. 121. At the time of her death, most of her prominent relatives, as befitted their noble status, chose suicide.

Suggested Reading:

(1) Langer, William L., ed., *World History.* Boston: Houghton Mifflin, 1948, 1980. p. 146.

Thecla

Co-regent of Byzantine Empire (c. 842)

She was the daughter of Emperor Theophilus, ruler of the Eastern Roman Empire from 829 to 842, and Empress Theodora. She was the sister of Michael III, who acceded to the throne as a child of three upon their father's death, and of Constantine, who died ca. 830, and four sisters: Mary, Anna, Anastasia and Pulcheria. When Michael came to the throne, their mother

Theodora served as regent. Apparently Thecla, the oldest surviving sister, was entitled to share in the regency of her mother, since she was portrayed on the coins together with Michael and Theodora and was named with them on official government documents of the period. But there is no indication that Thecla took any actual part in the conduct of government. When Theodora was forced to surrender control of the government in 856, her daughters were shut up in a nunnery. If Thecla was among them, she apparently did not remain long, because she soon surfaced as the mistress of Byzantine Emperor Basil I, who ruled from 867 to 886, who, in a fruit-basket-turnover of wives, took as his second wife Eudoxia Ingerina, Thecla's brother Michael's former mistress. Michael made Basil co-emperor in 866 but in 867 Basil repaid the compliment by having the drunken emperor murdered in his bed chamber.

Suggested Reading:

(1) Ostrogorsky, George, *History of the Byzantine State*. New Brunswick, NJ: Rutgers University Press, 1969. pp. 219, 232.

(2) Previté-Orton, C. W., *The Shorter Cambridge Medieval History*. Cambridge: Cambridge University Press, 1952, 1982. vol. 1, *The Later Roman Empire to the Twelfth Century*. pp. 249, 252-253.

Theodora

Empress, defacto co-ruler of Macedonian Dynasty, Byzantium (527-548)

A woman of humble origins, a former actress, in 525 she married Justinian, also born of peasant stock, who ruled Byzantium from 527 to 565. It is generally conceded by today's historians that the historian Procopius, who in 551, 553 and 554 wrote books on the ruler and his wife, unduly maligned them both. In fact, Theodora's unswerving will, superior intelligence, and acute political acumen lead many modern day historians to the conclusion that it was she, rather than Justinian, who ruled Byzantium. In 527 Justinian was made co-emperor with his uncle, the Emperor Justin, and was given the rank of August. At the same time, Theodora, who exercised considerable power and influence over him even at that time, was crowned Augusta. While Justinian's entire reign was troubled by wars in both the east and the west, and by frequent attacks from the north by barbarians, Theodora's spheres of influence, although not wholly confined to the domestic issues, concerned themselves with every facet of administrative, legislative and ecclesiastical matters. Her name is mentioned in nearly every law passed during the period. She was one of the first rulers to champion women's rights, passing strict laws prohibiting white slavery and altering divorce laws to make them more favorable to women. In 531 she arranged the dismissal of the praetorian prefect, John of Cappadocia, whose collection of revenues and general attention to the financing of Justinian's military campaigns she thought inadequate. In 532 two factions (the Greens and the Blues) united against Justinian and proclaimed the late emperor Anastasius' nephew Hypatius emperor. Justinian, believing all was lost, prepared for flight. But the indominable courage of Theodora prevented a *coup*. She persuaded Justinian to stand his ground, and those troops loyal to the emperor were able to quell the revolt. In the field of foreign affairs, she corresponded with and received diplomats and in general conducted any foreign policy that did not pertain to fighting battles. Her championship of the cause of Monophysitism, the Christian teaching emphasizing the divine nature of Christ, counterbalanced the orthodox view set forth by the Council of Chalcedon in 451, that human and divine natures coexist in the Christ. She died of cancer in 548, leaving her bereft husband, toward the end of his life, to grapple with the theological mysteries and questions she had posed. Following her death, although her husband ruled almost two more decades, no notable legislation was passed.

Suggested Reading:

(1) Browning, Robert. *Justinian and Theodora*. New York: Praeger Publishers, 1971.
(2) Ostrogorsky, George. *History of the Byzantine State*. New Brunswick, NJ: Rutgers University Press, 1969. pp. 25, 69, 73.
(3) Previté-Orton, C. W. *The Shorter Cambridge Medieval History*. Cambridge: Cambridge University Press, 1952, 1982. vol. 1, *The Later Roman Empire*. pp. 78, 185-188.

Theodora

Empress, regent of Eastern Roman Empire (A.D. 842-856)

Theodora was the wife of Emperor Theophilus, who ruled the Byzantine Empire from 829 to 842. The couple had seven children: Maria, Thecla, Anna,

Anastasia, Pulcheria, Constantine and Michael II (later called the Drunkard), who at the age of three acceded to the throne aupon his father's death (842) with his mother as regent. Her ministers and her brother Bardas advised her to restore orthodoxy which had been recanted by her late husband. She did so with a vengance: she reinstated icons (as pictures, not statues) and gave the Paulicians the choice of conversion or death. Paulicians who survived the ensuing bloodbath which her edict caused in Constantinople made a mass exodus to Thrace. Her government was then forced to undertake a new campaign against the Slavic tribes in southern Greece. After a long bitter struggle, the Slavs were subdued and forced to pay tribute and to recognize Byzantium supremacy. In 856 Theodora's brother Bardas, acting in secret agreement with her son Michael, murdered her advisor Theoctistus and had the senate proclaim Michael an independent ruler. Theodora was obliged to retire and her daughters were shut up in a nunnery. Ten years later, after she attempted an attack against her brother, she too was sent away to a nunnery.

Suggested Reading:

(1) Sullivan, Richard E. *Heirs of the Roman Empire*. Ithaca, NY: Cornell University Press, 1965. pp. 103, 125.

(2) Durant, Will. *The Story of Civilization*. New York: Simon & Schuster, 1950. vol. 4, *The Age of Faith*. p. 427.

(3) Ostrogorsky, George. *History of the Byzantine State*. New Brunswick, NJ: Rutgers University Press, 1969. pp. 215, 219-223, 225, 250, 575.

(4) Previté-Orton, C. W. *The Shorter Cambridge Medieval History*. Cambridge: Cambridge University Press, 1952, 1982. vol. 1, *The Later Roman Empire*. pp. 249, 252-253.

Theodora (or Augusta Theodora)

Empress, ruler of Byzantine Empire (1042 and 1055-1056)

Born c. 981, she was the youngest daughter of Constantine VIII, ruler of Byzantium from 963 to 1028, and his wife Helena of Alypius. Psellus described her as "tall, curt and glib of tongue, cheerful and smiling" and as having "a placid disposition and in one way . . . a dull one" and as "self-controlled in money matters." Her eldest sister Eudocia, pocked-faced from an early age, entered a nunnery. Her second sister, Zoë, was singled out by their dying father to be married to Romanus II, who, with Zoë, inherited the reign upon the emperor's death (1028). During their reign, Theodora was exiled to a convent in Petrion. She never married, but by some quirk of disposition, she seemed not to hold a serious grudge against her sister for her treatment. Zoë, always the adventurous one of the two, took a lover, Michael IV, and together they conspired to murder Romanus, whereupon Zoë married Michael and made him emperor. Although Michael IV treated Zoë poorly once he was installed, he nevertheless convinced her to adopt his nephew, Michael V, as her heir and his successor. Michael IV died, and Michael V came to the throne. But he made the mistake of exiling Zoë, arousing the populace against him. Michael quickly brought Zoë back, but the people were not appeased. They brought Theodora out of exile and proclaimed her empress (1042). She ruled alone briefly, then allowed her sister to join her and even gave her the more prominent role. But Zoë could not be satisfied; she seized power again by marrying a third time (Constantine IX, 1042-1055). Zoë died during this reign (1050), and when Constantine died (1055), Theodora was again summoned to take control. This time she superintended all affairs of state herself. She appointed all officials, dispensed justice from the throne, issued decrees, and gave orders. According to Psellus, during her reign, the Empire prospered and its glory increased. She died in 1056 at the age of 76, having named as her successor Michael VI, an aged man of the court suggested by her advisors, when she was on her deathbed.

Suggested Reading:

(1) Psellus, Michael. *Fourteen Byzantine Rulers*. tr. E. R. A. Sewter. Harmondsworth, Middlesex: Penguin Books, 1982. pp. 143-162, 261-271.

(2) Ostrogorsky, George. *History of the Byzantine State*. new Brunswick, NJ: Rutgers University Press, 1969. pp. 321, 326, 337-338, 576.

(3) Previté-Orton, C. W. *The Shorter Cambridge Medieval History*. Cambridge: Cambridge University Press, 1952, 1982. vol. 1, *The Later Roman Empire*. pp. 273-274, 277.

Theodora

Queen, ruler of the Empire of Trebizond (Trabzon) (1284-1285)

Trebizond, both empire and city, also called Trabzond, or, in ancient times, Trapezus, was located on the southeast coast of the Black Sea in northeastern

Turkey. The empire was founded in 1204, after the fall of Constantinople, by the Grand Comneni, Alexius and David, two grandsons of Emperor Andronicus I (ruled the Byzantine Empire 1183-1185). After the fall of their grandfather, the boys were taken to the Georgian court of their relatives where, in 1204, their aunt, Queen Thamar (r. 1184-1212), helped them to capture Trebizond and found an empire. Alexius I (r. 1204-1222) was the first ruler and the patriarch of the Trebezondian Commenian Dynasty, while David was killed in 1206 in battle.

Theodora was the youngest daughter of Manuel I (r. 1238-1263), a son of Alexius I. She was the sister of George (r. 1266-1280) and John II (r. 1280-1284), both of whom were deposed. After one year on the throne, Theodora was also deposed and her brother John was restored (r. 1285-1287).

Suggested Reading:

(1) Morby, John E. *Dynasties of the World*. Oxford: Oxford University Press, 1989. p. 56.
(2) Ostrogorsky, George. *History of the Byzantine Empire*. New Brunswick, NJ: Rutgers University Press, 1969. pp. 401, 426.
(3) Runciman, Steven A. *A History of the Crusades*, Vol. III. Cambridge: Cambridge University Press, 1987. pp. 126, 359, 398, 451.

Theophano

Empress, regent of Byzantine Empire (963)

Born the daughter of a publican, Anastaso, she was an extraordinarily beautiful woman who attracted the attention of the future Byzantine Emperor Romanus II, who married her ca. 956. When Romanus became emperor in 959, she took the name of Theophano. A historian describes her as "entirely immoral and immeasurably ambitious." The couple had two sons, Basil II and Constantine VIII. Upon Romanus' death in 963, Theophano assumed the regency for the small boys. Being a shrewd student of political affairs, she knew her regency could not last long, so she came to an understanding with the elderly Nicephories Phocas, offering herself in marriage to him. The supreme military command was entrusted to the brilliant General John Tzimisces, with whom Theophano conducted a heated affair. She cooperated with conspirators of Tzimisces who murdered her elderly husband in his bed chamber in 969, expecting that she and john would then be married. But the Patriarch Polyeuctus, in the sort of slap-on-the-wrist justice which was so often meted out to the powerful, demanded that, before John could become emperor, he should do penance for his part in the murder, and that he should expel Theophano from the palace. She died in 991.

Suggested Reading:

(1) Previté-Orton, C. W. *The Shorter Cambridge Medieval History.* Cambridge: Cambridge University Press, 1952, 1982. vol. 1, *The Later Roman Empire.* pp. 258-259.
(2) Ostrogorsky, George. *History of the Byzantine State.* New Brunswick, NJ: Rutgers University Press, 1969. pp. 284, 285, 293.

Tindu

Mongol queen of Iraq (1411-1419)

She belonged to the Jallarid dynasty, a branch of the Ilkhan dynasty which ruled Iraq from 1336 to 1411. She was the beautiful daughter of the great Mongol King Awis. During a trip to Egypt with her uncle, she caught the fancy of Mamluk King al-Zahir Barquq, who asked for her hand in marriage. Her father was more than happy to oblige, in exchange of Egyptian military aid against the invasions by Tamerlane's armies. But Tindu was not happy in Cairo, and because Barquq loved her very much, he allowed her to return to her homeland of Iraq. Eventually she married her cousin Shah Walad, ruler of Baghdad, and after his death in 1411, she acceded to the throne. She ruled until her death in 1419, at which time her son claimed the throne.

Suggested Reading:

(1) Mernissi, Fatima. *The Forgotten Queens of Islam.* tr. Mary Jo Lakeland. Minneapolis: The University of Minnesota Press, 1993, pp. 72, 105-106.

Tizard, Dame Catherine

Governor-general of New Zealand (1990-1996)

Catherine Tizard was born Catherine Anne Maclean on April 4, 1931, the daughter of Neil and Helen Montgomery Maclean. She received her education from Manamata College, in the north central part of North Island, and at the University of Auckland. In 1951 she married Robert James Tizard. The couple had four children and divorced in 1983. In the interim, she was a tutor in zoology at the University of Auckland (1967-1984), served on the Auckland City Council (1971-1983), and was a member of the Auckland Regional Authority (1980-1983). In 1984 she was elected mayor of the City of Auckland, a post she held until December, 1990, when she was named Queen Elizabeth II's representative, Governor-general of New Zealand. She continued in this position until 1996, when. in September of that year, she was appointed Chairperson of the Historic Trust. She lives in Auckland, New Zealand.

Suggested Reading:

(1) New Zealand Executive Government News Release Archive, Sept. 10, 1996.
(2) *Marquis Who's Who in the World.* 14th. edition. New Providence, NJ, 1997. p. 1461.

Tomyris

Queen of the Massagetae (c. 529/530 B.C.)

The Massagetae was a large, warlike half-nomadic Sakan tribe whose land lay eastward beyond the Araxes River in Eastern Persia. Tomyris was the widow of a Sakan chief and was both Queen and leader of the army. She had at least one son, Spargapises. Cyrus the Great, not content with his latest conquest of Assyria, turned his attention to adding the country of the Massagetae to his ever expanding Persian Empire. According to Herodotus, Cyrus, camped across the river from the Massagetae, first sent word to Queen Tomyris pretending to want her hand in marriage, but Tomyris, not so easily duped, refused. She went him word, "King of the Medes, I advise you to abandon this enterprise . . . . Rule your own people, and try to bear the sight of me ruling mine. But of course, you will refuse my advice, as the last thing you wish for is to live in peace." She then offered him an alternative: allow her army to withdraw a three-days' march from the river and then the two rulers could meet. Cyrus was at first inclined to accept this proposal until advised by Croesus against any compromise. Croesus suggested tricking the Massagetae by preparing a feast as a trap, luring the Massagetae to descend upon it and, once they had sated themselves and had drunk themselves into a stupor, his troops could come out of hiding and massacre them. Croesus pointed out, "It would surely be an intolerable disgrace for Cyrus son of Cambyses to give ground before a woman." Cyrus took his advice and the plot went off as planned, except for one small hitch: one of those captured in the plot was the queen's son Sargapises. When the queen learned of this, she sent word that her son be released or she would give him more blood than he could drink. Actually, Cyrus could not return Spargapises even if he had wanted to because the boy had committed suicide in captivity. The Massagetae attacked and massacred the Persians, including Cyrus. By Herodotus' account, the queen, learning that her son had committed suicide, filled a skin with blood and stuffed Cyrus' head in it, fulfilling her promise to give him more blood than he could drink. According to other accounts, Cyrus was only mortally wounded at the time and didn't die until three days later.

Suggested Reading:

(1) Olmstead, A. T. *History of the Persian Empire*. Chicago: University of Chicago Press, 1948. p. 66.
(2) Herodotus. *The Histories*. tr. Aubrey de Sélincourt. New York: Penguin Books, 1954, 1988. pp. 123-127.

Toregene (also Turakina, Toragina or Toragana)

Khatun, regent of Outer Mongolia (1241-1246)

A Naiman princess, she has been described as energetic but avaricious. She was the wife of Ogodei (or Ogotai or Ogodai), a son of Jenghiz-khan and ruler of the Mongolian Empire from 1229 to 1241. Jenghiz-khan had divided his realm among his four sons, making each a khan over the chieftains in his own realm; however, the khans then elected one great khan to rule over all. In 1229 Ogodei was elected great khan by the plenary Kuriltai. Prior to his death of a drinking bout in 1241, he had had a quarrel with his eldest son Guyuk and had sent him disgraced into exile. He had named as his successor his grandson Shiramon, whose father Kuchu had been killed fighting the Chinese. But Toregene, determined that Guyuk should have the throne, took over the regency. She summoned a Kuriltay (gathering of the official ruling body), which recognized her authority until a new great khan should be appointed. For five years she ruled while trying to convince the clan chieftains and princes of the blood to appoint Guyuk. During her reign, she chose as her advisor, not a Christian like herself, but a Moslem, Abd ar-Rahman. Gossipers accused Abd ar-Rahman of aiding in Ogodei's untimely demise. Toregene eventually convinced the Kuriltai of Guyuk's suitability, and she handed over the throne to him in 1246.

Suggested Reading:

(1) Grousset, René, *The Empire of the Steppes*. tr. Naomi Walford. New Brunswick, NJ: Rutgers University Press, 1970. pp. 268-269.

(2) Reischauer, Edwin O. and John K. Fairbank. *East Asia: The Great Tradition*. Boston: Houghton Mifflin, 1960. pp. 267, 270, 273.

(3) Runciman, Steven. *A History of the Crusades*. Cambridge: Cambridge University Press, 1952, 1987. vol. 3, *The Kingdom of Acre*. pp. 249, 251-252, 293.

Tou Hsien

Empress, regent of China (A.D. 88-97)

During the Later or Eastern Han Dynasty, dowager empresses and their eunuchs gained the power by choosing infants as successors to the throne. Tou Hsien, who came from a great land-owning family that dated back to the second century B.C., became all powerful at court by this ploy. Empress Tou altered the succession and, with her family, ruled as dowager empress from A.D.88 to her death in 97.

Suggested Reading:

(1) Reischauer, Edwin O. and John K. Fairbank. *East Asia: The Great Tradition*. Boston: Houghton Mifflin, 1960, pp. 125-126.

(2) Morton, W. Scott. *China: Its History and Culture*. New York: McGraw-Hill, 1982. p. 63.

(3) Langer, William L., ed. *World History*. Boston: Houghton Mifflin, 1940, 1980. p. 146.

Tribhuvana

Queen, Majapahit ruler of Java (1328-1350)

Tribhuvana succeeded her father, Jayanagara, who was slain by his physician Tancha. Her minister Gajah Mada, instigator of the assassination plot, became the empire's most powerful figure. In 1350 she abdicated in favor of her son, Hayam Wuruk, the Majapahit Empire's most famous king.

Suggested Reading:

(1) *Britannica Macropaedia*. Chicago: Encyclopaedia Britannica, Inc., 1983. vol. 7, "Gajah Maja". pp. 825-826.

Trieu Au

Vietnamese hill-people "ruler" (c. A.D. 248)

Although not a queen, Trieu Au was a leader at a time when Vietnam was not unified but was instead a territory occupied by the Chinese. Born in A.D. 222, she was orphaned and taken by her brother and his wife, who treated her cruelly, more like a slave than a sister. Trieu Au killed her sister-in-law, perhaps a Chinese, and escaped to the hills. A commanding and charismatic speaker, she took it upon herself to enumerate the indignities which her people had endured at the hands of the Chinese. She set up her administration in the hills and raised 1000 troops with which she launched a revolt against the hated Chinese. Wearing golden armor, she rode at the front of her troops on the back of an elephant. She was defeated in only six months and, in honorable fashion, rather than surrender, committed suicide by throwing herself into a river. She is remembered today in Vietnam by a temple built in her honor and by her defiant declaration, "I want to rail against the wind and the tide, kill the whale in the sea, sweep the whole country to save the people from slavery, and I refuse to be abused."

Suggested Reading:

(1) Karnow, Stanley. *Vietnam: A History*. New York: Viking Press, 1983. p. 100.

Trung Nhi and Trung Trac

Co-queens of Vietnam (A.D. 39-42)

Between 111 B.C. and A.D.221, Vietnam was in the hands of the Han Dynasty overlords of China. For more than a century the Vietnamese made no serious challenge to the Han rule. Then, in ca. A.D. 39, a Chinese commander murdered a dissident Vietnamese nobleman and raped his widow, who happened to be Trung Trac. She and her sister Trung Nhi organized the surrounding tribal lords and mustered an army which included at least one other outstanding woman, Phung Thi Chinh, who was pregnant at the time. The sisters attacked Chinese strongholds and either cleared out or massacred the enemy Chinese. Phung Thi Chinh reportedly gave birth to a baby but strapped it on her back and got back into the fray. The Vietnamese carved out an independent kingdom, purged of Chinese, which stretched from Hue into southern China. The Trung sisters were proclaimed co-queens of this new kingdom. They ruled until A.D. 42, when the Han emperor sent a large force to recapture the kingdom. Unable to meet such mighty opposition, the Trung sisters took the honorable route of committing suicide: they drowned themselves in a river. The Vietnamese still venerate the sisters at temples in Hanoi and Saigon. Madame Ngo Dinh Nhu, the sister-in-law of South Vietnam's President Ngo Dinh Diem, erected statues in their honor in Saigon in 1962.

Suggested Reading:

(1) Karnow, Stanley. *Vietnam: A History.* New York: Viking Press, 1983. p. 100.

Tz'u-an

Queen, regent of China (1862-1873) and (1875-1881)

She was at one time the senior consort of the Hsien-feng emperor, who reigned from 1851 to 1862, until another consort, Tz'u-hsi (Cixi), bore a son and heir, T'ung-chih. When the emperor died in 1862, the five-year-old boy became emperor with a council of eight elders acting as regents. Through clever plotting with Prince Kung, brother of the late king, the two dowager empresses managed to get the regency transferred to them. They then named Kung as the prince councillor. The women gradually brought about some westernization of the government and to put an end to much of the government corruption. The regency ended when T'ung-chih reached his majority in 1973; however, he died only two years later. Tz'u-hsi violated succession laws, which called for an emperor of the next generation, by adopting her three-year-old nephew as heir. Again the two empresses served as regents until Tz'u-an's sudden death in 1881, possibly from poisoning.

Suggested Reading:

(1) Morton, W. Scott. *China: Its History and Culture*. New York: McGraw-Hill, 1982. pp. 168-175.

Tz'u Hsi

See Cixi

Section U

Udham Bai

Queen, defacto co-ruler of Mughal India (1748-1754)

She was the daughter of Farrukh-Siyar, who in the twilight years of the Mughal Empire married Muhammad Shah (Rawshan Akhtar), ruler from 1719 to 1748, the fourth in a row of weak rulers. Under his leadership, the empire lost the province of Kabul to Persia's Nadir Shah and Katehr to another soldier of fortune, Ruhela. Several other provinces became practically independent. Her son, Ahmad Shah Badahur, born in 1725, was no stronger. He had already reached his majority when he crowned himself king upon his father's death (1748), but his mother knew that he was cut from the same cloth as his four predecessors. If India was to continue under the Mughals, someone besides the good natured, lackadaisical Ahmad Shah would have to take the reins. It was easy for Udham Bai to dominate her son completely. She did not encourage responsibility in her son, but in the end the weaknesses that she encouraged sealed her fate as well as his. She had as her cohort, the emperor's eunuch vicar and superintendent of the harem, Javid Khan. Despite their meddling, Ahmad Shah, who was easily intimidated, gave the Punjab and Multan to Nadir Shah's lieutenant, Abdali. Then, at a demonstration by the Marathas in Sikandrabad, Ahmad Shah, who invariably chose flight to fight, abandoned the women of his family, including Udham Bai, to captivity by the Marathas. He was blinded and deposed in 1754 by a force consisting of Doab Afghans and Marathas. He lived in confinement until his death in 1775.

Suggested Reading:

(1) Gascoigne, Bamber, *The Great Moghuls*. New York: Dorset Press, 1971. pp. 245, 250.

(2) Burn, Sir. R., ed., *Cambridge History of India*. Cambridge: Cambridge University Press, 1937. vol. 4, *The Moghal Period.* p. 462.
(3) Glubb, Sir John, *A Short History of the Arab Peoples*. New York: Dorset Press, 1969. pp. 235-236, 244.

Section V

Vaekehu

Queen, ruler of the Taiohae tribe (1891)

Remnants of the Taiohae tribe live in the Marquesas Islands, two volcanic clusters of islands 40 miles northeast of Tahiti. The main harbor and port on the northern island of Nuku Hiva is a town, also the administrative seat of the Marquesas, called Haka Pehi, or Taiolae, from the Polynesian tribe of Queen Vaekehu. The French annexed the whole group of islands in 1842. The French mission, backed by a military force, wiped out native culture by gradually weeding out recalcitrant chiefs, requiring that natives wear European-style clothing, and banning native songs and dances, musical instruments and tatoos. By 1890, the time of Queen Vaekehu, the native culture was well broken, and she ruled at the French behest. The introduction by the French of venereal diseases, tuberculosis, smallpox and leprosy all but obliterated the tribe. However, some improvement in their numbers has been made in this century, although their culture is lost forever. Queen Vaekehu's reign was documented in 1891 by F. W. Christian, who collected her genealogy for a paper entitled "Notes on the Marquesas," published in the *Journal of the Polynesian Society*, vol. 4, 1895, p. 194.

Suggested Reading:

(1) Suggs, Robert C. *The Island Civilizations of Polynesia*. New York: Mentor Books, NAL, 1960. pp. 53-54.

Section W

Wang

See Cheng-Chun

Wajed, Sheikh Hasina (or Wazed or Wazid)

Prime Minister of Bangladesh (1996-2001, 2008-)

She was born September 28, 1947, in Gopalganj, Bangladesh, the the oldest of five children of Mujibur Rahman, a Sunni Muslim, the founder of Bangladesh in 1971 and its first prime minister. He, along with more than a dozen members of his family, was gunned down in his home in August of 1975 by renegade army officers. Hasina and her sister were the only family members not present. She later became leader of the Awami League, the main opposition party to Prime Minister Khaleda Zia.

Her political career had begun in the 1960s during her days as a student activist at Edwn College. While at Government Intermediate School, she was elected vice president of the College Students Union for 1966-1967. In 1968 she married M. A. Wazed Mia, a nuclear scientist. They had two children, Sajeeb Wazed Joy, and Ssaima Wazed Hossain Putul. Later, at University of Dhaka, she joined the student wing of the Awami League, which she would lead a decade later.

During the liberation war of 1971, Hasina, her son, mother, sister, and brothers were placed under house arrest, while her father, Sheikh Mujibur Rahman was imprisoned in West Pakistan. After liberation, her brother, Sheikh Kamal, was groomed to become his father's successor, and Hasina withdrew from active politics. But the assassination of her family by officers of the Bangladesh army while she and her sister, Sheikh Rehana, were on a good-will trip to West Germany, changed her focus. She first sought refuge in the Uniter Kingdom and later was exiled to New Delhi, India, where in 1981 she was elected president of the Bangladesh

Awami League, and in May of that year, she was allowed to return to Bangladesh.

Soon after her return, President Ziaur Rahman was assassinated during yet another coup, leaving his widow, Khaleda Zia, in charge of the Bangladesh Nationalist Party. A few months later Lieutenant General Hossain Mohammad Ershad declared martial law and took command as President in a "peaceful" takeover. In 1983, Hasina, leading the Awami league, cobbled together an alliance with 14 other parties for the purpose of ousting Ershad from power. Hasina's eight-party alliance and Khaleda Zia's four-party one were most vocal in their opposition, such that Hasina was placed under house arrest twice in 1984 and once in 1985. In 1986, she agreed to participate the the Parliamentary elections held by dictator Ershad, for which she was roundly criticized. She served as leader of the opposition from 1986-1987, when the parliament was dissolved. In 1990 Hasina's eight-party alliance and Zia's four-party alliance finally ousted the Ershad military regime. In the first democratic elections in 1991 Zia's party coalition prevailed and she became Bangladesh's first female Prime Minister.

A "family feud" between the two leaders had begun with Mujibur Rahman's assassination, which was linked to followers of Khaleda Zia's husband, a former president who had in turn been assassinated in Chittagong in 1981. In 1995-1996 Sheikh Hasina Wajed launched a series of crippling strikes against the Khaleda Zia government, eventually bringing it down. Hasina became Prime Minister from 1996 to 2001, promising to create a government of national unity. A major achievement of Hasinas government was to strike a treaty between Bangladesh and India concering water rights from the Farakka Barrage, which had been built in the 1960s. She next pursued a peace treaty with the tribal rebels in the mountainous southeast of the country, where incursions against citizens have occurred for centuries. These rebel activities were reduced after the treaty, but the region remains a danger zone.

During Hasina Wajed's first year in office, Bangladesh's economy grew as foreign investment dollars poured in. But she failed to bring about much needed governmental and social reforms, and there was ample evidence that the bitter feud continued. During 1998 at least 31 opposition party politicians were murdered, leading former Prime Minister Zia to call for the same paralyzing strikes which caused her own government to fall.

During the last year of her rule, which had been criticized for harboring gangsters-turned-politicians, such as Jainal Hazari of Feni, Transparency International declared Bangladesh to be the most corrupt country in the world. Zia's party also accused the Awami league of politicizing the state-owned media.

Hasina's party suffered a landslide defeat in the 2001 Parliament elections. It won only 62 seats in the Parliament, while the Four Party Alliance led by Zia's Bangladesh Nationalist Party won more than 200 seats, giving them a two-thirds majority in Parliament. Sheikh Hasina and the Awami League rejected the results, claiming that the election was rigged. However, the international community was largely satisfied with the elections and the Four Party Alliance went on to form the government.

In her position as opposition leader, Hasina was the victim of assassination attempts that killed as many as 21 key party personnel, including Awami's women's secretary, Ivy Rahman. In 2006 the Awami League formed an alliance with Ershad's Jayiya Party, which would ultimately result in her party's return to power in the 2008 Parliamentary elections. But before the elections could occur, in April of 2007 came the announcement that Bangladesh police were investigating extortion charges against Hasina. Businessman Tajul Islam Farooq claimed that in 1998 he paid her a large sum in bribes before his company was allowed to build a power plant.

Earlier that month, murder charges were filed against her, claiming that she had masterminded the murder of four political rivals in October 2006. She was visiting in the United States at the time, and the interim administration attempted to block her return to Bangladesh. She vowed to return anyway, and a warrant was issued for her arrest. When she attempted to board a London flight back to her country, she was not allowed aboard the airplane. However, the next day the warrant was suspended, and two days later the ban on her re-entry was dropped.

At the same time Khaleda Zia was being pressed into exile, so the government's actions appeared to be an attempt to restructure the system without the interference of either woman. Two months after her return to Bangladesh, Hasina was arrested by state police, accused of extortion, and denied bail. The following day, July 17, 2007, the Anti-Corrumtion Commission sent notices to both Hasina and Zia demanding that both submit details of their assets within one week. On July 30 the Dhaka High Court suspended the extortion trial and ordered her release on bail. Another case was filed in September regarding the 1997 rewarding of a power plant contract. That same day a case was filed against her rival Zia. Still another charge was filed in January, 2008, but it was thrown out by the High Court on a technicality.

In June of 2008 Hasina was allowed to leave the coutry for medical treatment in the United States. She returned home in Novemebr to conduct her party during general elections in December. Her Awami League won the elections with an overwhelming majority, controlling 230 seats out of 299. She was sworn in for her second stint as Prime Minister on January 6, 2009. Meanwhile, her rival Khaleda Zia accused the election officials of bias. The rivalry brings to mind the ongoing feud between Frankish queens Fredegund and Brunhilde.

Prime Minister Hasina is a member of the Council of Women World Leaders. Her children both live in the United States.

Suggested Reading:

(1) "The 'Strongwomen' of South Asia"; see Mahmud, Arshad, "Zia's Faltering Rule" reprinted from *The Guardian* (London) in *World Press Review* December 1994. pp. 18-20.

(2) "War of the Ladies" *World Press Review* September 1998. p. 21.

Wu Hou (or Wu Chao or Wu Tso Tien)

Empress, defacto ruler of China (A.D. 660-684), regent of China (684-690), "emperor," ruler in her own right (690-705)

She was born in A.D. 625 and at the age of 13 came as a junior concubine to the court of T'ang Emperor Tai-tsung, ruler from 627 to 649. When he died, she was chosen by his heir and possibly already her lover, Kao-tsung (649-684), first as his favored concubine and then, in 655, as his empress. On her way to ultimate power, she is said to have poisoned one of her own sons, her sister and her niece, forced another son to hang himself, had four grandchildren whipped to death, ordered the execution of two stepsons and 16 of their male heirs, killed four daughters-in-law, 36 government officials and generals, and ordered another 3000 families to be slaughtered. By 660 she had eliminated all her opponents. The emperor was often too ill to attend to affairs of state for months at a time and relied entirely on Wu Hou. For the last 23 years of his life, Empress Wu Hou ran the country with consummate ability and efficiency. Military spending was reduced, the country experienced peace and prosperity, and commerce and agriculture thrived. When Kao-tsung died in 683, she became regent for their son Chung Tsung. But she had disagreements with the new emperor's wife almost immediately, so she deposed her son after only one month and installed her second son Jui Tsung, over whom she had more control. In 690 she simply usurped the throne for herself, naming herself "emperor," and ruled with great wisdom in her own name for 15 years. Described as self-confindent and assertive, she took great pains to encourage independent thinking and bold behavior in her children. So long as she remained strong, no one dared attempt to usurp her power, but when she reached the age of 80, her opponents grew more courageous. She was deposed in a palace *coup* in A.D. 705 and died in retirement ten months later.

Suggested Reading:

(1) Hook, Brian, ed. *The Cambridge Encyclopedia of China*. Cambridge: Cambridge University Press, 1982. pp. 189-190, 191.
(2) Bloodworth, Dennis. *The Chinese Looking Glass*. New York: Farrar, Straus and Giroux, 1967. pp. 90-92.
(3) Bloodworth, Dennis and Ching Ping Bloodworth. *The Chinese Machiavelli: 3000 Years of Chinese Statecraft*. New York: Dell Publishing Company, 1976. pp. 214-215, 218, 258-259.
(4) Grousset, René. *The Empire of the Steppes: A History of Central Asia*. tr. Naomi Walford. New Brunswick, NJ: Rutgers University Press, 1970. pp. 107-108.
(5) Morton, W. Scott. *China, Its History and Culture*. New York: McGraw-Hill, 1980, 1982. pp. 87, 89.
(6) Reischauer, Edwin O. and John K. Fairbank. *East Asia: The Great Tradition*. Boston: Houghton Mifflin, 1960. pp. 157, 170, 190.

Section Y

Yanjmaa, Sükhbaataryn

President of Mongolia (September 23, 1953-July 7, 1954)

She was born Nemendeyen Yanjmaa in 1893. She married Damdin Sükhbaatar (Damdiny Sühbaatar), a military hero who died at the age of 30 in 1923. In place of her father's name, Nemendeyen, she adopted the name of her late husband after his death, an unusual circumstance in Mongolia.

From 1940 to 1954, she served on the politburo of the People's Revolutionary Party of Mongolia. From 1940 to 1950 she was a member of the Presidium of the Little Khural, the executive committee of Parliament, or Great Khural. From 1941 to 1947 she was Secretary of the Central Committee of the People's Revolutionary Party. In 1950 she became a member of the Great Khural, where she served until 1962.

Following the death of President Gonchigiin Bumstend in 1953, Yanjmaa served as President of Mongolia from September 23, 1953 until July 7, 1954, when a new election was held and Jamtsarangün Sambuu was elected. She continued to serve in the Parliament until 1962. She died the following year.

Suggested Reading:

(1) en.wikipedia.org.
(2) www.FemalePresidents.com.

Ye-lü Shih (or Pu-su-wan)

Regent of Kara-Khitai (1163-1178)

The Kara-Khitai Empire was located in Eastern Turkestan. Ye-lü Shih was born Pu-su-wan (Chinese transcription), a member of a pagan Mongol line ruling in Muslim Turkic territory. She was the daughter of Ye-lü Ta-shih who ruled ca. 1130 to 1142 and his wife Ta-pu-yen. Upon the death of the king in 1142 the aggressive Queen Ta-pu-yen served as regent until their son, Ye-lü Yi-lie, reached majority. When he died in 1163, Pu-su-wan assumed the regency on behalf of her nephew, Ye-lü Che-lu-ku, son of her late brother. Although as ruler she was called Ye-lü Shih, for the sake of clarity she will be continue to be referred to here by her birth name. During her reign, her army entered Khurasan to plunder Balkh (1165). In 1172 she took sides in the dispute of a neighbor, the Khwarizmian Empire. Two sons of the late shah vied for the throne. The loser, Takash, sought refuge in her country. She charged her husband with the task of leading an army into Kwarizmia to reinstate Takash and drive out his brother, Sultan-shah. Once this was accomplished, she demanded payment of tribute under extremely exacting conditions. When Takash rebelled, she reversed her policy and attempted to reinstate Sultan-shah. Although the Kara-Khitai were unable to accomplish this, they lent him an army with which he conquered another land, Khurasan (1181). When Ye-lü Che-lu-ku reached his majority in 1178, Pu-su-wan retired.

Suggested Reading:

(1)   Grousset, René. *The Empire of the Steppes: A History of Central Asia.* tr. Naomi Walford. New Brunswick, NJ: Rutgers University Press, 1970. pp. 165-167.

Yolanda (or Isabella II or Yolanta)

Titular queen of Jerusalem (1212-1228)

She was born in 1212, the daughter of hereditary Queen Maria La Marquise, regent from 1205 to 1212, and King John of Brienne, ruler from 1210 to 1225. Queen Maria died the year Yolanda was born, and Yolanda (actually usually called Isabella, but here referred to as Yolanda to lessen confusion with other Isabellas) inherited the throne. Her father, who then had no legal right to govern except as regent, married (1114) Princess Stephanie of Armenia. Stephanie proved to be a malelovent step-mother. She died in 1219, reportedly as a result of a severe beating at the hands of her husband for having tried to poison Yolanda. In 1225 the young queen was sent off to Italy to become the second wife of Holy Roman Emperor Frederick II. On her way to Italy, she stopped in Cyprus to see her aunt, Queen Alice, for the last time. Both queens and their courts were in tears as Yolanda said goodbye to her "sweet land of Syria" that she would never see again. Frederick was 31 and she was 14. Although he was handsome and intelligent, he was also said to be cruel, sly, selfish, and given to erotic conduct of the basest sort. He sent his new wife to a harem that he kept at Palermo, where she was obliged to live in seclusion. In 1228, at the age of 16, she gave birth to a son, Conrad, and having given the emperor his heir, she died six days later, never having ruled the kingdom which had been rightfully hers all of her short life.

Suggested Reading:

(1) Runciman, Steven A. *A History of the Crusades*. Cambridge: Cambridge University press, 1987. vol. 3, *The Kingdom of Acre*. pp. 134, 173-177, 179-182, 221.
(2) Löwenstein, Prince Hubertus Zu. *A Basic History of Germany*. Bonn: Inter Nationes, 1964. p. 38.

Yolande

Empress, regent of Latin Empire (1217-1219)

Yolande was the wife of Peter of Courtenay, Emperor in name only of Constantinople from 1216 to 1217. She was the sister of both Baldwin I (formerly Count Baldwin IX of Flanders and Hainault), Latin Emperor from 1204 to 1205, and Henry I, Latin Emperor from 1205 to 1216. Yolande and Peter had three children: Marie, who married Theodore Lascaris; Robert, who ruled from 1219 to 1228; and Baldwin II, who ruled from 1228 to 1261. Her husband Peter was in Europe when his brother-in-law Henry died, and he set out for Rome where the Pope crowned him emperor. He was then on his way from Durazzo to Thessalonica when he was captured by Theodore Dukas of Epirus (1217). He died in captivity in 1218, never having ruled a single day. Yolande, who was the legal heir, became regent for her feeble son Robert. She died prematurely in 1219.

Suggested Reading:

(1) Ostrogorsky, George. *History of the Byzantine State*. New Brunswick, NJ: Rutgers University Press, 1969. pp. 430, 433.

(2) Langer, William L., ed. *World History*. Boston: Houghton Mifflin, 1980. pp. 281-282.

Yuan Yu

Regent of Sung Dynasty, China (1085-1093)

She was the mother of Sung Shen Tsung, ruler from 1067 to 1085. He had appointed as chief councilor Wang an-Shih, who carried out a program of radical "socialist" reform of the government. He cut the budget by 40 percent, raised the salaries of officials to make honesty possible, gave aid to farmers, made large assessments for public services. When Emperor Shen Tsung died in 1085, the grand dowager empress, ruling under the reign title of Yuan Yu, was regent for her grandson, Che Tsung, ruler from 1085 to 1100. Empress Yuan Yu, who was opposed to the reforms of Wang an-Shih, recalled the conservative ministers and rescinded the whole reform program. She died in 1093 and was succeeded by her grandson, Che Tsung.

Suggested Reading:

(1) Reischauer, Edwin O. and John K. Fairbank. *East Asia: the Great Tradition*. Boston: Houghton Mifflin, 1960. pp. 206-208.
(2) Langer, William L., ed. *World History*. Boston: Houghton Mifflin, 1980. pp. 365-366.

Section Z

Zabel (or Isabella)

Queen, ruler of Lesser (Little) Armenia (Cicilia) (1219-1269)

Little Armenia was located in modern day Turkey. Zabel was born in 1215, the younger daughter of Leo II (or Leon) the Great, ruler of Armenia from 1198 to 1219, and his second wife, Princess Sibylla of Cyprus and Jerusalem. Leo had no sons, and his older daughter Stephanie was the wife of John of Brienne, king of Jerusalem. On his deathbed (1219), he named Zabel his successor under the regency of Baron Constantine of Lambron. Since King Leo had earlier promised the succession to his niece Alice Roupen, married to Raymond of Antioch, Raymond put in a claim on behalf of his Armenian wife and their infant son. But his wife died, reputedly because of a battering he inflicted, and soon afterward, the baby died as well. On Leon's death, the Hethumid baron Constantine was elected Zabel's protector and regent. He imprisoned Leon's grandnephew, Ruben-Raymond, who had declared himself king, but who, with the death of his wife and son, had no further legal claim on the throne. With the consent of Armenian nobles, Zabel was married as a child to Philip, fourth son of Bohemond IV of Antioch. Zabel first married Philip of Antioch, but he did not comply with the marriage agreement: He refused, although already excommunicated by the Catholic Church, to embrace the separated Armenian Church as his father Bohemond IV had promised he would do. In addition, he spent as much time in Antioch as possible. Philip stole the crown jewels and sent them to his father. In 1224, as he set out again from Armenia for Antioch, he was arrested at Sis by Constantine, who demanded the return of the jewels as ransom. But Bohemond preferred to allow his son to die in prison rather than relinquish the jewels. Philip was poisoned at Sis a few months later. Zabel, broken-hearted, fled to Seleucia, and the Hospitallers, or Templars, who previously had openly favored the heretical Armenian, to avoid the shame of surrendering Zabel in person, handed the whole town over to the regent

Constantine. In 1226 Constantine arranged to have his own son Hethoum I (Hayton) of Lambron marry Zabel, although for many years she refused to live with him. Finally she relented, and in 1226 the two were crowned together. Bohemond IV, still seething over the murder of his son Philip at the hands of Constantine, tried vainly to persuade the Pope to arrange a divorce between Zabel and Hethoum so as to deprive Hethoum of the right to rule. The couple had at least five children: Leo III, who became King of Armenia on his mother's death in 1269; Thoros; Sibylla, who married Prince Bohemond VI of Antioch; Euphemia, who married John of Sidon; and Maria, who married Guy of Ibelin. In 1254-1255 Hethoun, an ally of the Mongols, journeyed to Karakorum and back by way of Samarkaland and Persia. His travels were chronicled by Kirakos Gandzaketse in an account which provides some of the best source material on early Mongolian life and culture. As Hethum the Great, he ruled from 1226 until 1269.

Suggested Reading:

(1) Chahin, M., *The Kingdom of Armenia*. New York: Dorset Press, 1987, 1991, pp. 275, 282-283.

(2) Runciman, Steven A. *A History of the Crusades*. Cambridge: Cambridge University Press, 1987. vol. 3, *The Kingdom of Acre*. pp. 164, 172-173, 230.

(3) Grousset, René. *The Empire of the Steppes: A History of Central Asia*. tr. Naomi Walford. New Brunswick, NJ: Rutgers University Press, 1970. pp. 281-282, 360-363.

(4) Egan, Edward W. et. al., eds. *Kings, Rulers and Statesmen*. New York: Sterling Publishing, 1976. p. 21.

Zabibi (or Zabibê)

Queen, ruler of an Arabian state (c.738 B.C.)

In ancient Mesopotamia the term "queen" was applied only to goddesses and to those queens of Arabia who served as rulers. If a king were ruling, both his spouse and his mother were also politically important. In 738 B.C. Azriyau, King of Sam'al (Ya'diya or Yaudi) of northern Syria formed a coalition of principalities to obstruct the advance of King Tiglath-Pileser III of the New Assyrian Empire (r. 744-727 B. C.). The coalition was defeated, and Tiglath-Pileser exacted tribute from rulers of all the important states of

Syria-Palestine, including Menahem, King of Israel, and Rezin (Rasunu), King of Damascus. Queen Zabibi, referred to in ancient documents as "Queen of the Arabs", was among those rulers, including another queen of the Arabs, required to send him tribute.

Suggested Reading:

(1) Roux, Georges. *Ancient Iraq*. Harmondsworth, Middlesex: Penguin Books, 1964, 1980. p. 285.

(2) Laessøe, Jørgen. *People of Ancient Assyria*. tr. by F. S. Leigh-Browne. London: Routledge and Kegan Paul, 1963. p. 113.

(3) Oppenheim, A. Leo. *Ancient Mesopotamia*. Chicago: University of Chicago Press, 1977. p. 104, 169.

(4) Olmstead, A. T. *History of the Persian Empire*. Chicago: University of Chicago Press, 1948. p. 22.

(5) Langer, William L., ed. *World History*. Boston: Houghton Mifflin, 1980. p. 33.

Zenobia

Queen, ruler of Palmyra, Syria (A.D. 266-272)

She was born Bat Zabbai, or Septima Zenobia. Arabians knew her as Az-Zabba. A beautiful and wise woman with aggressive energy, she became the second wife of King Odaenathus, ruler of Palmyra for Rome ca. A.D. 260 to 266. She bore three sons: Wahballat or Vaballath, Herennianus, and Timolaus. She reputedly instigated the murder of her husband and his heir by his first wife, and then became regent for her own son, ruling extremely effectively. At the time of her reign a certain Paul of Samosata was bishop of Antioch in Syria, when Antioch was subject ot Palmyra. Paul held the belief that Jesus was not God incarnated as man, but rather a human who became divine. His beliefs were thought by many to be heretical, and in 268 the church denounced his doctrine and attempted to depose him. But Zenobia's patronage mitigated harsh judgment against him and prevented his removal.

Not content to remain under Roman cliency, Zenobia decided to extend her power. In 269-270, she moved into Egypt and then occupied most of Asia Minor. In 271 she had her son proclaimed Augustus. Roman Emperor Aurelian, who had not taken her seriously up until her move into Egypt, marshalled his considerable forces and marched against her. He recovered Egypt and Asia Minor, then besieged Palmyra itself. After its surrender, Zenobia and a son fled to a waiting boat in an attempt to gain sanction among her Sasanian allies on the other side of the Euphrates. But she was apprehended. She and her two younger sons were taken back to Rome and paraded in golden chains in Aurelian's triumphal processsion (272 or 274). Wahballat's fate is unknown; Zenobia was granted a pension. It was not until after her defeat that Paul's sentence of deposition could be carried out. Conjecture exists as to the direction the Christian church might have taken had Zenobia prevailed against the Romans and Paul of Samosata had continued to promulgate his doctrine.

Zenobia later married a Roman senator and lived into old age in Italy.

Suggested Reading:

(1) Mommsen, Theodor. *Provinces of the Roman Empire*. tr. William P. Dickson. Chicago: Ares Publishers, 1974. pp. 106-110, 249.
(2) Peters, E. E. *The Harvest of Hellenism*. New York: Barnes & Nobles Books, 1996. pp. 588-601.
(3) Fusfield, Bob. *Zenobia, Queen of Palmyra*. Pacific Palisades, CA: Morningbird Press, 1997.
(4) Bowder, Diana, ed. *Who Was Who in the Roman World*. Ithaca, NY: Cornell University Press, 1980. pp. 586-587.

Zia, Begum Khaleda

Prime Minister of Bangladesh (1991-1996)

Born in 1945 to a middle-class family with no connections to politics, she was married at the age of fifteen, just after she finished school, to an army captain, Ziaur Rahman (Zia ur-Rahman), in a wedding arranged by her parents. She and her husband had two sons. Ziaur rose to become a Major General and during a military coup in 1975, he emerged as the country's "strong man", although a civilian, Abusadat Mohammad Sayem, remained as titular head of state for almost two years. In May of 1977 Gen. Zia held a national referendum which resulted in a 99 per cent vote in his favor. During his five-year rule, his wife Khaleda Zia showed no interest in affairs of state. But in 1981, following her husband's assassination in Chittagong, the Bangladesh Nationalist Party which he had founded drafted her to

lead it. It was generally believed that she accepted the challenge in order to avenge her husband's murder, which she believed was masterminded by Zia's successor, General Hussein Muhammad Ershad. She waged a tireless nine-year war against Ershad's corrupt regime, vowing not to take part in any elections under him. Finally, in 1990, he was brought to justice for some of his excesses and was sentenced to 20 years in prison. Zia was praised as an "uncompromising" leader. Her party was swept into power in the 1991 general election.

Unlike her counterpart in Pakistan, Benazir Bhutto, Prime Minister Zia took immediate steps to address the literacy problem in her country, where the average Bangladeshi received about two years of schooling, and only a third of the students were girls. She began agressively promoting education and vocational training, especially of girls, and expanding small, no-collateral loans to women-owned businesses. However, by late 1994, much of her popularity had eroded. The critical view was that, by concentrating all her efforts on staying in power, she had become increasingly isolated from the people. She was accused of pandering to fundamentalist causes when she refused to come to the defense of feminist writer Taslima Nasrin who had made fervent demands for women's rights and an end to purdah and other institutions of sexual repression. The Bangladesh government charged the writer with defaming Islam, forcing her into hiding in Sweden. Zia's most vocal opponent was leader of the Awami League, Hasina Wajed, born in 1946, daughter of Bangladesh's founder and first Prime Minister, Mujibur Rahman. By 1996 it appeared that Bangladesh's five-year experiment in democracy was failing. In late March of 1996 Zia gave in to public demands for new elections to be held and petitioned the president to form a caretaker government. However, although Zia's party retained control by default, only 15 percent of registered voters participated in the May elections, which were marred by widespread protests and violence that left sixteen people dead and several hundred injured.

Suggested Reading:

(1) Crossette, Barbara. "A Woman Leader for a Land That Defies Islamic Stereotypes". *The New York Times*. 17 October 1993: 3.
(2) "The 'Strongwomen' of South Asia" *World Press Review*. December 1994: 18-20.
(3) Baker, Deborah. "Exiled Feminist Writer Tells Her Own Story". *The New York Times* 28 August 1994: 4 E.

(4) "Shaky Democracy" *World Press Review*. May 1996: 24.

Zoë

Empress of Byzantine Empire (1028-1050)

Zoë was born in A.D. 980, the middle daughter of King Constantine VIII, ruler of Byzantium from 963 to 1028, and his wife Helena of Alypius. Psellus described Zoë as "very regal in her ways, a woman of great beauty, most imposing in her manner, and commanding respect." As her pock-faced older sister Eudocia had entered a nunnery, Zoë was named by her dying father to be married to Romanus III. The two inherited the reign when Constantine died in 1028, and Zoë exiled her other sister to a nunnery, probably at Romanus' suggestion. Romanus immediately lost interest in Zoë, even keeping her short of money. She took a lover, a peasant's son, handsome Michael IV, and together they conspired to murder Romanus in his bath. Zoë claimed the right to rule after Romanus' death, not for herself, but for her adored Michael, whom she married and made Emperor. Although Michael treated her badly, confining her to the women's quarters, he nevertheless convinced her to adopt his nephew, Michael V, as his successor. When Michael IV died in 1042, Michael V became ruler, but to avoid the possibility of usurpation of his power, he made the mistake of exiling the aging Zoë to the island of Prinkipo. Indignation at the treatment of the rightful empress swept through the land, and mobs quickly assembled to protest her exile. Michael quickly brought Zoë back and made a great show of his regard for her, but it was of no avail: the mob tracked him down in a local church and gouged his eyes out after he had been forced to watch as the same treatment was given to his minister. Meanwhile, the youngest sister Theodora had been brought back by another faction, which had proclaimed her queen, while across town another crowd had pledged loyalty to Zoë. Eventually Zoë made the first move of reconciliation, welcoming her sister back with an embrace. The sisters ruled jointly for a while, although Theodora bowed to her older sister's seniority and, if Psellus was correct, did not show the slightest rancor about having spent the best years of her life in a nunnery. Then in 1042 Zoë, ever warm-blooded and impulsive, seized power again by marrying, at the age of 64, the 42-year-old senator, Constantine Monomachus, who ruled with her as Constantine IX. More tolerant with the passing of years, aware that her own charms had faded, Zoë ignored her husband's open affair with Sclerina, a niece of his second wife. He gave his mistress the title of Sebaste, and she took her place beside Zoë and Theodora at all court ceremonies. Zoë died in 1050, and when her husband died three years later, her sister Theodora at last ruled alone.

Suggested Reading:

(1) Psellus, Michael. *Fourteen Byzantine Rulers.* tr. E. R. A. Sewter. Harmondsworth, Middlesex: Penguin Books, 1982. pp. 55-59, 63-65, 75-81, 87-240 *passim*, 250.
(2) Ostrogorsky, George. *History of the Byzantine State.* New Brunswick, NJ: Rutgers University Press, 1969. pp. 321, 323, 326-327.

Get Published, Inc!
Thorofare, NJ 08086
28 August 2009
BA2009240